SOCIALIST
POPULATION
POLITICS

JOHN F. BESEMERES

SOCIALIST POPULATION POLITICS

THE POLITICAL IMPLICATIONS

OF DEMOGRAPHIC TRENDS

IN THE USSR AND

EASTERN EUROPE

M.E. SHARPE INC
White Plains, New York

Copyright © 1980 by M. E. Sharpe, Inc.
901 North Broadway, White Plains, N.Y. 10603

Library of Congress Cataloging in Publication Data

Besemeres, John F
    Socialist population politics.

    Bibliography: p.
    Includes index.
    1. Russia—Population. 2. Russia—Population policy.
3. Europe, Eastern—Population. 4. Europe, Eastern—Population
policy. I. Title.
HB3607.B47   304.6'0947   80-65260
ISBN 0-87332-154-5

Printed in the United States of America

CONTENTS

LIST OF TABLES

PREFACE

During the 1950s and 1960s there was a dramatic decline in
birthrates in the USSR and the European Socialist[1] states. This
decline brought in its train agonizing reappraisals of population
policies and doctrines in virtually all the countries concerned.
Albania alone has been spared the soul-searching. Elsewhere national birthrates have fallen so low that the high fertility once held
to be an essential feature of socialism seems little more than a
nostalgic memory. And like the sinister Malthusians portrayed
in erstwhile Soviet critiques of Western demography, Soviet bloc
observers are now apt at times to view rapid population growth
and countries or peoples engaged in it with some reserve. From
regarding domestic population development with total unconcern
or untroubled confidence, most governments of Eastern Europe
have now passed over to or toward an active involvement reminiscent of the morbid preoccupation with physical function of the in-
trospective centipede.

Much of the public anxiety is focused on the socioeconomic problems presented by fluctuations, imbalances, shortages, and local
or temporary superfluities of manpower supply either currently
experienced or seen as in prospect. Most of the rest is expended
on the danger that at some point in the future, this or that country, republic, or region might pass into a phase of "narrowed reproduction" (i.e., population decline) of indefinite duration. In this
respect the Eastern European countries seem to be experiencing
something similar to the extinction scare evoked by intemperate
extrapolation of fertility trends in Western Europe in the 1930s.
That population decline or stagnation is disastrous both economically and in general tends to be taken as self-evident. On the other

hand, at the international level fertility decline has since the mid-1960s been accepted as a worthy objective for Third World countries, if coupled with appropriate socioeconomic policies in other directions. But for the Socialist countries themselves, the time when population might have to be restricted is not in sight.

While the specter of depopulation is obviously a strong emotional stimulant in itself, one suspects that it frequently serves consciously or unconsciously as a symbolic surrogate for anxieties about potential transformations in relative ethnic or national strength. The emotion may not be wholly irrational. Existing trends of differential fertility seem to suggest that major transformations are indeed in the making.

The British demographer Jack Parsons has recently coined the term "demophobia" to refer to all forms of acute anxiety about population trends.[2] Parsons sees demophobia and "competitive breeding" as threats to rational control of world population, which no doubt they are. The implication that "demophobia" is some kind of psychological disorder, however, seems to beg the question of whether the fear may not be partly or wholly justified. Given the relative comfort of their modern historical experience, Anglo-Saxon scholars are more inclined to believe in the solutions of liberal rationalism. By contrast, Eastern Europeans are readily persuaded that clouds on the horizon portend almost inescapable conflict or catastrophe; or that they are the harbingers of national rebirth or deliverance. In the present case, one way or the other, they may well be right.

My own view is that the demographic pressures that are building up in the Soviet Union and Yugoslavia are such as to threaten the integrity of the two states and political systems in question; and indirectly, to pose a threat to peace and stability (or if you like, the status quo) in their region and in the world. I am naturally not suggesting that demographic factors can effect such changes unaided. But in combination with other social and economic factors like ethnic tensions, employment pressures, and shifts in the international balance of forces, they appear to have a catalytic and explosive potential of enormous magnitude.

One should perhaps emphasize: catalytic and explosive. Demographic trends can aggravate the effects of other social forces and bring them to crisis point. But they also do much to determine the extent of the motor power brought to bear in any social collision. Demographic trends can create or

accentuate conflicts, stir them into active violence, and at
the same time, more or less rapidly transform the relative
strengths of the contending parties. To a large extent this
potency is a product of the twentieth century. It is only in
modern times that 3% natural increase rates have appeared
as a stable medium-term phenomenon; and that such dramatic
growth has been observed coexisting with Einkindsystem
norms within a single political entity. Even if the divergence
is not maintained beyond a few decades, the "astonishing
power of compound interest" will have had time enough to do
its work.

In the Soviet Union it seems almost certain that the traditional
imperial masters, the Russians, will be challenged in some or all
parts of their domain by the Moslem peoples they once subjugated.
This prospect seems equally inescapable whether one sees those
peoples as their victims or their beneficiaries. In addition, numerous other less crucial interrelationships will be affected.
Whether and how the Soviet regime will deal with these problems
is a fascinating theme for speculation.

In Yugoslavia the situation is similar though in some ways a
little more complex. The interplay of ethnic forces is less dom-
inated by a single group. But there too the dominant Slav element,
or rather elements, is under threat of partial dispossession by a
demographically burgeoning minority group of distinct ethnic and
cultural characteristics. The stability of the interrelationships
between the Slav groups is also affected. And the various cross-
currents thereby whipped up seem likely to involve external forces
in the ultimate dénouement.

Detailed explanation of and empirical justification for these as-
sessments of the Soviet and Yugoslav demopolitical futures can be
found in the relevant chapters. It may appear to some that my emphasis on the demographic factor in these chapters is at times one-
sided, if not indeed downright monomaniacal. But any essay which
focuses on a particular theme will at times produce optical illusions. One is dealing with that theme and not with others. The relative lack of visibility of the others implies no necessary underestimation of their importance. Out of sight is not necessarily out
of mind. In any case, I would assert positively that the demographic
factor in politics is itself very widely overlooked. In what follows
I have attempted to struggle with what I see as a common imbalance
in political analysis.

Studies of the politics of population involve serious demarcation difficulties. The area of overlap between politics and population is vast. On broad definitions of both one might well need to discuss a country's social and economic policies and politics in their fullest complexity to exhaust the subject. This book being addressed primarily to the political implications of the present size and growth tendencies of national and ethnic populations, certain thematic choices automatically follow. Such matters as, for example, internal and external migration, urbanization,[3] changing educational and occupational structure, health and education administration, gerontology or environmental pressures — all of which might quite properly be regarded as falling within the purview of the politics of population or population policy — will only be dealt with insofar as they affect the issues more directly connected with numerical aggregates. The range of issues actually touched on will vary from country to country. Thus, for example, emigration will be only of tangential interest in the case of the Soviet Union, whereas for Yugoslavia it will have to be given a special section to itself; the question of ethnic relations will be marginal for Poland but central for both the USSR and Yugoslavia. The reason for so delimiting the subject of study is partly pragmatic; considerations of manageability dictate that lines be drawn somewhere; and when, as in this case, the subject matter is amorphous and rich in ramification, a certain arbitrariness may be unavoidable. But drawing the line where it has been drawn has the additional advantage of focusing attention on those concerns which most people would regard as being relevant to population policy rather than social policy. The central issue of pro- or antinatalism is held in the foreground, and priority given to demographic rather than sociological, medical, or ecological problems.

Also, as its title indicates, the emphasis in this study is placed on the political impact of demographic trends rather than the demographic impact of political decisions. The latter approach has already received a good deal of attention.[4] But in any case, as it seems to me, despite the inherent interest of Eastern European states as demographic testing grounds, the political significance of population developments there far outweighs their importance viewed from any other perspective.

Finally, greater stress will be laid on politics than policies: on dilemmas, differences, and conflicts rather than on past or present measures taken by governments to affect the course of demographic events. Here the preponderance of literature in favor of the approach not adopted is overwhelming.[5] Commentators from the

Socialist countries themselves naturally are at pains to avoid direct discussion of the politics of population issues. Many Western observers, curiously, betray a similar reticence. Hence a politics-rather than policy-oriented approach seems opportune.

Broadly speaking, from the vantage point just outlined the areas of overlap between population and politics in Socialist Europe can be schematized as follows:

1. Socioeconomic policies: the policy implications of variations in labor supply, consumer demands, educational requirements, etc.[6]
2. Ethnic relations: the influence of demographic changes (and prospective changes) on the relative influence of ethnic populations within states.
3. International relations: the influence of demographic changes (and prospective changes) on the relative power positions of the nations concerned.[7]
4. Ideology: the effects of population trends on the world-views and self-images of the regimes in question.
5. Migration: the demographic changes caused and political issues raised by internal and international population movements.[8]
6. Population policies: the issues raised by the attempts of governments (or interest groups)[9] to influence population trends.

The relative weight accorded to these topics will, as was suggested earlier, vary from country to country as the data appear to dictate; and at times one or another of them will be discussed only very cursorily or dismissed altogether. With these qualifications, the above schema will be applied to each of the three main countries examined.

A further word should perhaps be said about the regional focus of this study. The USSR, Poland, and Yugoslavia have been singled out for more detailed consideration because they are the three largest and politically most important countries in Socialist Europe. And as was suggested earlier, it seems that demopolitical pressures could easily blow either the USSR or Yugoslavia apart, with considerable attendant hazard to other countries in the area. In Poland the prospects seem much less apocalyptic, at least to the outside observer. But Poland's case has the virtue of involving many of the issues common to other countries within the Soviet sphere of influence: the anxiety about national "survival" or national "greatness"; the receding labor surplus and the impending labor shortage; the abortion question; pronatalism and the rights of the individual, of women, and the family; (implicitly) the position

of the nation vis-à-vis the USSR and other regional oppressors or
rivals. Discussing the situation in Poland effectively conveys a
fair impression of the spread of views and considerations that obtain elsewhere. In addition, Poland presents some interesting and
largely unique features: a Malthusian phase in official thinking and
a powerful ecclesiastical lobby on family and population policy.

However, it should be borne in mind that the USSR, Poland, and
Yugoslavia, while the most interesting and significant, are also the
least typical. They happen to be the three countries in which population policy remains to some extent an open issue. Elsewhere,
while things are continuing to happen, the basic orientation of the
governments concerned is uniformly and explicitly pronatalist. To
help maintain a comparative perspective, reference is frequently
made to the other European Socialist countries (and also to China),
and a short section is devoted to summarizing the main features
of the scene there. Although Albania will also be referred to
periodically, generalizations can usually be taken as not including
it. Albania is an exceptional case and one, moreover, concerning
which neither the author, nor anybody else, the Albanians perhaps
included, knows very much. [10]

Chapters 1 through 3 will provide a general introduction to the
problems of population politics and policies and the Soviet Marxist
tradition on demographic questions. Chapter 4 will provide a cursory sketch of the main features of demographic development in
Eastern Europe and the Soviet Union in recent decades. Chapters
5-17 will attempt a detailed examination of the main features of
population politics in each of the three major countries in turn. And
finally, Chapter 18 will briefly summarize the main features of the
demographico-political scene in Eastern Europe as a whole, seeking in the process to give some broad impression of where the
three major countries fit into the overall pattern.

The basic argument of the chapter on the USSR was prepared in
1973, of the chapter on Poland in 1974-75, and that on Yugoslavia
in 1976. All parts of the work have been updated at least once
since then. It has not, however, been necessary to make basic
alterations, and I have generally refrained from adding much
more than some fresher citations and a few extra empirical
details.

Finally, perhaps a word of warning about the author's political and other prejudices, lest they should not prove immediately obvious. Though not, I believe, anti-Soviet or anti-

communist (insofar as those terms are meaningful), I do not like murder or any lesser forms of bullying or their conceal- ment after the event; and I am allergic to deliberate lies and obfuscations, toadying, and repetitive self-congratulation. Gov- ernments and their spokesmen are at least as prone to these vices as private individuals, and I believe all people of good- will anywhere have a legitimate right to denounce them when and wherever they espy them. At the same time, I am also allergic to another common Socialist failing, wearisome di- dacticism. I hope I have struck the right balance. I would also like to stress that any implicit or explicit criticism of aspects of the countries I am dealing with implies no necessary approval of political institutions, attitudes, or events elsewhere. One can cast out the mote in the Slovenian eye without being enraptured by the beam in the Haitian eye; to condemn Megagate is not to condone Watergate. To refrain or to pretend to refrain from any moral judgment of social and political events is usually intellectually dis- honest; insofar as it is not, it may indicate emotional sterility or lack of imagination. I mention these things as one who is often ex- asperated by the scientistic tendencies of the younger generation of Western writers on the Socialist world. Whether because of a lack of human involvement in the human affairs they are writing about, or perhaps because of a nervous inner ear trained on a hot line to some distant visas section, they seem bent on avoiding judg- ments altogether, or at least on conveying the impression that they have lived all their lives in the middle of the Bering Strait. This book tries to distinguish between objectivity and moral neuterism.

The other main warning I should issue is, I think, that I am a Slavophile. I find Slavs, in general, more rewarding people than Anglo-Saxons. And by virtue of many contacts over a number of years, I have developed a particular tenderness for Russians, Poles, and Serbs, the Slavic peoples I have had most to do with. As one with multiple attachments, it is often given to me to notice not only the ethnic prejudices and follies of the Slavs but also the second- ary ethnic prejudices of Western scholars specializing in this or that Slavic country or people. God grant that I myself should avoid such prejudices at all times.

Among the many dozens of people in East and West who have helped me in various ways during the course of my work on this book, I would particularly like to thank Professor J. Zubrzycki, Dr. T. H. Rigby, Dr. R. F. Miller, and Dr. L. Růžička of the Aus-

Preface

tralian National University, Professor J. A. Armstrong of the University of Wisconsin, and Dr. R. Pervan of the University of Western Australia. No one among them, however, has seen the final text, so all are innocent of any howlers the reader may find.

John Besemeres
Canberra, January 1980

PART ONE

THE DOCTRINAL AND DEMOGRAPHIC BACKGROUND

CHAPTER 1

POPULATION AND
POLITICAL STUDIES
IN WEST AND EAST[1]

The common ground between the study of politics and demography has not until very recently attracted more than passing interest from social scientists. This seems to have been particularly true in the case of political science. As of 1970 it was still possible for an American political scientist to assert that what he regarded as the two key problems of the remaining decades of the century, pollution and population growth, had not yet had a single article devoted to them in any major U.S. political science journal, either national or regional.[2] And in the introduction to a volume of the U.S. Commission on Population and the American Future Report devoted to political aspects of the problem, we find the observation: "It became quickly apparent to the Commission that political science had, by comparison with other social sciences — especially economics, demography, and sociology — little to offer by way of policy-relevant research."[3]

The other social sciences have not been overprecipitate in tackling these problems either. Bernard Berelson has estimated that over the 25 years from 1946 to 1971, the entries catalogued under "Policies" in the Population Index have not amounted to more than 2-4% of the total.[4] What is true of demography is undoubtedly true a fortiori of the social sciences less directly concerned with population matters. As for the demographers, their interest has been overwhelmingly in Third World countries and in the central question of fertility control. They have usually (with the notable exception of the French) been less interested in domestic policy considerations. And while the neo-Malthusian concern of recent years has been making Western population growth something of a political issue also, the attitude of most demographers to this latter

3

question has on the whole been less engagé.

Irrespective of whether their concern is primarily with Western or Third World population growth, Western neo-Malthusian movements and demographers have paid relatively little attention to such collateral questions as whether Third World countries might object to outside concern with their birthrates; whether there are good reasons for supposing that the Socialist countries will decisively alter their attitudes to world population questions and refrain from encouraging Third World resentments; whether antinatalist population policies in the West should be concerted with a similar "demographic disarmament" in the East, and so on.[5]

In any case, those Western demographers actively concerned with policy questions tend in the present climate to be more interested in fertility control than in fertility stimulation, which does not by and large predispose them to taking an interest in events in the Socialist countries, where exactly the reverse concerns are dominant.

Indeed, were it not for the almost unique character of the various thoroughgoing governmental programs that have been adopted by the Socialist countries from time to time, the interest of Western scholars in the area would probably have been quite negligible. As things are, there is a strong tendency for professional demographic interest in Socialist population policies to limit itself to requests to colleagues in Socialist countries to provide the required information.[6] Where the more sensitive areas of government policy are concerned (and "more sensitive" in the Socialist context needs of course to be broadly interpreted), it is somewhat naive to expect that Socialist colleagues will be able to speak frankly and fully about what they believe to be the moral or other shortcomings of their national demographic policies.[7] Moreover, Western demographers tend naturally to be primarily interested in the policies themselves and their demographic effects and antecedents rather than in the political context from which they have emerged and the political consequences they appear likely to entail.

The reasons for the recent surge of interest in the West in the political aspects of population are obvious enough: the Third World population explosion since World War II; the neo-Malthusian alarm about Western population levels (and allied ecological concerns) in wide circles of public opinion; the emergence of a radical feminist movement; the contraception and abortion controversies, and so on. However, the reasons for the earlier almost complete lack of interest are rather more elusive, especially in the case of Western

4

social science in general, and political science in particular.

In the Socialist countries, where there was a similar reticence about population policy until recently, the reasons both for the reticence and the recent spread of interest are a little more clear-cut and comprehensible. Soviet demography shared the fate of all social sciences under Stalin. For three decades or more it performed a residual and purely apologetic role as a neglected adjunct of government economic statistics. When it was not being neglected, it was being manhandled. At least one census was suppressed and the results of another left largely unpublished during Stalin's reign; and there were (and still are) large gaps in even the most basic Soviet demographic statistics.[8] The demographers themselves, of course, ran the usual heightened risks to life and career characteristic of all scientific endeavor in the thirties and forties. Official demographic doctrine was crudely oversimplified. Certain Marxist dicta as glossed by Stalinist interpretation became normative writ. When and insofar as the trend of facts did not square with them, the facts tended to be dispensed with before the theory. In these conditions it was difficult for any kind of demography to flourish, let alone that branch of it directly concerned with governmental decision-making. In addition, the Stalinist years saw a number of major demographic catastrophes befall the Soviet Union, so that considerations of prestige and national security were added to the usual Stalinist intolerance of objective information.[9] When demography began to reemerge as a discipline in the early 1960s,[10] it did so in the context of such spectacular fertility decline that policy-oriented discussion, either open or veiled, was bound to ensue.

In some of the other Socialist countries, particularly Poland, Czechoslovakia, and Hungary, demography and discussion of population questions reemerged from the Stalinist phase rather earlier.[11] But there too, and for similar reasons, there has been a notable expansion in policy discussions in recent years.

Thus in both the non-Socialist and Socialist worlds, we are presently confronted by a rapid increase in the literature on population problems generally and population policies in particular. The already rising tide was given further impetus by the organization of the 1974 UN World Population Conference in Bucharest, which had a much stronger orientation toward both international and domestic population policies than any similar gathering held previously. Large conferences devoted exclusively to population policy were held in Warsaw (international, largely Socialist) in 1972[12] and Belgrade (domestic Yugoslav population policy only) in 1973.[13] Among the numerous policy-oriented publications emerging from the Soviet Union in 1974 was one collective tome actually entitled <u>Demographic Policy</u>.[14] In recent years the Socialist demographic journals have begun to reflect this same growing interest; articles on policy issues are starting to proliferate. Statements by party and state officials on population matters are also becoming more and more frequent, if still relatively rare in certain of the Socialist countries. And as in the West, advisory commissions on population are being either established or widely postulated as necessary. Meanwhile in the Western and Third worlds, interest in population policy grows apace. A most notable event during World Population Year 1974 was the appearance of a large and comprehensive collective monograph volume on population policies in the developed countries.[15] The leading Western demographic publications are devoting more and more space to the subject, in relation to both the "capitalist" and "Socialist" countries. Even political scientists are beginning to offer some contributions. And at the governmental level there is an increasing awareness that population growth is a legitimate or indeed a necessary sphere of state involvement.[16]

While politico-demographic writing is expanding rapidly in both the Socialist and non-Socialist worlds, with many parallel features and for many of the same reasons, there are also some important and fundamental differences between the two literatures.

To begin with, of course, there is no such field as political demography or population politics in the Socialist countries, and it is unlikely that one will be recognized in the foreseeable future. What they do have, on the other hand, is what is known in Russian as <u>politika narodonaseleniia</u>, in the broader sense of the study or science of population policy. At least in relation to the Socialist countries, the main thrust of this discipline is not of course toward disclosing the political aspects of population development and policy but rather toward mapping what is actually being done by Socialist governments to solve perceived problems and cautiously evaluating the merits of possible alternatives within the guidelines of currently established orthodoxy. As practiced, the discipline has a fairly strong contemporary orientation; excursions into history have to be conducted with tact (owing to the strong distaste of Socialist authorities for being reminded of past <u>volte-faces</u>) and are in general avoided. There is a relative paucity of discussion of such normative questions as the permissible limits of state power, the ethics of coercing or otherwise inducing particular social or ethnic minorities to regulate their natural growth, women's rights in relation to the fetus, etc., all of which play such a prominent and increasing part in Western discussions of population issues. However, just beneath the surface one often senses a strong interest in these and other similar questions and a frequent and strong desire to make empirical discussion serve normative ends. Another characteristic feature of the Socialist literature is the overwhelming dominance of pronatalist values and preoccupations, something largely absent from Western demography at present and which therefore makes the Socialist framework of discussion of policy issues virtually noncomparable with the Western.[17] And finally, note should be made of the technocratic and nationalist style of Socialist writers on population policy: their concern is with their own countries, and their objective is to make their rulers understand what policies need to be adopted in the national interest. Though many of them seem to be concerned about the human aspect of the problems they are discussing, they will often go to considerable pains to conceal the fact and to present their case in the form of an empirical demonstration of the demographico-economic benefits that will surely flow from the course prescribed, or of the practical futility of policies in fact probably held in distaste for moral reasons.

Thus to sum up, while the Western and Eastern literatures on population policies are expanding equally rapidly, they are doing so in different directions. Socialist writers are, at the surface at least, pragmatic and technocratic rather than normative, policy- rather than politics-oriented, and nationalist and natalist rather than neo-Malthusian and international in their perspectives.

CHAPTER 2

POPULATION AND
THE MARXIST CLASSICS

Marxism and Population Growth

It seems that Marx and Engels might conceivably have chosen to impart a strongly demographic slant to their central theory of historical materialism.[1] Both in Marx's German Ideology and later and more explicitly in Engels's The Origin of the Family, Private Property and the State, the suggestion is made that human reproduction forms part of the base, the underlying reality from which all other social phenomena ultimately take their rise. It would appear, in other words, that at different times both inclined toward a demoeconomic version of historical materialism rather than the more monistically economic one with which their names are now associated. Engels went so far as to say explicitly that the determining factor in history, the production and reproduction of the immediate essentials of life, is "of a twofold character. On the one hand, the production of the means of subsistence, of food, clothing and shelter, and the tools requisite therefore; on the other, the production of human beings themselves, the propagation of the species." And he added: "The social institutions under which the people of a definite historical epoch and a definite country live are conditioned by both kinds of production; by the stage of development of labour on the one hand and of the family on the other."[2]

At other times, however, they were content to regard the social configurations arising around procreation as being determined by the base and not as some independent causative force.

The Origin appeared late in Engels's life and after Marx's death; but given Marx's plans to write something on Morgan's work (referred to by Engels only a few lines before the passage quoted

8

above),[3] it seems unlikely that Engels was thrusting an idea back onto Marx which Marx himself had wholly and consciously rejected somewhere between the first hints of it contained in German Ideology and his death.[4] Be that as it may, the fact is that few of the Marxist classics contain very much material that one could classify as demographic, and consequently it is difficult, generally speaking, to determine just what their attitudes to key population issues might have been. Moreover, most of what they do say on these subjects is said in the context of their recurring polemics with Malthus. The effect of this may have been to burden Marxism with a demographic doctrine which strictly speaking does not logically derive from the main body of Marxian thinking at all. For it seems clear that Marx and Engels were not objecting so much to Malthus's empirical demographic errors as to what they perceived to be his moral and political attitudes. Their response to Malthus has been aptly described as "apoplectic."[5] Marx and Engels were much given to forceful polemical prose, a field in which they displayed no mean ability. Yet even judged by their own exacting standards, in Malthus's case they seem indeed to have excelled themselves: "The crudest, most barbarous theory that ever existed," "a sin against science," "immorality brought to its highest pitch," "shameless and mechanical plagiarism," "this revolting blasphemy against nature and mankind," "this libel on the human race," "shameless sycophant of the ruling classes," "schoolboyish," "superficial," "fundamental meanness of outlook," "the contemptible Malthus . . . (who) always steals (his premises)," "a very model of intellectual imbecility winding its way casuistically through its own inner confusion," "difficult and clumsy style," "absurd commonplace" — such were some of the expressions chosen by Marx and Engels to characterize their adversary and his theoretical work.

Neither of the main recurring charges — plagiarism and conservatism — seems to have been fully apposite. As Malthus himself says in the first chapter of his Principle of Population: "The most important argument that I shall adduce is certainly not new."[7] He then proceeds to acknowledgments, pointing out that the argument may well have been stated by other writers he does not know. For on his own admission, Malthus's reading on population matters had been very modest to that point. His intention to represent the argument is modestly, even diffidently, stated: "I should certainly therefore not think of advancing it again, though I mean to place it in a point of view in some degree different from any that I have hitherto seen, if it had ever been fairly and satisfactorily answered."[8]

As to Malthus's alleged conservatism, it would seem that Marx and Engels were characterizing Malthus the symbol rather than Malthus the man.[9] For Malthus the man advocated among other things free universal education, free medical care for the poor, state assistance to emigrants, and direct relief to large families; and he opposed child labor in factories,[10] something which Marx saw as being an essential feature of the capitalist law of population.[11] Malthus undoubtedly shared some of the moral blindness of his time and class; and no doubt, too, he expressed himself at times with a deliberate antisentimentality that may well have contributed both to his fame and his notoriety. But to regard him as the archapologist of the most reactionary sections of the moneyed classes, as Marx and Engels consistently did, is at least an oversimplification. And as was suggested earlier, and will be further explained later, it is an oversimplification which, in subsequent and even more oversimplified and ossified forms, has had and continues to exert a momentous influence.[12]

Malthus's great and enduring merit was to dramatically call attention to the fact that either in the short term or in the long term, growth of population would, unless checked, outstrip any possible growth in the resources available to support that population. The Marxist reply to the alleged short-term danger varied from occasion to occasion. At times it was emphasized that population did not grow geometrically (Malthus had never said it did as a matter of empirical fact, merely that it would unless checked) and that Malthus had grossly overstated his case; at other times, that irrespective of how fast the population might be growing, productive capacity was growing faster, and that only the irrationalities of capitalist economic organization prevented this from being reflected in a steady growth of general well-being: "But science increases at least as fast as population," wrote Engels, "the latter increases in proportion to the size of the previous generation, and science advances in proportion to the body of knowledge passed down to it by the previous generation, that is, in the most normal conditions it also grows in geometrical progression — and what is impossible for science?"[13]

As to the long-term prospects of absolute or global overpopulation, Marx and Engels tended to be insouciantly or even jocularly evasive. Engels on one occasion declared roundly that "we are forever secure from the fear of overpopulation." On another occasion he referred to the inexhaustible regions fertilized by nature herself in southeastern Europe and western America and com-

10

mented, "If all these regions have been ploughed up and after that a shortage sets in, then will be the time to say <u>caveant consules</u>."[14] In fact, of course, given the nature of demographic dynamism, it would by then be much too late to sound any alarms. One makes this somewhat humorlessly pedantic observation since it is a common lay illusion that demographic processes can be reversed by five minutes of thought and ten minutes of evasive action; an illusion that was evidently shared by Engels, and more importantly, by many more directly influential figures who claim to be his intellectual legatees. In his reply to Kautsky, quoted below, Engels says of an extrapolation of population growth that it is of no greater worth than an estimate of the compound interest yielded by a <u>kreutzer</u> invested in the year 1 A.D., which by the nineteenth century would amount to the equivalent of a lump of silver larger than the earth.[15]

Despite their utopian visions, Marx and Engels's basic concern was, of course, with the present. Observing the onward march of the industrial revolution (as they were in better position to do than Malthus had been), they had no doubts about the ability of productivity to win the population-production race within any meaningful time span. Overpopulation was for them a nonproblem. They did not want to be bothered about vague hypothetical situations which might not arise at all, or if so, only at some future time after they would both be dead and buried. At a stage when Kautsky was expressing the keenest concern about the impending problem of overpopulation, the most explicit comment that could be coaxed from either of the founding fathers was this:

> There is of course the abstract possibility that the number of people will become so great that limits will have to be set to their increase. But if at some stage communist society finds itself obliged to regulate the production of human beings, just as it has already come to regulate the production of things, it will be precisely this society, and this society alone, which can carry this out without difficulty. It does not seem to me that it would be at all difficult in such a society to achieve by planning a result which has already been produced spontaneously, without planning, in France and Lower Austria. At any rate, it is for the people in the communist society themselves to decide whether, when, and how this is to be done, and what means they wish to employ for the purpose. I do not feel called upon to make proposals or give them advice about it. These people, in any case, will surely not be any less intelligent than we are.[16]

Elsewhere in this same letter Engels refers to the massive growth of food production in America, remarks of the population there that it will take more than thirty years to double itself, and adds: "That doesn't scare me!" The whole tone of the letter is one of jocose and robust common sense self-consciously contrasted with the chimerical fears of nervous intellectuals. As Petersen observes, "By such a comment, Engels avoided having to discuss in any detail either the economic significance of population growth or the moral system of the socialist society he was advocating."[17] And in consequence, it might be added, contemporary Marxist theorists and policy-makers have virtually no political, economic, or ethical guidelines within which to shape a specifically Socialist population policy.[18]

Similar references to the untapped bounty of the New World (and the Old) can be found elsewhere in the classic Marxist texts. It is evident that the contemporary expansion of science and land use both exerted a powerful impact on the founding fathers' minds — so powerful, in fact, that they seem to have experienced the greatest difficulty in conceiving of the earth's resources as in any sense finite. This extreme form of rationalist optimism was one of their more sturdy legacies to Soviet Marxism.[19]

Thus, briefly and colloquially, Marx and Engels pooh-poohed the short-term population/production dilemma (and in the days before population growth rates of more than 2% per annum had really established themselves may have been right to do so) and simply laughed off the long-term one. In doing so, however, they showed only a limited interest in demographic facts as such. To the Malthusian theory of an eternal conflict between inherently prolific reproduction and inherently less prolific production they counterposed the historical-materialist doctrine that the laws of population growth depended on and derived from the nature of the socioeconomic base, so that in successive historical epochs, quite different patterns might obtain. This allocation of demography to the superstructure, however, was not developed very much more than the conflicting theoretical strand, which tended to identify population as in some sense belonging to the base. Marx and Engels do not seem ever to have displayed any systematic interest in the overall demographic development of earlier periods, or indeed in macrodemographic statistics of any sort. Even a communist commentator has felt it necessary to make this point. Ronald Meek, the compiler of a most valuable compendium of Marxist obiter dicta on population questions, having noted that Marx and Engels maintained that every stage of historical development has its own law of population, goes on to comment:

It was not enough, of course, merely to assert this — it had to be proved (Meek's emphasis). Marx and Engels do not seem to have made any direct attempt to formulate the laws of population appropriate to earlier forms of class society; had they done so, they would probably have framed these laws in terms of the particular form of pressure of the direct producers against the "means of employment" which was generated by each of these types of society.[20]

Meek here puts his finger on another crucial feature of the Marxist writings on population. Not only were they not sufficiently interested to gather information about the demography of precapitalist societies, their interest in capitalist population problems was not strictly a demographic one either. The Marxist "law of capitalist population," if such it can indeed be called, was essentially a theory of employment under capitalism, a rider of the theory of the declining share of variable capital. The law says nothing about the actual movement of population as such — births, deaths, marriages, etc. And the comments made about these specifics by the masters en passant tend to be, from the theoretical point of view, unsystematic and rather elusive.[21] While the theory of the reserve army of the proletariat and the theory of growing immiseration (in some, at least, of their formulations) might be taken as suggesting that sooner or later population might be checked or indeed decline, their pragmatic view appears to have been that the solid increase characteristic of the Western European, and more particularly the Anglo-Saxon, world of their time would continue.[22] It is not altogether clear why they thought so. Marx did note, along with many others, that the rich get richer and the poor get children, and even formulated the principle that "not only the number of births and deaths, but the absolute size of the families stand in inverse proportion to the height of wages."[23] But he does not appear to have made any systematic attempt to explain why this should be so, beyond suggesting that it reflected the greater employability of minors and the high mortality of laborers exhausted by their brutal exploitation, which in combination created a social need for "rapid renewal of the generations of labourers," a need which the laborers obligingly met by marrying early. Early marriage, it is suggested, represents an attempt by the working classes "to conform to these circumstances," i.e., their own relatively high mortality. It is not clear whether Marx is here implying some kind of drive for species survival by the working classes or rather asserting that early marriage, "a necessary consequence of the conditions in which the labourers of modern industry live,"[24] stems quite independently from the sociological patterns of working-class life, the drunkenness and sexual excesses so vividly described by Engels in his The Condition of the Working Class.[25] The fragments of a theory that we find here are ingenious and suggestive. But apart from the obvious objection from hindsight (that class differentials in fertility and mortality alike have since flattened out without capitalism collapsing), it is also less than clear what is meant to be cause and what effect. Do the working classes reproduce to meet the requirements of the law of diminishing profits, as Marx seems at times to be suggesting? If so, is it just an accident that their life patterns tend to favor the kind of reproduction that the capitalists require? Or are the requirements of the latter an independent causative factor? If so, in what relation to one another do the two (or more than two) causative factors stand?[26]

The fact is that the Marxist theory of population was never more than a sketch for a theory of population, and a sketch in which few of the elements were truly demographic. But what Marx and Engels did say was sufficient to establish a strong and surprisingly durable prejudice within the German Social Democratic tradition against Malthusianism or anything that might ever be taken or mistaken for it.[27] The view that Malthus was a scoundrel and a fraud to attribute all the ills of capitalism to population growth (itself an oversimplification) somewhere merged into the view that population growth in itself was a good thing and proletarian, and efforts to restrain it wrong and bourgeois or petit bourgeois.

Lenin seems to have absorbed this strand of the German Marxist tradition in its more virulent form (a point to which we shall recur a little later). Apart from that, he does not appear to have added very much to Marxist teachings on population, Socialist commentators notwithstanding.[28] His principal writings on demographic matters are actually concerned with the Russian social structure of his time and migration, particularly internal migration. As this is not relevant to the central natalist concerns of this book, there is no point in discussing his contribution any further in the present context.

Marxism and Demographically Relevant Social Issues

As has already been noted, the list of social phenomena that might be regarded as demographically relevant is virtually endless. For present purposes, however, the discussion shall be limited to a few summary observations on three somewhat untidily overlapping topics: the institution of the family; the rights and role of women in socialist society; and the question of fertility con-

14

trol and the means to its achievement.

The classical Marxist writings on the place of the family in the socialist society of the future are ambiguous on certain key issues. Engels, the main contributor to the classical opus on this subject, was, whether for personal, intellectual, or other reasons, most ambivalent about marriage as an institution. His disdain for bourgeois marriage and his interest in primitive women-sharing arrangements seem at times to suggest that he might have gladly consigned marriage to the category of impermanent superstructural phenomena.[29] At other times he betrays a romantic, not to say ingenuous, enthusiasm for the joyous potentialities of marriage if and when it were to be stripped of economic calculation and based on what he called individual sexual love.[30] On the whole, however, he leaned toward radical revision of the institution. In particular he foresaw the disappearance of the indissolubility of marriage ties. "If only marriages that are based on love are moral, then also, only those are moral in which love continues. The duration of the urge of individual sex love differs very much according to the individual, particularly among men; and a definite cessation of affection, or its displacement by a new passionate love, makes separation a blessing for both parties as well as for society. People will only be spared the experience of wading through the useless mire of divorce proceedings."[31]

Another feature of traditional marriage which Engels felt sure would vanish was patriarchal male dominance.[32] In the family, wrote Engels, the husband is the bourgeois, while the wife represents the proletariat. Whereas once "in the old communistic household" the woman's economic role had been a public one, with the advent of monogamy and the emergence of the family as an economic unit, her work ceased to be the concern of the society: "The wife became the first domestic servant, pushed out of participation in social production."[33] While the diversification of the economy and employment opportunities brought by industrialization presented her with some opportunity for economic independence, this independence could only be seized by her if she were prepared to neglect her family duties. The solution to this dilemma lies in the re-communalization of the family as an economic and social unit: "Private housekeeping is transformed into a social industry. The care and education of the children becomes a public matter. Society takes care of all children equally, irrespective of whether they are born in wedlock or not."[34]

The precise extent of the communalization of the family as a social unit, however, was something that Engels left unclear. As if in trepidation before the changes he seemed to be endorsing, he chose at this point to add his celebrated excursus on the emergence of the higher value of individual sexual love, which he saw as being the basis of sexual, if not progenitive, relations in the society of the future. What patterns might be expected to emerge from the application of these principles can only be a matter for conjecture. Would lovers live with one another, and if so, would their children live with them, and if so, to what age? Would all household functions be taken over by society, and if so, who would perform them? If any disputes did emerge in the sphere of sexual or family relations, on what basis would they be resolved? Engels conceded that all that could be safely conjectured at that stage were improvements of a negative kind, then asked: "But what will be added? That will be settled after a new generation has grown up.... Once such people appear they will not care a rap about what we today think they should do. They will establish their own practice...."[35]

These were, in the event, prophetic words, perhaps the most prophetic of all Engels's comments on the family, if Soviet developments are to be taken as any test of their validity. For while the writings of the two founding fathers were somewhat ambivalent, it is clear that their basic orientation was toward radical change. And this indeed was the path that Soviet policy-makers took at the outset. That they later retreated from this path cannot, however, be simply categorized as expedient abandonment of declared principles. For not only did Marx and Engels themselves shrink before condemning the institution of marriage outright; Lenin also spoke on the issue. And while it is not clear that his views directly affected the evolution of policy on these matters, they were sufficiently unequivocal for us to assume that they may have had some restraining force during his lifetime; and they were quite certainly very influential after his death.

It is probably true to say (as Geiger does)[36] that Lenin was not greatly interested in problems of family policy. Indeed this must have been true, since the libertarian strand in Bolshevik policy during the first fifteen years or so (which was later to be identified as the left-wing deviation on family matters) could scarcely have endured had Lenin regarded the issue as of first importance. He was certainly in favor of liberation of the woman within the family and her absorption into economic activity; and he certainly recognized that to this end far-reaching communalization of domestic labor would be necessary. But he was most impatient with any attempts to introduce radical new sexual notions into party policy. While he did pay lip service to the traditional Engelsian doctrine on the subject, it seems fairly clear that he regarded the whole question as being one that good communists should ignore; and insofar as they did not, he seems tacitly to have felt classical doctrines to be rather an embarrassment. In nonpublic discussions with some of the sexual radicals among the female members of the Bolshevik movement, he made his impatience and his essentially conservative approach to these questions clear.

In two letters to Inessa Armand[37] he characterized "women's demand for free love" as a bourgeois demand, indicated that he understood this slogan as at best excluding any question that there might be such a right as freedom from childbirth and freedom to commit adultery, and suggested that she ought to contrast the base and vile marriage without love of the bourgeois not with any fleeting poetic passions, but rather with "a proletarian civilian marriage with love." The line ought, in any case, to be subordinated to the political needs of the moment.

In his celebrated conversation with Klara Zetkin some five years later,[38] by which time he had become the leader of a successful but still beleaguered revolution, this same approach was spelled out even more clearly. He deplored the interest shown by women comrades (and indeed the public in general) in sexual matters, dismissed Freudianism as typical of the kind of fashionable theory that "flourishes luxuriantly in the dirty soil of bourgeois society,"[39] admitted that the Russian youth movement was equally preoccupied with sexual matters and that he himself had been accused of philistinism in his attitude toward them, but made clear nonetheless that if this was modernity, he wanted none of it. Zetkin reports him as saying that "nothing could be more false than to preach monkish asceticism," then a moment later as characterizing himself as "nothing but a gloomy ascetic."[40] Kollontai's celebrated doctrine of the glass of water he rejects with the equally celebrated rejoinder that no normal person in normal circumstances will "lie down in the gutter and drink out of a puddle or out of a glass with a rim greasy from many lips." Then he says: "Drinking water is, of course, an individual affair. But in love two lives are concerned and a third, a new life arises. It is that which gives it its social interest...."[41]

Having again protested that he has no intention of preaching asceticism, Lenin goes on in scoutmasterly fashion to recommend healthy sport and bodily exercises as a substitute for sexual excesses. All energy should be concentrated on the revolution. The revolution cannot tolerate orgiastic conditions. "Dissoluteness in sexual life is bourgeois, is a phenomenon of decay. The proletariat is a rising class. It doesn't need intoxication as a narcotic or a stimulus. Intoxication as little by sexual exaggeration as by alcohol."[42]

Lenin's views on divorce were very much what one would expect. He did on one occasion assert that "one cannot be a democrat and a socialist without immediately demanding full freedom of divorce, for the absence of such freedom is an additional burden on the oppressed sex, woman"; however, he went on at once to add that "the recognition of the right of women to leave their husbands is not an invitation to all wives to do so!"[43] One is therefore led to wonder what might have been Lenin's reaction in a situation in which the "freedom" of divorce was seemingly being regarded as an invitation to divorce; a situation in which more and more young people were "reeling and staggering from one love affair to the next,"[44] to the detriment of their revolutionary obligations.

While most of Lenin's observations on sex and the family were made in a context of intense political struggle, to the dictates of which many other matters had to be temporarily subordinated, it seems doubtful that he would have had any stomach for free love or any version of it even in more placid times. He seems indeed to have been the kind of person who feels uneasy when the subject of sex is raised. It is not necessary to agree with any of the more extravagant psychohistorical speculations that have been hazarded about his personal makeup to conclude that here he represented a view well to the right of the overall trend of party policy and thinking at this time. And if this discussion of his views has given them greater weight than his own estimate of them or his contemporary influence on the course of social policy might appear to warrant, this has been done consciously, and for two reasons: first, to indicate that in sexual and family matters the Marxist-Leninist tradition, if not the Marxist one, had a definitely conservative as well as a radical face; and second, because it would appear that his views were typical of the kind of thinking that was subsequently to become party orthodoxy in the High Stalinist phase of Soviet family and population policy.

Having briefly glanced at the views of the pioneers of Marxism-Leninism on women and the family in general terms, it remains to say a few words about their attitudes toward the most demographically relevant question of all, namely, fertility control and the means to its achievement.

While their attitude toward Malthus and his views on overpopulation might suggest that Marx and Engels regarded birth control as unnecessary if not positively undesirable, it would seem that in actual fact they adopted a neutral position. Despite the fact that the neo-Malthusians were already very active (particularly in England) in the last decade of Marx's life (the celebrated Besant-Bradlaugh affair took place in 1876-77), neither Marx nor Engels seem to have ever explicitly commented on the movement.[45] Similarly, they appear to have maintained a discreet, Victorian silence on the technical aspects of the problem. Lenin's sparse observations accordingly represent the only scriptural authority on the subject. As was noted earlier, whatever the provenance of the anti-neo-Malthusianism[46] of the German Social Democratic movement, it appears to have been something which Lenin accepted without question and injected into the Russian tradition. The classic text here is Lenin's article "The Working Class and Neo-Malthusianism."[47] In it Lenin makes a forceful assault on those who would justify legalized abortion in terms of preventing the suffering of the future offspring. The point he makes in the article is not so much the Marxian one that this kind of argument puts the blame for social evils on the wrong shoulders, but rather that this represents a miserable and petit bourgeois pessimism which Lenin contrasts with the life-affirming vigor of the proletariat: "...why not have children so that they may fight better...than we against the living conditions which are deforming and destroying our generation.... We are already laying the foundations of the new building and our children will finish its construction."

Having thus justified rapid demographic growth among the proletariat in terms of the heroic tasks awaiting them, Lenin goes on to say:

That is why — and that is the only reason — we are unconditional enemies of neo-Malthusianism, which is a trend proper to the petty-bourgeois couple, hardened and egotistical....

It stands to reason that such an approach does not in any way prevent us from demanding the unconditional repeal of all laws persecuting abortion or laws against the distribution of medical works on contraceptive measures and so on. Such laws are simply the hypocrisy of the ruling classes. These laws do not cure the ills of capitalism but simply turn them into especially malignant and cruel diseases for the oppressed masses.

The freedom of medical propaganda and the protection of the elementary democratic rights of men and women citizens is one matter. Quite another is the social doctrine of neo-Malthusianism.

While Lenin shows himself in this article to have been conscious of a distinction between the practice or advocacy of birth control and the theory that excess births are the root cause of all working-class misery, or to paraphrase, between what he at one point calls "neo-Malthusianism (artificial measures to prevent conception)" and at another "reactionary and impoverished 'social neo-Malthusianism,'"[48] the distinction seems to be in constant danger of disappearing. Small wonder that the literal-minded neophytes of later years failed to perceive any distinction whatever. People should be allowed the right to birth control by various means, up to and including abortion (though Lenin made clear that he regarded a high incidence of abortion as a very bad thing); and this right should certainly be made available to the working classes, since the existing laws turn the already serious ills of capitalism into "especially malignant and cruel diseases." At the same time, Lenin enjoins the working classes not to make use of any such right, but rather to multiply and go forth to the construction of a new society and leave birth control to the moribund classes. Given this strange and somewhat contradictory combination of attitudes, it is difficult to say what policy measures Lenin might have felt necessary were he to have survived at the helm of the Soviet state to the 1930s, when abortions in Moscow were outrunning live births by three to one. My own inclination is toward the belief that other things being equal, he would have sided with the conservatives on population and related social-policy issues. And were he to have felt that the circumstances amounted to an emergency situation, it is all the more likely that he would have done so. As with divorce, there is just a hint that Lenin's approach to the problem is basically instrumentalist, that is to say, that he was more concerned with what the party line should be from the point of view of his general political goals than the inherent rights and wrongs of the particular issue at hand: "It stands to reason that such an approach does not in any way prevent us from demanding...." If Stalinism was indeed Leninism-when-the-chips-are-down writ large (and indelible), it could be argued that the subsequent development of Soviet family and population policy represented a retreat from Engels, and presumably from Marx also; but not from Lenin.

CHAPTER 3

POPULATION
AND SOVIET
SOCIAL POLICY

In this chapter I shall present a schematic outline of the course
of Soviet social policy in areas of direct demographic relevance
from the time of the revolution up to the mid-nineteen fifties,[1] then
attempt to assess its significance from the point of view of numerical or quantitative population policy. Policies on population matters throughout the bloc were broadly uniform up to about 1956,
and one can regard everything done to that time in the USSR as
forming in some sense part of a common tradition of influence
both in the USSR and elsewhere in the Socialist world.

Despite Lenin's relative conservatism on family policy, the period before and just after his death saw the passage of some of the
most far-reaching if not the most far-reaching reform legislation
that has ever been passed anywhere on these matters. This legislation seems all the more remarkable when it is borne in mind
that Russian prerevolutionary laws on family and related matters
had been strongly conservative. Within weeks of the October Revolution, ecclesiastical control over civil status had been withdrawn,
and within a year, a new codified family law was introduced providing for rigorous equality between the partners to a marriage,
including the right to seek divorce.

At the same time, the status of illegitimate children was greatly
improved.[2] In 1920 abortion was legalized and the medical profession apparently enjoined to perform the operation for anyone wanting it.[3] In 1926 a new Family Code was enacted for the RSFSR
which, among other things, accorded de facto relationships equal
rights with legally registered marriages and made divorce dependent simply upon one or the other party registering a desire for it.[4]
During this same period there were many other measures taken

21

and statements made which clearly indicated an official determination to radically alter the institution of marriage and the family if
not positively to abolish it. Thus bigamy, adultery, and even incest
ceased to be crimes, familial rights of inheritance were restricted,[5]
efforts were made to encourage women to enter into economic
and political life on an equal footing with men, communal household
services were established, and in the Komsomol and elsewhere,
an ethos was allowed to develop in which it became acceptable, if
not actually praiseworthy, to do all one could to overturn the old
norms of sexual and family life. Geiger has summarized the situation as follows: "In the first decade or so after the Revolution it
was rather generally though vaguely agreed that the family was not
worth much as an institution and would eventually disappear."[6]

While Geiger's formulation may perhaps err slightly on the side
of overstatement, broadly speaking it does capture the trend of
official thinking, at least in the early years after the revolution.
Kollontai, the radical feminist associated with the so-called "glass
of water" theory, has since been retrospectively identified as belonging to a left-wing deviation on this question also. Nonetheless
both she and another dissenter from Lenin's views on family policy,
Inessa Armand, occupied for a time the position of secretary of
the Women's Department of the Central Committee.[7] And Kollontai
may well have continued in that position beyond 1920 had she not
incurred the party leadership's displeasure by her left-wing activities on other and more crucial issues.

But though in terms of legislation 1926 marks the high point of
radicalism, already by the midtwenties, voices of caution and even
downright dismay were beginning to make themselves heard. The
1926 legislation itself was passed against considerable if not very
politically weighty opposition from speakers representing what
might be schematically described as traditional views and rural
and feminine interests.[8] But even before that, well-known party
and state leaders had made attacks on certain consequences of the reforms, notably the alleged spread of abortions and sexual indulgence.[9]

As the twenties wore on there was a tendency for more conservative views to gain in official favor and currency. Thus in 1923
Lunacharsky was defending the sphere of private relations not
only from state interference but also even from pressure of public
opinion; and in 1927 the same Lunacharsky was deploring sexual
inconstancy and urging greater attention be paid to "that which until
the present has been called private life."[10] Then, coinciding with
the full blooming of Stalin's personal dictatorship in the midthirties

(and presumably, therefore, in some measure reflecting his personal approach to these matters), there came a complete reorientation of official policy. After an extensive press campaign lasting
for about two years, during which lax morals in sexual and family
relations were pilloried in fairly traditional terms, legal innova-
tions began to reflect the new approach. A 1934 law held parents
responsible for their delinquent children. Then in 1935-36 legal
fees were introduced for divorce to underline the official disapproval of marital instability. In 1936 abortion was made illegal,[11]
penalties for nonpayment of alimony were increased, various forms
of state aid to mothers were introduced or expanded, and a large
program of crèche, kindergarten, and maternity ward construction
was foreshadowed. In 1941 a tax was introduced on the earnings
of single people and married couples without children.[12] And in
1944 there was further legislation substantially extending child
allowances and similar benefits, introducing a string of honorific
titles for fecund mothers, rendering divorce much more difficult
and costly to obtain, increasing the taxes imposed on childless
adults, and withdrawing the legal recognition of quasi-conjugal
rights formerly accorded to de facto wives and single mothers.[13]

Concurrently with these legislative developments there occurred
a marked shift in the overall propaganda approach toward sex and
family matters. The Bohemian experimentalism of the early post-
revolutionary years was totally expunged, and the Victorian decorum
so attractive to many Western clergymen took its place. Sex became a taboo subject, and premarital or extramarital breaches of
traditional monogamous morality were now frowned on.[14] The
simple family virtues were much extolled; children were exhorted
to respect their parents, while the latter were entrusted in large
measure with the ideological as well as the material welfare of
their offspring. Though women were not encouraged to abandon
their jobs for the home (a development which neither they themselves nor the state could afford), traditional sex roles within the
family were by and large reasserted. The purpose of marriage
was declared to be the creation of a "strong, many-childrened
family,"[15] unmarred by the "obscenity" of bourgeois divorce,[16]
a family which was at once loyal to itself and loyal to the state.
Sexual licence of any kind was a sign of bourgeois corruption. Insofar as such phenomena continued to exist in the Soviet Union,
they were survivals of the capitalist past.[17] In a word, the "revolutionary sublimation" of Zalkind and the benevolent parental despotism
of Makarenko had become received — and mandatory — orthodoxy.

The 1944 legislation was probably the climactic point in the Stalinist policy of restabilizing the family, at least from the point of view of its demographic objectives. In 1947 the generous family allowances of 1944 were halved and not thereafter increased.[18] In other respects, however, existing policies were maintained. In 1949 all remaining legal rights and duties arising from de facto marriage were annulled, and divorce was made a good deal harder to obtain by an authoritative Supreme Court interpretation of the law which directed lower courts in effect to be much less lenient than they had been prior to that date.[19]

Soon after Stalin's death, however, the authoritarian structure of his family legislation began to crumble. In early 1954 there was a public attack on the discriminatory aspects of the 1944 legislation whereby men were granted impunity from paternity and support suits.[20] Later in the same year certain exemptions to the tax on the childless were introduced,[21] women were exonerated from criminal responsibility for abortions performed on them,[22] and simultaneously a ground swell of more general criticism of the 1944 provisions on divorce and paternity began.[23] Then in 1955 abortion was abruptly relegalized without prior public discussion or any accompanying official comment.[24] In 1956 the public debate on the Family Code blossomed into forthright criticism of many of its aspects by a number of well-known Soviet figures. After a number of vicissitudes, the divorce reformers were finally triumphant, partially in 1965 and more substantially, though not completely, in 1968.[25]

During this post-Stalinist phase a good deal of the earlier ideological ballast surrounding the family was jettisoned: there was less talk of the holiness and purity of Soviet marriage, rather less rigorous prudishness and repressiveness about matters relating to sex, a greater emphasis on women's rights, and correspondingly lesser degree of tolerance of the old patriarchalism and double standards. Sound family life and concomitant values continued to be favored, but without the politically tinged fanaticism of the later Stalinist period.

At this point it will be appropriate to break off this sketch outline of the main historical trends in Soviet family and population policy and to make some attempt at assessing the significance of those trends in terms of our central natalist point of reference.

The reforms introduced in the early years of Soviet rule represented the implementation of a platform that might have been proposed by a number of other radical movements, not necessarily communist or even Marxist, had they only succeeded in conquering state power as the Bolsheviks did. The thrust of the legislation was toward increasing the civil rights of the oppressed minorities of patriarchal class society and, in some measure, toward deliberately weakening the family as an institution. It seems clear that no populationist considerations of any kind entered into the initial reckoning. The legalization of abortion and the tolerance extended to family planning activities (at a time when they were illegal in most of Europe) were certainly not intended to restrict population growth. Indeed, in a certain sense they appear to have been policies adopted without any very great inner conviction or commitment. Abortion was legalized in response to what was described as an epidemic emergency and was never greatly encouraged thereafter. And observers seem to be agreed that the use of contraceptives was never actively fostered either.

If, however, natalist considerations were not prominent at the outset, they seem definitely to have become so subsequently, most probably in the early 1930s, as falling birthrates and the demographic consequences of collectivization began to penetrate the official consciousness.

Reference was made earlier to the difficulty that is often experienced in disentangling demographic from social considerations in the analysis of motives underlying particular policies. There is probably a universal tendency for governments to downplay any quantitative, as opposed to qualitative, demographic ambitions they may have. Be that as it may, it is certainly true that the Soviet authorities have often been less than fully explicit about their populationist motives. There is a good deal of evidence to support the view that these were a major influence, if not the major influence, on several of the key policy decisions taken or not taken in the 1930s and afterward. In relation to the 1936 and 1944 legislation, Juviler cites several official statements in support of the view that, as he says, these edicts "marked an extension of Stalin's social engineering for a strong family, and, especially, for a higher birth rate."[26] But much of Soviet comment on these issues has tended to be evasive, preferring to stress that the main concern of the Soviet state is to care for the interests of its citizens. The family planning expert, Dr. Abraham Stone, has said that whenever he asked Soviet officials to explain the reasons for this or that shift in abortion policy, the reply was always the same irrespective of the direction of the shift: "For the benefit of our Soviet women."[27] Wolffson, the erstwhile liberal on family matters, explained in an article published in 1936 that the birthrate was rising in the USSR, but in virtually the same breath justified the prohibition of abortion on the grounds that this practice had been "depriving the country of its posterity."[28] Another commentator on the 1936 legislation, Svetlov, referred to an alleged rise in the Soviet birthrate (itself a falsehood or, at best, a distortion), arguing that this was a clear sign that abortion had come to be felt to be unnecessary under Soviet conditions, and accordingly could be safely abolished.[29] Juviler also cites a number of instances of reluctance on the part of those debating family law reform in the fifties and sixties to refer to natalist considerations in public, though these were evidently very prominent in discussion behind the scenes and between the lines.[30]

Both the 1936 and 1944 parcels of measures were introduced after dramatic and simultaneous declines in natality and increases in mortality.[31] It would be naive in the extreme to regard this circumstance as accidental. Given the great brutality of the measures that were being taken against the population contemporaneously, and given the relatively low priority social welfare enjoyed under Stalin's rule,[32] it would again be naive in the extreme to accept the official Soviet claim that the principle purposes of that legislation were humanitarian. Western commentators have usually inferred that the population issue was paramount. Significantly, this was the view taken by the well-informed Western communist observer Rudolph Schlesinger, who, in introducing his collection of documents on Soviet family policy, declared his overall approach to the subject in the following terms:

> We shall concentrate most of our attention upon the original issue, the emancipation of women and the overcoming of the traditional institutional framework which prevents that emancipation, and on the modifications of the attitude taken on this issue in connection with the growing preponderance of the population question.[33]

While the population factor does indeed appear to have been paramount, it should be emphasized that other important issues and problems were involved. The radical family legislation of the 1920s had evoked considerable discontent among wide segments of the population which had not (and indeed have not yet) accepted the new sexual morality that most of the original Bolsheviks advocated. If that morality was not "bourgeois" in the doctrinaire sense apparently intended by Lenin, it was certainly urban and nonproletarian, inasmuch as workers and peasants usually either rejected it (especially if they were female) or naively abused it.[34] And among those

26

who abused it there was widespread recourse to rationalization in terms of traditional male double standards. Their perception of the new freedoms was that these were the old illicit freedoms now sanctioned by official approval. Their misinterpretation was naturally widely resented by victims and deplored by moralists; and not only by those still under the influence of the church. Nor was abuse of the new laws confined to men and resentment confined to women. Many women took advantage of the new and generous provisions for alimony to father their children on the nearest and best-off males with whom they could claim to have been in some fleeting union. Moreover, there had been in the early years a marked tendency for the authorities to distrust the family as an institution and to seek to set children against their parents. This "Morozovism" was no doubt universally resented by the adult population, irrespective of sex. Thus as Stalin's plans for gigantic destruction and reconstruction developed in the 1930s, together with the massive resentments they must have unleashed, he may well have deemed it discreet to adopt a policy which would tend to diminish discontent in areas of life less relevant to his main economic and political purposes.

But more important than that was the need to bring stability to the basic social unit of society. If it were not to be or could not be reconstructed along with everything else, it was better to strengthen it and make of it a prop for the regime, the more so as it was now unlikely that the family would nurture opposition to the new order in quite the same degree as it was believed to have done just after the revolution. As things stood, the loosened family ties were bringing the authorities nothing but trouble. Already in the twenties there were numerous social problems that were the direct result of or had been severely aggravated by the new legislation. An article published in 1926 referred to the courts as being "buried under alimony cases."[35] War, the abolition of the institution of adoption, and the spread of evanescent liaisons were producing armies of besprizorniki, or vagrant children.[36] Public facilities like canteens, laundries, orphanages, and daily child-care institutions that were supposed to be making the old-style family economy obsolete were in fact hopelessly inadequate in numbers and quality; and their oft-projected massive expansion was for the foreseeable future economically unfeasible, particularly given the magnitude of the tasks accorded priority by the leadership.[37] Easy divorce encouraged irresponsibility not only toward one's family but also toward one's work: the husband skipping about the country to avoid his obligations toward his family or families was obviously a less reliable and conscientious worker than one tied to one spot and with mouths other than his own to feed from the proceeds of his struggle with the norms. The best guarantee of a disciplined and reasonably healthy labor force was to have a sound family struc- ture in which both parents and children would find social security and strong motivation to endeavor.

Thus the restabilization of the family served important objectives of social and economic policy as well as purely demographic policy in the narrower, numerical sense. But the protestations of some Soviet sources notwithstanding, it was probably the latter element that was decisive.

It may be helpful now to make some brief assessment of the overall significance of the Soviet population policy tradition. It might appear at first sight that it has now described a more or less complete circle from radically liberal beginnings through a phase of Victorian conservatism back to something more akin to the starting point, where society is left to order its sexual and family life with only a modest degree of state regulation. This ap- pearance may yet prove to have been illusory. The official mood of the fifties and sixties on these matters has nothing of the ideo- logical strain of social laissez-faireism of the early years of the revolution. At a time when official and unofficial attitudes on sex and the family are undergoing extensive liberalization throughout the world, the trends in Soviet official opinion represent something less than an avalanche. The most recent reforms of family law were introduced after a long, hard struggle against tough opposition. The attitude toward contraception remains cautious and unenthusi- astic. Abortion has been relegalized, but the official view of it has always tended to be that it is basically a regrettable and tem- porary necessity. For the rest, official policy on sexual matters remains conservative. The chances of a reversion to the Stalinist approach seem to be diminishing, but slowly and not very surely. One wonders whether the slender element of principled liberalism within it might not again be eclipsed some day by raison d'état.[38]

This having been said, it remains true that since the demise of Morozovism, sexual and family relations have always represented an important pocket of autonomy within the Soviet system. And after Stalin's death the reintroduction of "Leninist norms" into the relevant area of social legislation has resulted in the significant further expansion of that area of autonomy. Rigby speaks of "an acknowledged personal-family-domestic sphere, to which the system

28

concedes a major influence over such societally important matters as quantitative and qualitative[39] changes in the population, child-rearing, personal consumption and leisure activities."[40] In the light of the far-reaching claims made on the individual at the height of the Stalinist period, the truly noteworthy thing is perhaps that these claims were <u>not</u> extended to complete control of human re-production (as they were, for instance, in the otherwise less totali-tarian or mono-organizational — to use Rigby's term — Nazi Germany);[41] that the claims that actually were made at the height of the Stalinist phase have since been withdrawn, or at least have become markedly less obtrusive; and that both in the tradition of Marxist-Leninist theory and the practice of the Soviet state, there is strong authority with which this sphere of personal autonomy can be defended.

CHAPTER 4

POPULATION TRENDS
IN THE USSR AND
EASTERN EUROPE[1]

The Soviet Union before 1945

The Soviet Union is a vast country of great ethnocultural, and hence demographic, diversity which its political uniformism has not eliminated, but rather, if anything enhanced. It is also a country which has seen more demographic disturbances and disasters in this century than almost any other in the world. These two circumstances make generalization difficult. But the overall figures for the USSR,[2] though they are misleading as regards the non-European peoples, do nonetheless give some picture of the developments that have taken place in the numerically dominant European populations.

Just before World War I, both birth and death rates in Russia were very high, oscillating around 46 and 28 per thousand respectively, and having been at even higher levels only a decade or so earlier. In recent years these same two measures for the USSR as a whole have been hovering around 17 to 18 and 8 to 9 per thousand. Imperfect as they are statistically, these figures speak for themselves. East Slav fertility was undoubtedly higher than was known anywhere in Western Europe. Now it ranks among the lowest in Western or Eastern Europe. A good deal of this decline had already occurred by the outbreak of World War II, though this was to some extent masked by the temporary fertility revival achieved by the restoration of restrictive abortion legislation in 1936. The birth and death rates per thousand for 1935, the only ones available for the years just preceding the policy change, were 28.6 and 16.3. Fertility appears to have been declining in this period faster than mortality, so that before the pronatalist measures of 1936, natural increase must have been diminishing. Far more important than fertility trends, however, were the effects of the world wars, the Civil War, the collectivization campaign and famine, and the Great Purge. No "official" figures are, of course, available, but statistical inferences suggest staggering total losses, particularly if allowance is made for temporary decline in birthrates. Petersen has estimated the total population deficit "correct to the nearest 10 million" at 80 million.[3] Even if we assume that half of the "nonbirths" and extraordinary infant mortality he includes in his total were later effectively "replaced" (which is very unlikely), and that his lower margin of error is the correct one,[4] we are left with losses amounting to substantially more than the present population of Great Britain and equivalent to about one half the number of Russians at present living in the USSR. Though certain of the nationalities suffered particularly heavily from aberrant Stalinist policies, it would probably be safe to assume that a disproportionately high percentage of the total came if not from the Russian, then at least from the European population.

Eastern Europe before 1945

It is customary to emphasize the social, cultural, and economic diversity of the East European countries when lumping them together for political analysis. The usual warning is no less apposite in the demographic context. Before World War II the Czech lands and the region now known as East Germany were, demographically as in many other respects, similar to the countries of northern and northwestern Europe, with low birth and death rates and relatively small natural increase. Hungary occupied intermediate positions, while Poland, Romania, and Bulgaria, at least at the outset of the interwar period, had only just embarked on the process of demographic transition from high to low birth and death rates. By the end of the interwar period, however, marked change had occurred there too, with crude birthrates below 30 per thousand, and in the case of Bulgaria, nearer 20 per thousand. Yugoslavia then, as now, encompassed virtually the entire range of demographic phenomena observed throughout the area, while Albania appears to have been following a pattern of high fertility and relatively high mortality, with natural increase substantially less than it has since become.

The economic effects of the Great Depression (which were felt longer and more sharply in the area than in Western Europe) accelerated the secular trend toward fertility decline, and by 1938 natural increase rates were everywhere (Albania excepted) of the order of 1% per annum or less, a modest enough rate, though roughly twice the average for the countries of northern and western Europe at that same time.

The war produced enormous loss of life and touched off major migratory movements in Eastern Europe. Civilian losses amounted to four times the European average (even excluding the murder of the Jews).[5] With some notable exceptions (Czechoslovakia, Bulgaria, and Hungary), birthrates also declined during the war years. The immediate postwar migrations also tended, in general, to involve net population losses. The peace negotiations resulted in considerable territorial revisions. It is impossible to recapitulate even the broad outlines of these developments here.[6] Perhaps their most important feature was to greatly increase the national homogeneity of the countries of the region, which before the war had with few exceptions been plagued by apparently insoluble ethnopolitical problems. Until recently observers of the area were sometimes apt to think that the combination of mass migration and centralist policies and controls had gone a long way toward solving these problems. More recently it has been forced on our attention that this may not be the case. And as shall be indicated elsewhere, current demographic trends are not, in general, conducive to their solution.

Population Trends in the USSR and Eastern Europe since the War

Fertility and Natural Increase

As elsewhere in Europe, the postwar years saw birthrates in general higher than those prevailing in the 1930s. In Poland, which had suffered the greatest losses in total population of any country in the region, there was a spectacular baby boom which persisted for a full decade before subsiding. In the Soviet Union, too, the drastic postwar shortage of young males was more than compensated for by extremely high male fertility.[7]

By the midfifties, however, this wave had all but exhausted itself, and the secular trend toward fertility decline apparent throughout the area before the war had set in again. This trend seemed to be sharply accelerated by the liberalized abortion legislation introduced first in the Soviet Union, in 1955, and adopted by almost all

32

the other Warsaw Pact countries — Bulgaria characteristically
leading the way — before the end of 1957. East Germany, in catastrophic demographic plight owing to the heavy outmigration of
young men via West Berlin, did not liberalize its abortion arrangements till 1972 (by which time many of its neighbors were reverting
to restrictive regulations). Apparently thanks in some measure to
this, its age-specific fertility rates remained steady and for a time
even improved slightly. Yugoslavia liberalized its abortion laws
decisively in 1960.[8] Albania, stubbornly independent in all things,
did not alter its legislation; and it too — though probably not mainly
for this reason — has maintained very high and stable fertility
levels almost to the present.

The areas occupied by Moslem peoples in the Soviet Union and
Yugoslavia apart, a spectacular slump in birthrates now ensued,
matched in the opposite direction by burgeoning abortion rates.
The prevalence of abortion differed substantially from country to
country, but the upward trend till well into the sixties at least was
everywhere the same.[9] Hungary had for many years before 1974
the highest recorded abortion rate, which ran at times well in excess of its birthrate. In Romania and the Soviet Union, though no
adequate statistics have been published, the rates must be (in the
case of Romania must have been)[10] very much higher. Elsewhere
abortion rates were more moderate, but the same tendency toward increase in its incidence and the same decline in fertility were apparent.

By the midsixties the Socialist countries were starting to break
world records for low birth and natural increase rates. Hungary
recorded an average of 13 births per thousand population over the
years 1962-65, and in Bulgaria, Czechoslovakia, East Germany,
and Romania, crude rates also fell below 15 per thousand in at
least one year. More recently the Soviet Union has been saved from
such indignities only by its youthful age structure and the fecundity of
its ethnic minorities. In the early 1970s similarly low natality was
confidently predicted for Poland by many of its demographic experts. And comparable rates have for some time now been a commonplace in the relatively more developed republics of Yugoslavia.

To some extent the declining crude birthrates reflected reductions in the proportion of women in the main fertile age groups (as
the relatively depleted cohorts of the depression period of the thirties and in some countries of the war years entered the child-bearing
age groups). As age structures began to improve in the late 1960s,
a certain steadying of the crude rates became perceptible. Alarmed
by the drastic deterioration of the situation, some states initiated

pronatalist measures, which have contributed to checking fertility declines and in some cases may even be bringing about substantial recoveries, at least in the short term.[11] And in recent years there has been throughout most of Socialist Europe a general, not as yet very well understood, increase in age-specific fertility rates. But in many countries or regions fertility rates remain around or below replacement levels; and in several cases (Hungary before 1974, Bulgaria, and parts of Yugoslavia and the USSR) they have probably been hovering in that area for a number of years.[12]

The fertility decline, dramatic in the more developed areas, has not affected all regions of the bloc. In many of the traditionally Moslem areas of settlement, fertility has actually increased since the postwar years and is only now beginning to show signs of falling from its very high levels. This is most notably true of Soviet Central Asia and the Caucasus region and parts of Yugoslavia and Albania. In these same areas the application of public health measures and improved medical and hospital facilities have brought a simultaneous reduction of mortality levels down to those prevailing in the more advanced regions. Thus in the bloc as a whole and in Yugoslavia and the Soviet Union individually, one is confronted in effect with something approaching the full gamut of vital rates existing in the Eurasian land mass today.

From what has already been said, it will be clear that there have been large discrepancies in natural increase rates between the different countries, regions, and peoples of the bloc. Thus in 1972 the range within the Warsaw Pact countries was from -2 per thousand in East Germany through 9.6 per thousand in Romania to 25.2 per thousand in Albania.[13] The range within the Soviet Union in 1972 by individual republics (and remember that virtually all of them have a substantial Russian minority which will serve to damp down extremes) was 3.2 per thousand in Latvia through 6.3 per thousand in the RSFSR (which comprises over half the total population and contains four fifths of all ethnic Russians) to 29.0 per thousand in Tadzhikistan; all this within a deceptive national figure of 9.3 per thousand.[14] In Yugoslavia the spread was no less extreme, from 2.1 in the Autonomous Province of the Vojvodina, through 4.6 and 5.5 in the Republic of Croatia and Serbia proper, respectively, to 27.4 per thousand in the heavily Albanian Kosovo Autonomous Province.[15] Kosovo has a large (roughly 18%) and much less fertile Serbian minority, which again tends to derogate from the contrast that is really involved.

It may bring out the magnitude of the differences better to consider changes in the population of the principal national groups within individual republics/provinces of the Soviet Union and Yugoslavia as between the last two censuses of 1961 and 1971 and 1959 and 1970 respectively. Thus whereas the Russians increased by 13%[16] in the USSR as a whole (the Russians being especially prone to outmigration from the RSFSR, to take the figure for their "own" republic would be slightly misleading), the numbers of each of the five major Central Asian republican nations increased within their respective republics by almost 50% or more.[17] The Serbs increased by 4.3% and the Croats by 5.4%, whereas the Albanians increased by 43.1%.[18]

A word or two should perhaps be added to the above remarks on the fertility decline in the Socialist countries to put them in some kind of overall European perspective. In the early and midsixties, as mentioned earlier, all the low birthrate records were going to the Socialist countries, and the overall postwar fertility recovery in the Western world seemed only just beginning to falter slightly. Since then, while crude rates and, in some measure, actual fertility have steadied or shown tentative signs of recovery in many of the low-fertility Socialist countries, there have been spectacular fertility plunges in many Western countries, with crude birthrates frequently slumping despite age structure changes that would lead one to expect a demographic echo of the postwar baby boom.[19] Two of the most spectacular drops occurred in Finland[20] (where crude rates went from 28 to 12.2 per thousand between 1947 and 1973) and West Germany,[21] which wrested the world record from Hungary's grasp and latterly seems bent on disappearing off the graph paper. Even France, traditionally the most earnestly pronatalist country in Western Europe, and one which was slower in moving into this present slump, is now again causing its helmsmen concern.[22] The steep and general downturn in Western birthrates ought to be of some consolation to the Socialist countries. After their giddy burst of overtaking the West in the early and midsixties, they must be cheered to find so many capitalist nations outpacing them on the slippery slope down to demographic perdition.

Other Population Trends

For present purposes less needs to be said about trends in other demographic indicators. Mortality rates are low throughout the area, and given normal circumstances, are unlikely to vary widely in the future. Infant mortality rates remain high enough in Albania and Kosovo Province in Yugoslavia for further major improvement to be possible. This would temporarily dilute the effect of inherent fertility declines (assuming that they come) on natural increase rates. In the more developed countries, particularly East Germany with its aged population and its middle generations depleted during the pre-Wall era, mortality is relatively high in absolute terms, though not according to age-specific rates. The general tendency in the area as a whole is toward moderate increase in crude mortality rates. In recent years this same tendency has extended to age-specific rates for males in the older age groups, suggesting that the Socialist countries are entering the phase of affluent mortality patterns. Up till the early sixties much was made for propaganda purposes of the Soviet Union's (then) unusually low death rate, which was felt to indicate, like vigorous natural growth, the beneficent operation of the "socialist law of population." Since then, with a general aging of the society and (perhaps) improved death registration in some republics — so that more dead souls actually enter and bulk out the statistics — Soviet death rates have ceased to be in any way remarkable. Echoes of the old pride in longevity are still sometimes to be heard in population pronouncements, but less frequently than at one time; and the ring of assertive confidence now seems to lack real conviction. Indeed, in the Soviet Union the recent increase in age-specific death rates has evidently been sufficient to prompt the withholding of data about infantile mortality and life expectancy from public view.[23]

The aging process has been proceeding everywhere except in the countries and regions of continuing high fertility. So far the growing numbers of pensioners have been compensated, as it were, by declining cohorts in the younger age groups, so that dependency ratios have on the whole deteriorated little.[24] There is a general tendency to aging within the labor force, though not in every case. In East Germany there has even been a marked improvement in the age structure of the able-bodied section of the population latterly, as the pre-Wall migrating generation approaches middle age.[25]

The abnormalities produced in the sex structure of certain of the populations (notably the USSR, East Germany, and Poland) are also of course working themselves out. The massive postwar Soviet deficit of twenty million or so males is gradually diminishing and passing up the pyramid to age groups where it is economically, militarily, reproductively, and perhaps generally less keenly relevant. Thus while the Soviet Union's able-bodied age structure actually was in quite significant decline in the 1960s, this was largely counteracted by improvements in the sex ratio of the work force.

With forced-draft industrialization programs being implemented throughout the area and collectivization introduced everywhere (though discontinued and largely disbanded in Yugoslavia and Poland), there have been massive flows of population from country to town and extensive urban development. The proportions of urban and rural population have been drastically altered everywhere in a very short time.[26] Despite the simultaneous feminization of the rural work force, female employment ratios in the socialized non-agricultural (i.e., urban) sectors are running high and tending to increase further. Intolerable strains have been placed on urban housing stocks; severe housing shortages are endemic to Eastern Europe. All these factors have an impact on the demographic situation. As to housing, though long-term correlation studies might not seem to suggest it, opinion surveys into planned numbers of children in urban families have come up almost unfailingly with the conclusion that housing conditions are a major subjective factor involved in family limitation. High female labor force participation rates are also contributing to fertility decline, the more so as domestic services to aid the housewife (from crèches to supermarkets) are uniformly unsatisfactory. One urban study carried out in Bucharest in the 1960s, for example, revealed an average number of wanted children of 1.3, and 0.7 for women with higher education.[27]

Turning to collectivization, it is perhaps "not accidental" that Poland and Yugoslavia, the two noncollectivized countries, have had higher levels of fertility than the other countries. While Yugoslavia's position in this respect undoubtedly owes something to its partial membership in the Moslem world, this is not true of Poland, where for a decade or more rural fertility has been supporting overall rates hindered by very low urban indices.[28] Poland and Yugoslavia appear in fact to have the highest urban/rural fertility differentiation in Europe.[29]

Since the massive population movements following World War II, to which reference has already been made, not a great deal of either short-term or permanent external migration has occurred in the area.[30] East Germany's flooding outmigration has now been staunched to a trickle (nonetheless East Germany is not expected to regain its postwar level of population in this century). There have been some spasmodic flows of deportations and exchanges or permitted emigration of ethnic groups: Turks from Bulgaria and Yugoslavia; Jews from Romania, Poland, Bulgaria, and more recently the Soviet Union; Germans from Czechoslovakia and Poland;

a substantial inflow of Poles from the Soviet Union into Poland in the late fifties. All of these movements were, so to speak, exceptional. No state in the area (apart from Yugoslavia) has extended toleration to emigration as such. And apart from inflows of ethnic groups identifying with the metropolitan nation concerned, none has any problem with immigration. Thus paradoxically, during a period when intra-European migration movements reached a level of unprecedented intensity, with labor moving across state frontiers almost as freely as goods, Soviet bloc rigidity continued to box up relative labor shortages and surpluses in autarkic national cells. There is now some official realization of the benefits of international movements of labor, and the first cautious beginnings have been made. But like nonswimmers at the water's edge, the Socialist governments have confined a large proportion of their experiments to daily commuting between border towns. It seems quite conceivable that by the time any bolder plans are approved, the general and growing labor shortages throughout the area will smother them at or soon after birth.

For the moment, then, there is a clear resolve, for whatever reason, to avoid letting large numbers of nationals of any country run loose in another. As a prominent Soviet writer on Comecon labor exchanges has put it, "For the time being, as for the foreseeable future, priority is given to those forms of coordinated utilization of labor resources in the Comecon countries which do not involve their international movement."[31] One of the problems involved is, of course, that there is a strong ideological presupposition that any socialist country can find rational and productive employment for all its citizens and that the bad old days of economic emigration are over. Another is the fact that fewer and fewer countries have labor surpluses to dispose of. The one exception here, Yugoslavia, is reluctant to participate fully for political reasons (and in any case, it is difficult to conceive Yugoslav workers who have seen Paris or Stockholm being content with Pilsen or Katowice). The Romanians, for their part, have simply refused to join in.[32]

If, however, some form of expanded Gastarbeiter system were to be devised in Eastern Europe, with migrant laborers from within or outside the Socialist countries, the demographic and political consequences of such a development could be no less momentous than the economic. On this particular issue bureaucratic rigidity may be masking sober pragmatism. The Yugoslav case illustrates some of the more serious complications that might ensue.

Here, as in so many other things, Yugoslav events help us to imagine what could conceivably happen elsewhere under Socialism if circumstances or policies were to change. The Yugoslav economic emigration in a very short time assumed massive proportions. Estimates vary, but it is clear that at its peak there were at least a million Yugoslavs "temporarily" (as official documents always maintained) employed outside the country. The economic and political strains caused continued for long to be outweighed by the very tangible benefits reaped in the form of hard-currency capital inflow (remittances in 1978, for example, amounted to a figure of $2.8 billion)[33] and mitigated (rather than reduced) domestic unemployment. But ultimately, and perhaps inevitably, official policy toward emigration changed. These matters will be discussed more thoroughly later. For the moment, however, by way of briefly illustrating the kind of demographic-political problems that can be unleashed by free emigration from a Socialist country, perhaps it might be mentioned that before the change of policy (or perhaps more relevantly, before the onset of the post-1973 recession in the Western economy and the consequent decline in the demand for labor in the Common Market countries), the annual outflow from Yugoslavia was of dimensions comparable with those of the country's natural increase; that Yugoslav observers are still skeptical as to how many of these emigrants will return; that the overwhelming majority of those who left were in the fertile age groups; that the national composition of the emigrants did not reflect that of the population as a whole (although the divergences in this respect narrowed as time went on); and that the noncoercive measures undertaken by the Yugoslav government to reduce the outflow of workers were less than successful until they were reinforced by the aftereffects of the oil crisis.[34]

PART TWO

POPULATION POLITICS IN THE SOVIET UNION

CHAPTER 5

USSR:
THE LABOR FORCE

While it was once held that socialism virtually automatically assured that everyone could work and work productively, Soviet bloc countries now admit to both labor shortages and surpluses. Labor shortages have actually become endemic to the whole bloc in some form or other. Soviet-type economy is notoriously profligate with labor resources for systemic reasons.[1] There are also strong ideological pressures militating against dismissal of redundant workers, which reinforce the inbuilt tendency to hoard labor. Various measures undertaken with the aim of releasing labor power for use where it is most needed do not seem to have yet produced radical improvement;[2] nor has automation. The secular tendency appears to be for the problem to become more rather than less acute. The declining birthrates in the late fifties and sixties will bring this problem to near crisis point following 1980, as annual increments to the work force drastically diminish, and their regional distribution becomes more and more anomalous.[3] Planners are becoming increasingly aware of the need to budget carefully for what they have always previously regarded as virtually a free good.[4] One gains the impression that it was pressure from this group above all that provided the necessary political context for public calls for pronatalist policies in the Soviet Union and Poland and their adoption elsewhere.

Throughout Socialist Eastern Europe (with the exception of Yugoslavia), discussions of demographic trends are closely tied up with discussions of economic policy and strategy, in particular, with questions of labor supply. (See, for example, the titles of the books cited in Note 6 below.) Most pronatalist advocates argue in terms of economic, especially manpower, factors. Prominent pronatalists

43

include among their number such men as Kasimovskii[5] (head of the Labor Resources Research Laboratory of RSFSR Gosplan) and Kazimierz Dzienio, the head of a unit responsible for manpower planning in the Polish Planning Commission, who has become a noted authority on population policy matters both within Poland and elsewhere in the Soviet bloc. East Germany refrained from adopting abortion reforms at a time when it was the only European socialist country with a labor shortage. Hungary, Czechoslovakia, and Bulgaria all adopted pronatalist policies as labor shortages began to affect them in the 1960s. It may be significant that in Poland and the Soviet Union, the two main countries where strong pronatalist policies have not yet been adopted, the late 1960s and the 1970s saw a large inflow of manpower onto the labor market as their large respective postwar "baby booms" reached school-leaving age.

It may seem an illogical response to a present labor shortage to lay plans for increased numbers of work-force entrants twenty years or so hence. But this time lag and other elementary demographic calculations are often overlooked. And in any case the influence involved need not have been one of tightly logical cause and effect; the apparent "disappearance" of manpower (itself often not due to past fertility decline but rather to long-term policies of extensive rather than intensive development) may simply have oriented policy-makers more toward demographic concerns.

The quantities and distribution of the Soviet labor force are a vast and intricate subject.[6] The general picture is, briefly, that the Soviet Union is threatened by a demographically accentuated overall labor shortage, acute in some regions and tempered by looming unemployment in others. The problem of labor scarcity is particularly pronounced in the Baltic states (where natural increase has been very low for decades), certain urban and rural parts of European Russia (where there has been heavy outmigration of the young and where population stagnation or decline has set in), and virtually all of Siberia and the Far East (where migration policies have foundered on the reluctance of Europeans to travel there or, having done so, to remain there).[7]

The labor shortages are associated with a number of other chronic labor problems in a relationship of dialectical aggravation. The Soviet press expresses regular concern about excess labor turnover and poor labor discipline. Efforts to curb these phenomena tend to be frustrated by the eagerness of industrial managers to take on new workers irrespective of their performance in earlier

44

jobs or their reasons for having left them. Similarly, "elemental" migration movements in (centrally) undesired directions are facilitated by labor shortages. It is difficult to police measures aimed at holding workers in a labor shortage area when there will be no lack of employers elsewhere quite ready to turn a blind eye to irregularities.[8] And of course, even in areas where labor resources are plentiful, as in Central Asia, there may nonetheless be an effective shortage of industrial labor, of workers with the right skills and dispositions.[9]

The authorities have responded to the growing shortages by a variety of measures aimed at increased utilization of existing labor reserves, in particular of housewives and old-age and invalid pensioners. While it is still hoped to further exploit reserves of this kind,[10] work-force participation rates have already reached such high levels in most of the country that little further increase would seem feasible.[11] Meanwhile the systematic siphoning of the younger age groups from rural areas has so drastically altered the age-sex structure of the agricultural work force that that source too is virtually exhausted in most areas. Thus it would seem that the only future possibility for augmenting the labor force will be natural increase. But the last of the more numerous postwar birth cohorts have already entered the work force, and it is estimated that since about 1975, the annual increments from this source have been drastically diminishing. To make matters worse, the proportion of these increments concentrated in Central Asia is growing spectacularly.[12] Pressures seem to be mounting on the labor market from all sides more or less simultaneously.

In Soviet writings the word unemployment remains taboo;[13] however, the subtly different concept of "surplus labor" has been gaining acceptance and its presence in various areas commented on. Though some of the Western border regions of the Soviet Union (notably Moldavia, Western Ukraine, Belorussia, and Lithuania) continue to have some rural overpopulation, the main concentrations of underemployment are in the Caucasus and Central Asian areas, both of which have high rates of population increase and, at least until recently, substantial net immigration balances. In fact, in the 1960s trends in migration worked toward enhancing the demographic imbalances that differential fertility and the distribution of natural resources were creating in Siberia and Central Asia. Siberia, where Soviet plans required an enormous accession of manpower, was by and large an area of emigration, while Central Asia and the North Caucasus, where apart from in Kazakhstan there was already a manpower surplus (at least in agriculture), were registering a net inflow.[14]

It is possible that this trend may have now been modified to some extent. The 1970 Census results suggested a degree of net outflow in 1968-69 from Central Asia (including Kazakhstan) and the North Caucasus region and substantial net inmigration into the RSFSR.[15] All of these trends were in marked contrast to the overall pattern of movement in the 1960s, as derived by other statistical analyses. Whether we are dealing here more with a statistical anomaly than a change in prevailing migration patterns remains to be seen. Most Soviet sources on migration continue to be sparing in their citation of hard data.[16]

But it would seem that some migration into the labor surplus areas is continuing. Meanwhile, as noted earlier, the numbers of able-bodied in Central Asia have been increasing very much more rapidly than elsewhere and will continue to do so for the foreseeable future. The numbers actually seeking employment there could increase even faster if hitherto reluctant rural dwellers and housewives begin to join the urban work force at increased rates. Given the growing pressure on what are for the most part scarce fertile land resources in the area, and also the Soviet emphasis on liberating women from "feudal survivals," both developments seem bound to transpire sooner or later. For the moment, however, there have been and are, paradoxically, shortages of industrial labor in various parts of Central Asia, and even — in some parts of Kazakhstan — of rural labor. These shortages have in the past been filled by Europeans, for a combination of political and economic reasons. Some Soviet observers are keenly aware that this policy may be unwise, and that it would be better to recruit local people into urban jobs and improve their qualifications as necessary.[17] But there are still widespread illusions, apparently, that the supply of European labor is inexhaustible and can go on being shipped into Central Asia ad infinitum. In his article in Voprosy ekonomiki cited earlier, Professor Bachurin, the deputy chairman of USSR Gosplan, mentions that according to the 1978 plan, more than 90% of all workers involved in resettlement will be drawn from the Ukraine, Belorussia, and Moldavia and sent to the RSFSR and Kazakhstan.

It should be emphasized that the Central Asian peoples have the worst command of Russian of any of the major nationalities.[18] They are also among the least mobile peoples in the Soviet Union. In 1968-69, while 6.7% of Russians and 5.0% of Ukrainians changed their place of residence, only 2.7% of Tadzhiks and 1.4% of Uzbeks and Turkmen did so.[19] No doubt both of these factors increase their reluctance and inability to enter the urban work force. Outside the northern regions of Kazakhstan, however, they are in a majority overall, a majority, which, as we shall see, is increasing with dramatic speed. It is possible that as this and other demographic and sociological trends deepen, the indigenous peoples may come to see the present terms of their acceptance into the work force as onerous.

Most of the problems created by manpower shortages and maldistribution can be tackled in either of two ways: in Soviet parlance, by economic or administrative methods. The essential difference between them is of course that the first method seeks to manipulate economic values and indicators so as to make sufficient numbers of people perceive as being in their own best interests the kind of behavior the government wishes to encourage; whereas the second castigates undesired patterns of economic behavior as harmful or even wrong, selfish, philistine, etc., and proposes legal penalties for them. Soviet commentators on social and demographic policy frequently distinguish a third approach, namely, moral exhortation. However, given the by all accounts declining impact of purely moral exhortation on Soviet citizens, and bearing in mind that moral exhortation is not infrequently combined with or apt to merge into "administrative measures," we can probably safely pass over it in this brief discussion. While there is no logical reason to assume that government measures would adhere to one of these approaches to the exclusion of the other, it is obviously a matter of the greatest moment for the future of Soviet society which of them will tend to become predominant in the years that lie ahead.

At first glance it might seem that the present situation of serious and growing labor shortages favors the proponents of economic measures and the emergence of some measure of de facto or even de jure employees' sovereignty. If the manpower is simply not there, production increase can only be achieved by increasing productivity. And in turn, productivity can only be increased in a sophisticated economy by essentially economic stimuli. Any orientation toward raising productivity and efficiency, it has often been claimed, must lead to decentralization of economic decision-making and hence to a general liberalization of economic and social arrangements. Be that as it may, if labor is a scarce commodity, its value is bound in some sense to rise and the bargaining power of the laborer to increase. And indeed, it could be argued that this

enhanced bargaining power is already evident in the official tolerance (however reluctant) of the flitting, weak industrial discipline
and "anarchical" migratory flows which mark the scene at present.

On the other hand it is evident that every "economic" or "liberal"
solution to a problem has a potential "administrative" or illiberal
counterpart. In place of pay-loadings to attract or retain workers
in labor-scarcity areas, one can use central job allocation of
school-leavers and a labor-book system; and if the latter already
exist but are not achieving satisfactory results, one can simply
sharpen their teeth. One can raise kolkhoznik wages, or one can
write restrictive clauses into the collective farm charter. One
can offer long-service benefits, or one can attempt to penalize
both the worker defecting from his place of work and any subsequent employer he manages to find.

Perhaps on balance the indications are at present that the Soviet
leadership has chosen or has been driven to adopt a basically more
economic approach. But the possibility cannot be excluded that in
the future the choice may fall on a thoroughgoing and detailed
system of labor control with computerized recordkeeping, centralized allocation of manpower, and an elaborate network of sanctions.
The Leningrad-Kaluga experiment may yet make a comeback.[20]

The real test of Soviet policy in this area will come in the 1980s,
when virtually all spare labor resources other than farm-bound
non-Russian-speaking peasants in Central Asia and the Caucasus
will have been exhausted. Women and rural migrants, the traditional safety valves, have been fully exploited in the last two decades. Young school-leavers accounted for 29.1% of total manpower
growth in 1961-65, but over 90% in 1971-75.[21] And now that source
is also abruptly disappearing. In these circumstances, given the
traditional Soviet reliance on extensive growth factors, economic
growth could be sharply diminished. Certainly some Western economists see this as a likely outcome. The Soviet authorities have
been laying increased stress on increasing labor productivity. But
old work habits — both of management and employees — die hard.
Bachurin has drawn attention to the fact that in 1976-77, labor productivity plans in Soviet industry were not fulfilled.[22]

If in the 1980s policy-makers were to find both that labor resources were shrinking and that productivity still lagged (though
by definition its relative contribution will of course increase), and
that on top of that they were plagued by the traditional indiscipline
and inefficient vices of their labor force, they might well begin to
think in terms of radical alternatives of one kind or another.

CHAPTER 6

USSR:
ETHNIC RELATIONS

In this chapter the crucial question of the effect of demographic trends on ethnic relations in the USSR will be considered. The possibility of severe racial tensions emerging in the USSR at some time in the future is discussed. As some observers are inclined to question the assumptions on which such reasoning is based, it may be as well to spell them out. Those readers who believe the USSR not to be immune to the sociopsychological diseases of the rest of mankind may prefer to turn immediately to the second section of this chapter (p. 57).

Some Theoretical and Historical Considerations

A very large literature has developed on the sociology of plural societies and ethnic politics. Despite this, unity of conceptual approach or, indeed, of basic terminological usage has not yet been achieved.[1] The term "ethnic relations" is variously applied. Some use it to denote an area separate from and complementary to that of racial relations within the broader field of communal relations: others use it in a more generic sense to refer to all of what followers of the first definition would identify as "racial and ethnic relations," i.e., relations between communities within a state that are conscious of belonging to different racial or national groups; and others again use it in a still broader generic sense to refer to almost any social group within a state or community that is not defined in terms of age, sex, or nonascriptive socioeconomic function or status (thereby including, for example, caste groups, tribes, and confessional communities). In this book the term is being used

49

in the second of these three senses (i.e., the less sweeping of the two more generic usages). Accordingly, no attempt will be made, for example, to systematically examine the extent or importance of purely religious, regional, or residual tribal affiliations in the Socialist countries. Discussion will be restricted to and largely framed in terms of the "nations" and "nationalities" recognized by the regimes in question.[2]

A major shortcoming of the literature on the political sociology of ethnicity from the point of view of present concerns is that it has not hitherto devoted a great deal of attention to systematic treatment of the demographic factor. Observations made on the matter tend to be brief and axiomatic. Among writers who do make reference to the demographic factor there is a tendency to dismiss it as of lesser importance. It is often pointed out that small minorities can dominate a polity, and that therefore no very strong correlation between demographic and political strength can be established. One well-known authority on plural societies (M. G. Smith) indeed suggests that demographic expansion is more likely to reflect the pattern of interethnic accommodation than to independently influence it.[3]

Obviously the demographic ratios of ethnic groups within a state are not likely to correspond precisely to their relative political strength. But perhaps there is a tendency in the existing literature to overemphasize the lack of correspondence between the two. Most of the instances of domination by a tiny minority are drawn from societies which have not yet been touched by the worldwide rise of ethnic awareness, or in which the ethnic groups in question represent quite different levels of socioeconomic organization. The ongoing process of modernization and the to some extent independent ethnonationalist revolution seem likely to make such power structures obsolete.[4] The confidence once felt by some outsiders that in South Africa "white supremacy may well continue indefinitely"[5] was not always shared by the South Africans themselves, who tend, moreover, to be keenly aware of the discrepancy between white and black numerical strength.[6] And Smith's suggestion that demographic patterns only repeat and reinforce power relations previously established, whatever its empirical validity outside premodern African situations, seems to overlook the point that power reinforced is effectively new power acquired.

As no established typology of ethnic politics systematically incorporating the demographic factor has yet emerged, the discussion that follows here and in later chapters will not pursue any precise, predetermined contours but rather will attempt to describe those features of the topology which seem most striking to the unaided eye. Obviously the term "ethnic relations," even in the slightly restricted sense indicated above, covers some fairly disparate phenomena. I shall not attempt to draw clear-cut boundaries for the concept, which is quite remarkably resistant to definition. But I shall make a distinction within this general category between potential or actual nationality conflicts and racial ones. Such a distinction, though often made in the specialist literature[7] (and nearly always made in the less specialist literature), is not an easy one to maintain with a high degree of precision and consistency. In addition to the difficulty of defining the outer limits of ethnic, as opposed to other intergroup, tensions, one has the further problem of the word "racial." Like "ethnic," "racial" tends to be used in a variety of senses. Sometimes it is used coterminously with what I have chosen to call "ethnic";[8] sometimes it is used to refer almost exclusively to black-white situations; sometimes in a scientific sense to refer to biologically identifiable human types; and sometimes to refer only to those situations in which one at least of the contending groups consciously and explicitly uses pseudo-scientific "racial" arguments to justify its attitude toward the other or others.[9] Here the term will be used to refer to that subgroup of ethnic relations in which in- and out-groups are recognized on the basis of certain perceived physical characteristics (as opposed to cultural characteristics, in the case of "national" distinctions). Racial conflicts, it is suggested, have a number of features which tend to differentiate them from other kinds of ethnic conflict. Where nationality conflicts tend to derive from rational (if mistaken) apprehensions concerning the sharing of power, wealth, or prestige within a community, racial conflicts characteristically involve an element (on at least one side) of disinterested revulsion. Where racial feelings are involved, there tends to be stricter spatial or social segregation. Where members of an in-group may see certain positive or at least respect-worthy human qualities in an out-group perceived as being of the same race, in racial antagonisms one side at least is likely to view the other as almost totally without human virtues.[10] Indeed, in racial conflicts it is common for one side at least to question the very humanity of the other.[11] In non-racial conflicts competition is the predominant mode of interaction, whereas in racial ones there tends to be a clear demarcation between superior and inferior, recognized either positively or negatively by both sides. Racial conflicts tend to have their origins more typically in a history of colonial subjugation or slavery rather than autonomous migratory movements; hence the genealogy of conflict tends to be rather more embittered. Racially plural communities are more likely to be composed of large majority and small minority rather than roughly equal numbers. Owing to the high visibility of physical, racial differences, as opposed to cultural ones, there is a tendency for group perceptions in racial situations to be sharper and more strongly and more frequently reinforced by experience. And despite the potentially blurring effects of miscegenation, those differences and perceptions of them tend to be less mutable over time. Finally, I believe it can be laid down as a general proposition that racial relations are often marked by a greater degree of hostility than ethnic relations.[12]

But paradoxical as it may seem, while racial tensions may tend to involve a greater degree of hostility, they do not necessarily lead to a greater amount of hostilities. Whether and in what conditions ethnic or other intergroup tensions reach the stage of violent conflict is another extremely complex question in itself. Without going into the matter too deeply, from the point of view of the demographic aspects of interethnic relations, one point should be made. It is that while in the case of nationality tensions, the development of rivalry or conflict will be more directly related to the relative power positions of the groups concerned, and therefore to some extent to the demographic ratio between them (and in particular to large or decisive changes in that ratio), in the case of racial tensions, no real objective threat need yet be presented to the dominant partner for the situation to ignite.

In the case of nonracial conflicts, we have basically a 50-50 situation, in other words, one in which the relative demographic and/or political strengths of two peoples within a state are fairly evenly balanced, and the question thus arises kto kogo (who is to [dominate] whom), whether by war, the ballot box, or other process of decision. Despite its apparent claim to precision, the 50-50 should not be taken too literally. Depending on the degree of socioeconomic difference between the two communities, a demographic balance of 35-65 might equally well raise a 50-50 type problem. And, of course, the regional subdistribution of a population may lead to what is overall a majority-minority situation acquiring 50-50 dimensions in particular areas. Thus, for example, in the context of Soviet Central Asia (a case to be discussed at some length below), we have a dominant Russian minority at the regional level, a dominant Russian majority in many key urban areas, and a 50-50 situation maturing in the city of Tashkent.

In the case of racial conflicts, on the other hand, any increase in numbers (or even any apparent increase in numbers created by a change in migratory and settlement patterns) may be critical. Thus the growing urban visibility of Jews in many parts of Europe led to the great waves of anti-Semitism of the nineteenth and twentieth centuries, even though there were few regions where Jews threatened to present anything approaching even a localized 50-50 problem (unless, of course, one takes the analysis to the level of urban district or occupational group). In several countries of European culture, the proportions of Catholics in the community have risen to, or toward, the 50-50 area without provoking much more than Masonic mutterings. And before too much is made of the spectacular counterexample of Northern Ireland, it ought to be remembered that despite the fact that men of demonstrably Irish cultural stigmata have been living among the British and in numerous well-publicized cases blowing up the British for many years (reports of bombing phone warnings almost invariably mention the Irish accent of the caller), migration from Ireland to Great Britain is still completely unrestricted and, indeed, completely uncontrolled.

The types of extreme violence that occur in racial and nonracial conflicts also tend to differ: on the one hand civil war, on the other the lynching or the pogrom.

This follows logically from the earlier proposition that multiracial states tend more typically to consist of communities of widely differing size. Evenly balanced multiracial societies are probably rarer because they are more unstable than other kinds. And most multiracial mixes have arisen from partial European settlement of non-European areas, complete European overrunning of areas of non-European settlement, or the import of non-European slave labor. Both pogroms and lynching are only really practicable where there is a strong overall strategic majority or an effectively concentrated local one. The aggression involved is bullying rather than defiant or competitive. While the majority group may be beginning to fear rather than despise the minority involved, the fear is coupled with a realistic certainty that the aggression will achieve its objectives. Civil wars are a more "valorous" undertaking.[13]

While the type of violence occurring in racial and nonracial conflicts may differ, the damage done to the fabric of society may be equally great in both types of cases. Scapegoating of despised minorities seems to be closely associated with (whether causally or epiphenomenally) destruction of the rule of law and the spread of police-state methods and the underlying social patterns that support them. Insofar as differential fertility can easily lead to the greatly increased visibility of a pariah or scapegoat group, the importance of demographic factors in racial conflicts may be even greater than in the case of nonracial ones.

The distinction between racial and nonracial ethnic conflicts, though widely recognized and used, is not one that appeals to all students of these matters.[14] Marxists in particular are reluctant to accept that any kind of ethnic stratification can be of "decisive" importance anywhere;[15] a fortiori that there might be a subcategory of ethnic divisions that are even more important again. And it must be acknowledged that the distinction is indeed not without its difficulties. It would appear, for example, that one is not dealing here with some kind of clear dichotomy but rather with a dispersed bipolar distribution, or even perhaps some kind of spread along a continuum. In any one case all the potential elements of ethnic distinction (both physical and cultural) may work to reinforce one another; or they may tend on the whole to cancel one another out. Alternatively, they may be reinforced by socioeconomic cleavages or crosscut and thereby attenuated by those cleavages. Racial differences may also vary both in their objective, physical and in their subjective, psychological salience. There is, moreover, the usual difficulty of neatly categorizing the incidence of irrational subjectivity. For the ultimate definition of "racial" (like that of "national" or "ethnic") must be in terms of "racial is as racial does." Individuals may believe they are Napoleon; and social groups moved by analogous "pathological" thought disturbances may, despite the absence of any distinguishing physical stigmata, nonetheless believe themselves to be racially different from and superior to some among their neighbors; and in such an event cultural stigmata may be perceived and responded to as though they were physical. Such a development is particularly likely to take place under the pressure of socioeconomic collapse or an ongoing ethnic conflict which acquires a momentum and escalating ferocity of its own. Thus the division between racial and ethnic is not clear-cut either theoretically or empirically, and particular situations may be hard to allocate unequivocally to either type. But while some cases, like that of Serbs and Albanians or Ukrainians and Jews, may contain some elements of both, there is an obvious and basic difference between, for example, the relations between Czechs and Slovaks, Croats and Serbs, or Flemings and Walloons, on the one hand, and that between Slovaks and Gypsies, Russians and Central Asians, or White and Black Americans, on the other.

If one accepts the general division between racial and nonracial types of ethnic antagonism and some broad categorization of the two types along the lines suggested here, it remains to be considered where the patterns of interaction formed by the main ethnic constituents of the Soviet Union should be located. Are ethnic tensions likely to be more or less racial in type? And what circumstances are likely to mitigate or exacerbate their intensity?

It is often emphasized that Russians were never racially prejudiced in anything like the manner that other European colonizers were. And sometimes, also, that whatever the vices of the tsarist regime in this respect, the policies and structural reforms that have been carried into effect by the Soviet regime have so radically altered the situation that ethnic tensions have ceased to be a significant problem in the Soviet Union. The latter of these two views is most prevalent among fundamentalist pro-Moscow communists, the uninformed, and those whose principal concerns are not with Soviet affairs. However, it is undoubtedly true that the pattern of development of interethnic relations in Russia and the USSR is almost without parallel outside the Soviet bloc (and without exact parallels within it).

If we compare the situation in tsarist Russia with our model of a racial situation, we find that Russo-Turkestani relations seem to be something of a borderline case. In some of the northern areas of what is now Kazakhstan, where Russians appeared as early as the sixteenth century, intermarriage became common and the peasants there of Russian stock could scarcely be distinguished from the indigenous steppe dwellers.[16] Even later, after Russian conquest of the area, the Russian attitude seems generally agreed to have been less overbearing and superior than that taken by other European colonists elsewhere.[17] And while the degree of intermingling that occurred in most of the area in the late tsarist period (as since) was minimal, this was not so much a consequence of Russian as of Moslem attitudes. Tsarist administrators, like their Soviet successors, were eager to promote sblizhenie (ethnic rapprochement),[18] but the autochthonous peoples resisted it. The rare cases of intermarriage did not necessarily lead to Christianization and Europeanization: Russian women tended to adopt the Islam of their husbands.[19] Russian peasant settlers were not always noticeably better off than Central Asians; and sometimes they were worse off. Economic exploitation of the indigenous peoples tended to take the form of selective dispossession rather than serfdom, slavery, or complete expulsion. And tsarist administrators seem, in some periods at least, to have displayed a degree of genuine tolerance toward the Moslem religion. Moreover, the physical differentiation between Slavs and Central Asians is less marked than that observable in some other colonial contexts. Thus, all in all, there are reasons for expecting the Central Asian racial context to be less volatile than many others. This having been said, it should nonetheless be emphasized that certain other features of the situation point in a different direction. The distinguishable and relatively unchanging physical stigmata are there, and so is the recent history of colonial subjugation and administration. And despite the efforts of the Russians and the partial exception mentioned above of the Kazakh steppe-lands, spatial and social segregation existed in the past and, as we shall see, persist into the present.[20] There is, moreover, a history of recurring violence between Europeans and Central Asians, during the period of annexation in the nineteenth century, during the Basmachi revolt of 1916, and again during the collectivization period and the purges of the 1920s and 1930s.

Similar considerations probably apply, if in lesser measure, to the Azeri and the other Moslem peoples of the Caucasian and Transcaucasian regions. In the case of the Armenians and Georgians, it can probably be maintained that the ethnic tensions involved, being mitigated by common cultural traditions, are less racial than national in character (however intense). With two exceptions, the remaining major nationalities seem best classified as identifiably "European" and therefore only nationally, and not racially, distinct. The two exceptions are the Tatars and the Jews. It is quite possible that the Tatars (particularly the Crimean Tatars) may again turn their undoubted political skills to some Soviet variant of pan-Turkic, or pan-Islamic, activity.[21] Moreover, the hostility of some of the Tatar communities to Soviet Russia is well documented and not likely to abate. All in all, it seems that the Tatar communities can generally speaking be classed with the Central Asians,[22] with the proviso that some at least of them have, like the Kazakhs, traditionally displayed a relatively greater readiness to intermingle with Russians and assimilate to Russiandom. To that extent, of course, we may be nearer the border-line area between racial and ethnic differences.[23] The Jews, on the other hand, must be classified as being in very large measure a racial or quasi-racial minority in the Soviet context, despite their greatly diminished physical visibility as such.

Thus, while the Russians may be less prone to racial (if not na-

tional) animosities than Anglo-German or even Latin peoples have
been, there are excellent reasons to believe that they are not free
from these widespread human failings. And there is ample evidence that the USSR is not the emergent paradise of ethnic harmony
and integration that it has at times been presented as approaching.
Any attempt at more precise evaluation of Soviet propensities in
this regard is difficult or even pointless given the almost complete
blotting out of information on the subject after the 1920s.[24] Some
evidence bearing on these matters has been collected again in recent years by Soviet scholars. Reference will be made to some of
that evidence in the pages ahead. However, in general it will be
simply assumed that the peoples of the Soviet Union share some of
the ethnocentric vices of humanity, with those probable modifications to the general pattern that have been outlined in the preceding
discussion; and that although these vices may not always find overt
expression, they can nonetheless be reasonably assumed to be present where other evidence would suggest it. In what follows attention
is focused rather on the demographic aspects of ethnodemographic
problems in the Soviet Union; here, at least, some relatively plausible and precise-looking information is available. In the subsequent course of the discussion, however, due consideration shall
be given to the possibility that in the future, severe national or racial conflicts may arise, worsen, or emerge in the Soviet Union,
aggravated by demographic developments which in themselves are
already, within a modest margin of error, safely predictable.

Ethnic Relations in the USSR:
the Demographic Factor

Partly perhaps because of their once very high birth and natural
increase rates, the Russians tend to have been thought of in the
past as a people of virtually unlimited demographic capacity. This
image seems to have been shared by the Russians themselves. As
Blok wrote:

> Mil'ony — vas. Nas t'my, i t'my, i t'my.
> Poprobuite, srazites' s nami!
> Da, skify — my! Da, aziaty — my, —
> S raskosymi i zhadnymi ochami!
> (We are millions. There are hordes and hordes and
> hordes of us.

57

Try to contend with us!
Yes, we are Scythians! Yes, we are Asiatics —
With slanting and avid eyes!)

The image in fact appears to have survived the reality. It has been suggested to the author by a Soviet bloc demographer that the cliché notion "Nas mnogo" ("We are many") embedded in the Soviet Russian consciousness has been a considerable obstacle to efforts to achieve a more active pronatalist policy in the USSR in recent years.

Although the Russian settling of Siberia at least has actually always proceeded at rather a slow pace, the Russians have indeed applied first military and then demographic force majeure to a considerable number of peoples and extensive areas in the east of their empire. As late as the early 1960s, the trend still seemed to be all in one direction, with the Russians further increasing their advantage all the time, and all the other peoples apparently doomed to cultural extinction or sblizhenie (convergence) and then sliianie (merging), to use the Soviet formulation that held sway in the later Khrushchev years.[25] Then between the censuses of 1959 and 1970 it became apparent that the earlier picture of universally advancing Russification was by no means the whole truth. Demographic trends which had earlier seemed capable only of slowing down the process now threatened to halt or reverse it. Russia's manifest destiny suddenly began to seem less manifest. I shall now discuss some of the salient features of those trends.

The declining USSR fertility has been largely declining Russian and Slav fertility. The population of the Russian Republic, the RSFSR (which contains 83.5% of all Russians), has declined from being 56.3% of the population in 1959 to 53.8% in 1970 and 52.6% in 1977.[26] There is no reason to suppose that this trend will be reversed; on the contrary, it seems more likely that it will intensify. By 1990 the RSFSR will probably contain less than half of the total Soviet population. The immediate result of this milestone being passed will doubtless not be the automatic issuance of a constitutional charter for the nationalities. But that this prospect has political significance is borne out by the fact that the simple statistic relating to 1970 given above was not included in any of the volumes of the official 1970 Census results.

The proportion of Russians within the USSR as a whole has also declined, from 54.7% in 1959 to 53.4% in 1970, another detail which was not found worthy of inclusion in the 1970 Census Results. Before the 1970 Census and again before the one currently being pre-

pared for 1979, there has been speculation that the results would
show the Russians as being in the minority. It seems unlikely in
fact that the results will show that. But setting aside for a moment
the question of whether there might be any tendency to overcount
Russians in censuses conducted under present Soviet conditions,
there are two points which should be made. First, that the total
of Russians evidently includes some proportion of assimilation
gains. And second, that Russian increase rates in the first years
of the 1959-70 period were relatively high and unlikely to be re-
attained. It follows from this that we can expect the Russian decline in the future to be greater barring an increase in assimilation
gains (which is possible) or the application of Soviet experience in
conducting elections to census procedures. To my knowledge, no
Soviet projections of population by republic (much less by nationality) have been published, which is itself suggestive.[27]

A further basic point to note is the decline in the relative strength
of the Slav population within the Soviet Union as a whole, from a
total of 77.1% in 1959 to 74.6% in 1970.[28] This trend too is likely
to accelerate and is less likely to be padded by assimilation, since
the great bulk of the assimilation going on in the Soviet Union at
present is occurring among the Slavic population. This statistic
is scarcely explosive as yet; but if present trends are maintained
or even enhanced, it could begin to be so within a couple of decades,
given the recent extreme dominance of Slavs in the Soviet political
leadership.

It may seem to some that the "if present trends are maintained"
is an extremely problematical "if." It is much less so than it may
appear. High fertility societies in contemporary medicodemographic
conditions have a kind of inbuilt spring mechanism which, barring
natural or other catastrophes, makes further dynamic natural increase in the short term inevitable. Even if inherent fertility rates
were to decline rapidly over the next two decades in the high-fertility
areas of the USSR (and the present indications are rather that the
decline will be gradual), the present age structure of those populations will ensure that rapid increase will continue and last decades
longer than the fertility-mortality pattern which originally set it in
motion. Central Asians have been exposed to contraception and
abortion for some time now, and also to propaganda aimed against
early marriage and other sociocultural factors tending to maximize
fertility. The results to date have been only modest, and there is
no very good reason for supposing that a dramatic transformation
is about to occur. Soviet commentators frequently maintain that

Central Asian fertility rates will soon go the way of those in Armenia and Azerbaidzhan. Ultimately, no doubt, they will. But the fact remains that between 1958 and the mid-1970s, Central Asian fertility declined scarcely at all; in some cases it actually increased.[29] If and when they do describe the Armenian pattern, it will be, so to speak, after the deluge, not before it. Soviet population policy seems for the present to be hamstrung on the nationalities issue. But even if the government were to adopt and press with reckless abandon a differential fertility policy aimed at reversing the existing trends, by the time their policy began to bite (assuming that it was successful), the pattern up to the year 2000 (and indeed beyond) would largely have been set anyway. The time for the Soviet government to have acted in this matter was a decade and a half ago, if not earlier.

The pattern of development in the individual republics is often more striking than that in the country as a whole. Between the 1926 and 1959 censuses the proportion of Russians in the different union republics (including the RSFSR itself) increased universally; and over the same period there was a dramatic accession of new Russian settlers into the newly acquired republics of Latvia, Estonia, Lithuania, and Moldavia. In many republics the increases were very steep. This was particularly true of Latvia, Estonia, Kazakhstan, and Kirgizia, where the proportion of Russians between the midthirties and 1959 increased from 12 to 26% (Latvia), 7 to 22% (Estonia), 20 to 43% (Kazakhstan), and 12 to 39% (Kirgizia). The increases were substantial also in the Ukraine (9 to 18%), Turkmenia (8 to 17%), Tadzhikistan (from an insignificant percentage to 13%), Uzbekistan (6 to 14%), and the RSFSR itself (73 to 83%), while the Moldavians and Lithuanians suddenly found themselves with 10.2% and 8.5% of Russians, respectively. Only in Belorussia and the Caucasian republics were the changes of modest dimensions.[30]

Since 1959 the pattern has been radically transformed at a number of points. The Russian proportion of the population has, it is true, increased in all the Western republics, i.e., in the Baltic states, Belorussia, Moldavia, and the Ukraine. But in every case except Belorussia (where the earlier rate of increase had been very small), the rate of further relative increase of Russians has been greatly reduced;[31] and while the respective periods involved are not strictly comparable, the drop in the rate of increase is too sharp not to reflect a trend. Several different factors are involved here, but the key one is manifestly the declining numbers of underemployed Russians physically available for colonial settlement or transfer as urban workers.

The picture in the Western republics is in fact a mixed one. In the case of Estonia and Latvia, it would appear that some caution may have been exercised for a time in deference to the national sensibilities of the peoples concerned. There was a report in 1967 to the effect that mass immigration into the Baltic states had grown so intense that the authorities had been forced to close the borders.[32] This may have been a concession from the post-Krushchev leadership. If so, it was short-lived. In Latvia between 1971 and 1975, the net migration balance was 76,100, which represented 69% of all population growth in the country. The comparable statistics for 1966-70 were 68,600 and 36%, and for 1961-66, 78,100 and 42%.[33] In Estonia after the "moratorium," immigration rose rapidly again in 1969 and 1970[34] and has continued in the seventies along roughly similar lines to Latvia, with probably something like half the total increase in population deriving from immigration.[35] In both Estonia and Latvia fertility has remained below replacement level for many years now.[36] The future strength of "Russians" there is likely therefore to depend crucially on who, culturally, absorbs whom — the beleaguered natives or the Slavic newcomers.

In Lithuania in the 1950s and 1960s, the indigenous population substantially recovered from the ravages of war and successive occupations. The extent of Slavic immigration was in any case more limited there than in Latvia or Estonia. Between 1959 and 1970, of a total population increase of 417,000, only 50,000 resulted from migration.[37] Lithuanian fertility has been declining rapidly in recent years, almost to replacement levels;[38] but even so there seems to be no prospect of the kind of Russian demographic dominance in the country as may be looming elsewhere in the Baltic.

As for the Ukraine, the statistics do not bear out any picture of galloping Russification enveloping pockets of intelligentsia and rural resistance. The numbers of Russians, and more particularly Russian-speakers, are going up substantially — much faster than in the RSFSR itself; but the percentage of people choosing to identify themselves as Ukrainians for census purposes declined only from 76.8 to 74.9%. And in this case, unlike in the case of changes of similar magnitude mentioned earlier, it is by no means certain that the trend will continue. The case of Belorussia (to which I will recur below) is similar.

In the Caucasian republics, where Russian demographic inroads have always been relatively modest, between 1959 and 1970 there were declines in the proportion of Russians in every case. In Armenia the proportion dropped to 2.7% and is probably still falling; this seems scarcely enough even as a flag-showing mission. In Georgia the proportion of Russians is also declining in the capital, Tbilisi, as the Georgians reported in their republican newspaper in 1971 (though there was no need to do so). This is indeed a note-worthy development, though not as exceptional as earlier trends toward Russianization of the republic capitals might have suggested.[39] In Azerbaidzhan the percentage drop was the largest in the Caucasus — from 13.6 back to 10%. The absolute total of Russians in the three Caucasian republics as a whole has stagnated, which would suggest that there was no central aspiration to strive for ultimate Slavic domination, as would seem to be the case in Latvia and Estonia.[40] There are obvious geopolitical reasons why this should be so. Given the pattern of interwoven settlement and keen ethnic hostility between the main nations in the area (and on the other side of the Soviet border), it ought not to tax the diplomatic skills of the Soviet leadership too greatly to maintain their dominant control there by traditional imperial methods. In Central Asia, by contrast, the peoples involved, whatever their differences, have much stronger linguistic and cultural ties and a much more formidable extramural ally in China.

The fertility of the main Transcaucasian nationalities has been declining fairly rapidly in recent years. First the Georgians and more recently the Armenians and the Moslem Azerbaidzhani have passed more or less rapidly into the latter stages of the demographic transition. But Georgian fertility remains substantially higher than Russian, and it remains unclear whether Armenian and Azerbaidzhani fertility will fall to the same levels as have been observed in European USSR. In the meantime substantial differences between Slavic and Transcaucasian natural increase rates persist and are extremely likely to go on doing so for decades yet.[41] In these circumstances any reversal of present shifts in republic national composition seems most unlikely.

In the Central Asian republic where Russiandom registered some of its most spectacular advances before 1959, there was also a decline in the proportion of Russians in every case. For the time being, the high flow of immigration into the area in the 1960s, coupled with the probably quite high but declining natality of the European immigrants, has succeeded in keeping the numbers up. But there seems little prospect that this position can be maintained for very much longer. With the exception of some of the northern and eastern oblasti of Kazakhstan, the Russian hold in the area is tenuous and confined to the cities. Whether Russian social and economic (as distinct from political) dominance of the area can be maintained when the major influx of indigenous people into the cities gets under way seems dubious. And any attempt to detach the region of demographic conquest in the north will not be a simple undertaking.

Writing just after the 1959 Census, Boris Lewickyj said: "The Central Asian republics are in the worst situation. The Kazakh Republic is now Kazakh only by name ... whilst the Kirgiz [too] are on the way to becoming a national minority in their own republic."[42] This statement undoubtedly reflected the general trend of opinion at the time. And yet even in Kazakhstan, where the inflow of Russians and Ukrainians (who assimilate to Russiandom very quickly away from the Ukraine) after the 1959 census was probably more intensive than anywhere else, the proportion of Russians and Ukrainians together has declined from 50.9 to 49.6%, while the Kazakh figure has gone up from 30.0 to 32.6%. By the 1980s, barring untoward developments, these two statistics can be expected to be racing in opposite directions. The Kazakhs have evidently recovered from their colossal losses during the collectivization era (there was an absolute decline of nearly one quarter in the Kazakh population between 1926 and 1939)[43] and are now engaged on a peaceful reacquisition of their own land in accordance with the best traditions of Stalinist population doctrine, for which they can scarcely be subjected to open censure. Though their fertility is probably slightly below that of most other Moslem peoples in the region,[44] it is not apparently diminishing very much. Moreover, it would appear that Russian outmigration from the republic is now occurring, and that in future, migrant workers will be increasingly drawn from within Kazakhstan or from the Central Asian republics.[45]

Elsewhere the picture is similar. In Kirgizia the Kirgiz increased from 40.5% in 1959 to 43.8% of the population in 1970, while the Russians and Ukrainians together declined from a total of 36.8 to 33.3%.[46] The Tadzhiks in Tadzhikistan went up from 53.1 to 56.2%, while the Russian and Ukrainian combined total was down from 14.7 to 13%. In Turkmenistan the titular nationality increased from 60.9% in 1959 to 65.6% in 1970, while the Russians' and Ukrainians' combined proportion declined from 18.7 to 16.1%. And in Uzbekistan the Uzbeks increased from 62.1 to 65.5% of the total, while the Russians and Ukrainians were down from 14.6 to 13.4%. It should be reemphasized that these developments have

taken place despite the fact that the total number of Russians in
Central Asia as a whole increased by 36.9%,[47] a figure which is
of course far and away higher than the overall Russian increase
of 13.1% for the same period. Thus Russiandom has been commit-
ting more forces to the battle, as it were, than it can really afford
to lose, without being able to turn the tide. All the massive Russian influx into Central Asia is likely to achieve in the long term
is a growing aggravation of the employment problem (as local demographic pressure on the job market builds) and, probably, increasing resentment among the indigenous peoples. Only in northern Kazakhstan have the foundations been laid for a Karelian-type
annexation.[48] And there it may be more prudent to be forbearing.
In six of the seventeen oblasti of Kazakhstan, the Kazakhs form
less than 20% of the population (in 1959 the Karelians formed 13.1%
of the population of the Karelian ASSR). But nowhere are they in
significant further decline.[49] Moreover, a Karelian solution for
the northern oblasti would obviously severely strain the situation
in the south. For these reasons it does not appear likely.

In some ways, perhaps, the most surprising decline of all, though
modest in dimensions, is the diminution of the percentage of Russians within the RSFSR from 83.3 to 82.8%.[50] For here the Russians might be expected to make their largest gains from assimilation. Moreover, with one or two exceptions, they are not confronted in their own republic by any strong national groups with
large net increase rates. If observers were once ready enough to
dismiss the chances of Central Asian peoples surviving as anything
other than half-assimilated rump minorities in their own homelands, their attitude toward the future of the ethnic groups in the
RSFSR was even more peremptory. And yet even this does not
seem to be being borne out by events. Of the sixteen autonomous
republics of the RSFSR, the proportion of Russians declined between
1959 and 1970 in all but five.[51] In two of those five the increase
was marginal. In the remaining three, with the arguable exception
of the Yakut Autonomous Republic, Russian demographic as well
as political domination of the area was not really in doubt anyway.
In some potentially not unimportant areas on the Volga and in the
North Caucasus area, the indigenous peoples have made significant
gains. I shall enlarge on this point later.

Two other general statistical perspectives may be worth reviewing at this stage. In the period before the Stalinist Gleichschaltung
of the nationalities, and during it, considerable concern was expressed about pan-Moslem and pan-Turanian tendencies. As the

nations which are now staging rapid demographic advances almost all belong to one or other or both of the Moslem and Turkic families, it may be valuable to consider the collective magnitudes involved in each case. Some people are inclined to assume that as religion has been suppressed for so long in Soviet Asia, the old cultural and potentially political affinities have been or soon will be permanently obliterated. This seems a rash assumption. Concerning pan-Turanianism, suffice it to note, in justification of the exercise, that a Soviet linguist has seen fit to claim that nearly all of the Turkic speakers of the USSR can understand each other,[52] and also that there have been some moves toward undoing some of the cellularization of the Turkic languages that was wrought in the Stalin period.[53]

Between the 1959 and 1970 censuses the total number of those belonging to the Moslem nations, according to my reckoning, increased from 24,785,000 to 35,004,000, while that of the combined Turkic peoples rose from 23,050,000 to 32,108,000, of which all but 2,504,000 also belonged to the Moslem community. As the two groups do overlap to a large extent, it will be economical to consider the demographic prospects vis-à-vis the European population of just one of them, the Moslems.

As was mentioned earlier, no Soviet projections of population by republic or nationality are apparently available. What might be done, however, is to improvise a single simplified projection for the Moslem population to the year 2000 just to ascertain roughly what order of magnitude is involved.

The increase from the 1959 to the 1970 Census (35.0 million – 24.8 million = 10.2 million) implies an average annual increase of 3.16% per annum. Taking this figure as the starting point and assuming that natural increase will have declined linearly to 1.0% per annum by 2000 (which is a rather strong assumption and one which should more than compensate for any tendency to overstate the 1970 natural increase level by taking the average for the previous decade, when rates were probably declining slightly), estimated Moslem population in the year 2000 will be about 65 million. Baldwin's 1973C series projection of the total Soviet population for 2000 is 307 million.[54] The roughness of the procedures adopted to assess future Moslem population should not be contrasted with any mysterious prescience imputed to the Census Bureau's projections. The major defect of the whole operation consists in a tendency to understate probabilities on the Moslem side and slightly overstate them on the overall Soviet side. What has been done in effect is to assume a very modest decline in the fertility of A plus B while assuming a very solid decline in the fertility of B. Given that B (i.e., the Moslem part of the Soviet population) is probably contributing a good two fifths of total Soviet annual population increase at present, this could easily cause significant underestimation of relative Moslem strength by 2000. I am following this procedure in order to forestall any impression that might otherwise be created that the case is being overstated.

Taking these very cautious rough estimates for what they are worth, we can now compare the proportion of members of the Moslem peoples within the total Soviet population for 1970 and 2000: for 1970 the percentage is 14.5, and for 2000 it is 21.3. And be it emphasized once more: these figures are so cautious as to be almost foolhardy.

The Russian increase of 13.05% between the 1959 and 1970 censuses was one of the lowest of any major people within the Soviet population, despite their presumable assimilation gains. Even that figure was achieved largely thanks to the relatively high natality of the early sixties before the fertility decline really took full effect. Subsequent increases are not likely to be relatively as great, not even in the current phase, despite the fact that the age structure is at present particularly propitious. But even assuming that the Russian element were to cling tenaciously to its present 53% of the total Soviet population to the year 2000 (a quite unreal assumption on present indications), that would give it a total of some 163 million in our hypothetical population of 309 million.

There is a tendency for observers to juxtapose the likely Russian and Moslem or Central Asian figures and conclude that the Russians may not be expanding very fast, but that nonetheless they have the numbers and are not likely to be overrun. Thus Geoffrey Jukes, for example, writes:

...even if the present trends should continue, a drastic change in the balance between races will not occur. Should the present differential rates of increase continue for the rest of the century, the Soviet population would rise to about 320 million of which Central Asians (a smaller group than "Moslem peoples" — J.F.B.) would constitute about 63 million, while there would be about 170 million Russians. It is therefore unlikely that the Soviet leaders have yet begun to have nightmares over the prospect of being swamped by their internal segment of the "teeming masses" of Asia.[55]

Jukes indicates by his use of the word "even" that he feels that the trends are bound to tilt back toward the Russians before 2000.

While I suspect that his calculation is at least as likely to over-estimate future Russian numbers as future Central Asian numbers, it is the political evaluation he makes of those magnitudes which seems least convincing.

To begin with, it implies a false juxtaposition of 170 million Russians and 63 million Central Asians. In fact the juxtaposition will be of 63 million or whatever Central Asians and 11 or 12 million Russians in the relevant area. It is not necessary to postulate any Central Asian march on Moscow. It will be sufficient if they march (metaphorically) on Tashkent, the "capital of Central Asia," as a Kirgiz (n.b. not an Uzbek) poet recently apostrophized.[56]

It might be objected that the use of generic notions like "Moslems" and "Central Asians" is an indefensibly loose procedure. However, for the most part the propositions being made in collective form about their demographic behavior and ethnopolitical attitudes are equally valid for each individual nation. And, in addition, it is reasonable to assume that some such collective self-identification is made by many representatives of those peoples themselves.[57] It is not being suggested that the "Moslems" or "Central Asians" are bound to form a tightly knit bloc in all matters of sociopolitical relevance. But there is a good deal more basis in language, history, culture, and current political experience for some kind of Moslem "negritude" concept to take hold in the USSR (implicitly or explicitly) than there is in Africa itself.

The confrontation is likely, then, to be worked out in a local context. French numerical superiority on the mainland was not sufficient to maintain the position of the colons in Algeria. The Russians have the advantages of contiguous borders and an efficient central control system; but the capacity of the latter to contain racially tinged socioeconomic confrontations of the type which seem to be maturing in Central Asia is yet to be demonstrated.

The relative quietism of the Central Asian educated classes in the recent past ought not to be presumed a permanent feature. The Russian domination of the urban work force, and with it the key sectors of social and economic life, is likely to be challenged in the next decade or two, particularly as the increasingly massive indigenous birth cohorts of the 1960s and 1970s come onto the labor market.[58] Moreover, the number of educated Central Asians is increasing even more explosively than the population as a whole and will continue to do so.

Education of less-privileged minorities of any kind tends to be politically destabilizing. A sophisticated Soviet rejoinder might be that if education is coupled with opportunities for social mobility as in Soviet Central Asia, there should be no problem. Quite apart from the specific questions of (a) to what extent the Central Asian peoples have really been fully admitted to all fields of socioeconomic endeavor, and (b) whether Soviet planning will be able to provide adequate employment for the enormous bulge in the labor force that is currently developing, it is not clear as a general proposition whether social mobility does in fact tend to reduce ethnic resentments. As Kuper put it, "...mobility may have very different consequences. ... In a racially structured society ... appreciable upward mobility may in fact stimulate revolutionary change."[59] Where social mobility is blocked, of course, the situation is likely to be worse again. In this context it should be noted that the levels of urbanization achieved by the Central Asians according to the 1970 Census are only comparable with those of such countries as Liberia, Zambia, Paraguay, and West Malaysia, and that in certain respects the educational gap between the Russians in Central Asia and the Central Asians themselves is widening.[60]

Accordingly, it seems more than likely that Arutiunian's much-quoted finding that the Tatar intelligentsia of the Tatar ASSR is more prone to chauvinism than the working class[61] is likely to be equally applicable to Central Asia. And here, as in so many other things, the reasonable expectation surely is that the numbers of chauvinists are going to grow.

Soviet writers usually maintain, of course, that "bourgeois nationalism" is diminishing and destined ultimately to disappear. Experience elsewhere, however, would seem to suggest that as societies grow more socially and economically sophisticated, far from abating, ethnic tensions and chauvinist excesses actually tend to increase: Belgium, Yugoslavia, Uganda, Ireland, Canada — to name a few instances almost at random. Nor would these phenomena appear to be confined to any particular type of socioeconomic system. The efficient Soviet control system may keep such stresses in check or even wholly out of sight; but they may still exert a concealed influence in normal times or flare into overt prominence when circumstances change.[62]

The problem is unlikely to be relieved by outmigration of the Central Asians in large numbers. For one thing, they seem the least inclined of all the Soviet national groups to leave their homelands.[63] It is similarly unlikely to be relieved by assimilation. The Central Asians have hitherto also been the least assimilable of all the nationalities. Their level of proficiency in Russian re-

mains very low. Other than among the Kazakhs very few advance
Russian as their native language or as a competently spoken second
language. And statistics on mixed marriages confirm that most of
the Moslem peoples are more likely to intermarry among themselves than to marry Europeans.[64]

Perhaps the most difficult and singular feature of the Central
Asian situation, however, is that trends there seem to point to an
inevitable future change in the dominant national group. In the
cities of the western republics (with the partial exceptions of the
Ukraine and, more recently, Latvia), the Russians have been at
most politically and not demographically in the ascendant. In Central Asia, on the other hand, they have often formed a large majority in the cities. Demographically this pattern is bound sooner
or later to change radically. While the Soviet government may or
may not deem it expedient to reduce the numbers of Russians and
Russian-speakers in Riga or Tallin at some time in the future,
they will not be outnumbered there as a result of future trends in
fertility or migration among the Baltic populations. In the cities
of the Ukraine and Belorussia, even if their demographic presence
were to be weakened (which does not seem imminent), their assimilatory gains could quite possibly continue to offset any losses. In
the Caucasian republics they have never seemed likely to outnum-
ber the indigenous populations. But in Central Asia they will have
to resign themselves to rapidly becoming a minority in urban
areas which in some instances must once have seemed as Russian
as Novgorod or Vologda. The social position of the Kirgiz in Kir-
gizian cities is clearly not the same as that of the Georgians in
Georgian cities.[65] But as the Kirgiz begin to move into their cities
in greater numbers, they are bound sooner or later to aspire to
such a status, and then a destabilizing transformational phase must
inevitably ensue. Irrespective of whether any implicit or explicit
challenge is issued to central authority, a great many economic,
administrative, and most important of all, psychological adjustments will have to occur on both sides. In analogous situations
elsewhere in the world, the European element has politically and
often demographically withdrawn completely. This last-resort
defusing technique would not seem a realistic possibility in the Soviet case for the present. But it could be argued that something
analogous has been happening in the Kosovo Province of Yugoslavia
in recent years.[66] There would seem to be, therefore, no inherent
reason why similar developments could not occur in the USSR as
well at some time in the future.

Currently the internal political kon'iunktura in the USSR favors the Great Russian element. This seems likely to continue for the foreseeable future. But should the demographic or the political situation change sufficiently, and in particular should some future leadership opt for a substantial degree of decentralization, the relative strength of the Central Asian nations could greatly increase, as developments in Yugoslavia after the decline of the "Great Serbian chauvinist" Ranković suggest. While one would not wish to argue that the Serbs lost the position of dominant (large) minority-cum-near-majority which they held in prewar Yugoslavia (and to a lesser extent up to 1965 in Socialist Yugoslavia) due to their relative demographic decline (they claimed to form over 50% of the population after the 1931 census, were 42.1% according to the 1961 census, and only 39.7% according to the 1971 census), it is probably true that their demographic behavior is making it difficult for them to hope to reachieve hegemony in the future, and also that the Russians are stronger in the USSR than the Serbs are in Yugoslavia partly because the Russians were and still are a real majority, whereas the Serbs were at best a phony majority.

In fact, the Serbs' relative decline at censuses reflects their growing political weakness rather more than their declining fertility. But the longer the relative demographic decline of the Russians lasts, the more conceivable it becomes that political decentralization will emerge as a serious possibility. Should such a decentralization occur, of course, we may well learn after the event that Russian demographic strength had also been exaggerated by previous censuses, just as Serbian numbers were.

The international political situation may also work increasingly to the benefit of the Central Asians. Indeed, it has already done so. The Sino-Soviet conflict has unleashed propaganda campaigns on both sides aimed at the Central Asian and Sinkiang minorities of the respective adversaries. Third World pressures (Islamic? OPEC?) on behalf of the Central Asians could also emerge as a factor, particularly if the Sino-Soviet rivalry in this domain were to intensify. For demographic reasons the Soviet Union is likely to become more and not less vulnerable on this point.

Similar considerations apply to the Turkic peoples as to the Moslems. Only the Finno-Ugrian family seems to be supplying a steady flow of assimilated Russians to the point where its own (rather higher) fertility does not represent any kind of local threat. Though there again it is interesting, and perhaps significant, that most of these ethnic groups are now showing net gains rather than losses.

The Finno-Ugrians remain substantial and in some cases rapidly increasing communities which could yet experience a renaissance of national identity.

To date, although there have been guarded hints from demographers and journalists, including some apparently writing with official sanction, that there is a need for a differential population policy that would counteract some of the "unfavorable" trends that have been described above, nothing very much seems to have happened. An important part of the problem is of course that official ideology at the present stage of its development does not permit expressly nationalist justifications for policy. Nor can it be admitted that ethnic relations in the Soviet Union can by their very nature be anything but harmonious. Thus while tacit deviations from this norm can of course be practiced or tolerated, it is difficult to launch full-scale propaganda and administrative campaigns that fly directly in the face of it. While policy-makers hesitate, events move inexorably onward. They have in any case gone too far for major future changes to be averted. In this situation the leadership seems to have placed its money (with what conviction can only be conjectured) on the only wager available, namely linguistic and cultural assimilation.

Official commentary on population developments contains innumerable indications of the official hope that while the number of Russians may decline, that of Russian-speakers will increase. This seems a forlorn prospect. The number of Russian-speakers is increasing at a more satisfactory rate. But the difference for the time being is marginal and not enough to indicate a trend. The number of Russians, as was mentioned earlier, dropped from 54.6% to 53.4% between 1959 and 1970. The number giving Russian as their native tongue also dropped in the same period, from 59.5% to 58.7%. The fact that this decline is smaller than the other, and that the number of non-Russians giving Russian as their native language showed a solid absolute increase, seems scarcely sufficient to warrant optimism. And in conditions where the great Russian language is being ceaselessly extolled, it may well be that this modest increase is more indicative of a stiffening of national resistances than anything else.[67] In any case, the nationalist speaking the colonial language is a sociological cliché. As Walker Connor puts it: "Care must be taken not to confuse assimilation regarding overt characteristics, such as language and dress, with psychological assimilation; advances in the former need not be accompanied by advances in the latter."[68] Warnings against over-

estimating <u>overt</u> compliance with assimilatory norms seem particularly apposite to the Soviet case. It is, of course, also true that
spreading Russian may have the paradoxical result of further facili-
tating contact among speakers of Turkic languages who might otherwise have found communication slightly more difficult.

The present situation confronting Soviet Russian policy-makers
in the nationalities sphere is rather like that of a thrifty woman
seeking to patch holes in a ragged pair of trousers using swatches
ripped from the trousers themselves. To prevent exposure at one
point involves the necessity of exposure at another. In such a situation it is evident that there must be an allocation of priorities.
The behavior of the Soviet government to date, however, seems to
suggest that it has not fully grasped this fundamental truth; or alternatively, that population policy considerations are still given low
priority. They have made or at least failed to prevent onerous population investments (to avoid the preempted term "demographic
investments") in areas where the interest rate is negative, and
where the only final net yield is likely to be trouble. It is true that
they have shown themselves eager to populate their crucial western
and far eastern border areas as well. But while in the west they
may in places be proceeding with an excess of zeal and haste, touch-
ing off keen and perhaps explosive resentment in the process, in
Siberia and the Far East, where the demographic and political
threat is more external than internal, their policies have misfired,
and sponsored immigration has been rendered largely nugatory by
spontaneous emigration. To the external observer it would seem
that they are also confronted by a danger that a band of continuous
non-European (and largely Moslem) settlement might redevelop
right across from the North Caucasus area to the Turkestan-Sinkiang
border.[69] With the possible re-Kalmuckization of the Kalmuck
ASSR on the north coast of the Caspian, only Astrakhan Oblast, with
its solid Russian majority, is left holding the lines. Developments
in the Turkic (both Moslem — Tatar and Bashkir — and non-
Moslem — Chuvash) and Finno-Ugrian autonomous republics in
the Volga-Urals area are not wholly without their dangers either.
This area is only separated from the north of Kazakhstan by a narrow neck of territory formed by Orenburg and Cheliabinsk oblasti,
where there are modest but by no means negligible non-Russian
minorities. "Elemental" migratory tendencies in the area would
need to be kept under control. Presumably this much is being done.[70]

Perhaps the most remarkable thing about current demographic
trends in the context of the nationalities issue is the way in which

certain Asian peoples, vanquished long since, are now staging a
revival and, by virtue of economic advance coupled with demographic dynamism, reasserting a claim to some part at least of the
lands in which they were once the masters, regaining thanks to the
pax sovietica what they once had been forced to cede in military
defeat. Where previously the demographic strength of economically
weaker peoples tended to be held in check by warfare and other
Malthusian checks stemming from conditions imposed on the losers,
currently the reverse applies. Political and economic strength no
longer imply demographic strength; rather the contrary. In the
context of multiethnic states this may lead to curious results. In
the international arena a similar development is being observed,
but there national military, economic, and strategic considerations
may, at least in the short term, prevent the growing populations
of Latin America or Asia from generating any corresponding increase in political weight. But not all these considerations need
be relevant in the case of multiethnic states. If the nonwhite component in the U.S. population were to rise from its present 12% to
25% or 30%, say, and its incidence to be largely reconcentrated in
a relatively few states, would this, politically, be a matter of indifference?[71] Obviously the American system is more conducive
to minority politicking in many ways. But the American system
does not as a matter of principle seek the relatively more rapid
social and cultural development of the minority peoples in the way
that the Soviet system does.[72] Moreover, it deprives ethnic minorities of their language with an alacrity and lack of effort that
must excite the keenest envy in Moscow.

It would seem that the importance of the problem of the nationalities in the Soviet Union will grow at a speed at least commensurate
with their demographic advance, and that the major problem area
in the future will be Soviet Central Asia. It is ironic that this
should be so when, numerous brutal episodes notwithstanding, the
record of tsarist and Soviet administration has been better there
than in most other places. And it is, of course, thanks to the relative Soviet tolerance of linguistic and cultural heterogeneity and
their efforts at least partially to bridge the gap in development between different parts of the country that the necessary bases for
Central Asian "nationalism of a new type" exist. A relatively good
record, however, has not yet been an effective guarantee for any
colonial power.

As pressures build up in the Central Asian demographic cauldron,
several things might conceivably happen. As the indigenous element

in the cities grows and competition for jobs (with competence in Russian one of the factors) grows with it,[73] Russian reemigration from the area may set in amid harsh feeling all around (as has happened in Kosovo in recent years, where the Serbian population, originally in significant measure a political immigration, has been stagnating in the last decade because of net migration losses). Apart from the local impact of any such dénouement, which can readily be imagined, it may have the effect of sharpening Russian distaste for "Asians," already reported to be running high in the wake of the Sino-Soviet conflict and the rather heady propaganda that has sometimes been circulated in connection with it.[74] This in turn might be expected to have a strong impact on the Soviet Russian view of the world in general, leading quite possibly to some measure of reorientation toward Europe and the West. Perhaps we are already witnessing something of the sort in détente (if for different reasons). Moscow might also respond by effecting a closing of ranks among the European or possibly the Slav or simply Russian element in the population, as during World War II, perhaps too, with some of the same religious and traditionalist concessions. This, one suspects, if coupled with an appropriately reformulated "Soviet" traditionalism, could appeal much more strongly to the Russian population than the rather watery ideology they are being offered at present.[75]

Alternatively, if the Europeans on the whole were to stay[76] and the Central Asians were to be forced to seek work in European USSR (something which they have been extremely reluctant to do voluntarily), their eventual appearance in rather large numbers in the cities of the European USSR might lead to tensions of a different sort. Soviet Europeans are not likely to love them very much more than the Swiss, for example, love their economic immigrants. The result might be similar to that triggered by the arrival of colored Commonwealth immigrants in liberal, tolerant England. An "unshakable brotherhood" line would surely be maintained at first; but if popular resentment of the newcomers rose to high enough levels, it might well find tacit approval in the same way that popular anti-Semitism does now. The overall result might be much the same as in the paradigm described earlier in which the Central Asians stayed at home and the Russians returned: growing indigenous socioeconomic strength in Central Asia and growing European resentment of the Central Asian peoples both there and elsewhere. Even if five to ten million Central Asian workers were to make their appearance in the European parts of the USSR by the 1990s, their numerical preponderance in their homelands would not be materially altered. Such a situation — with large but demographically not dominant settlements of colonizers in the colonies, and large minorities of the colonials in the (still-ascendant) metropolitan country — would probably be without precedent in the history of European colonialism. Elsewhere, in Britain, France, and Holland, for example, the main influx of racially distinct colonials began flowing into the metropolitan country only after the sensitive issue of national independence had been resolved. Thus if the Central Asians do migrate in substantial numbers to the European parts of the USSR, we will have, so to speak, a potentially Wolverhampton situation at home and a Salisbury situation "abroad" simultaneously.

What the cumulative impact of such a combination might be can only be a matter of speculation at this stage. It may be that race relations in the USSR are inherently better than elsewhere (though I doubt it); perhaps they lack some of the key stigmata of racial, as opposed to ethnic, tensions (though again I doubt it); and the Soviet Union may conceivably display superior political wisdom or a greater degree of efficient ruthlessness in handling the situation. But the situation itself will be structurally unique. It is difficult to escape the conclusion that in this matter discretion would be the better part of wisdom: that the Soviet authorities should at least ensure that only limited numbers and selected sociological samplings of Central Asians ever arrive in the European USSR. In respect of this objective, at least, the regime is as well equipped as any that has ever existed. But it may prove beyond them to hold the Central Asians in their own republics through the 1980s and 1990s without accepting widespread unemployment there. Moreover, their record in directing migratory flows along approved channels in the past has been surprisingly unimpressive.

In general, few viable policies seem obviously available to help forestall the dangers implicit in the present differential ethnic growth rates. The current line — avoiding wholly overt Russian chauvinism while pursuing mildly repressive policies in respect of nationalist threats as they arise, furthering intermingling in the hope of thereby spreading assimilationist trends,[77] imposing the use of Russian wherever possible in schools, journalism, science, and public life, maintaining and within demographic limitations increasing the Russian physical presence in all the union republics (outside the Caucasus), making the means of family limitation available and hoping the Central Asians will sooner or later come round to using them, speaking meanwhile loudly and often of fraternal relations, Soviet patriotism, and, hopefully, of an emergent Soviet people in the singular — this line, though it may be the product of inertia, bemusement, stalemate, or lack of imagination or concern, may not nonetheless be the worst alternative. More pessimistic and more optimistic prognoses of future trends in Soviet policy both suggest themselves as plausible up to a point.

Perhaps the greatest danger inherent in the situation from an external viewpoint is the possibility of further radical deterioration of the Soviet polity. Soviet constitutionalism is a tender plant; but the cautious re-Stalinization of recent years notwithstanding, it would probably be true to say that for the first time in Soviet history, established ways of doing things are starting to emerge, group interests of a kind to be regularly affirmed, and the place of experts (including social scientists) recognized. The present de facto Soviet constitution seems to debar riding too roughshod over the interests of any one major nationality, for instance. It also debars Russification that is both brutal and overt, repression on purely racialist or nationalist lines without ostensibly nonracialist or nonnationalist justification, or the preservation or fostering of economic inequality between nations and republics. This fragile rule of law wears very thin at certain points and is sometimes openly flouted with institutional authority, as the World University Games excesses of 1973 illustrate.[78] And in general the case of Soviet Jewry would seem to suggest that the society is currently generating both elite and popular needs for a convenient and ethnically more or less visible scapegoat. If and when Central Asian industrial workers come to live cheek by jowl with Slavs and others in European cities of the USSR, and not in their traditional quarters in the cities of Central Asia,[79] they may well assume certain of the Jews' social functions, particularly if large numbers of the latter were to emigrate.

As both the intense idealism and the intense hostility toward the capitalist enemy seem to have largely disappeared from Soviet communism, it is in need of psychological and emotional fuel to recharge its batteries and restore some of its earlier dynamism. Once resident in European USSR in sufficient numbers, while presumably pressing for more voice in their own homelands, the Central Asians could be the kind of part-scapegoat, part-real-but-manageable-enemy that could encapsulate and serve as a convenient focus for anti-Chinese sentiments and anxieties. It should be remembered, however, that scapegoating requires a consciousness of overwhelming superiority. This is more likely to be felt by the

popular masses than their rulers in the kind of situation that has
been adumbrated. Any Soviet government, however chauvinist,
would remain aware that bad ethnic relations at the center would
strain the political situation at the periphery (where the hypothetical metropolitan minority would, of course, be a solid majority).
For this reason, they would be fearful of permitting Black Hundreds
methods to be applied to the "Asians"; would be, that is, as long
as political modes remained more or less rational.

The liberal alternative in anything seems unlikely in the Soviet
Union at present. But this may be only a transient perspective.
In any event, at least as far as the Central Asians are concerned,
relative liberalism may make pragmatic good sense in the context
of foreign policy. Reference was made earlier to the propaganda
war that has been raging across the Sino-Soviet border with both
sides aiming at influencing the national minorities of the other.
While this does not affect all the peoples involved equally, as long
as the two sides continue to be adversaries, certain limits are
placed on their conduct of nationality policy in the vicinity of their
common border. The Soviets have, for example, shown particular
tenderness toward the small community of Moslem Uighurs (most
of the 179,000 of whom are recent refugees from China), even allowing them to publish large amounts of various kinds of literature
in their Arabic script, a most significant and, one would have
thought, risky deviation from their usual linguistic policy in Central Asia.[80]

The Chinese, meanwhile, have proceeded to Latinize their Uighurs as a countermeasure.[81] Though the Chinese have shown considerable sensitivity about the members of their minority groups
having been, as they always allege, abducted across the border by
the Soviets, demographic reasons at least would suggest that on
the whole, this is an area of policy in which the Soviet Union has
much less freedom of maneuver. The Chinese minorities only
amount to some 5% of the total population of the CPR, and the relative overall proportions are likely if anything to change in favor
of the Han Chinese. The latter, moreover, are having and will
have little difficulty in demographically swamping the minority
areas adjoining the Soviet Union. The Russians have pursued similar resettlement policies; but if one of their purposes in doing so
has been to achieve demographic dominance in Central Asia, they
will manifestly not succeed. In this situation they may perceive
that it is in their interest to make a virtue of necessity by keeping
their nationalities positively happy as well as fostering disaffection

among the minorities on the other side of the border. If so, they
may then find it expedient to give the Central Asians more say in
their own affairs; they might also decide to refrain from hindering
tendencies toward national consolidation among the Turkic peoples
of the area, possibly even sponsoring a little more international and
internal Moslem religious activity than has hitherto been permitted.

The Soviet leadership seems to be aware that the most dangerous
time for any government is when it begins to improve. However
they may formulate this adage in their own minds, they are unlikely
to forget its wisdom completely within a generation or so of 1956.
If they do opt for liberalism in their nationalities policy, it is likely
to be restricted geographically to the areas of greatest need. And
of course, the three alternatives of continued immobility, liberalism, and neonationalist radicalism are only three cardinal points
within a multitude of possibilities. Actual future policies may well
prove to be a hybrid of them or of others I have failed to anticipate.
All I have been concerned to do was sketch some possibilities which
seem to be inherent in the present situation in order to bring out
the full importance of contemporary demographic trends.

A Note on Ethnic Assimilation
in the Soviet Union[82]

Reference has been made at several points to assimilation tendencies within the Soviet Union. This, of course, is another enormous subject in itself, but perhaps it would be useful to briefly
summarize some of its main features as they affect, or are likely
to affect, the relative numerical strength of the peoples of the USSR.

It has been pointed out earlier that the regime does in fact pin
a good deal of hope on the beneficent workings of assimilation processes. It has also been indicated that the main sources of Russian
"converts" are the Ukrainians and Belorussians and, in lesser
measure, various other mainly European national groups, notably
the Finno-Ugrian peoples. It was noted that the proportion of people identifying Russian as their native language was declining more
slowly than the proportion of people identifying themselves as Russians. Russian is being pressed on the national minorities to an
increasing degree. The minority languages appear in general to
be losing ground in the sphere of book and periodical publishing.[83]
Particularly determined attempts are being made to expand Russian teaching especially as a second language[84] but also, de facto,

as a first language at points where resentment and resistance is weakest or most fissiparated (in Dagestan schools, for example, where the multitude of local languages provides reinforcing practical reasons for the move).[85] Census materials from 1970 were unfailingly presented in such a way as to underscore the importance and popularity of Russian as the (a) language of international communication in the Soviet Union and beyond, as the language of science and culture, and also as an adopted language. Much sociological research on nationalities problems is now being organized.[86] A Scientific Council for Nationality Problems has been created within the USSR Academy of Sciences. The new council's stated areas of research interest betray a clear policy orientation. In general the quantity and quality of sociological writing on nationality questions advanced considerably in the late sixties and early seventies. Demographic research has formed a similar pattern, with growing numbers of monographs appearing that are devoted exclusively or largely to ethnic differentials.[87] In sociological and demographic enquiry a good deal of attention is devoted to the subject of mixed marriages, whose incidence, it is always emphasized, is increasing greatly.[88] No less a person than Brezhnev himself has commented on the importance of this beneficent development.[89]

There is a very large degree of wishful thinking or displaced anxiety in the confident assertiveness shown in Soviet press comment on this subject. In fact assimilation trends hitherto have not been particularly favorable to the Russians, certainly not when one considers their dominant position in the Soviet Union as a whole. The Ukrainians and Belorussians have always been a good source of additional Russian increase. It may well be that they are now "defecting" in smaller numbers than they did in the 1920s and 1930s (between the 1926 and 1939 censuses, the number of Belorussians increased much more slowly than that of the Russians, and the Ukrainians registered a 10% decline;[90] some of this difference may have been due to the greater damage inflicted there by the collectivization and subsequent upheavals, but much of it may also have been due to assimilation). The decline in the proportion of Belorussians and Ukrainians who gave their national language as their native language between the 1959 and 1970 censuses is significant (from 84.2 to 80.5% and 87.7 to 85.7%, respectively),[91] but the absolute numbers of native speakers continue to show a solid increase; and in the case of the Belorussians, the rate of increase of Belorussian-speaking Belorussians is only slightly slower than the overall increase (including assimilation gains) of Russians.[92] Neither nation is showing any signs of disappearing, as is not infrequently suggested, although both are obviously exposed to great pressure and a real, if long-term, threat.

Few other major nationalities have registered similar declines of native-speaker proportions within their ethnic group totals over the same period. Of the twenty-two nationalities numbering over one million, the only other such exceptions are the Germans, the Jews, and the Poles.[93] The Germans, it should be remembered, are exposed to particularly repressive cultural conditions as well as physical dispersal and may well feel, moreover, that not to give Russian as their native language would be unusually imprudent. The Poles form a marked exception among the major national groups in that they tend to give as their native language the language of their host nationality rather than Russian or Polish: in the Ukraine, more than four times as many give Ukrainian as either Russian or Polish, while in Belorussia the corresponding figure is roughly six times as many.[94] As for the Jews, they are, of course, the classic illustration of how fallacious it can be to mechanically identify language with ethnic identity. Over four fifths are now self-declared native speakers of Russian with results in terms of ethnic identification that we read about daily in our newspapers.

In Central Asia the chances of large-scale assimilation seem virtually zero. The native peoples' command of Russian is (outside parts of Kazakhstan) worse than anywhere else in the Soviet Union, and their devotion to their own language, as measured in the proportion of people giving their own national language as their native language, higher.[95] Though much is made of the allegedly high incidence of mixed marriage in the area, there is good reason to suppose that the great bulk of it is between European and European or non-European and non-European.[96] Cross-cultural intermarriage is certainly increasing, but from such low levels as to be virtually negligible outside a few urban centers, where it is minor. Rather significantly, the great bulk of the cross-cultural marriages are between indigenous men and European women. According to one study, 887 Turkmenian men married non-Turkmenian women, while only 162 Turkmenian women married outsiders.[97] A similar pattern appears to obtain in most Moslem areas of the USSR. Moreover there is evidence that the offspring of these marriages normally identify themselves as indigenes rather than Europeans. While Russian numbers are undoubtedly boosted by intermarriage with the Finno-Ugrian peoples of the RSFSR or indeed the Orthodox Turkic-speaking Chuvash,[98] it seems that in Central Asia, though

the numbers involved so far are small, it is the Slavs who are the
net "losers." Thus a study carried out in Dushanbe, for example,
revealed that 82% of adolescents in families with a Tadzhik father
and Russian mother adopted the father's nationality.[99] Elsewhere
the proportion may be even higher. According to the Soviet ethnog-
rapher Bromlei, nearly 90% of all teenagers in Turkmenian-
Russian families identify themselves as Turkmenian.[100]

In fact there tends to be a large measure of informal apartheid
in Central Asian cities dating from tsarist times, when the tendency
was to build separate cities for the European settlers away from
the existing ones. Data on Russian-language skills among Central
Asian rural dwellers suggest that there is even less mingling in
rural areas. While it is likely that there is prejudice and "blame"
on both sides, most Central Asian peoples have good reason to as-
sociate the Russians with national and personal or family disasters
suffered by them in the recent past. Major historical and sociopolitical conflicts and grievances apart, it would seem that the Russians
have the usual European knack of not endearing themselves to non-
Europeans. It is unlikely that floods of mutual passion will suddenly be undammed by exhortatory Kazakhstanskaia Pravda edi-
torials. The most that could reasonably be hoped for in the distant
future, one would have thought, would be decorous relations marked
by a kind of some-of-my-best-friends tolerance. Had the cultural
repressions of the 1920s and 1930s been directed more toward language and had they been followed up by resettlement programs, the
regime might have achieved a better distribution of Russian speakers among the Central Asians (as it has done, for example, with
the displaced Koreans of Central Asia);[101] but this would not necessarily mean assimilation. Very probably the racial factor intro-
duces additional barriers whose surmounting cannot be measured
by linguistic affiliation anyway. If the Central Asians are to be
viewed by the Europeans as an inferior people, i.e., if tensions are
to be more racial than national, intermarriage will always produce
more Central Asians no matter what language the progeny speak:
"The powerful fictions invented through application of a descent
principle are further demonstrated by the treatment of children of
mixed marriages. Regardless of phenotype, such children are affiliated with the racial group of the lower-ranking parent."[102]
These words were actually written about mixed marriages in the
United States. The situation in Soviet Central Asia may develop
differently, but this remains to be seen. It also remains to be seen
whether the products of mixed marriages will, as Soviet commen-

tators seem to imply, transcend national exclusivisms and represent perfect specimens of emergent Soviet narodnost'. There are good historical and sociological reasons for doubting it. To quote Walker Connor again: "The progeny of ethnically mixed marriages do not necessarily exhibit less national consciousness than do either of their parents; they often exhibit more."[103]

Even in the Baltic states, where Russification seems to be making great inroads and where the racial factor is absent, assimilation trends are somewhat ambiguous. Taking all three republics together, we find 36,192 self-identified members of the respective titular nationalities giving Russian as their native language, while 18,671 Russians give one or other of the Baltic languages as their native language.[104] These figures are difficult to interpret with confidence, but they are consistent with substantial degrees of assimilation away from Russiandom as well as to it. A recent Soviet source suggests in fact that half of the children of mixed families in the Baltic states opt for the local nationality and half for Russian.[105] Clearly the pattern there differs markedly from that in the other Western republics or the autonomous national units of the RSFSR. It seems, in other words, that if Russia is to dominate the Baltic states, it cannot rely on assimilation processes to do the work for it unaided.

Among the numerous minor (less than one million) ethnic groups in the Soviet Union, the degree of linguistic tenacity displayed in recent years is no less surprising than their demographic expansion. Few apart from the Finno-Ugrian groups have shown declines of more than a few decimal points in the proportions giving the national language as their native one in 1959 and 1970. In many cases that proportion has actually increased.[106] Here, too, on present indications, the sources of potential Russians are small as a proportion of the whole and almost negligible in absolute terms.

The spread of fluency in Russian to wider sections of the Soviet population and the growth of ethnic intermarriage may bring certain benefits, including perhaps greater cultural tolerance and stability, to the Soviet Union. There is little reason at present to expect that they will set up a landslide of assimilation that could counteract the demographic landslide in the opposite direction. And they are least likely to do so precisely in those regions where counteraction, from a Russian point of view, is most required.

The results of the 1979 Census may throw a few more oblique shafts of light on this subject. But even if it were to show signs of accelerated linguistic and other assimilation, caution would still be warranted. As a senior official in the RSFSR Ministry of Education said, "...he who knows Russian in the Soviet Union has an advantage whatever profession he chooses."[107] Similarly, no doubt, he who says he is a Russian. There have been suggestions that Soviet citizens of non-Russian parentage should have the choice of declaring themselves Russian if they should so desire.[108] Article 36 of the new Constitution speaks, unlike its predecessor, of the opportunity all Soviet nations have to use their mother tongue and the languages of other nations of the USSR. But the Yugoslav example (as we shall see later) illustrates how patterns of self-identification can change as social and political pressures ebb and flow, and how tenacious underlying allegiances can be. Russian absorption of national minorities in the Soviet Union is a phenomenon one could easily overestimate.

CHAPTER 7

USSR:
INTERNATIONAL POLITICS

Now it is true that international migration is not an important factor for the Soviet Union, though it has been so at times for Tsarist Russia. (...) But there
can hardly be any doubt that migration would help to solve some of China's economic problems, and if directed towards the Soviet Union it might also help in
the development of that country's Far Eastern areas.[1]

In this brief discussion I shall for the most part avoid reference
to the existing literature on the connections between population and
international politics.[2] Thus far this literature has been limited
in large measure to occasional essays and reflections and has
perhaps for this reason accumulated relatively few undisputed
maxims, other than those that were in any case largely familiar
to most thoughtful students of international politics.

In proceeding on the assumption that differing rates of population
growth may be relevant to the relative power positions of the nations concerned, I should perhaps emphasize that I am not thereby
attributing any very definite importance to military manpower as
such. In an age of mutual assured destruction, a large population
may be of limited value. Even if we have now proceeded from MAD
to MCC (mutually contemplated counterforce), mere numbers are
probably still not crucial, either in terms of overall demographic
strength or military manpower. In any case the Soviet Union has
not in the past registered any public anxiety on the issue. For
much of the 1950s and 1960s, in fact, the tendency was to reduce
the numbers in the Soviet armed forces.[3] While this apparently
reflected Khrushchev's personal views as well as extreme shortages of young manpower as the depleted World War II birth cohorts
entered work-force and military age, it was surely of some significance that the decision was taken to prefer economic to military

use of the available manpower reserves. Faced by the emergence of China as an active adversary in the late 1960s, the Soviet Union was able to quickly raise its force levels (including manpower) on the Eastern border. Moreover, projections indicate (rather surprisingly) that Soviet prime-age military manpower will go on increasing until 1984.[4] The situation, however, is about to change drastically.

Discussion of these matters is not made any easier by the circumstance that we do not really know how many people there are in the Soviet armed services. But whatever the precise number, it is clear that another and more prolonged dearth of recruits than that of the early 1960s is about to descend. Moreover, it will occur at a time when the USSR's commitments (particularly on its Eastern borders) are greater and more sensitive, and when the labor shortage cannot be met by migration of peasants or greater female employment. In these circumstances, as Feshbach and Rapawy have commented, "the Soviet Party and Government are faced with an increasingly acute competition for manpower between the civilian economy and the military."[5] Whatever the effects of this may be on the Soviet Union's inherent capacity to safeguard or extend its interests, it will clearly be an important and disruptive influence on the unity of the political establishment in the years ahead. If military recruitment rates of 18-year-old males were not to change, Feshbach and Rapawy estimate that the numbers of 18-year-olds available for the civilian labor force would decline from 399,000 in 1978 to −204,000 in 1987.

They also draw attention to the fact that the proportion of these recruits stemming from the Central Asian republics (including Kazakhstan) is going to increase sharply, from an estimated 16.8% in 1975 to 27.4% in 2000, and 34.6% if the Transcaucasus is included.[6] While these estimates are apparently based on the unlikely assumption that fertility will everywhere remain at 1972 levels, the results they give are not likely to be far wide of the mark. The 1970 Census results are so arranged, accidentally no doubt, that one cannot readily estimate future military cohort proportions by nationality. But my own rough estimate is that the numbers of "Moslems" among recruits by about 1990 will be roughly one quarter, probably increasing steadily thereafter.

Feshbach and Rapawy emphasize the linguistic problems these trends will present to the Soviet forces and question the suitability of Central Asian recruits in units employing advanced technology.[7] These are serious difficulties, though it is of course true that the

younger Central Asians are better educated and markedly more
fluent in Russian than their parents were.

Perhaps more serious are the problems they will pose for the
unity, morale, and reliability of the Soviet forces. Central Asian
troops have their special advantages, as their prominence in Czechoslovakia in 1968 indicated. But could the leadership feel just as
happy about their deployment on the Chinese border? If any sort
of Harlem-Notting Hill tensions were to develop from Central
Asian migration as adumbrated in the last chapter, would this have
any consequences for armed services efficiency? Do these manpower trends in fact make Soviet commitments in Eastern Europe
and on its Asian borders such as to overstrain its capacity? Should
the leadership respond by increasing the Central Asian component
in the officer corps? What effect would this ultimately have on the
unity of outlook and perspective of the High Command? In an area
where so little is known, only speculations rather than judgments
can be essayed. But it is evident at least that it is an area fraught
with difficulty if not danger for the Soviet authorities.

Turning to consider the USSR's position more directly vis-à-vis
the outside world, the discussion is bound to become even more
imprecise and inconclusive than it has already been. I am assured
by competent experts on strategic studies generally, and on Soviet
strategic thinking in particular, that very little advanced theorizing
exists on the connections between national population size and military capability in the nuclear age. It is significant that the most
thorough Western discussion of linkages between population and international conflict (Choucri's Population Dynamics and International Violence) also devotes relatively little attention to this point
and appears not to cite any military opinions. But there are at
least five areas in which population trends may influence international politics: the military or psychologico-military impact of
numbers; the effect on international ethnopolitical conflicts; the economic consequences of differential growth; the effects on national
prestige; and the possible "spillage" of demographic pressures
across borders.

The military-strategic aspects of population growth are both
highly technical and highly problematical. In an age of mutual de-
terrence, it was suggested earlier, margins of overkill may not be
of inherent strategic importance; but because of their psychological
impact, they may seem so and therefore become so. Certainly they
seem to be striven for with unabated zeal. Analogously, though it
may be difficult to foresee in what way differential densities, mag-

86

nitudes, or rates of growth of population might affect the outcome of any armed conflict between, say, the USSR and China, it is clear that they are likely to be felt to be of importance if the numbers involved are large.

Extremes in population growth may also cause or contribute to changes in relative economic potential if trends are maintained over a period of time. While rapid population growth is held to be an obstacle to economic development, it is evident, for example, that if, say, by 2025 East Germany is still languishing[8] at or below its 1946 level of 18 million while Poland has increased its population from 23 million to 50 million, there is likely to have been a shift in their relative economic weight in favor of the latter that is at least partly due to the manpower factor. There is also the factor of economic size as a necessary basis for major defense-spending programs. A country of modest economic attainments, but rich in human and natural resources like the USSR (or India), can more readily afford the kind of military expenditure that modern weapons technology appears to dictate. This is a function of sheer economic size, not efficiency; and it may appear to a country like Brazil, for example,[9] that rapid growth in human resources, however unhelpful from the vantage point of per capita income levels or urban social problems, nonetheless expands the base on which national "greatness" rests.

The size of a country's population is, in any case, an important element in determining its relative prestige. This is a view prominently displayed in demographic writing at all levels throughout the Socialist bloc. Where other forms of national expression are inhibited, Olympic gold medals or census results may acquire an even greater significance. And though the Soviet Union (or, if one prefers, Soviet Russia) has relatively greater outlets for nationalism, it too is susceptible to the prestige aspect of population growth. Respect for numbers is not confined to the Socialist countries, however, and they are probably right to see things in this light.

Finally, in the case of the relationship between the Soviet Union and China (if not Japan), there is the question of whether population pressures building up in one country are not bound sooner or later to "spill over" into another, thereby unleashing political or military conflict. Here again we are dealing with what are ultimately still imponderables, though ones about which a great deal has been and no doubt will be written.

Thus Stuart Kirby, for example, has written:

Still deeper, more primitive or primary motivations underlie the matter. 800 million Chinese, rising soon to over 1,000 million, are in dire need of Lebensraum; in the direct sense of more land for settlement of huge numbers, or the less direct sense of access to natural resources which would sustain China's industrialization. One of the simplest and most immediate directions in which the Chinese may look . . . is the whole area called Siberia, largely unpopulated and with huge untapped resources.[10]

It is not a disqualification of this kind of view to demonstrate that the density of China's population is less than that of Europe, or that migration, as a solution to overcrowding, is likely to be economically more expensive and demographically less effective than domestic birth control measures.[11] For it is sufficient that either the Chinese or the Russian leaderships be deceived by such a "great illusion" for it to become an effective influence on the course of events.

Having sketched these blurry guidelines, it remains to consider the Soviet Union's position in terms of them. It seems clear, to begin with, that population trends as between the Soviet Union and either Eastern Europe or the West are unlikely to exert much influence on the course of events in the immediate future. The demographic strength of the Moldavians is obviously not irrelevant to the future of Romanian-Soviet relations. Some Poles may feel an important moment has been reached if and when they overtake (numerically) the Ukrainians. As the number of home-born Poles grows in the Western Territories, the hopes of German revanche grow, perhaps, ever slimmer. The brief period in which the U.S. population seemed to be overtaking the Soviet one raised something of a flutter in the breasts of some U.S. demographers — and their Soviet counterparts no doubt.[12] But basically, taking the USSR, the USA, and East and West Europe as blocs, their relative positions of strength seem destined to remain the same insofar as demographic factors can influence the outcome. The fertility decline in the USSR has been matched by that in East Europe (and, after a pause, by that in West Europe and the United States as well). If the Soviet Union can no longer place itself at the top of developed countries' population increase league-tables, as it still could when the 1959 Census results were published,[13] this is a prestige item of predominantly domestic significance.

To the south of the Soviet border, demographic trends seem more or less matched on the Soviet side, and the Russian core of the USSR (i.e., the RSFSR) is not in any case exposed. Moreover, there are no major political threats stemming from that quarter. One can conceive of a Persian Pan-Iranianism aspiring to expanded relations with Soviet Tadzhikistan or a Pan-Turanianism reaching out from Turkey to Yakutia which might be more than mere nuisance value in the future. Some observers believe in fact that there is a possibility that a unified Turko-Iranian Moslem state might emerge in Soviet Central Asia were circumstances propitious. This argument is based on the fact of extensive bilingualism among the Iranian speakers in the area and the common historical and cultural traditions which the two groups of peoples share.[14] But none of these possibilities will be brought into being by extra-Soviet demographic trends alone, nor perhaps even exacerbated by them. To be effective they would depend heavily on demographic and other domestic developments within Soviet Central Asia itself. If the latter were not conducive, external pressures from the south would probably not amount to much. In any case, the Soviet Union would not be wholly bereft of possible countermeasures.

This leaves Siberia and the Far East. Here one has on the one hand the USSR struggling to get its numbers up but in vain, and on the other China straining intermittently to keep its numbers down, but also experiencing difficulties. Of course, China is not eager to reduce her numbers in the area bordering on the Soviet Union, where, reportedly, the latest antinatalist rigors are not applied, and where in any case the Chinese government is bent on greatly increasing the Han Chinese component by fostering inmigration. As a result of these policies, the ratio of Han Chinese to Mongols in the Inner Mongolian Autonomous Region has reportedly risen from 3 to 1 (in 1947) to 15 to 1 in 1971; and of Han to Tibetans to 2 to 1 in Tibet as of the mid-70s. In Sinkiang the Han proportion of the population has risen from 5.5% in 1949 to 45% in 1966.[15]

Then there is Japan, a country with a relative surplus of population and capital and by tradition eager to find a home for both if the conditions are right. The similarities between the Soviet situation and that which has produced the Australian psychological syndrome of "the vast unpopulated north" and "populate or perish" are very striking. Australia, however, does not have 60 million of its potential adversaries living adjacent to an exposed strip of strategic territory along a land border. It is interesting and perhaps symptomatic that Soviet scholars are apparently not unaware of certain parallels between Australia and Siberia.[16]

The vital question here is whether population pressures are bound to or likely to issue forth into political conflict. And second, if so, whether relative manpower strengths are likely to affect the outcome of any future conflict. In other words, once the Chinese have achieved the level of nuclear deterrent sufficient to constrain the USSR from using or threatening to use nuclear weapons against them, will their relative manpower superiority be a crucial factor? There are far too many issues involved in these questions for even a sketch summary to be worth attempting. In any case they exceed this writer's competence. Perhaps it is enough to say that the USSR feels it to be of the greatest importance to build up and populate its border areas with China. A Council of Ministers' decree of May 1973 offered special financial and other inducements (including the promise of motor vehicles specially suited to primitive border terrain) for settlers prepared to go and live along the Chinese border.[17] If anything like population parity throughout the area is aspired to, however, official hopes must be doomed to frustration. It could perhaps be achieved locally in some of the less habitable parts of the Asian hinterland, but certainly not in the Far East section of the border. There, and in general, the demographic trends in favor of the Chinese are so colossal as to paralyze the imagination. This may be worth bringing out with a few rough statistics. They cannot be anything other than rough, since most people, including Chinese politicians, tend to be a few years out of date with their Chinese population estimates; and those estimates themselves are unlikely to be very precise.

Until the early '70s, the figure of 700 million was still in official use, though all observers agreed that the real figure must be in the vicinity of 800 million if not more. Huang Shu-tse, China's chief delegate at the UN Population Conference in Bucharest in 1974, asserted that the Chinese population had increased from 1949 by 60% "to nearly 800 million" in 1974. If earlier official statistics were correct, however, a 60% increase would have made the Chinese population about 880 million by 1974.[18] A member of the press party which toured China with the Australian prime minister in 1976 reports that the figure of 900 million was often used by Chinese spokesmen as an estimate of national population.[19]

To give an estimate of annual increase for China's population is a hazardous undertaking. Two of the leading authorities on the subject, Leo Orleans and John Aird, suggest widely disparate figures for 1974, Orleans proposing a rate of 1.4% and Aird 2.2%;[20] Aird's base figure, moreover, would be much higher. Orleans arrives at a net annual increase of about 11.2 million, whereas all of Aird's four variants are in excess of 20 million. Orleans' reasoning seems slightly more engagé than Aird's, and one suspects it may reflect in some measure either his own optimism or that of the Chinese officials he spoke to. In any case, a compromise figure of 15 or 16 million seems not unreasonable for the purposes of the exercises which are about to follow.[21]

Thus, taking our compromise figure for what it is worth, one can say that the entire Russian increase between 1959 and 1970 of circa 15 million (which, it will be remembered, probably includes a solid element of assimilation) is, on a fairly cautious estimate, only about the same as the current annual increase in China; and unlike the latter, it is positively known to be declining fast.

The total population of West and East Siberia and the Far East (some 26 million in 1974) could probably be exceeded by the Chinese in natural increase in about a year and a half, give or take a month or two.

The Chinese could accumulate a natural increase equal to the entire Russian population in less than a decade, even if we assume a large decrease in estimated current levels of natural increase between now and the end of the decade and take the Russian figures for the end of it rather than the beginning.

It should be noted that there is nothing known to demographic science that would enable the Russians to materially alter this situation in the foreseeable future, though the trend could well become or be later proved to have been more unfavorable. Even if the Soviet government were to adopt a pronatalist policy of Romanian severity, and even if we were to assume that it would be equally successful (and there are reasons for doubting this), it would thereby only elevate Russian fertility to a level which would probably still be well below current Chinese crude birthrates. After the initial surprise effect had worn off, there would probably be a rapid decline back to about half or two thirds of present Chinese levels (within five years or so) and the prospect of further decline.

Little is definitely known about the Chinese population other than that it is very big and probably increasing rather fast. There has been no census since 1953, and official statements, as noted earlier, tend to be conflicting, nontechnical, and sometimes inherently implausible. It is curious, given the manifest unreliability of the data, that so many people are inclined to credit the Chinese with spectacular successes in fertility control. The Chinese themselves seem more cautious about their own claims, as is illustrated by their extraordinary action in trying to suppress all data relating to their

population in the UN publications prepared for the Bucharest World
Population Conference. Many of the assertions that have been made
by local Chinese spokesmen are plainly nonsense (e.g., the local
birthrates of 5 per thousand mentioned by J. Parsons in Planet,
August 22, 1974)[22] and cast doubt on the validity of all the others.
One would have thought the only statement about Chinese population
that can be made confidently is that very little is known.[23]

In the 1970s there have been reports alleging the introduction of
some particularly stringent birth-control measures in China, including compulsory abortion;[24] and the authorities have published some
fragmentary data which suggest a considerable decline in fertility
levels. Recently, for example, it has been claimed that live births
amounted to eight million fewer in 1978 than in 1971.[25] This characteristically oblique statistic implies a decline of just under one
per thousand per annum in the birthrate, a significant though not
unprecedented trend. Foreign observers in some cases remain
unconvinced.[26] In any case, even if the trend is maintained, Chinese natural increase rates will remain substantially higher than
those of European USSR for some time to come, probably until at
least the next century.

In the absence of reliable data, informed guesses can vary widely.
Thus, for example, two estimates attempted by outside sources for
1970 range between 753 million and 871 million. For 1980 preferred
projections by these same sources range between 887 and 1,060
million.[27] Since then the author of the lower of the two, Orleans,
has increased his 1980 hazard to 934 million. Even accepting with
him that Chinese natural increase is now only 13 per thousand and
that it is declining steadily, this would give a total figure of close
to 1,150 million by the year 2000.

It seems to me obvious that whatever projection they intimately
prefer, these figures at least must be disturbing to the Soviet leaders. While their precise political or military meaning is extremely
difficult to assess, the probable Soviet attitude toward them can be
more readily conjectured. They have been quoted here because they
form a crucial part of the Soviet geopolitical context,[28] if one that is
usually left implicit, both by Socialist and Western commentators.

Not all Western analysts have failed to grasp the nettle of es-
saying a precise evaluation of the population factor in Sino-Soviet
relations: Choucri and North have reported that

In extensive but preliminary statistical analyses of Chinese and Soviet Russian
reactions to each other's capabilities and power over the past 20 years, we

found that Soviet conflict behaviour toward the People's Republic (defined in terms of actions and events and measured systematically over time) is associated first and foremost with the size of the Chinese population rather than with indicators of technological growth and economic development. The correlation between Russia's actions toward China and the size of the Chinese population is .71. . . . At the same time China's behaviour toward the Soviet Union is strongly associated with the Chinese population size. The correlation is .86. . . . The correlation between China's violent behaviour toward the Soviet Union and the size of the Russian population is .89 . . .[29]

If "preliminary analyses" are capable of producing such impressive precision of judgment about what some might have regarded as imponderables, then the noncomputerized among us can presumably only join the Russians in quaking before the inevitable. However, queries do suggest themselves. What counts as evidence of Soviet awareness of Chinese population size and increase rates and vice versa? Is the course of the Sino-Soviet split related to the (virtually nonexistent) Chinese demographic statistics available at that period, and if so, in what way? Tantalizingly we are offered no details of how these and other problems were overcome.

Soviet commentators, though presumably for different reasons, are also disinclined to address this question in explicit detail. One does, however, see the occasional oblique comment. Thus, for example, the point that "other things being equal, a country's position in the world is determined by the size of its population" has been made explicitly by the forceful Soviet demographic commentator V. I. Perevedentsev.[30] Perevedentsev calculates that if existing growth rates are maintained, the USSR, from constituting 8.6% of the world's population in 1940, will have declined to 5% by the beginning of the twenty-first century. Another observer is even more candid, referring to the "senseless territorial claims of the present leaders of the Chinese People's Republic" in the context of "the notorious living space theory earlier adopted as an ideological weapon by the German, Italian, and Japanese fascists."[31] But comments even of this kind are fairly unusual.

It is surprising, given the apparent seriousness of the situation, that the military have not yet apparently made any very great public contribution to the demographic debate. A passage in a recent book by Boris Urlanis might even be read as a reproach to the military, or at least as an attempt to secure their support for an active population policy:

All this indicates that neither at present nor, it would seem, over the next decades will human resources cease to be an essential element in the military potential of a country. Indeed, as technology develops and becomes more complex, the role of the fighting man will increase still further.

From the foregoing it follows that defense interests cannot remain indifferent to the flow of demographic processes.[32]

The slightly stilted prose no doubt reflects the delicacy of the subject matter. A rare contribution to the demographic debate by someone identified with the armed forces (a staff-member of the Lenin Military Academy) makes no reference to either the question of military manpower or the interethnic balance.[33] Of course, it may well be that these matters are adjudged so delicate that all reference to them in the military context is either avoided or suppressed. In this connection a remark made by the sociologist Levada in a sociological house journal is of particular interest:

When the Supreme Soviet passed the new military law, Marshal Grechko, in explaining the reasons for the change in call-up age, said that it ensured that young 20-year-olds would return to civilian life, which would in turn have a favorable effect on family relations. This factor, as we can see, is also taken into account, and it is natural that specialists, in particular military specialists, are interested in the normal development of the population.[34]

Perhaps when the Russo-Ukrainian Soviet officer corps begins to be confronted by recruit detachments a good quarter of which are comprised of representatives of the Moslem peoples, they will become more energetic in their support of the demographic lobby.

CHAPTER 8

USSR:
IDEOLOGY

Actual population trends since World War II have wrought havoc
with the Stalinist version of the Marxist "laws" of population.
Marx's original pronouncements on the subject were sporadic,
unsystematic, and conveniently flexible. Basically, to recapitulate,
he had held that population movements were dependent on the underlying socioeconomic reality; that different patterns might
therefore be expected to prevail in different socioeconomic systems; that overpopulation was a purely relative thing; that in the
capitalist context, overpopulation was no more than an ideologically
distorted apprehension of the reserve army of the unemployed; and
that with the demise of capitalism, the "problem" of overpopulation
would disappear. Though he declared that different laws of population were applicable to different systems, Marx in fact confined
his attention to capitalism. He seems to have been inclined to assume that the numerical growth of the nineteenth century was likely
to persist, but he wisely refrained from dogmatic commitment.

Not so his Soviet successors, as we have seen. In the 1930s, as
the capitalist countries experienced sharp declines in birthrates,
they drew the inference that higher rates of growth must be one of
the essential features of socialist population development. And
finding Marx's polemical outbursts against Malthus strangely con-
genial, they petrified their slightly obsessive accusations into base
dogma: that there could never be any absolute overpopulation; and
that fertility control was unnecessary and to enjoin it upon people
was "barbaric"[1] and "cannibalistic."[2]

Whatever plausibility the Stalinist "law of population" may have
had in the 1930s, it was decisively rebutted by the course of vital
events after 1945 as (a) Western birthrates rose substantially in

most countries; (b) Soviet bloc birthrates, after initial resurgences, fell; and (c) Third World natural increase rates slid inexorably upward from high to higher, and future world population estimates began to resemble science fiction.

The Soviet ideological response to all this was complete immobility till about the midsixties. Then in late 1965 a switch to a more flexible line was negotiated. The shift, though quite abrupt, had been preceded by a few signs that reappraisal was pending. The American UN diplomat, Richard N. Gardner, commenting on the course of the debate in the General Assembly in December 1962 on the "Population Growth and Economic Development" resolution, notes that:

This Communist line (needless to say, anti-Malthusian — J. F. B.) was poorly received by the Assembly. At least one representative of a less developed country chided the Soviets for favouring planning in all sectors of economic life except the human sector — the one most important in its implications for economic and social growth. The negative Soviet statement in the population debate was followed by a significant shift in the Communist line. When it came time to vote, the Soviet bloc did not oppose, but merely abstained on the General Assembly resolution. What is even more surprising, the Soviet representative at the recent meeting of the Economic and Social Council commended the United Nations for its work in the population field, agreed that population growth is an urgent problem for less developed countries, and announced the willingness of the Soviet Union to provide technical assistance in the demographic field.[3]

Gardner goes on to suggest, rather surprisingly, that this change in line may have been connected with a personal interest in the dangers of overpopulation on Khrushchev's part. As of 1961, however, Khrushchev had still been an emphatic anti-Malthusian.[4] Gardner does not cite any source on Khrushchev's change of heart, but he may of course be right. Nonetheless, it would seem that the decisive breakthrough came only after Khrushchev's fall, in late 1965 or early 1966, when efforts began to be made by official sources to publicize the new trend in official thinking, and a consistent pattern in UN voting emerged.[5]

The new line was clearly reflected in a series of articles published in Literaturnaia gazeta in 1965 and 1966.[6] While the Soviet leadership could not be taken as endorsing all the ideas that appeared in the discussion, the discussion itself could not have occurred at all previously. There was considerable comment on these developments in the West at the time,[7] and the realistic hope seemed to be emerging that West and East might cooperate in addressing the world population problem. These hopes have proven

premature, however. The World Population Conference held in
Bucharest in 1974, at which the Russians found themselves facing
a challenge from China on the left, saw a retreat to more traditional ideological postures. While official doctrinal statements
about population since 1965 have been rather more pragmatic, and
strong traces of the old myths persist and have evidently not entirely lost official favor.

It is fascinating to speculate on which factors were most decisive
in bringing about the change of line in the 1960s. Many were undoubtedly involved. As already noted, theory and reality had been
split far asunder. But this in itself was unlikely to have forced a
change. One element clearly involved was the belated recognition
that Third World countries increasingly preferred to receive assistance from the UN or elsewhere toward curbing fertility rather
than be reassured that there was no problem and that all they need
be on their guard against were scheming Malthusian sterilizers.[8]
Soviet-type social reforms had by then been urged on them for at
least a decade as a remedy for all ills (including population pressures) with only partial success. More and more Third World
countries, meanwhile, were going over to the Malthusian enemy.
It was high time to hedge bets and cut losses.

The well-known Soviet demographer of the older generation,
Smulevich, has made an unusually explicit comment on this political
aspect of Soviet demographic doctrine. Having characterized the
earlier Soviet posture on population matters and the advice Soviet
commentators traditionally gave to Third World countries, namely
to forget about population policies and concentrate all their efforts
on social and economic reforms, Smulevich says bluntly: "This
incorrect and inflexible position often harms us politically."[9] Another hint that the pressure to revise policy came from those concerned with or about relations with Third World countries can be
seen in the fact that one of the first Soviet spokesmen to sound a
liberal note on population issues at the UN was a Soviet diplomat
stationed in New Delhi and seconded to a UN Population Conference
held there in December 1963.[10]

Given the importance of the international dimension in this issue,
it is probably significant that the break came just after the Belgrade
World Population Conference of 1965, to which the Soviet Union
sent a large delegation. While the fact that the USSR sent a delegation of twenty-seven (compared with one of three at the previous
World Conference in Rome in 1954) might be taken as suggesting
that a change of line was already in the process of taking place, it

seems likely that those who were present were impressed by the pressure of international and Third World opinion and later fulfilled an at least catalytic role in bringing about the politico-ideological reorientation. It must have been becoming increasingly embarrassing to the Soviet authorities on such occasions that they were rubbing shoulders almost exclusively with Spains and Portugals, and finding even Latin American spokesmen moving to their left.

Another event at the congress which might conceivably have made an impact on the Soviet delegation was a paper presented by Roderich von Ungern-Sternberg on the consequences of future population growth in (among other places) China. According to the published abstract of his paper, he argued that:

...Thus the people of China will continue to suffer heavy population pressure, and, in times of poor harvests, shortage of food. History demonstrates that such conditions can easily degenerate, causing an explosive exodus towards countries offering attractions to space-starved and hungry people. Such a movement may take place ... peacefully if access to suitable countries is open to them. But it can also degenerate into a military migration.[11]

What the Soviet delegation thought of this paper is not, to my knowledge, recorded. But it is very possible that similar thoughts had been occurring to the Soviet political leadership for some time past. In the context of the Sino-Soviet conflict, the ideological shift again came at a significant time. The first fully public airings of dissension had occurred not long before, in 1963. Then with Brezhnev's accession in 1964, there was a brief period in which it seemed that some kind of accommodation was being sought, after which, however, the Chinese reaffirmed their attitude toward "Khrushchevism without Khrushchev." It was shortly after this again that the Soviet government let it be known unequivocally that it was no longer necessarily opposed to fertility control campaigns in underdeveloped countries. It is not being suggested, of course, that the Soviet Union may have varied its position in the hope of somehow affecting the course of demographic events in China, merely that political and population developments in China in combination exerted some influence on their overall frame of mind. Soviet ideology had always been basically optimistic about general economic and social trends in world development. China's joining the Socialist bloc made all kinds of international statistics seem like dramatic confirmation of the spread of Socialism. (Even today, Soviet reluctance to abandon hope for Chinese socialism is nowhere more evident than in statistics.[12]) Two of the articles which appeared in Literaturnaia gazeta

early and late in 1965[13] (before and after the ideological shift)
neatly illustrate the change that seems to have occurred in official
thinking somewhere in the interim. The first was ostensibly a
comment on a typically neo-Malthusian piece that had appeared in
Readers' Digest. The author of the comment, one Cheprakov, conceded that in some parts of the world population growth was a
serious problem at present. But with social and economic reforms,
he assured his readers, the "unlimited" capacities of science and
technology would speedily solve it. The article contained strong
denunciations of capitalist Malthusians and bore the splendidly
characteristic title "A Threat — but for Whom?" Equally characteristic were the author's limited interest and uncertain competence
in basic demography, and his special field of academic concern,
which was described in an editorial introduction as contemporary
monopoly capitalism. The second article, by the demographer
Boris Urlanis, was in effect a not very muted polemic against the
first. It treated the population problem at length and with considerable seriousness, mentioning China as having the highest absolute
annual increase of population in the world, and supplying illustra-
tive statistics. From the article the impression emerged that Urlanis agreed that there was a threat but was agnostic as to whom
it could most affect. The note of strident self-confidence and pug-
nacity that radiated from Cheprakov's article was wholly absent
from Urlanis's.

One final international factor which may have played a role was
the development of U.S. government policy on international population matters in the 1960s. It should be borne in mind that although
the United States has been one of the strongholds of neo-Malthusianism,
governmental attitudes took a very long time to evolve in the same
direction. It is possible that the U.S. government's entry onto the
scene of financial aid for population programs and the positive response to these initiatives by many Third World countries forced
Soviet policy-makers to review their somewhat dog-in-the-manger
attitude.[14]

Another element which was maturing in the situation during the
1960s, of course, was the population pressure within the Soviet
Union itself. Rapid, though declining, Russian increase had always
tended to reduce the visibility of Central Asian and Caucasian fertility (between 1926 and 1939, in fact, only four peoples exceeding
100,000 in number — of which, at the time there were thirty-five —
registered population increase rates higher than that of the Russians).[15] Apart from that, the growth of the Asian nationalities of the

USSR actually began to further increase after about 1950. As was mentioned earlier, it seems to have been only in the 1960s that the full scope (if not the implications) of this development began to be noticed either in the Soviet Union or outside it. There is no unequivocal evidence known to me that the turnabout in Soviet population doctrine affecting the Third World stemmed from any arrière-pensée as to its own domestic explosion. But it does seem inherently likely. And it is significant that some of the demographers associated with the overturn of the Stalinist dogma on population in 1965-66 have also been among those who have cautiously raised their voices in favor of a differentiated population policy to damp down the present interethnic extremes in fertility.[16] And no less significant, perhaps, that the former head of the Census Division of the Central Statistical Agency (the main center of opposition to the new doctrinal tendency), P. G. Pod'iachikh, has argued most forcefully against any differential population policy. In a tract aimed against the reemergent demographic profession in general, and D. I. Valentei and his associates in particular, Pod'iachikh makes this trenchant attack on proposals for a differentiated population policy:

This would mean that large families in Central Asia, where the standard of living is still lower than in the Baltic states, would not receive as high allowances, while in the Baltic states, where the standard of living is higher, families would receive high allowances. It is easy to see that this arrangement places the peoples of the Baltic states and those of Central Asia in an unequal position and is not in accord with the existing policy of raising the welfare of all members of socialist society.[17]

The Central Statistical Agency has continued to take the conservative line in debates on doctrinal population issues. Thus in an article marking the USSR's achievement of a population of 250 million, we find the deputy director of the Central Statistical Agency, L. M. Volodarskii, suggesting that the Soviet population ("we") is growing rapidly and referring contemptuously to attempts in "bourgeois" countries to "frighten" people with the prospect of overpopulation and starvation.[18] In this connection it is significant that Volodarskii headed the Soviet delegation to the World Population Conference in Bucharest in 1974.

One other important development connected with the change of line was the reemergence in the mid-1960s, the Central Statistical Agency notwithstanding, of a thriving school of Soviet demography, after a recess of some three decades. Though the demographers remain scattered through various ad hoc subsections of other departments, and though their long campaigns for a specialist demographic journal and a central demographic institute have not yet been rewarded with success, their general level of activity since the midsixties has been impressive. Khrushchev personally seems to have been an unreconstructed vulgar anti-Malthusian,[19] and it is unlikely that the relevant party authorities could have been readily persuaded of the need for the radical expansion of academic demography during his time. It seems probable, therefore, that it was his political demise that created the kind of open situation which permitted the atomized demographic fraternity to close ranks and apply effective sectional pressure.[20]

Thus to sum up, the pattern of development the facts seem to suggest is as follows: With the fall of Khrushchev a period of flux ensued, during which new alliances and lines of influence were formed. This process lent itself to the emergence of new ideological and sectional pressures. One of these was that of the academic demographers, who sought both to establish their discipline and to convey to the new leadership their concern about certain key policy implications of their professional assessment of Soviet and world population trends. The new leadership, whether because of a desire to attract the support of the previously alienated, or because of a disposition to make greater practical use of the social sciences,[21] or both, gave some initial encouragement to the demographers. As bureaucratic routine reestablished itself, however, the traditional custodians of demographic orthodoxy, the apparat statisticians, regained some at least of their former influence. And with the emergent competition from China for the favors of the anti-Malthusian Third World and, perhaps, on realizing the difficulties of any policy response to differential fertility within the USSR, the Soviet leadership decided that the best and most comfortable ideological position would be one of minimal adjustment. Accordingly, since the watershed year of 1965, while the Soviet ideological stance on population matters has been more flexible, it has remained ambivalent. Generally it is held that the world population problem can only basically be solved by thoroughgoing economic and social reforms, but that appropriate demographic policies can make some contribution. Accusations of Malthusian cannibalism have disappeared, but less drastic hard-line versions continue to make their appearance, if less frequently.

Thus, for example, a report on the 1972 ECAFE population conference held in Tokyo expresses great distaste for the emphasis on birth control introduced into the proceedings by U.S. and Western European delegations. No family planning programs could "seriously" affect the level of fertility:

When the imperialists were forced to clear out of their former colonies, they left behind them nothing but the poverty and deprivation of the masses. And now they are trying everything to hinder the economic and cultural development of these countries, intimidating them with talk about "the demographic explosion" and seeking to persuade them that their poverty stems from excessive population growth.[22]

This small sampling contains several typical features of the old Stalinist line: the suggestion that imperialism is solely responsible for the present-day poverty throughout the Third World; the denial that any such thing as a "population explosion" exists; the attribution of bad faith and devious cunning to all advocates of family planning; the use of the opprobrious term "birth control" to describe it (which in Russian suggests bureaucrats or indeed policemen stationed by the bedroom door);[23] and the failure to mention DDT or penicillin as having played or as playing any role whatever. While versions quite as crude as this one are rare, it would probably be true to say that Soviet participation in recent international population politics has been less "liberal" (for want of a better word) than the developments in the midsixties might have led one to expect. One important reason for this, as noted, is the somewhat opportunistic and demagogic stance adopted by China, which, while introducing Malthusian rigors at home, continues to take the most vigorous "antiimperialist" line internationally, a line which has shown itself to be popular with some Third World countries at least, particularly in Africa and Latin America.[24] The Soviets may feel obliged in this situation to maintain a "radical" position.

At the national level the notion that there is a specifically socialist law of population is usually still clung to, but its actual content tends to be reduced to a few general propositions illustrating growth in popular well-being, the spread of education, high levels of employment, and so on. Despite the very low birthrates prevailing in the RSFSR and the other European republics, attempts are sometimes still made to present the USSR as a land of flourishing fecundity, as the numerous articles published in the Soviet press in August and September of 1973 in honor of the arrival of the 250-millionth Soviet citizen illustrate. From a reading of these articles it emerges clearly that the topic was made the subject of a mandatory recommendation to editors and that certain lines of approach to it were fairly clearly mapped out for them.

It should be emphasized, however, that much of Soviet demography is free of this kind of equivocation and claptrap and addresses itself in a straightforward manner to real problems, not hesitating at many points to implicitly challenge official doctrine and suggest modifications.[25] Though the reemergence of Soviet demography came well after similar developments in the East European countries, and although its practitioners have to perform verbal genuflection to a bureaucratic Marxism rather more often perhaps than their bloc colleagues, the science is now flourishing vigorously.

Thus the picture here, as elsewhere in post-Stalinist ideology, is one of repressed disarray, as official pragmatism and dogmatism seek to contain strong currents of potentially competitive professionalism that are alternately dammed and released and at times channeled into use with watchful caution.

CHAPTER 9

ISSUES AND
DILEMMAS IN
USSR POPULATION POLICY

For present purposes population policy is being taken to mean those measures adopted by a government (or, where appropriate, party) aimed at affecting the numbers, distribution, and ethnic composition of the population. Obviously, as noted earlier, many social policies might influence population developments without that having been the intention, and many observers regard social policies with incidental demographic impact as population policies. Here, however, I shall be speaking about population policy in the narrower sense of deliberate and conscious pursuit of demographic ends. And given the absence of an explicit and detailed policy line in the USSR at present,[1] the discussion will focus on the issues confronting policy-makers and "lobby" groups.

As the power of the state to increase life expectancy is limited in normal circumstances and is in any case not usually exercised for demographic reasons or objectives, population policy may be said to boil down to two issues:

  i) pro- versus antinatalism; and

  ii) migration policy, both external and internal.

Of these the second, though briefly referred to in some sections of this study, has not been a central theme; here too attention will be concentrated on the first.

A distinction is not always drawn, though it should be, between Soviet population theory or doctrine and population policy. As they correspond roughly to theory and practice, it should be evident that they may diverge; and, in fact, in the Soviet case they have very frequently done so. Thus in the thirties, while averring at the ideological or doctrinal level that socialism was conducive to high fertility, the Soviet government introduced measures designed to prop

up fertility, which had already begun to sag. And without dethroning
the Leninist pronouncements that it was a mother's right to decide
how many children she should have, or the numerous earlier expressions of concern for the damage done by illegal abortion, the
authorities nonetheless proceeded to promote fertility by abolishing
legal abortion. Similarly, the midsixties shift in doctrine discussed
in the previous section did not lead, or at least has not yet led, to
any reformulation of domestic population policy. In the international sphere the USSR has withdrawn from its previous alliance
with the Roman Catholic Church and now gives some, if limited,
support to international efforts to limit population growth. But the
approach to the key domestic issue — to be or not to be pronatalist,
and if so by what means, to what extent, and in what parts of the
country — remains cautious and basically irresolute, though a
variety of opinions and suggestions are being permitted to be heard.

It would probably be true to say that it is only recently that the
concept of "population policy" as a distinct and autonomous sphere
of public concern has gained full acceptance in Socialist countries.
While in Hungary, Czechoslovakia, and to a lesser extent, Bulgaria,
the notion has been freely in use for nearly two decades, and politicians are prone to speak in terms of it, elsewhere there is caution. Though Soviet demographers frequently use the phrase, Soviet politicians have virtually never done so. Brezhnev's use of it
at the Twenty-fifth Party Congress may therefore be a turning point.[2]

While the term may be of uncertain status, and the practice ambiguous and inconsistent for the time being, there can be no doubt
that the Soviet Union has followed very vigorous and unequivocal
population policies in the past. It will be recalled that after the
collectivization disasters of the 1930s, the Soviet government abolished legal abortion and introduced unmistakably pronatalist measures, which were further strengthened in the wake of the drastic
human losses and fertility decline of the 1941-44 period by a combination of moral and material incentives strangely reminiscent of
Stakhanovism. After the war had ended and the birthrate evidently
(no birthrates were published until 1950) been restored to acceptable
levels, the financial inducements were reduced and later left unchanged as average wages rose and thus were allowed to decline
into relative insignificance as a proportion of family income.

The official attitude toward birth-control measures has usually
been divorced, it was noted in Chapter 3, from national population
considerations. That this can at least sometimes be disingenuous
is clearly demonstrated by the circumstances of the abortion re-

strictions of 1936 and the legislation on the family that accompanied them. But the fact remains that there is a strong tradition in Soviet social policy, supported by unequivocal and well-known statements by Lenin, that it is a woman's right to decide whether she will or will not have a baby, and that this is probably one of the factors militating against the present pressures for a more active pronatalism.

There are other and stronger obstacles to decisive action on population policy, however. One is that any effort to increase fertility involves present sacrifices. Either the mothers are to be given financial support sufficient to make them want to spend more time raising families than working and earning money, or the network of crèches and kindergartens and other auxiliary services must be extended radically so that child-bearing need not interfere with the mother's work for more than a few months, and she will feel more able to combine the two. Either solution is bound to be costly; and if in the short term the first of the two is less expensive in that heavy capital outlays are not involved, and easier to apply instantaneously, it must also be remembered that it involves a greater drain on the female labor force if successful. As labor shortages are already acute, it is difficult to reach a decision to plan for more plentiful supplies in the relatively remote future by accepting aggravation of the shortages of the present.[3] If planners and economic administrators have somehow contributed to the climate of pronatalist agitation that has been much in evidence in recent years, they probably also include in their ranks formidable opponents of any solutions involving the expenditure of much money or the removal from the work force of large numbers of young women.

A crucial, if not the crucial, factor inhibiting decisive action appears to be the nationality issue. Economic, social, and political reasons would all prompt the Moscow leadership to wish to restrain fertility in Central Asia and the Caucasus while promoting it almost everywhere also. Ideally, of course, they would like to reduce non-European numbers while stimulating larger European families wherever they might be resident. This second variant is scarcely practicable. But even the first seems to have run up against political objections. The issue has certainly been referred to in public, but so far it would appear that no such proposals have been made by ranking politicians, as opposed to academics and publicists. And as was noted earlier,[4] there is evidence of explicit opposition to any such proposals in official circles. Indeed, there are some signs of divided counsels at all levels. Thus a Kommunist article by the prominent Central Statistical Administration official, Boldyrev, devoted to the passing of the 250-million mark, steers a precarious tightrope course between various possible views of the situation and commends all in turn, apparently contradicting itself more than once in the process.[5] Though Boldyrev refers only to "differences of opinion" among demographers, one can probably assume, given his gymnastics, that the differences of opinion are to be found at higher levels as well. The compromise Boldyrev's diplomatic equivocation seems to point to on balance is a mildly pronatalist policy, oriented in some moderate way that is not made clear toward the low-fertility areas of the country. The only measures that appear to have been taken lately (of which more in a moment) seem more social than demographic in their objectives. After so many years of unsuccessful agitation, it is to be expected that any new initiatives wrung at last from the reluctant allocators of finances will be too parsimonious to have any decisive effect.

A further factor involved may be demographic ignorance in leading decision-making circles, or putting essentially the same point another way, the inability of the demographic lobby to succeed in making the leadership sufficiently aware of the seriousness of the demographic situation. The relative stability of demographic indices in the 1970s may have made their task harder. How many Soviet policy-makers, one wonders, could give a rough account of the current state of crude demographic indices by republic? And how many are able to grasp the difference between net population increase and more analytic measures of fertility? Conversations with Soviet bloc demographers suggest that their awareness is only partial and intermittent.

Even official spokesmen on demographic matters sometimes convey the impression that they have a less than vivid perception of the existing demographic situation in the USSR. The prominent Central Statistical Administration official referred to earlier, Boldyrev, may be a good case in point. His grasp of demographic realities seems at best to be one that might be termed "bureaucratic commonsensism." The reasons he has given against adopting a pronatalist policy probably represent a good deal of prevailing official orthodoxy. Interestingly, he seems to be under the impression that America is officially antinatalist (an evident misreading of the politics of the setting up of the Commission on Population Growth and the American Future) and believes this to reflect official concern about finding jobs for the postwar baby boom. "This," he concludes, "is evidently the reason for the population stabiliza-

107

tion program currently being pursued in the USA." Boldyrev implies that what is good enough for the mighty United States should be good enough for the USSR.[6]

But a lot of what may look like ignorance could of course equally well be bemusement before the complexity of the dilemma, coupled with a desire to keep the matter quiet. Certainly not the least important aspect of current Soviet population policy is the evident official determination to keep the unfavorable trends of overall and differential fertility away from the public's notice. To some extent we are dealing here with the Cheshire cat's smile of the old ideological tenet, now half-abandoned, that socialism is conducive to fertility and that Socialist populations develop according to their own immanent and beneficent laws. In popular articles by government or Central Statistical Office spokesmen, statistics are presented to the general reader with the manifest intention of misleading him if possible.[7] Whether this is a measure of the concern felt or merely force of habit is difficult to say. But the tendency to gloss over probably does again suggest that no very decisive new policy steps are to be expected for the time being.

The measures that have been actually taken or foreshadowed in population policy in recent years have the same apparent tendency to avoid the most crucial issues. Two of the main ones — the extension of full maternity-leave entitlements to kolkhoz women irrespective of length of employment,[8] and the introduction of child allowances for families whose total income amounts to less than 50 rubles a head[9] — both appear to be egalitarian measures of social policy rather than population policy as such. Insofar as either of them should have a pronatalist effect (which was probably not specifically intended), that effect will tend to be greater in those areas of the country where fertility is already relatively high. The Central Asian and Caucasian areas are both strongly rural and relatively less well off (particularly in terms of family income per head since dependency ratios there are much less favorable). It seems unlikely that advocates of a planned and differentiated policy will be pleased by this development. To them it must seem like a dissipation of scarce funds where they are least needed.

Brezhnev's report to the Twenty-fifth Party Congress in February 1976 does not really suggest that population policy has achieved a preeminent position in the thoughts of key policy-makers. While it is no doubt a sign of the times that the report contained a fleeting reference to the need to develop an effective demographic policy as being one of the tasks of social science, this allusion found no reflection in the section of the five-year plan guidelines devoted to "the development of science"; and the measures actually foreshadowed for improving the working mother's lot seem both vague and modest and unlikely to amount in practice to any radical departure from the existing drift of policy.[10] Population policy is still being treated as something for future decision (an attitude on the part of the authorities actually fostered by the demographic community's eagerness to get its research programs funded and its voice heard before policy is decided).

Given the evident official reluctance to spend too much money on population policy measures,[11] the question arises whether more economical and necessarily therefore coercive measures might not be resorted to. For the time being, Soviet policy remains liberal: divorce and abortion rates exceed and probably exceed (respectively) those prevailing anywhere else in the Socialist bloc; and while both are not infrequently deplored, there do not seem to be any campaigns which would presage their prohibition, as in Romania in 1966. Nor has one heard any reports of withdrawal of contraceptive devices from sale, though their use continues to be rare by Western standards.[12]

A Soviet commentator has expounded the principles said to underlie government attitudes in these matters:

The legal norm banning abortions, issued without profound study of the demographic situation and without due consideration being given to the natural causes of natality decline in that period (the author is referring to the 1936 legislation — J. F. B.) could not have been sufficiently effective (quite apart from the question of principle involved) and accordingly was revoked in 1955. In changing the law the legislator correctly pointed out that reduction in the number of abortions could better be ensured by further expansion of state measures supporting motherhood.... From the foregoing it can be concluded that in such matters of demographic policy, it is essential to apply not prohibitions but rather measures designed to encourage a particular pattern of behavior on the part of citizens by improving the nation's living conditions; this follows directly from the CPSU's directives that are consistently carried out in our country.[13]

One might well be skeptical about the amount of principled liberalism in official policies, however. The attitude toward contraception is reserved, as we have seen. And specifically there has been some stalling on the pill, though the stated reasons at least were ones of medical caution.[14] Contraceptives are likely to strike Soviet planners as being almost as far removed from virtuous heavy-industrial producer goods as anything could be. And there may well also be some apprehension as to what the consequences might be for the sagging birthrate if even further methods of averting births were to be made available. Skepticism about the sincerity of medical objections to the pill and other contraceptives is surely justified given the known deleterious effects of abortion, particularly when it reaches epidemic forms as in the USSR. Such skepticism has in fact found its way into official Soviet publications: "The problem of an effective, reliable, and absolutely harmless contraceptive has not yet been solved anywhere in the world. But it would appear nonetheless to have been solved a great deal more effectively than one might suppose judging by the quantity, quality, and assortment of contraceptives that are available for sale in our pharmacies."[15]

Moreover, the overall trend within the bloc seems to be quite clearly toward more decisive measures, particularly in the sphere of abortion legislation. While the extreme Romanian solution is usually said (somewhat misleadingly) to have failed, the Czechoslovak, Hungarian, and Bulgarian precedents may be more influential. There the governments have successively introduced more moderate restrictions on the availability of abortion; and at least in the case of the first two, it would seem that these measures may be succeeding where others have been at best palliative or inconclusive.[16] And while we have the rather surprising counterexamples of East Germany, which finally legalized abortion despite its very low fertility and acute labor shortage, suffered a drastic slump, and now seems to be recovering from it without manipulating the abortion laws; and Poland, where the periodic agitation for the repeal of liberal abortion legislation seems to have been (temporarily at least) again defeated, the overall climate of opinion does seem to be shifting toward robust solutions.

Most Soviet demographic commentators generally seem to agree on the need to forestall any attempts to apply "administrativnye mery" (administrative measures — a standard Soviet euphemism for repressive policies), which, they emphasize, are counterproductive. They proclaim loudly and prophylactically the Soviet Union's allegedly steadfast policy of always leaving decisions about family size to the parents:

Demographic policy in the socialist state is based on observance of the principle of "family sovereignty." This means that the fullest freedom is extended to citizens in deciding matters relating to family formation, the freedom in other words, for parents to decide on the number of children they will have. It follows from that that all children should be born wanted children in families and to mothers who await them with joy.[17]

It may also be that in adopting a parcel of administrative measures, the Romanians (who ideologically speaking have been sent about halfway to Coventry just at present) have made their wholesale adoption elsewhere in the bloc just that little bit less likely. Certainly the response of Socialist demographic opinion elsewhere to the Romanian solution has been cool.

One possible development which could decisively influence the course of events would be the accession to power in Moscow of more or less overt Russian chauvinists. The former editor of the right-wing samizdat journal Veche, Vladimir Osipov, in an interview given to some American correspondents, declared that the Russian people might die both morally and physically; the latter, because the contemporary Russian woman is having only one or at most two children. Osipov added that in his view, "the problem of human rights is less important than the problem of the dying Russian people."[18] If, as Kruczek suggests, Osipov's views reflect those of a growing faction within top party circles, we could witness a dramatic change of line on demographic no less than other issues. Osipov himself has since been arrested and sentenced to eight years imprisonment. But a samizdat article by Agurskii suggests that this may have been because Osipov and the other Christians attached to Veche refused to let themselves be used by what Agurskii identifies as the neo-Nazi faction within the regime.[19]

If there are rabid Russian chauvinists among Soviet demographic commentators, they contain their emotions fairly well. But many do evince a considerable degree of "Europocentric" concern about population trends in their country. It is this factor which unites many of them behind demands for four key objectives: (i) the creation of a central demographic institute along the lines of the government commissions existing now virtually throughout Eastern Europe, which would coordinate demographic research and make policy recommendations to the authorities; (ii) the establishment of a regular demographic journal; (iii) extensive funding of a broad program of demographic research, without which, as it is usually emphasized, policy decisions cannot but be ill founded; and (iv) the introduction of a "differentiated" population policy which would tend to close the gap separating vital rates in the different regions of the country. While demographic research is indeed expanding rapidly, the remaining postulates have still not been satisfied, despite repeated invocations over a lengthy period of time.

One Soviet source suggests that Valentei's Center for the Study of Population Problems within the Economics Faculty of Moscow

University, "in accordance with a decision of Gosplan, the State
Committee of the Council of Ministers for Science and Technology,
and the Presidium of the USSR Academy of Sciences, performs
the role of the main organization responsible for working out the
socioeconomic bases and methods of managing and regulating the
development of the population."[20] Valentei's institute and Valentei himself have for some time exuded an air of primus inter pares.
But it should be noted that they have rather less than a royal charter (neither the Central Committee nor the Council of Ministers
are referred to as having endorsed the decision to give them special status). Their formal and their real position do not seem to
be comparable with that of the government population commissions
of East Europe. Indeed, recent reports suggest that Valentei's
writ does not run much beyond Moscow.[21]

Whether all demographers would be delighted if Valentei's Center were to become the focal point of an official demographic apparatus is not clear. But most demographers feel the need of some
such body (other than the Central Statistical Administration). The
question of the need for more demographic research and publications is naturally even less controversial. There are, on the other
hand, some dissenters from the proposition that a differentiated
population policy is needed. Some observers are not convinced
that the fertility levels in European USSR are catastrophic. Others
feel that whatever the various levels may be, a uniform policy must
be maintained. But by and large, most are of the view that a differential policy is urgently required. They have in fact been putting
this point of view openly for many years, but without success.
Thus a book published in 1967, for example, draws attention to differential fertility trends and calls for "differentiated demographic
legislation" to meet the situation, "since what is appropriate, for
example, in the Ukraine or the Baltic region has turned out to be
quite inappropriate in Central Asia or Azerbaidzhan. The decree
of the Presidium of the Supreme Soviet of July 8, 1944, has in certain respects become outdated."[22]

Whatever response, if any, the Soviet government may finally
offer to this dogged agitation, it is clear that it will be faced with
a difficult and intractable problem if the fertility scissors do not
begin to close more rapidly in the near future. If the situation in
the high-fertility areas were indeed to develop in the direction of
confrontation, it is difficult to conceive of anyone other than perhaps China benefiting therefrom. Past fertility trends have in effect already assured the Central Asian peoples of future demo-

graphic dominance within their own homelands. Continued high
fertility in the future will bring them small additional social and
political advantage and a great deal of economic hardship. While
it was suggested earlier that the current population policy may
not necessarily be the worst of the available alternatives (on the
let-sleeping-dogs-lie principle), it does seem nonetheless that
some kind of differential approach could and should have been applied long since. For such a policy to be implemented without
giving rise to additional tensions, it would probably be necessary
(and would be in any case wise) to accept some modest degree of
devolution in social policy decision-making, with republics receiving central allocations of budgetary funds which they might then
dispose according to their own judgment. The rather wealthier
and less fertile republics could afford to disburse more on child
endowments if they so desired, while the high-fertility republics
might find it in their own best interests to adopt policies aimed
rather at restricting population growth. Proposals along these
lines have actually appeared in print in the Soviet Union. A report
of a lecture on Yugoslav demographic problems given by the well-
known Yugoslav demographer Miloš Macura at the Soviet Academy
of Sciences carefully drew attention to the many parallels between
the Soviet and Yugoslav demographic situations. Noting that Yugoslav child-endowment was formerly paid only to the poorer (malo-
obespechenym) families (the decision to do the same in the USSR
having been already clearly foreshadowed at the time of writing),
the writer continued:

Since 1969 child allowances have been decentralized; every republic or autonomous province (emphasis added — J. F. B.) independently determines how many
families will receive allowances and how much they will be. In those republics
where the birthrate is very low, the allowance is higher and received by a
larger number of families. Thus these payments will have not only a social but
also a demographic significance.[23]

Given the traditional Soviet reluctance to accept dispersal of decision-making, it seems unlikely that this recommendation will
be heeded.

Hitherto the discussion has been conducted in terms of the prospects for active pronatalism. The reason for this is that the
chances of a swing toward antinatalism seem to be effectively ruled
out. There are undoubtedly pockets of antinatalist, or rather antipronatalist, thinking and sentiment among Soviet demographic observers and officialdom, but they seldom come into the open.

113

Boldyrev's implicit commendation of what he believed to be Nixon-
ian antinatalism is a rare example of its kind. Some demographers
emphasize that they are not in favor of rapid population increase
(particularly when they are discussing Central Asia), but I know
of none who would advocate stationary reproduction (i.e., holding
fertility at replacement rates), much less ZPG (net population
growth of nil) at the earliest possible juncture. While it is now
recognized that fertility-limitation policies may be of some value
to developing countries, it is virtually never suggested that the
Soviet Union itself should limit its population growth. The same
taboo is observed elsewhere in the bloc as well, which would suggest that ZPG is ideologically out of bounds. The official attitude
on this point seems for the most part to be quite genuinely held by
unofficial commentators also. While often heterodox on other matters, they nearly always share their governments' belief in the inherent and self-evident justice of national demographic expansion.[24]

Given its "vast unpeopled spaces," its labor shortages, its dis-
rupted internal ethnic balance, and its fertile and not always
friendly continental neighbors, Soviet Russia must be the industrial
country least likely to be susceptible to ZPG-type arguments. And
as long as the Soviet attitude remains what it is, the similar stands
taken in Prague, Budapest, and elsewhere are unlikely to alter.
At a time when many serious observers believe that a halt must
be called to population and economic growth, it is perhaps a matter of concern that the USSR and the other Comecon countries are
proceeding so unreflectingly along the path of demographic mer-
cantilism.

In a round-table discussion of "Man and his Environment" published in Voprosy filosofii, population actually was mentioned by
one or two of the contributors as a relevant factor. The amount
of space devoted to it, however, was markedly less than would be
the case in any comparable Western discussion. Urlanis, the only
demographer among the thirty-four or so participants, criticized
the way in which these matters had been neglected in the Soviet
Union: "We ought not to avoid these problems either. As Acade-
mician Kapitsa said, we live not in a separate apartment but in a
communal one ... (and) this apartment is already extremely densely
populated.... There is no need to dramatize the situation, but it
is essential that population problems should be studied. It is most
regrettable that we should somehow be standing aside from these
most pressing contemporary problems." Significantly, however,
Urlanis goes on to hedge his bets, adding that while it is important

that the whole world should appreciate the difficulty and complexity of population matters: "The question arises in various forms; in some places natality needs to be diminished; in other places it needs to be increased."[25]

Isolated remarks like these aside, however, there are few public signs of the emergence within the Soviet Union of a global perspective on global population problems. If ZPG is to be our salvation, it will probably have to come without intentional Soviet-bloc participation.

In the time that has elapsed since the Twenty-fifth Congress, little has happened. Clause 35 of the new Soviet Constitution, when it finally appeared in June 1977, contained two phrases, not present in the original draft, which promised to reduce the workweek of young mothers and in general to provide them with conditions which would make it possible for them to combine work with motherhood. There is nothing specifically pronatalist about these sentiments. "Antipronatalists," like Piskunov and Steshenko in the USSR or Jerzy Urban in Poland, would be quite happy to endorse them. Nor are they a new departure, as policies of this kind were promised at the Twenty-fifth Congress. It remains to be seen how generously and in what precise form the Soviet government will redeem these promises.

Demographers continue to press for urgent action on various aspects of the problem of divergent population growth rates, purporting to take the Twenty-fifth Congress directive about developing an effective demographic policy as an almost personal commission. One commentator simply asserted that the Twenty-fifth Congress had adopted a pronatalist demographic policy.[26] The CPSU, like many political organizations, has long been an ardent supporter of motherhood and, moreover, has a traditional image of itself as encouraging and inspiring fecundity. But by Bulgarian or Czechoslovak standards, the congress was Malthusian.

The tireless Perevedentsev continues to press for rational solutions: increased family size in the European USSR[27] and the encouragement of outmigration from the crowded kishlaks of Central Asia.[28] Valentei, whose long-term efforts to achieve acceptance of his broader notion of population policy (as opposed to the narrower demographic policy) received an implicit rebuff at the congress, continues nonetheless to advocate his broader approach and the various elements it has embodied: detailed, long-term planning of population processes and labor force movements; a differential fertility policy to relieve the existing difficulties; government by or at least on the advice of experts for "free and conscious, able and qualified" workers, and so on.[29]

Apart from the references to demographic problems and the need for a "scientific" policy to deal with them made at the Twenty-fifth Congress, the Soviet authorities have shown few signs of heeding this advice. In June 1977, in response to an interviewer from Le Monde who had asked whether population growth in national republics might not entail certain "structural changes," Brezhnev declared that population growth in the national republics of the Soviet Union was not a source of concern:

On the contrary it gladdens us, because it reflects, first of all, the mighty upswing in the economic level of our republics, including the enormous growth in the well-being of the population of the former outlying areas in tsarist Russia and the colossal progress they have achieved on the path of socialist transformations. In the long run all this strengthens the single alloy that we call a new historical community — the Soviet people.[30]

Perhaps the most significant thing about this reply was that it was published, together with the rest of the interview, on the front page of both Izvestia and Pravda. With a national census planned to follow a year and a half later, this decision could scarcely have been in any sense inadvertent. Perhaps the results of the census will reopen the issue. But for the moment the policy is that there is really no problem; or if there is, that one should behave for the most part as if there were not. Journal comment may now begin to reflect this approach.[31]

Like the interviewer from Le Monde, I believe that population trends will bring about structural changes in the Soviet Union. It is interesting to know that Brezhnev, at least, is not planning to make any.

PART THREE

POPULATION POLITICS IN POLAND

CHAPTER 10

POPULATION POLITICS
IN POLAND

This chapter is divided into the following seven subsections:
(a) demographic background; (b) evolution of policies on population
matters[1]; (c) economic policies; (d) ethnic relations; (e) international politics; (f) ideology; and (g) current population policies:
debates and dilemmas.

Demographic Background[2]

In the postwar period Poland's population development has followed a path basically similar to those traced out by many other
of the rather less developed European countries, both Socialist
and non-Socialist: an initial increase in the birthrate, followed by
steady and at times rapid decline, with an uncertain stabilization
emerging only recently; initial rapid decline in general mortality
rates, followed by stabilization at low levels, then stagnation and
slight increases in both general mortality and age-specific mortality for older age groups (particularly males), with infant mortality, however, continuing its decline from rather high initial
levels; a sharp initial increase in net population growth followed
by decline and a shaky stabilization roughly parallel to that occurring in the birthrate; increasing nuptiality but also increasing
divorce; massive migration from the villages to the towns (including a vast statistically "concealed" component in the form of
worker-peasants commuting daily); sharp increase in the urban
work force and a particularly sharp increase in the level of qualifications and employment rates of young married women.

External influences on population development in socialist coun-

tries tend to be limited. With the notable and to some extent temporary exception of Yugoslavia, all frown on emigration,[3] and none
has yet been confronted by the problem of alien immigration. Once
the immense upheavals occasioned by the war and the westward
displacement of Poland's borders were finally smoothed out, Poland settled down to the usual Socialist pattern of nugatory immigration and a thin persistent leak of emigration, which, during
more liberal phases, broadens to a stream. In the late 1950s there
was a brief period of repatriation of Poles from the Soviet Union
to blur the pattern; and more recently there has been a tendency
for elderly Westerners of Polish origin to return to their homeland
to spend their later years and their warmly welcomed hard-currency
pension checks. During the Gierek years there has been an increase
in emigration generally and some outflow of Germans to the Federal Republic. But the numbers involved have not to date been
enormously significant.

Given its special relevance to numerical concerns, the pattern
of natural increase in postwar Poland may be worth a few additional
comments. These will focus on fertility, since it is fluctuation in
the level of fertility rather than mortality that determines natural
increase rates in more developed societies. Poland's natural increase in the first fifteen years or so after the war was exceptional,
both in relation to its own prewar experience and to the levels prevailing in other European countries of comparable development.
Natality remained extremely high till about the midfifties, and natural increase until about 1960, when natality decline began to accelerate, and declining mortality reached a point where further
improvement was impossible. Up to that point, however, Poland's
natural increase had been comparable with that of many Third
World countries. The decline, when it came, was all the more
drastic. In twelve years the crude birthrate fell from 29.1% (in
1955) to 16.3% (in 1967), and natural increase fell from 19.5% to
8.5%.[4] The net reproduction rate (NRR), 1.52 in 1955, slipped to
1.01 (i.e., only just above the replacement level) by 1969.[5] The
general fertility rate (GFR) (i.e., number of births per thousand
women in the population aged 15-49) fell from 98 in 1955 (the second highest in Europe) to 58 in 1965 (the fifth lowest in Europe).[6]
To a considerable extent the decline in the crude birthrate was
due to changes in the age structure of the population, as the less
numerous cohorts of the depression and war years reached the
most fertile age groups. But as the declines in the GFR and NRR
indicate, other factors were also at work. Among them, one might

mention the rapid growth of industrialization and urbanization (in Poland in recent years there has been a very large gap between rural and urban fertility),[7] the spread of education and the aspirations and attitudes it engenders, the sustained urban housing crisis, expanded employment of young married women in urban areas, the legalization of abortion and increased availability of contraceptives, and the later and more explicitly antinatalist measures adopted by the government after 1959. Since the late 1960s there has been a slight increase both in the crude birthrate and in certain more analytical measures of fertility. A casual reader of the Polish press in 1976-78, however, would scarcely gain this impression. It has been a frequent view among Polish demographers (and even more frequent among lay observers) that this stabilization will be only temporary, and that further decline is to be expected.[8] As the NRR for the country as a whole currently stands at 1.07 (1976),[9] this would mean that the population might soon be no longer reproducing itself, though owing to the present age structure of the population, and depending on the extent of the further decline postulated, there would, of course, continue to be a surplus of births over deaths for some time to come.

One of the consequences of Poland's erratic fertility fluctuations since the war has been that the abnormalities created in the population's age structure by past catastrophes have been further accentuated. The plunge in age-specific fertility rates occurred when the very small World War II birth cohorts were reaching the childbearing age groups, while the postwar baby boom and the stabilization of inherent fertility in the 1970s have both occurred at a time when the size of the main child-bearing cohorts would have ensured a large birthrate in any case. The consequent differences between the birthrates for different years not far removed from one another are very great. (Thus 782,000 children were born in 1957, but only 599,000 were born in 1962, and 520,000 in 1967.)[10] This is the characteristic "undulatory effect" (falowanie) much commented on and deplored by Polish observers. In the age pyramid this phenomenon takes the form of dramatic bulges interspersed with deep indentations. The succession of these demographic "highs" and "lows" has most disruptive effects on economic and social life.

Evolution of Policies on Population Questions

At the end of World War II, a Poland emerged which differed drastically from its predecessor state territorially, politically, and demographically. Its population had been reduced from over 35 million to 23.6 million,[11] and its very large ethnic minorities (amounting to roughly one third of the population in the 1930s) had been virtually eliminated by the combined effects of war, genocide, territorial and population shifts, and deportation. The population of Polish stock had also been decimated by a similar catalogue of disasters and upheavals. Though the total extent of the Polish state had been reduced, population density had been reduced also. There were, moreover, large expanses of formerly German territory in the west, where the autochthonous Polish population was either of modest or negligible dimensions. These regions now had to be settled and thereby consolidated as Polish. In such circumstances, with a threat of national extinction (to be understood quite literally) having been narrowly averted, and a future threat from German revanche needing to be forestalled, it was perhaps inevitable that a strongly pronatalist mood should emerge in both the nation and its new rulers. The burgeoning birthrate was greeted with great popular and official enthusiasm and approval. It was indeed one of the few issues on which complete unanimity of views could be attained. The government's attitude was expressed more in the form of rhetoric, propaganda, and a general policy orientation; no systematic and explicit pronatalist program was ever enunciated.[12] But the overall economic policies of the time were certainly calculated to reinforce the natural demographic revival that usually occurs after a war, as postponed marriages are concluded and postponed progeny hastily brought into the world. The revival of economic activity in the cities (including trade, services, and some private enterprise in the early years) and the redistribution of old land and the subdivision and allocation to eager peasants of vast tracts of new land were also conducive to the formation of a pronatalist climate. The introduction of social services on a larger scale no doubt exerted a similar influence.[13] The years of reconstruction before the forced-draft industrialization phase began were years of relative prosperity and must have done a lot to give apparent substance to the optimism fostered by the regime in demographic as in other matters. The means of family limitation were not in any case readily available, and little publicity was given to them. Abortion was prohibited for all but exceptional cases.[14] And government policies in housing and other matters favored people with larger families to an extent that came ultimately to be keenly resented by many members of the less fecund urban intelligentsia.

Then with the general liberalization of life in most parts of the

Soviet bloc that took place in the mid-1950s, abortion legislation
was liberalized in the Soviet Union, and it became easier for advocates of a similar step in Poland (as elsewhere in the bloc) to
put their case publicly and make representations in the appropriate
quarters. In 1956, after a lengthy campaign of press articles de-
picting the evils of barn and back-street abortions, making good
use of the claim that the church was the main adversary and surprisingly little overt use of the fact that similar legislation had
been passed in the USSR (surely a most remarkable sign of the
times), the reformers won. At the same time, efforts were made
(largely by the same people) to place family planning on an official
footing with government approval and financial support. In 1957
the Family Planning Association (then the Association for Conscious
Motherhood) was formed and permitted to develop links with western "neo-Malthusian" organizations and activists. Contraceptives
began to be produced in substantial quantities, and a press campaign for their acceptance was launched.[15]

At this stage (1957-58), however, the official support was less
enthusiastic than it was later to become. From the press of those
years, one gains the impression merely that a group of family
planners had gained the support or active tolerance of the government rather than that the latter itself was setting the pace. Moreover, the link between family planning and an antinatalist population
policy, while urged occasionally in some quarters, had not yet received any obvious official recognition.

The first articles deploring Poland's high fertility, pointing out
its economic disadvantages, and proposing counteraction made their
appearance in economic journals and the popular press during the
course of 1957.[16] Whatever the disclaimers of their authors, in
the context of the Soviet tradition in these matters they can only
be described as Malthusian. While some contributors to the discussion sought to evade this label, none really tried to relate themselves to the Stalinist doctrines on population; no doubt any attempt
on their part to have done so would have been futile. Yet despite
their Malthusianism, they were ultimately to win the day. After a
lengthy period of public discussion, the authorities were finally won
over more or less unequivocally to the antinatalist side. In 1959,
faced with one of Poland's recurrent meat shortages, Gomułka hit
upon, or more probably was led to, the idea that if he had fewer
subjects to cater for, his economic problems, among others the
tasks of maintaining food supplies and providing jobs for the demographic "high" that would be "invading" the labor market in the

latter part of the sixties, would be much more manageable. And accordingly, at a Central Committee plenum devoted to the meat crisis, he pronounced categorically that Poland's population growth rate was excessive. Having compared Polish natural increase with that prevailing in other European countries, Gomułka protested: "And yet there are still people in Poland who belly-ache (psioczą) against socialism because of the lack of meat on the market. If capitalist England had the same natural increase as Poland does, its standard of living would be falling constantly." Gomułka then made perfunctory mention of "our young nation" and "our optimistic future," but in the same context hastened to emphasize that "our numerous children" placed "considerable burdens and difficult obligations on us, their fathers." "The natural increase of population prevailing in Poland at present," concluded Gomułka, "is a serious obstacle to the growth of the nation's living standards."[17]

It was in these circumstances, then, that Poland embarked on its heretical antinatalist policy. The abortion legislation was further liberalized, and Catholic and other dissenting doctors were prevented from imposing their views on reluctant mothers.[18] The activities and views of the family planners were given enhanced support. And simultaneously, the flow of antinatalist articles in the press became freer, more emphatic, and more authoritative in tone. An intensive campaign against the "wave of brats flooding Poland" (zalewająca Polskę fala bachorów) was maintained thereafter for some months.

The reorientation of policies that occurred in 1957-59 seemed to produce spectacular results. The birthrate had already begun to decline from its high point in the midfifties, but by the late fifties and early sixties it was fairly plummeting down. To what extent the new policies accentuated or prolonged the fertility decline involved in this trend is difficult to determine, but certainly there was a marked change in public attitudes, both official and unofficial. Aspirations concerning family size changed dramatically, as did the popular attitude toward large families, which now became harshly censorious.[19] With the exception of anti-Germanism, there can have been few other propaganda lines which were quite so successful with the population. Many Catholics who would not accept other anti-Church views nonetheless accepted this one, and did so despite the most outspoken and sustained condemnation of government policy by Church spokesmen, headed by the redoubtable Cardinal Wyszyński.

Successive slumps in the birthrate were greeted with small but unmistakably gratified communiqués from the Main Statistical Office.[20] As the birthrate fell further and further, the matter ceased to be treated as one of great urgency, but the basic official line remained unaltered to the end of Gomułka's ascendancy. Despite the abruptness of the fall in the birthrate, and despite the fact that urban reproduction rates had dropped well below replacement levels, there was relatively little critical discussion of the matter in the press in the second half of the 1960s, apart from in the publications of the PAX (proregime Catholic) organization.[21]

It was in fact only after the fall of Gomułka in 1970 that this, like so many other of his policies, came up for serious review. In recent years, particularly during 1971-72 and again from late 1976 to 1978, the issue of pro- and antinatalism has been intensively discussed in the popular press and scientific publications. The overall attitude of the Gierek regime in the 1970s has been one of relatively weak but growing interest in population policy as such and a mild though intensifying pronatalism, mitigated by financial caution and a commitment to egalitarianism in social policy. More will be said about this in the last section of the chapter.

Thus having been initially pronatalist like all good Stalinist regimes, Poland became for a time the only Socialist state in Europe to espouse Malthusianism. Now, together with Yugoslavia and the USSR, it is one of the relatively few not to be pursuing an emphatically, not to say desperately, pronatalist policy.

Economic Policies

The central problem posed for economic planning and policy by demographic developments in Poland has been the disruption occasioned by the successive waves of demographic "highs" and "lows," which lead to alternate phases of excess strain and underutilization in a number of different fields: the labor force, the educational system, social services, and so on. Thus as the postwar baby boom began to reach school age, it was felt necessary to organize a patriotic school-building campaign financed by public subscription. By the late 1960s, however, the high was already being replaced by a low, and some schools were even being closed down for lack of pupils.[22] The baby boom had meanwhile passed on to adulthood, and in consequence Poland's lagging housing industry was beginning to be further taxed by the exceptionally large generation of young people now making their presence felt in the marriage

statistics.[23] And most spectacularly of all, in 1959, as we have
seen, Gomułka had been precipitated by a shortage of meat on the
domestic market to decide that the Poles' excessive propensity
to consume was related to an excessive propensity to reproduce
and that to curb the former it was essential to curb the latter.

However, it is in the sphere of manpower planning and labor
policy that the most crucial demographico-economic disturbances
are seen as occurring.[24] Gomułka came to power during a period
of alarms about unemployment,[25] and throughout his period in office, this same problem was continually threatening to recur.
Though the causes of the unemployment of 1956 were not directly
demographic, it had become apparent to economists by the later
1950s that the arrival of the postwar baby boom on the job market
would pose a considerable strain on the Polish economy's capacity
to absorb them.[26] Gomułka's concern to restrain consumption reflected an awareness on the part of the leadership that jobs would
have to be created for the large cohorts of school-leavers expected
in the later sixties. To create the jobs, it was felt, large investments would be required; and given Gomułka's ideological predilec-
tion for heavy and extractive industries, i.e., for the capital-intensive rather than labor-intensive sectors of the economy, to create
those jobs did indeed require very heavy investments.

The high presented another major problem to economic planners.
Poland, like the other socialist countries, had (and indeed still
has)[27] a marked tendency to use labor inefficiently. Intermittently
throughout the Gomułka period, campaigns were conducted to reduce
so-called surplus employment.[28] At times, particularly during the
late 1950s, these campaigns were given greater impetus by shortages of urban labor, shortages which were to some extent demographically conditioned. At other times, as in the late 1960s, the
policy of restricting employment was adopted in order to prevent
large increases in labor supply from creating their own kind of
fait accompli of inflated employment and reduced productivity. It
always seemed to be either that the only way to escape the Scylla
of overemployment was via the Charybdis of unemployment, or
that the only way to escape the Scylla of the impending labor surplus was to rush into the embrace of the Charybdis of overemployment. Overemployment, lest the Western observer should think it
obviously the lesser of the two evils, was associated in Polish conditions (as in Socialist conditions generally) with gross inefficiency,
low and stagnant productivity,[29] low and stagnant wage levels,[30]
absenteeism,[31] lack of industrial discipline,[32] inflationary pres-

sures,[33] and in the opinion of some, such symptoms of disorgani-
zation and demoralization as drinking on the job, industrial acci-
dents, and smoldering worker discontent (a potent factor to be
reckoned with in Poland).[34]

Faced with these unattractive alternatives, the Gomułka regime
finally decided in the late 1960s to strive for greater efficiency
even at the cost of accepting a certain measure of planned unemployment in the 1970s.[35] They might conceivably have succeeded
in escaping with this heresy as well had they convinced the working
class that some substantial number of their members might benefit from this new dispensation; but Gomułka, who was in any case
no diplomat, was not even aware that there was any need to nego-
tiate. In the event, he was not removed by higher ecclesiastical
authority but hoist with his own petard of 1956 — a near revolution.

In this, as in many other aspects of economic policy, Gierek reversed Gomułka's approach and acted swiftly to avert the looming
unemployment that his predecessors' plans had accepted.[36] Under
Gierek employment has burgeoned to such an extent that even the massive labor force increments of 1971-75 and 1976-79 have been fully
absorbed and a labor shortage "created"; indeed Gierek has had to re-
gress to the widely criticized Gomułka expedients of imposing administrative limits on permissible employment levels and latterly of planning reductions in total employment,[37] i.e., planning unemployment.

In the near future it will be the turn of the demographic low of
the 1960s to begin to make its own kind of impression on the labor
market. What form the already existing labor shortages will assume then is still a matter for conjecture. Polish economic demographers, like their counterparts elsewhere, plead for demographic considerations to be taken fully into account in the formulation of policy; and there is probably a growing awareness of these
matters now among the Polish leadership. But a solution of the
problem may require more drastic economic measures than the
present somewhat battle-scarred administration would care to
hazard. There is less talk of radical economic reform now than
ever.[38] Immigration of Arab or other Gastarbeiter scarcely seems
likely — that proposition is in any case as ideologically unsound
as the suggestions referred to earlier that Poland's labor surplus
might be exported temporarily or permanently, as before the war.
Poland does supply a certain amount of labor power to its neighbors,
mainly on a crossborder commuting basis;[39] but the abolition of
this and similar arrangements would scarcely make much difference to its situation even in the short run. In any case the outflow

127

of German "autochthons" has latterly increased and is therefore likely to cancel out any such gains. The labor power of women and pensioners is relatively less exploited in Poland than in the Soviet Union or the GDR, but there are strong influences militating against their further mobilization. Female work-force participation rates have already been emphatically denounced by Polish commentators as too high both for social and natalist reasons; and indeed, they could scarcely go on increasing at their 1970s rate of 6% per annum much longer.[40] Gierek has repeatedly pledged a new deal for women, part of which is said to be the chance of getting part-time rather than full-time employment; recently benefits for mothers have been foreshadowed which would take them out of the work force. Moreover, the party is committed to lowering rather than maintaining, much less increasing, the pension age, a commitment which it in fact has already begun to honor.[41]

Subject to shifts in political circumstances, it is possible that the forthcoming sharp[42] and demographically determined decline in labor supply could play the role of midwife to Poland's long-canvassed and repeatedly shelved decentralizing economic reform. But other solutions — attempting to impose greater industrial discipline by administrative fiat, for example, as in Czechoslovakia[43] or in the USSR in the 1940s and 1950s, or simply struggling through with a minimum of structural alterations and a maximum of central "parameter" manipulation and ad hoc administrative campaigns — seem rather more likely.

Ethnic Relations

Before the war Poland suffered from one of the most intractable complexes of ethnopolitical problems of any country in Europe. There were, among others, large Ukrainian, Belorussian, German, and Jewish minorities, amounting in sum to about one third of the total population. The Ukrainians and Germans were particularly militant and represented, moreover, explicit irredentist claims supported with varying degrees of overtness by two of Poland's former partitioners. In many of the cities the Jewish element was large and increasing much faster than it was assimilating, while at the same time, its presence in certain very visible professions and activities was growing faster again. After the slaughter, famine, murder, and deportations of and following World War II, Poland finally emerged with what has been officially described as

about 99% ethnic homogeneity.[44] While this claim is certainly exaggerated (it implies a negligible number of Germans, an assessment which the Warsaw authorities have now tacitly conceded to
be false), it is certainly the case that the only major ethnic issues
in Polish politics have been largely of the régime's own manufacture.

Little information is available on Poland's remaining ethnic minorities; and what information there is is approximate, out of date,
and somewhat dubious. Questions concerning nationality are not
asked at census enquiries.[45] According to one estimate made in
1963[46] there were 180,000 Ukrainians, 165,000 Belorussians, 31,000
Jews, 3,000 Germans (sic), and a number of other small groups.
The Belorussian minority in what was formerly the Białystok voi-
vodship in the northeast is of sufficient size and compactness to
provide some pretext for incorporation of part, at least, if not all
of the area in, say, an extended Soviet Belorussia (if other circumstances were propitious), and to that extent is a potential internal-
cum-external problem. The Ukrainians are, or perhaps it would
be more accurate to say have been, more scattered;[47] and while
Ukrainian nationalists have claimed parts of what is now southeast
Poland on partially ethnic grounds, they too seem unlikely to cause
much domestic trouble without outside intervention or encouragement. The East Slav minorities have apparently been blue-printed
for cultural extinction by assimilation, and press comments noting
with apparent satisfaction the first signs of this development have
appeared.[48] This probably reflects a vague feeling among both official and unofficial Polish circles that having lost so much territory and population in the East, the least that should be done is to
forestall any further possible inroads, and that the best way to
achieve this is by a policy of assimilation. The Polish concessions
to the traditional Leninist doctrine of "national in form, socialist
in content" are minimal.

The German and Jewish minorities represent complex political
problems, but at this stage those problems too are more likely to
be external than domestic. So few Jews remain now that one feels
that even the demagogic skills of the erstwhile Partisan faction of
the party would be taxed by the task of reconverting them into the
bogey they were made to represent in 1968. The Germans have
never played any role as a national group in postwar Poland, and
it seems unlikely that they will start to do so now. Their only
political ambition in People's Poland seems to be to emigrate, and
in this they are evidently succeeding.

Thus, insofar as demographic developments in the minority communities can be assessed given the absence of reliable data, they seem to be working toward diminution of any internal political problem these ethnic groups might represent. The Ukrainians and Belorussians are probably diminishing as a result of assimilation, and the Jews and Germans are certainly diminishing as a result of emigration.

International Politics

In the previous section it was suggested that Poland's ethnic minorities (and Polish ethnic minorities abroad) were of greater international than domestic political significance, and that for them to become the source of domestic political pressures, external interference or intervention would be necessary. It was suggested, in particular, that at some future stage a Soviet government might wish to exploit the Belorussian or Ukrainian minorities for purposes of its own, to help bring a recalcitrant Polish government to heel or, more drastically, to perform further surgery on Poland so as to permanently alter its borders and/or its position in the Socialist commonwealth of nations. If this were to happen, the Poles might have cause to regret their policies toward their East Slav minorities. But the direction of influence might easily be the reverse one, either with or without active Polish connivance. Restiveness in the western republics of the USSR (especially the Ukraine, Belorussia, and Lithuania) might be aggravated by activity among the corresponding minorities in Poland. It is conceivable that some Polish government might one day consciously foster such activity. But far more likely, at least in the foreseeable future, is some kind of largely involuntary embroilment on the pattern of the Czechoslovak Ukrainian minority's swelling and subversive influence on the Soviet Ukraine in the days of Dubček: a liberal Polish government promising a new deal for various groups within its own society might find its Belorussians and Ukrainians developing excessively close relations with their fellow countrymen across the Soviet border.[49]

None of these possibilities seems imminently likely. And with the further decline of the numbers involved, they will probably become less likely rather than more so.

The international problem presented by the German community, on the other hand, has been a very real one. For nearly five years after Brandt's historic visit to Warsaw in 1970, arguments raged back and forth about how many Germans there were, how many should be allowed to emigrate ever or at any one stage, and (under various polite and euphemistic verbal smokescreens) how much the West German government should pay for them. The outflow of Germans from Poland that began in 1971 for a time grew slower and slower. Then on August 7, 1975, following a meeting in Helsinki between Gierek and the West German Chancellor Schmidt, an agreement was signed to which was appended a protocol declaring that 120,000 to 125,000 Polish citizens would be permitted to leave Poland in the next four years. Since then most of them have in fact emigrated. The figure of 120,000 is, it should be noted, a compromise. In 1973 the Red Cross reported that it had received 283,000 emigration applications.[50] German and Polish estimates in the past have varied wildly at both extremes from virtually zero to over a million. That being so, there will probably be a further round of negotiations to determine how many more should be allowed to go and for what considerations. How many Germans there really are in Poland, and how many among those that have left have been more German than Polish are ultimately metaphysical questions. But basically the more that go the smaller the problem, either domestic or international, that remains.

The Polish diaspora in Western countries poses a number of interesting questions that are not without their political aspects. However, the subject is too diffuse and remote from present concerns to warrant even brief discussion here. There remains the question of the Polish minorities in Czechoslovakia and the Soviet Union. The Poles in Czechoslovakia have been the cause or at least the occasion of a good deal of conflict in the past. However, they are a small and numerically stagnant group,[51] and it seems most unlikely that Polish nationalism, for all its capacity for suicidal unwisdom, will ever again work itself up into the fine careless rage of 1939, when it joined in the dismemberment of Czechoslovakia, ostensibly for demographic-irredentist reasons.

In recent years, though, we have been reminded, if reminders were necessary, that the Polish minority in the USSR is by no means a dead issue. And here, paradoxically, it would appear likely that it is in part the rapid demographic decline reported in the Polish community there that is the cause of the trouble. The Soviet and Polish governments seem over the years to have had a tacit agreement to assimilate and absorb those of each other's nationals as are still resident on the wrong side of the border. The

number of people identifying as Poles in Soviet censuses has declined rapidly, and the number claiming Polish as a native language
has declined even faster. The real number of Poles in the Soviet
Union is no doubt also in some measure an irreducibly abstract
question; in any case it is an extremely complex one. But while
some of the Poles identified at earlier censuses may have been
Catholic Belorussians or Uniate Ukrainians, and others may have
been Soviet citizens who knew some Polish, wanted to emigrate
from the Soviet Union, and saw their opportunity to do so in the
repatriation of Poles organized in the late 1950s, there can be
little doubt that the figures are likely to greatly underestimate the
number of people who would identify as Poles in an open situation
and have quite a good deal of justification for doing so.[52] And
there can be little doubt, either, that the Poles are subjected to
conditions as nationally and culturally repressive as those suffered
by any other major ethnic group in the Soviet Union. Late in 1974
a number of extremely prominent Polish intellectuals called upon
the authorities to take a greater interest in defending the cultural
rights of the Polish community in the Soviet Union.[53] This issue
is potentially an explosive one and could be acutely embarrassing
to the Gierek regime. Further reported declines in the size of the
Polish community in the Soviet Union might conceivably have the
effect of making the problem worse. Whatever course future Polish agitation (and possible government representations to the Soviet leadership in private) might take, the Soviet side will not be
without weapons to use in its own defense, quite apart from its
usual ones of diplomatic force majeure. They could, for example,
ostensibly and ostentatiously hand the whole problem over to the
republic leaderships in Kiev and Minsk and leave them to handle
relations with the Poles. Polish-Ukrainian amity in particular
would almost certainly not prove robust enough to bear the strain.

Let us now consider the possible effects of Poland's demographic
development as a nation on her position on the international scene.
Since the war Poland's population has in fact increased faster than
that of almost any other European country. Between 1950 and 1968
Poland alone accounted for 55% of the total Eastern European population increase, while constituting only about 31% of the total population even at the end of that period. Already it has become twice
as populous as East Germany, though it was only some 25% larger
just after the war.[54] Its position relative to Czechoslovakia has
also improved over the same period (not to compare it with the
prewar Czechoslovakia, whose large German ballast was more a

source of weakness than strength). Given that its GNP has also increased at a more rapid rate than that of its two neighbors,[55] it is evident that the demographic factor has contributed to strengthening its relative power position without itself having given rise to any obvious countervailing factors that might have canceled out that effect. Poland's relative demographic strength vis-à-vis both East (and West)[56] Germany seems destined to go on increasing for the immediate future; and depending on the durability of the current Czech demographic revival, it may well again do so vis-à-vis Czechoslovakia. These two countries have been Poland's closest partners (apart from the Soviet Union) in recent years. Gomułka seems to have striven for some kind of special relationship with them, and there have been signs of a similar orientation on Gierek's part as well. If Poland were able to maintain its present birthrate or increase it, it is likely that barring ecodisasters, this would contribute to its further enhancing its relative weight within this triangular subgroup in the future.

Polish crude birthrates have largely risen and fallen with those prevailing in the USSR as a whole in the postwar period. However, RSFSR statistics indicate that Polish birth and natural increase rates have recently been well above those prevailing in the Russian population.[57] Were net reproduction ratios available for the ethnic Russian population, they would almost certainly have been below those of the Polish population since the 1960s. These facts and probabilities are unlikely to be unknown to participants in Polish demographic debates or wholly absent from their calculations, however unrelated these might be to the practical politics of the near future. The Polish gains vis-à-vis the Ukrainians since the war may also have been a source of satisfaction to some.

The latent geopolitics of Eastern Europe (i.e., what might be expected to happen in the event of some shrinking of the Soviet or Russian role, for example, or some expansion of the German one) is an inviting field for speculation. But demographic developments in Eastern Europe itself (i.e., excluding the Soviet Union for the moment) are not apparently working toward such a transformation, and so any elaborate consideration of future contingencies would not be germane to the present discussion.

Nonetheless, in considering population debates in Poland or any of the other East European countries, it is essential to keep this "make-believe" dimension in mind, as that is certainly what most of the actual participants are doing. It is this factor, I believe, that gives those debates much of their peculiar piquancy, their

ability to rouse the greatest fervor, attract the widest public attention, and to evoke anxieties and national neuroses which might
otherwise seem wholly inexplicable to the outside observer.

"How can we feel sure of our frontiers and of peace in Europe
when there are 198 Germans to the square kilometre and only
88 Poles?" cried Cardinal Wyszyński, the Catholic primate of Poland in a sermon delivered in 1959. "If we want a strong Poland,
we need a further 25 million people. Not 30 but 50 million Poles
can find living-space in our country. That is Poland's raison
d'état. Only then will we be a nation which by its numbers, its
work and its diligence earns everyone's respect...." Though he
did not, of course, mention them by name, there can be little doubt
that Wyszyński also had the Russians at the back of his mind when
he made his remarks.[58] It is noticeable that most Polish demographic commentators who allude to the "national future" argument
in this way follow Wyszyński in conspicuously failing to locate Poland's place as being necessarily within the Socialist bloc.[59]

Ideology

Since 1956 Poland has treated a number of tenets of Soviet Marxist theory and practice in cavalier fashion: decollectivizing agriculture; tolerating the church within relatively liberal repressive
limits; permitting a far broader spectrum of foreign information
and ideas to circulate within the country than is permitted by any
of its neighbors (with the obvious exception of Czechoslovakia circa
1967-69), and so on. While Gomułka retreated from some of his
1956 "program," this was in large measure because he had not
written that program in the first place. His subsequent withdrawal
from it was as much dictated by personal prejudice as by intraparty
or external pressures. But in certain matters he continued to dissent from the Soviet model with the same tenacity he had shown
in 1949.

This stubborn adherence to heretical ideas and policies was also
apparent in the Gomułka regime's attitude toward population issues.
Though other East European regimes also permitted or fostered
considerable revivals of demographic research before the final
rehabilitation of the science in the Soviet Union in the early and
mid-nineteen sixties, and did not prevent them from at times
treading on potentially dangerous ideological ground, no other country flew quite so boldly in the face of approved doctrine as Poland

did. While certain decencies continued to be observed, in the form, for example, of demographic articles devoted to Marx's demographic views views and the socialist law of population, the general tone of scholarship, and more particularly of journalism and official pronouncements, was one of at times stridently Malthusian pragmatism.[60] Rapid population growth was a social and economic bugbear, reflecting primitive mores and leading to a lowering in the standard of living and unreasonable burdens on the state budget.[61] The world generally, and the underdeveloped countries in particular, were faced by a serious demographic crisis. In respect of population growth Poland was in effect an underdeveloped country. The birthrate was no longer held to be anything to be proud of; on the contrary, it was something to be ashamed of individually and struggled with nationally. In that struggle "subjective" and superstructural factors like propaganda and the spread of contraception had an important role to play. The fact that Poland was a socialist country was of limited relevance; the nature of the problem remained basically the same.

And so the Polish public was regaled with the horrors of the population bomb exploding both within and beyond the nation's borders.[62] Following on the slump in the domestic birthrate, this theme died away in the latter part of the Gomułka period, and to that extent a partial return to orthodoxy occurred. But there was no return to the classical anti-Malthusianism of the early 1950s. And many traces of heretical thought have survived. Thus, for example, an antinatalist contribution to the domestic population debate in 1972 bore the title "Who Wants to Live Standing Up?"[63] And at the international level, while Polish discussions of world population problems now tend to follow the more liberal version of the current Soviet line, they do at times deviate quite markedly from it.[64]

While Polish Malthusianism was softening, so too was the pristine rigor of Soviet anti-Malthusianism. After the midsixties the two sides tended to move closer together. But for some years before that, while Moscow was maintaining that the world had no population problems, only social and political ones, Warsaw had been conceding that the world was threatened by a population explosion. It had, moreover, permitted its Society for Responsible Motherhood to affiliate with the International Family Planning Federation, a notoriously "Malthusian" organization, and to cultivate other similar international links. And while the Soviet Union was rejoicing in its last years of high natural increase and asserting

that this was not a problem but a natural and desirable state of
affairs for a socialist state, in Poland the official view was that
high natural increase was a basically pathological condition and
one that had to be cured at all costs.

It should not be thought that this was a particularly contentious
issue as between the Soviet and Polish leaderships, or even between
their ideologists. The Polish authorities simply went their own
way and avoided issuing challenges on the matter. The heresy in
their position was more evident in propaganda for domestic consumption than at loftier theoretical levels, where at times attempts
were made to distinguish between Polish antinatalism and Malthusianism. But preservation of the pure Soviet orthodoxy prevailing
up to the midsixties would have been quite impossible. To do so
would have entailed arguing that high population growth was a feature of socialism and therefore must be a good thing, despite the
fact that the Polish government had said that for Polish purposes
it was not. Then in subsequent years it would have been necessary
to go on maintaining that the high population growth actually still
existed, despite the fact that in Poland, where there was an antinatalist policy, and in all the other socialist countries, where there
was not, fertility and population growth were declining dramatically.
It was actually this turn of events, of course, more than any other
that ultimately led to the doctrinal revision in the Soviet Union itself. Already by the mid-nineteen sixties, in fact, relatively few
Soviet bloc demographers were still prepared to defend the cruder
aspects of the old official line.[65]

It remains to consider what forces pushed the Gomułka regime
into heresy on this particular question. The economic reasons
have already been briefly mentioned, and they were undoubtedly
important. But similar rates of natural increase had occurred in
the Soviet Union, for example, without producing any such ideological volte-face. The relative freedom of Polish intellectual life in
the late fifties was probably another important element in the situation, since it was thanks to that that the neo-Malthusian current
of thought was able to develop among Poland's economists to the
point where it was able to affect the thinking of those closest to the
leadership. But perhaps the most crucial single factor involved
was the determined opposition of the Church to this particular aspect of government policy. As was noted earlier, the Catholics
made use of the anti-Malthusian card in their opposition to the
abortion reform in 1956.[66] They thereby preempted the position
of Soviet orthodoxy for themselves, thus to some extent discrediting

it, so to speak, and giving the regime an added incentive to coun-
tenance ideological revision on the population question. As relations between Church and state deteriorated in the years after
1956, Gomułka no doubt became less and less inclined to see eye
to eye with the Church on this matter; and their outspoken and continued opposition must have enraged him.[67] The change in the policies on abortion and contraception of late 1959 were accompanied
by a sharp and concentrated campaign against the Church,[68] which
suggests that they had perhaps become more of a thorn in the authorities' side by that stage than even the "situation in the meat market."

The authorities' option for a fairly explicit neo-Malthusianism
is not really surprising given the logic of Church-state politics in
People's Poland. Indeed, were the Orthodox Church in the USSR as
powerful and pronatalist as the Catholic Church in Poland, one can
well imagine that the Soviet leadership might at some point have
been converted to Malthusianism also. As for Soviet tolerance of
this deviation, it is not inconceivable that they were quietly gratified that one of their traditional enemies was thus constraining itself.

Debates and Dilemmas in Population Policy[69]

As was mentioned earlier there has been a considerable amount
of discussion on population issues in Poland in recent years. Candid as it sometimes has been, the population debate in Poland in
the 1970s has not of course explicitly broached all the matters
raised in the discussion so far, which was aimed at mapping the
politico-demographic context with special attention to those features of it to which the protagonists themselves make least explicit
reference. For convenience of exposition, I will divide the themes
that actually are broached into the economic, the social, and the
political. All stem ultimately from the one central complex of
dilemmas: whether Poland should adopt a pronatalist policy (there
are no antinatalists any more, it seems, only at most antipronatalists); for what reasons it should or should not do so; how and
on what basis such a policy should be formulated; and by what
means it should be implemented.

Economic Issues

The rationale of Gomułka's antinatalist policy was that the rapid
population growth of the time was placing too great a strain on the

country's capacity to invest and thereby reducing its capacity to comfortably consume. The slower the population grew, the sooner it would become possible to supply everyone with the necessary ingredients of the good life; excess expenditures on demographic investments and investments to provide jobs for outsize cohorts of school-leavers were holding back living standards.

When the rapid decline in fertility in the 1960s brought no very dramatic improvement in living standards, the plausibility of this argument was greatly weakened. While people were obviously and by definition adopting it at the microeconomic level, there was a growing feeling that the chronic weaknesses of the Polish economy, particularly in its consumer sectors, had more to do with incompetent management and misconceived priorities than with demographic or any other pressures. As a 1972 commentator put it, trenchant after the event: "The attempt was made to explain the weakness of the economy in terms of an excess of children.... That of course was sheer lies."[70]

While most economically oriented participants in the population debate stress that they do not advocate a return to the earlier fertility pattern even if such a thing were possible, they do argue that the economic optimum is a "moderate" rate of increase. They also emphasize the importance of maintaining an even flow in the birthrate and avoiding the convulsive and economically disruptive fluctuations that have characterized the postwar period. They draw attention to the impending labor shortage in Poland and the impossibility of solving it demographically except in the long term. This, they say, is the consequence of the antinatalist population policy followed by the government in the 1960s, at the very time when it should have been doing all it could to keep fertility as high as possible so as to prevent the stunted birth cohorts of the war period from "echoing" and thereby perpetuating the imbalance in Poland's demographic structure. For similar reasons it was often argued that Poland should refrain from pursuing a strongly pronatalist policy in the 1970s when the most fertile cohorts were much more numerous, as this, if successful, would only produce in turn an enhanced echo of the baby boom and a repetition of all the successive problems that it caused. Poland should wait till the boom passes before introducing its pronatalist program.[71]

It was indeed a remarkable feature of Gomułka's population policy that it was pursued through the very period when it was least necessary. There was a joke circulating in Poland in the sixties to the effect that Gomułka, who was celebrated for both his austerity and his stubborn and misplaced intellectual overconfidence, had decreed that after his death a simple grave was to be erected to his memory bearing the words: "Władysław Gomułka, economist." The epitaph "Władysław Gomułka, demographer" would have been equally appropriate.[72]

In addition to the dangers of exaggerated fluctuations in labor supply in the long term, and severe overall shortages in the short term, the economic effects of changes in the age structure of the population are often greatly stressed. Low fertility sustained over a number of years reduces the proportion of younger people within the population and correspondingly increases the proportion of the aged. This pattern of demographic "ageing" is actually characteristic of all developed societies, and judged by European standards, the Polish population remains comparatively young. Nonetheless, many Polish demographic commentators present these trends as being rather threatening.[73] The dependency ratio (i.e., the ratio of dependent age groups to the active population), they point out, will decline, and the economic burden on wage earners will increase, the more so as increasing numbers of young people are kept out of the labor force until they are well into their twenties by expanded postsecondary education. Moreover, with the breakdown of the old three-generational family, the state will be required to disburse increasing amounts on the upkeep of the old. Apart from that there will be a tendency for the work force itself to age, as its younger cohorts become proportionately weaker. And in an age of unprecedented technological change, it is important that the work force should be supplemented by large cohorts of highly trained young people able to successively transform the permanently obsolescent economy they inherit.

Though economic arguments of this type are often put in conjunction with others, social, "national," or even overtly political, it is difficult to escape the impression that there is an excessive amount of econocentrism in Polish demographic thinking, as indeed there is throughout the Socialist world. In Gomułka's policies the primacy accorded economic over human concerns at times reached caricature proportions. But one suspects that while those policies have now been sharply criticized from a social no less than an eco-demographic viewpoint, among the reasons operating at the official level toward a review of policy, concern about future difficulties in finding the necessary human fuel for sustaining policies of economic growth occupied a dominant position. The postgrowth mentality has scarcely begun to affect the Socialist world. Even in Poland, despite its neo-Malthusian traditions, thinking of the ZPG type has only recently begun to be mentioned in print, often with a kind of breathless and shocked disapproval. Relatively few writers betray awareness of what a Yugoslav demographer has referred to as the "truism" that in the long term, the only acceptable rate of population growth must be around zero.[74] It is not clear for how long their "moderately increasing" population, allegedly so essential for maximal economic growth, will have to go on increasing. Nor is it clear how the problem of "ageing" of the population will ultimately be tackled if and when that so fervently desired "moderate increase" ever smooths out to nothing. Few seem worried, either, about what will happen if and when, as Soviet ideologists have long foreshadowed, the limits of life expectancy are radically extended: how will the economically optimal age structure of the population be maintained when all men can become centenarians?[75] The economic justification for the labor-force arguments is in any case seldom given empirical form: how the economies of such low-fertility countries as Sweden or Belgium survived to the post-Gastarbeiter age is not explained. The idea that the upper working-age limit could be somehow raised or, alternatively, not lowered is relatively seldom explored.[76] Few advance the counterproposition that the economy should be adapted to the human resources available rather than vice versa; and those that do are usually not economists. In economic pronatalist advocacy there is, in short, something of a tendency toward a technocratic steamrolling of human values, for all that the ultimate objective is ostensibly the prosperity and well-being of all.[77]

Social Issues

The economically oriented among Polish demographic commentators are fairly much agreed that a pronatal policy is a necessity; their only disagreement is likely to be as to details of strategy, timing, or feasibility. Those who are skeptical of their approach tend to counter it with what are essentially social or political arguments. And in general it is at the level of social and political issues that a greater complexity and differentiation of views appears.

In the context of policy debates, the distinction between the social and the economic or political is apt to become a little more blurred at the edges than usual. The discussion here will be in terms of three interrelated problems or groups of problems: the role of women in society; the family; and living standards. (The

position of women, in other words, has not yet become a fully
fledged political issue in Poland. The vexed question of living
standards, while obviously being also economic and, at times,
highly political, is nonetheless so closely connected with the other
two problems that it is impossible to separate them.)

Those who raised the alarm about impending depopulation often
sounded a concurrent alarm about the decline of the family and
family life in general: the affective, procreative, and social functions of the family, it was said, were following its economic functions into extinction;[78] the family itself was breaking up, there
was nothing to replace it, and the end product would be chaos;
traditional sexual roles were in disarray; the divorce rate was
growing and so were the numbers of failed and moribund marriages;
children with growing frequency were returning to empty houses;
juvenile hooliganism and problem behavior were becoming commonplace; childless and one-child families were leading to egotistical and unsocialist attitudes; materialism and a miniaffluence
(mała stabilizacja) were becoming the order of the day; there was
a decline in respect for parents and virtually none for the old, who
were being cut adrift and left to float to miserable and irrelevant
deaths in complete isolation from their erstwhile families and the
community; and numerous other evils like alcoholism, mental disorders, and antisocial attitudes were to be seen as the consequences
of the weakening of the family and the moral fiber which it had once
transmitted from generation to generation.[79]

Views of this kind are naturally particularly prevalent among
Catholic publicists,[80] but are by no means confined to them. The
discussion mentioned in Note 79 was published in a weekly put out
by the official atheist organization. Another weekly closely associated with the 1972 campaign on behalf of the family, Kultura, has
generally been regarded as having close links with officialdom. Its
then editor-in-chief, the late Janusz Wilhelmi, who actively associated himself with the campaign both for the strengthening of the
family and for raising the birthrate by means including restrictions
on abortion, was elected a member of the party's Central Auditing
Commission at the Sixth Party Congress in 1971. The Gierek leadership has in fact repeatedly affirmed its support for the family.
On March 6, 1975, for example, Gierek declared: "There can be
no socialist society unless the family is strong, stable, and spiri-
tually healthy. We reject the theories arising in capitalist countries about the allegedly inevitable crisis of family ties."[81] And
in June 1978 he attended a conference devoted to the "preservation

and development of the family," where he foreshadowed the formation of a committee of experts to report on the present state of the
family in Poland.[82]

This has not always been the attitude of the authorities. Poland,
like the Soviet Union before it, once flirted with radical reappraisals of the family[83] but then lapsed back into verbal support of the
institution coupled with a practical indifference. This indifference
was particularly evident in Gomułka's time, when, together with
the creation of a markedly antinatalist climate (which was obviously
not profamily in its implications), numerous other policies were
followed whose implicit message was that the family was really
rather a nuisance. Despite the planned absorption of large numbers
of women into the work force, the situation in regard to child-care
institutions in Poland remained worse throughout the 1960s than
in virtually any other Comecon country.[84] The expansion of the
housing program was very slow in relation to needs, and toward
the end of the decade an actual decline in the rate of housing construction was recorded at the very time when large numbers of
postwar babies were reaching marriageable age.[85] Moreover,
large numbers of very small flats were built to substandard speci-
fications in urban settings that were often most uncongenial to
family life.[86] Again these were common Socialist failings, but
they were ones in which the Gomułka administration tended to out-
fail its rivals.[87]

The minute Gomułka and his government fell, these and similar
aspects of everyday family existence and basic living conditions
came in for the most withering criticism. (There had of course
been some more cautious criticism earlier as well, but without
any unequivocal allocation of political responsibility.) Much of it
was directly related in due course to the population issue. How
could one possibly expect the Polish family to flourish and to reproduce itself when it was forced to live in such wretched conditions, with all hope of perceptible improvement postponed to the
remote future, and the only chance of partial escape in the short
term consisting in restricting family size to the barest minimum?
Critiques of Gomułka's population policy and his general living-
standard policy became so closely interwoven that it was often
difficult to see what the main motivation of any given critic was.
Was he using the issue of population policy to push more effectively
for socioeconomic reforms, or was he advocating an energetic
boosting of living standards to promote the greater demographic
glory of the fatherland? The fertility decline seemed a most dra-

matic vindication of all the unfortunate urban dweller's resentments. He was probably right in sensing that the stagnant consumer economy (coupled with rising expectations) was a major
factor in producing the slump in the birthrate. And if he was right,
the only way to solve the demographic problem was to first solve
the problems of the standard of living. The two issues dovetailed
most pleasingly.[88] Similarly, the advocates of a revival of family
life, even the least materialistic among them, usually felt that
some greater concern for the family's material well-being would
not be amiss. If having children were not such a major inroad
into the parents' resources of time, energy, and money, the chances
were greater that they would venture having a second and a third.
As the Catholic economic commentator Andrzej Wielowieyski argued: In Poland even to have one child is a terrible shock for
young working parents, and so it is not surprising that many stop
there. Yet a family of three, two parents and one child, is not a
real family; correct upbringing is impossible where there are no
brothers or sisters. Accordingly, the moral health of the family
is dependent in some degree on the prior success of a pronatalist
policy.[89]

Of all the hapless consumers of Gomułka's Poland, it was the
young mother who had most to complain about. While Soviet Socialism has brought a kind of professional and social liberation to
women that has been much more rapid and far-reaching than any
equivalent development in the West, it is also true in another sense
that Socialism has replaced the exploitation of man by man by the
exploitation of woman by man. As elsewhere, women in Poland
have been driven onto the labor market more by economic duress
than incentive.[90] And simultaneously they have been left (for social rather than what might conventionally be called political reasons)[91] with an only slightly diminished share of the usual domestic burdens of running a household. To further aggravate the situation, the state of basic trades and services in Poland in the 1960s
(and 1970s) was probably as bad as anywhere else in the Soviet
bloc;[92] and it is everywhere bad, as is often admitted. In these
circumstances the Polish woman, like so many of her sisters elsewhere in Socialist East Europe, cast her vote at the abortion clinic
or the private gynecologist's office.

A great deal of the Polish population debate has turned on the
question of how to make the woman's role more tolerable. Many
of the contributors have been women. Radical feminists in the
West would probably find their attitude unenlightened, since their

criticism, though often vigorous, is less than revolutionary. Open declarations of sexual war would in any case probably not be allowed by the censorship (irrespective of its sex). But there are few detectable signs that any women see their struggle in quite such bellicose terms. The occasional press items on Western feminism tend to be jocularly deprecating.[93] Women writers condemn men for their indolence in the house, but far more vigorously for the attempts that are sometimes made (and made I think invariably by men) to reassign them a place in the kitchen or otherwise to put the burden of the nation's "future" disproportionately on them.[94] The defenders of the family have included among their ranks several who believed that a restoration of the patriarchal family was essential both to the health of the family and the health of the national birthrate. The women who responded to these suggestions with indignant rebuttals (in which they were joined by several male commentators) may well have had middle-class perspectives and interesting intelligentsia jobs, but they were probably not too untypical of other working women nonetheless. Survey results suggest that it is male Polish industrial workers who are in favor of their wives not working, not the wives themselves.[95]

Elsewhere in the socialist camp in recent years, pronatalism has sometimes been accompanied by a return to older conceptions of the family, complete with sentimental rhetoric about the joys of motherhood, due emphasis on traditional male and female roles in and out of the house, reduced employment of young women in the most fertile age groups, and an elaborate cult of babies. While the Gierek leadership has greatly stressed its intention of strengthening the family morally and materially, it has not so far adopted any kind of Kinder Küche Partei approach. It has, however, foreshadowed a very explicit system of child-care benefits to draw young mothers out of the work force. At least one female commentator has commented unfavorably on this proposal.[96]

Political Issues

The population issue that raises perhaps the greatest passion is abortion. Gomułka's adoption of an explicit and emphatic antinatalist policy was, it was suggested earlier, partly caused by Church opposition to the abortion legislation of 1956. Throughout the Gomułka era Wyszyński and lesser Catholic representatives, including some from the otherwise proregime PAX organization, maintained a barrage of criticism of government policy in this area (largely unpublished in the case of the official Church spokesmen). Abortion was denounced as being literally murder. It was held to be a grave threat to the morality of the young. And it was said to endanger the health and reproductive capacity of the mother and, thereby, of the nation. This latter argument, vigorously stated even before the decline in the birthrate had gone very far, naturally became more frequent as events seemed to be offering their support.

After the fall of Gomułka the Catholic publicists were joined by other critics of the abortion legislation, who adduced very similar arguments to attack it.[97] From this the inference seems clear that there was a party ban on raising the issue of abortion in Gomułka's time, and that this ban was lifted after his removal. The antiabortionists showed themselves to be quite a formidable alliance of national, religious, medical, and aesthetic objectors. But after a lively debate, and despite the trend toward partial or complete restriction of abortion in other East European countries (where it had similarly been legal since about 1956-57), the counterreformers were defeated.[98] The main ripostes against them, however, did not obviously emanate directly from the top leadership, which may have conceivably been sitting on the fence to some extent while giving its support in the meantime to the defenders of liberal abortion. The latter, it should be said, did not usually defend abortion as such but saw it rather as a regrettable phenomenon that they hoped would soon diminish. However, they did challenge the propriety of state interference in what they held to be a sphere of individual freedom. And they frequently asserted that such interference, insofar as it was aimed at achieving spectacular pronatalist successes as in Romania, would be unsuccessful. The language at times was rather forceful, which may indicate strong personal feelings, but may also indicate that there was continuing high-level opposition to any change in the law. As one prominent demographer wrote bluntly:

Population policy cannot be conducted with the aid of administrative rigors (i.e., repressive measures), and accordingly the views heard calling for withdrawal of the legislation legalizing termination of pregnancies must be regarded as ill-advised.[99]

This particular commentator was as much a pronatalist as many of the antiabortionists. Virtually all the qualified demographers are pronatalists, but virtually all, too, are firmly opposed to any form of "administrative measures" being applied to the problem. Thus, while the economic bias of the demographic profession does lead some of them toward the technocratic econocentrism referred to earlier, it can also be said that in this matter they place a very firm stress on the rights of the individual.

The solution favored by the demographers, as indeed by most other contributors to the discussion, is to remove at least some of the economic disincentives to having children. Most favor generous child allowances, preferably graduated fairly steeply by birth order, and a variety of other social services and economic policies aimed at lightening the load of the young mother. Many such measures have been adopted or foreshadowed by the government, but not usually in the amount or form that the pronatalists would have liked, and the satisfaction they express about them seems at times to be mingled with a trace of reserve. One rather enigmatic lacuna in the economic pronatalists' program is that they do not seem to have any contingency plans in the event their policies are applied without success. Would the devotion of some to individual rights then waver?[100]

If many pronatalists are ready to defend individual rights on the abortion issue, and family planning generally, few seem to question the state's ultimate right to make all the macrodecisions and to decide what the birthrate should be; though they do frequently emphasize that those decisions should be made after careful research and due consultation with experts. And few participants in the debates on either side seem to question the state's right to unleash another barrage of propaganda (as in the sixties but this time pronatalist) to achieve that rate. But there are some skeptics. One journalist commentator spoke of the need to create a pronatalist climate in the population by manipulating media and cultural output, but at the same time deplored the stupidity of mass propaganda, suggesting that it was counterproductive anyway.[101] Another journalist, Ernest Skalski, went rather further, speaking with the greatest distaste of any attempts to make people "feel ashamed" of having only one child, as an earlier discussant had proposed. This he described as "arrogant social pedagogy," a description which, of course, sounds very like a condemnation of all propaganda campaigns aimed at adults (and be it noted, in passing, that in this domain Gierek's regime has probably outshone its predecessor). Attacking another debater who had declared that "citizens are obliged to think about the (needs of the) state in broader categories" (i.e., to be aware that they should have more children than they really want if the state sees it as necessary), Skalski described this kind of thinking as a "perversion" and went on: "The conviction still

146

cannot establish itself in our journalistic writing that man is first and foremost a value unto himself and not an instrument of policies; policies are meant to serve him and not vice versa."

Skalski's article, which bore the sarcastic title "I Suggest You Have Three Children," adhered to the usual stylistic convention of suggesting that it is journalists (or economists, demographers, historians, doctors, lawyers, etc.) who are to blame for the ills of Socialist society, and not the system, the government, or particular politicians (other than displaced ones, of course, who may be mentioned in season); but it was nonetheless a very spirited and noteworthy defence of private values.[102]

From time to time an interesting trace of class attitudes intrudes into the debate. Most if not all of the contributors are, of course, members of the intelligentsia, whatever their more remote social origins. Not only is this quite often evident, it is even at times made unabashedly explicit. The fertility of the intelligentsia in Poland, as elsewhere in the Socialist world, is markedly below that of other social classes and groups,[103] unlike the position in Western Europe, where equivalent groups like the urban better-to-do and the professionals have tended to increase their fertility in recent decades to the level of or above that of the urban proletariat.[104] Many members of the Polish intelligentsia feel that they are, objectively speaking, the salt of the earth.[105] This feeling sometimes reaches the surface of the population debate in the form of a conviction that it is vital to the nation's interests above all to raise the intelligentsia's birthrate.[106] Concern is often expressed too about the high birthrates rife among what in Polish is referred to as the "social margin," and which we would call the lumpenproletariat.[107] Here too they felt that what was required was a selective and differential population policy to encourage the fit and discourage the unfit. This note of social eugenics was struck with a considerable degree of caution. Other more medically eugenic proposals have also been aired at times, again, for the most part, very cautiously.[108] The caution no doubt reflects some measure of concern both about the possible consequences to the society and the possible consequences to the proposer.

From the foregoing it should already have been evident that several major definable interest groups have been involved in the population debate: the Church and Catholic laity, disinterested pronatalist nationalists, the demographers, the economic planners, women's righters, the intelligentsia, doctors, the party-state leadership, and so on. Here again we are obviously dealing with blurry

and overlapping edges: the demographers are often nationalists
and sometimes Catholics; the economic planners may feel strongly
conscious of their allegiance to the intelligentsia or their loyalty
to the party-state leadership, etc. And within the recognizable
groups, a considerable shading of opinion is often noticeable. Thus
within the Catholic contingent there is a very wide variation between the principled intransigence and strong language of Cardinal
Wyszyński, at one extreme, and the mild claims and conciliatory
tone of Sejm Deputy Hagmajer (PAX), at the other.[109] Some demographers are economic pronatalists; others evoke nationalist
arguments; others again seem to regard maintaining population
growth as an "axiomatic thesis not requiring any particular proof";[110]
while still others gently query the pronatalist enthusiasms of their
colleagues without quite dissociating themselves from them.[111] The
medical group is a particularly heterogeneous one, whose vested
interests and orientations have tended, moreover, to shift over
time. In the late 1950s there was often said to be a faction interested in maintaining abortion in an illegal or at best semilegal
state in order to profit therefrom. Other doctors both then and
now are undoubtedly irritated by the strain legal abortion places
on the scarce public resources they are required to administer.
Many are undoubtedly concerned about the medical aspects of legal
abortion, believing it to be harmful; and among these the more de-
voutly Catholic are likely, of course, to see the medical dangers
even more clearly than their colleagues. Now, after years of respectable and quite legal private abortion practice, a great many
gynecologists would undoubtedly feel threatened by any severe restrictions on the availability of abortion. While the profession on
the whole was clearly against legal abortion when it first came in,
their position at present is more difficult to assess in any gener-
alized terms. One journalist writing against abortion in the non-
Catholic Kultura has asserted that the views of the medical profession on the harm done by legal abortion are "shocking."[112] Yet the
attitude of those associated with the Ministry of Health and the
medical powers-that-be (insofar as that attitude is independent and
can be safely inferred from the Sejm committee hearings mentioned
earlier) is rather that the legislation has been medically successful.

One particularly interesting division which has emerged during
the 1970s debate is that between the pronatalist demographic lobby
and a group of academics concerned with a subdiscipline or field
known in Polish as polityka społeczna, i.e., social policy.[113] This
field, which not surprisingly has had a rather checkered history in

People's Poland, concerns itself with the sociological analysis of existing social policies and the consideration and cautious advocacy of improvements. It has now been joined by a subdiscipline of demography which calls itself polityka ludnościowa (literally, population policy),[114] and which aspires to provide a similar service to the government in its own field. The practitioners of both profess a basically technocratic-loyalist view of their society: the existing structures can be accepted but should be made more rational; and the way for them to become more rational is for the politicians to listen to our advice.

Thus we have the familiar spectacle of two groups with elitist aspirations competing for the ear of the powers-that-be. As the two spheres of demographic and social policy are inextricably interwoven, it follows that the potential spheres of influence of the two groups are also inextricably interwoven. The basic contention of the demographers is that the nation's economic and national future is at stake; the "social politicians," if the neologism may be permitted, argue that Poland's resources are modest and the needs of her underprivileged great, and that therefore any diversion of funds from social services toward the problematical objective of raising the national birthrate would be unjustified. To date it appears that the social politicians have on the whole had relatively greater influence on the decision-makers. Most of the Gierek government's moves in social legislation so far have been aimed at redistribution of wealth and the relief of hardship rather than pronatalist objectives per se.

The different tendencies within the debate can be traced in some cases to organizational strongholds as well. The official Catholic and PAX papers have both supported a pronatalist policy with restrictions on abortion. As noted earlier, Kultura, a weekly widely believed to have close relations with high authority, has given considerable prominence and support to the pronatalists and antiabortionists, while also opening its columns to their adversaries. Życie Literackie, another prominent cultural weekly, was antipronatalist, as was, even more markedly and militantly, the liberal weekly Polityka.[115] The trade union daily Głos Pracy represented a kind of down-to-earth version of the polityka społeczna line. The popular Warsaw daily Życie Warszawy, which had been closely identified with the change of policy on abortion and the campaign against the high birthrate in the 1950s, adopted a low profile in 1972, then unexpectedly in 1976 led the pronatalist radicals back into the fray. Trybuna Ludu, the party daily, was noncommittal or judiciously and moderately pronatalist, throughout, but without countenancing repeal of the abortion legislation.

Similarly, among government and academic institutions there are certain identifiable cleavages. Most pronatalist demographers urged the creation of a central organization coordinating research and making policy recommendations. But as between representatives of the Main Statistical Office (GUS), the Polish Academy of Sciences Committee on Demographic Sciences, the Planning Commission, and the Ministry of Wages, Labor, and Social Affairs, there was some difference of opinion about where this might be located.[116] And within the group of participants in the debate oriented in some way toward the Planning Commission, there appeared to be further signs of rivalry between those concerned with establishing a Department of Social Planning and those who found the need for a Government Population Commission attached to the Planning Commission more urgent (this division reflected that mentioned above between polityka ludnościowa and polityka społeczna).[117]

The attitude of the middle and upper echelons of the party-state apparatus to the debates seems to take the form of straddling and reconciling conflicting pressures coming from below. During the Gomułka era there was a period after 1959 when the authorities saw population as a clear-cut issue and maintained a fairly explicit line on the matter. While this line became less emphatic in the later 1960s, it was not formally altered. The Gierek leadership, on its accession, planned to make major changes in social policy generally. These plans do not appear to have had a specifically demographic component at the outset. However, the climate was suitable for a public debate and rethinking of population policy to proceed, and official permission for same was presumably granted.

Having thus sought out public and professional opinion on the matter, the authorities seem to have avoided favoring any one faction in the ensuing dispute. When the public discussion was temporarily reined in, the government's attitude continued to betray signs of ambiguity and compromise. While the social policy orientation seemed to be dominant for the time being, the pronatalists were given not only the satisfaction of expecting incidental demographic spin-offs from the new social legislation, but also the hope that more specifically and explicitly pronatalist programs might be adopted later. Speaking at the Seventh Trade Union Congress in November 1972, Gierek said: "We should create in this country the kind of socioeconomic conditions and moral and psychological climate that will favor the development and optimal sizing of the family. That is our obligation to the future."[118]

But though representatives of the Polish leadership have now begun to use the language of population policy (something which their colleagues in Hungary, Czechoslovakia, Bulgaria, and else- where — but not in the Soviet Union — have been doing for vir- tually two decades), it is still debatable just to what extent they can be said to have a population policy at all. In these matters it is easy to lose oneself in semantic trivia; but if one regards a population policy as being a policy aimed specifically at affecting the numerical demographic development of the country in question, a case could be made for the proposition that apart from a declared hope that the population might continue to increase satisfactorily, and that certain of their social welfare policies, adopted for egali- tarian or other reasons, might also serve to achieve this, they still have no very clear-cut demographic policy. A semiofficial exposition of Poland's population policy written in 1975 includes the remark that: "I doubt that Polish population policy can be sum- marily defined as pronatalist."[119] As late as mid-1978 a party commentator on the proposed child-care benefits, reviewing simi- lar measures undertaken in recent years, said that while they ob- viously may have an effect on social attitudes toward fertility, "nonetheless considerations of social policy appear to predominate when decisions are made regarding family benefits."[120] The anti- natalism of the Gomułka days has been buried, and social and eco- nomic policies are infinitely more oriented to family and consumer needs. This seems to have had a positive impact (if slight to date) on both rural and urban age-specific fertility in Poland. But it seems likely that Gierek, Jaroszewicz, and their colleagues are on the whole more concerned with preventing a renewed outbreak of the troubles of 1970 and 1976 than of the gloom and inactivity in the maternity clinics in the 1960s. The child allowance was in- creased in 1974 but weighted to favor the poor rather than the fe- cund as such;[121] paid maternity leave has been extended, and op- tional postmaternity leave has been greatly extended, but only now are the authorities thinking of reinforcing it by a generous pension allowance, as was done a decade or more ago in the more pronatal- ist neighboring states.[122] And although young marrieds have been given some credit concessions for furnishing their flats[123] and some preference in waiting lists, the problem of getting to the top of the waiting list remains formidable.

The Gierek administration has made some efforts to make up for the inactivity of the Gomułka government in the face of the oncoming marriage "high." But its efforts have been unequal to the task. There are now some 40% more marriages being contracted annually than in Gomułka's last years. The situation in housing and crèche construction, two of Gomułka's lowest priorities, has consequently worsened during the last decade. Though some 30% more flats were completed in 1977 than in 1969 or 1970, the number of flats has still not overtaken the number of marriages, and waiting periods of ten years are commonplace.[124] With crèches things stand even worse. Only 26,000 new places were created in 1970-77. Given that roughly 350,000 more children were born in Poland in 1974-76 than in 1967-69, and given the galloping urbanization and feminization of the work force, the Gomułka shortfall has been sharply aggravated, as a party spokesman has admitted.[125] This failure to provide anything like adequate crèche facilities is doubtless a powerful factor pushing the Gierek administration toward acceptance of the Hungarian innovation of three-year paid child-care leave. While the Hungarians, Czechs, and others were moved mainly by pronatalist aspirations, it seems likely that the Polish authorities have been pushed toward it by economic and administrative necessity.

While it is still debatable just to what extent the Gierek regime does have an unequivocal pronatalist policy, it is clear that it has been moving in that direction steadily throughout the 1970s, both at the declarative and substantive levels. And if it has moved slowly, this may have been due not so much to its resistance to the idea but rather to the fact that most experts, including the pronatalists, were counseling a measured approach. It was mentioned earlier that many people urged that Poland should adopt a pronatalist program in earnest only toward the end of the 1970s, when the first depleted cohorts of the demographic low of the early 1960s would begin reaching marriageable age. And despite their other differences, almost all demographers agreed that intensive and extensive research must be funded and reported before any effective population policy could be devised. The government was also warned that any population policy, to be successful, would have to be carried out in a complex manner, in many different spheres of life simultaneously. The devising of such a policy, as well as its subsequent implementation, would require a permanent government body, partly scientific, partly administrative, to coordinate research, advise on policy, and later check on how the policies once decided on were being administered. For a long time these demands seemed to fall on deaf ears, but at last, in May 1974, the formation of the

Government Population Commission was announced.[126]

Then in June 1978, as mentioned earlier, a special committee of experts was appointed to prepare a report on the state of the family. Simultaneously a Council for Family Affairs was created, attached to the government. From the context and commentaries surrounding these decisions, it was clear that the numerical strengthening of the Polish family would be an explicit objective of the new bodies. Thus in the institutions of government, as in social policy, there has been a gradual accumulation of pronatalist elements.

The statements by Polish leaders on population policy have also become gradually more explicit. Thus in a speech made by Gierek on the occasion of Women's Day in March 1975, he proposed the figure of 40 million people for the year 2000 as a minimal "objective," for the achievement of which, as he added a little inaccurately, "the natural increase rate must become greater." While we have not always had to pursue an active (i.e., pronatalist) demographic policy, said Gierek, "today it has proved to be a necessity. For this reason it is essential that a broad program be developed which would prescribe forms of assistance for families rearing children, and in particular for large families.[127] The Minister for Health and Social Security, Marian Śliwiński, declared in 1976 that "the objective of an offensive (i.e., pronatalist) population policy should be to ensure that there is for as long as possible a moderately increasing population."[128] Then at the Second National Conference of the PUWP in January 1978, when the child-care benefits were foreshadowed, and again at meetings of the Politburo and of Gierek with a number of social policy activitists in the Sejm in late June 1978, explicit reference was made by top party leaders to the desirability of encouraging larger families.[129]

Thus both official declarations and policy initiatives are continuing to veer steadily toward a greater pronatalist commitment. The speed of the trend, however, is unlikely to satisfy the radicals. The Church in particular has been maintaining its opposition to the state's policy of abortion on demand, both on religious and political grounds. In January 1977 the Polish bishops presented a memorandum to the government which set out their views on the current state of the family in Poland and proposed what was in effect a comprehensive pronatalist program.[130] Later in 1977 a right-wing nationalist dissident group began to campaign actively for reversal of the present abortion laws.[131] The moves the authorities announced in 1978 were no doubt intended partly to preempt opposition from these quarters. The opposition will not be so easily placated, however, as the Polish Bishops' Letter of December 31, 1978, devoted to the Revival of Family Life in Poland illustrates. In it the faithful are enjoined not to fear children and above all to abjure "the monstrous crime of infanticide" (i.e., abortion).[132]

It would appear then, all things considered, that Polish population policy will continue on its sedate progress toward the extreme pronatalism of its Socialist neighbors, goaded on by Catholic and nationalist ginger groups. As labor supplies dry up after 1980, and the demographic "low" of the 1960s begins to echo in the birthrate after 1985, more radical measures may be considered. So far, policy on the means of fertility control has been liberal, though one wonders at times whether this might not be partly due to reluctance by the authorities to concede to Church pressure on the abortion issue.[133] Perhaps by 1990 the party will be ready to take Pope John Paul the Second's word for it.

PART FOUR

POPULATION
POLITICS
IN YUGOSLAVIA

CHAPTER 11

YUGOSLAVIA:
DEMOGRAPHIC BACKGROUND

The demographic-political situation in Yugoslavia bears some strong resemblances to that in the USSR. In each case we have a numerically strong and politically dominant "post-Christian" Slavic element which is in greater or lesser measure divided against itself, and substantial ethnic minorities largely of Moslem culture whose loyalty to the existing status quo is questionable. In each case there are dramatic divergencies in demographic behavior between the main national groups. And in each case it appears that demographic trends are bound to aggravate, if not indeed to precipitate, severe socioeconomic stresses and conflicts. The relative success of the Soviet and Yugoslav regimes in resolving or containing these conflicts will be a most interesting test of the respective viability of two polities, which, in many respects, represent the antithetical extremes of modern European Communism.

During the twentieth century various parts of Yugoslavia have been successfully affected by the social metamorphosis known as the demographic transition,[1] in which, typically, first death and then birthrates fall from high to much lower levels, giving rise to a period of accelerated natural increase in the process. The more developed regions of Yugoslavia, Slovenia, Croatia and parts of Serbia began this phase in the last century,[2] and all had effectively completed it by the mid-1960s. In Bosnia and Hercegovina, Macedonia, and Montenegro the transition began later and is only now approaching its completion. In Kosovo death rates started falling some decades ago, but birthrates did not begin to follow them until very recently.[3] The pattern throughout the world has been, roughly, that the later a country or region embarked on the demographic transition, the more rapid the decline in its death rate was likely to be. In consequence, more or less sustained periods of low mortality and continued high natality have ensued, giving rise to the Third World phenomenon popularly identified as the "population explosion." Yugoslavia, like the USSR, has its own Third World, and its own domestic population explosion. As a result of it, and of ethnic differentials in demographic behavior, certain less prominent national communities, notably the Bosnian Moslems (a Serbo-Croat—speaking group since the late 1960s officially recognized as a constituent nation of the Yugoslav Federation) and the Shiptars, or Albanians, have greatly increased their relative numerical strength in Yugoslavia overall and, even more significantly, within their respective territorial units. Other national groups have remained numerically stagnant or shown only weak increase during recent decades. An extreme example may bring out the magnitude of the relative changes that this kind of development can involve: the Hungarians at the 1921 Yugoslav Census outnumbered the Albanians by 468,000 to 440,000. Yet in the year 1972, according to the official Yugoslav demographic yearbook, there were roughly ten times as many Albanians born in Yugoslavia as Hungarians.[4]

With such regional and ethnic differentiation as this, it makes little sense for the most part to speak of overall trends in the Yugoslav population. Nationwide demographic indicators indicate little and in fact serve rather to conceal the nature of trends in particular regions. The material presented in the Appendix has accordingly been chosen with a view to illuminating the disparate paths taken by the main subpopulations in the postwar period. As generalizing comment is so difficult and so deceptive, these introductory remarks will strive where possible to draw attention to the most politically relevant regional deviations from the overall Yugoslav norm.

Natality in Yugoslavia fell from the relatively high (by the European standards of the time) 36.7 per thousand in 1921 to 25.9 in 1939, rose again to 30.3 in 1950 (the peak year of the postwar baby boom), and fell rapidly thereafter to 17.7 per thousand in 1977 (still relatively high by European standards).[5] The decline in mortality has been more steady, and as a result the postwar years saw the period of most rapid natural increase in Yugoslavia's history. Since then natural increase has also fallen rapidly, dropping to less than ten per thousand in 1969 for the first time since the Yugoslav state was established.[6] These magnitudes do have, I believe, some national political relevance, whatever their imperfections as demographic measures in the pure sense. The postwar baby boom (a phenomenon common to all regions) arrived on the labor market in the early and mid-1960s, at a time when Yugoslavia was already struggling with growing unemployment (a problem to be discussed in greater detail in the next section). The period of rapid national population growth of the late 1940s and early 1950s probably also served to reinforce in the minds of the Communist leadership the traditional Stalinist doctrine that high rates of natural increase are a sign of national vigor inherent to Socialism, and to postpone the time when any of them could perceive that lagging population growth might conceivably be a problem either at the national or the republican level. National indicators probably deceive politicians in the USSR and Yugoslavia, just as they do the casual external observer of demographic statistics.

It will be observed from Table 20 in the Appendix (p. 289) that in recent decades, the regional differentials in natural population growth have actually been increasing, despite the almost universal trend toward decline in birthrates. Thus in 1950-54 Macedonia's natural increase was twice that of Croatia, whereas in 1970-73 (despite the rapid intervening decline in Macedonian fertility), the difference was nearly fourfold. In 1950-54 Kosovo's natural increase was less than two and a half times that of Vojvodina. By 1970-73 it was ten times as great. Such comparisons as these are demographically crude and to some extent misleading. In the emotionally charged atmosphere of Yugoslav nationality politics, however, demographic oversimplifications have at times been common. And in any case, more discriminating statistics, when they are available, frequently suggest almost equally alarming inferences.

The postwar baby boom in the more developed republics tends to divert attention from the fact that even by the early 1950s, very large discrepancies existed between the inherent fertility levels of the different national groups. In the census year of 1953, the general fertility rates of the different national groups ranged from 72.5 (Hungarian), 83.1 (Slovenian), 91.0 (Croat), and 101.8 (Serbian) to 170.5 (Yugoslav, undetermined — i.e., Bosnian Moslem) and 228.2 (Albanian).[7] By 1961 an even greater gap had opened, as the fertility rates of the more developed nations had fallen quite sharply, while those of the two main Moslem groups had remained relatively stable: 59.5 (Hungarian), 70.9 (Slovenian), 74.8 (Serbian), and 80.6 (Croatian), compared to 164.3 (Yugoslav, undetermined) and 223.9 (Albanian).[8] Since then the divergence between Albanian on the one hand and Serb, Croat, and Slovenian fertility on the other has largely been maintained.[9]

At the same time, the potentially very significant gap between Macedonian and Albanian fertility has dramatically widened. In 1953 the GFR for the ethnic Macedonian population in Yugoslavia was 143.0 (compare Albanian 228.2); by 1961 the Macedonian rate had dropped to 99.0 (compare Albanian 223.9). I have not yet seen any Yugoslav computation of GFRs by nationality for the census year 1971 or any other year since. But it is quite certain that the gap between Macedonian and Albanian fertility has widened still further, since while both have declined, the Macedonian decline has so far been a good deal steeper. My own (not strictly comparable) calculation of the GFRs for the two national groups within the Macedonian republic as of 1970 gives a figure of 69 for the Macedonians and 183 for the Albanians.[10] According to a Yugoslav source, the respective GFRs for Macedonians and Albanians within Macedonia in the census years 1953 and 1961 were 144 and 100 and 251 and 223. Thus the Albanian rate in Macedonia, from having been rather less than twice that of the Macedonians in 1953, was by 1970 nearly three times as great.[11]

Since 1961, on the other hand, Bosnian Moslem fertility seems to have fallen quite sharply (though statistics may exaggerate the steepness of the decline — see Note 12 below), and the gap between Moslems, Serbs, and Croats in Bosnia and Hercegovina is consequently closing. But even so it remains significant, at least for the two major groups, the Moslems and the Serbs. Again according to my own calculations, the respective GFRs for Moslems and Serbs within Bosnia and Hercegovina in 1970 were 96 and 63.[12] Before the gap closes completely (assuming that it does), further significant changes in their relative demographic strength can be expected. The Serbs can likewise derive little comfort from the GFR for Croats in Bosnia and Hercegovina in 1970, which I calculate to have been 81. The GFRs for the three national groups within the republic in the census years 1953 and 1961 were respectively as follows: undetermined Yugoslavs (i.e., Bosnian Moslems) 180 and 172, Serbs 138 and 105, and Croats 124 and 127.[13]

Outside Bosnia and Hercegovina and Macedonia the momentum and direction of change in relative ethnic fertility levels can be gauged reasonably well from the statistics on Net Reproduction Ratios by republic and province presented in Table 21 of the Appendix (p. 290).[14] The political implications of these trends will be discussed in greater detail below.

The reasons for the sharp postwar fertility decline in Yugoslavia

are no doubt very similar to those operating elsewhere in Eastern
Europe: rapid industrialization and urbanization, increasing educational levels, growth of female employment in the towns,[15] the
chronic urban housing crisis, the total inadequacy of child-minding
facilities,[16] the secularization of life-styles and the decline of
clerical influences, the progressive liberalization of abortion
legislation, changes in family structures and values, and so on.
Most of the factors involved are closely related to one another,
and many form part of the general socioeconomic modernization
that has been proceeding in Yugoslavia since 1945. Before 1939
some 75% of the Yugoslav population lived from the land. By the
1971 Census only 38% were still dependent on agriculture for their
support.[17] Urbanization has not gone ahead at quite the same
speed: like many other countries at a similar level of development,
Yugoslavia has a massive army of some 1.4 million "peasant-
workers" commuting to the cities daily to work in factories and
returning to their farms at night or at weekends. Puljiz estimates
that together with their households, the peasant-workers made up
about 3 million, i.e., more than one seventh of the total Yugoslav
population.[18] Nonetheless the rate of rural-urban migration in
recent decades has been very substantial. It is estimated that in
the period from 1948 to 1953, an average of 203,000 left the land
annually; between 1953 and 1961, an average of 229,000; and from
1961 to 1971, an average of 217,000.[19]

Under the impact of the declining birthrate of recent years, the
Yugoslav population has begun to "age," with the proportion of pensioners in the total population increasing, and the proportion of
children decreasing.[20] One region in which this trend has scarcely
begun as yet, however, is Kosovo, where the extremely high fertility of the Albanian population is keeping the age pyramid very
broad at the base and economic dependency ratios unfavorable.
Fifty-three percent of Kosovo's population is under the age of 20,
and only 7% over 60, whereas the corresponding figures for Serbia
proper are 31% and 14%, and for the Vojvodina 30% and 15%. Such
dramatic differences in dependency ratios as these figures imply
naturally contribute considerably to maintaining and extending the
differences in national income per head between the various regions.[21]
Thus, as with fertility, regional differences in age structure are
striking and of considerable socioeconomic and political significance.

The educational and occupational composition of the population
as a whole has altered considerably in the postwar period, as might
be expected, with levels of schooling and vocational training increasing

substantially overall, and the proportions employed in secondary and tertiary activities advancing at the expense of farming. Again there are the usual regional differentiations, with the less-developed areas continuing to lag behind. The more rapid population growth of these areas has led to rural overpopulation actually being accentuated, despite the draining off of manpower to the cities. Unlike other Socialist commentators, Yugoslav writers are uninhibited in discussing this matter. One source suggested the figure of 2 million for the surplus of rural labor in the country as a whole.[22] An estimate for Kosovo in 1970 placed the surplus there at 180,000, or well over 10% of the total population.[23] In this connection it is worth noting that Kosovo, much of which is mountainous terrain unsuitable to agriculture, is now by far the most densely populated of the eight republics and regions (it was one of the least densely populated in 1921).[24] Given existing trends in fertility and migration, its relative disadvantage in this respect seems bound to worsen.

The regional distribution of population in Yugoslavia has shifted considerably in this century as a result of war and migration. There is no time to discuss either of these topics in satisfactory detail. Suffice it to say concerning the first that Serbia (and Montenegro) lost one fifth of their total population during World War I alone;[25] and that during World War II (in which Yugoslavia sustained an extremely high casualty rate), the burden of mortality was again unevenly distributed, though less so, no doubt, than in 1912-19.[26]

A few cursory observations should also be made about interregional migration within Yugoslavia. Until the last couple of decades, internal migration tended to favor Serbia proper and Vojvodina exclusively, all other regions recording net outflows. Since the mid-1950s Slovenia and Croatia have also been showing a positive internal migration balance.[27] The main patterns of interregional movement have, of course, been from the less-developed south to the north. Serbs from all regions, but particularly from Bosnia and Hercegovina and latterly from Kosovo, have tended to gravitate to Serbia proper and Vojvodina, as have Montenegrins and, though in much lesser measure, representatives of other ethnic groups.[28] Croats from Bosnia and Hercegovina have also tended to emigrate to Croatia, thereby leaving the Moslems in the region (who have no metropolitan area outside the republic to attract them) in a relatively stronger position.[29] The Macedonians, perhaps because of their ethnic and linguistic distinctness, have maintained an even balance between immigration and emigration.

It should be stressed that Yugoslav statistics on interregional migration over recent decades are incomplete and depend heavily on indirect and in some cases misleading census data. The figures are all based on cumbersome, oblique, and incomplete computations. Data on prewar and war-time migratory movements are apparently scanty, and the very important cumulative effects the latter have had on the present distribution of settlement in Yugoslavia will probably never be known. Partly because of Yugoslavia's relaxed (by Socialist standards) internal administration, direct monitoring of population shifts has not been systematically carried out. Slovenia is alone among the republics in keeping reasonably adequate records of current migratory movements.[30] Moreover, since the war Yugoslav censuses have applied the criterion of permanent rather than present residence.[31] As a result the growing numbers of intra-Yugoslav "Gastarbeiter" in the more developed regions (particularly Slovenia) are systematically overlooked, though many of them may regard themselves as permanent settlers. No reliable estimates have been published of the numbers or ethnic composition of those involved in these supposedly temporary movements, and it seems quite probable that none exist.[32] These facts need to be borne in mind when considering the migration tables included in the Appendix.

Another area in which official statistics are inadequate and conceded to be so (or accused of being so) by many Yugoslav commentators is international migration. There has at times been hot dispute about the total numbers and ethnoregional affiliations of the emigrants. In the early stages of the mass emigration that followed the economic reforms of 1965, Croatia, Slovenia, and parts of Bosnia and Hercegovina were particularly affected, and Croatia's share of the diaspora is undoubtedly still disproportionately high. Official estimates of the total numbers involved are approximate and at times conflicting. But at its highest point, in 1974, the Yugoslav economic emigration evidently amounted to some 1.1 million workers, the vast majority of them between the ages of 20 and 45.[33] A recent estimate made after the effects of the post-1974 economic recession in Western Europe had made themselves felt (through reduced employment in general and discriminatory measures against immigrant workers in particular) put the figure for Western Europe at "more than 600,000," suggesting a current total of between 750,000 and 800,000.[34] The Yugoslav Gastarbeiter phenomenon is, of course, one without parallel in the Socialist world. Its demographic-political significance will be outlined in greater detail in Chapter 13.[35]

CHAPTER 12

YUGOSLAVIA:
THE LABOR FORCE AND
EMPLOYMENT POLICY

Strange as it may seem, those responsible for Yugoslavia's first five-year plan apparently took no account of population growth whatsoever.[1] It was only with the 1957-61 plan that the demographic factor began to be systematically represented in planning documents.[2] But while it was thus formally taken cognizance of, key decisions about economic strategy continued to be reached without much regard to natural fluctuations in labor supply. In 1965 Yugoslavia embarked on a radical economic reform, one of the main purposes of which was to restrict employment in the socialized sector in order to facilitate increase in productivity.[3] Partly at least as a result of these policies, employment stagnated, and there was virtually no increase in the numbers of employed for four years. Between 1945 and 1964 employment in the nonrural Yugoslav economy had expanded at an annual average rate of 10%. The numbers of employed in 1968, however, were actually lower than in 1964 (3,579,000 compared with 3,608,000).[4] In the meantime, the mass exodus from the farms set irrevocably in motion by postwar modernization continued to spill rural school-leavers and others into the towns.[5] And given its youthful age structure, the existing work force was not being depleted by natural wastage at a very high rate.[6] Moreover, the middle sixties saw the entry into the able-bodied age group of the first of the large cohorts of school-leavers born during the postwar baby boom.[7] During the late 1950s and early 1960s, when the depleted war-time cohorts had been reaching working age, annual increases in employment had been very high. Now, at the precise time when demographic considerations favored a strategy of extensive rather than intensive (i.e., labor-intensive rather than capital-intensive or productivity-

oriented) economic growth, the choice was made to severely limit
new employment and to favor policies leading to the drastic paring
down of existing employment. While the reform did not of course
aim at the total stagnation of employment that actually occurred
in the years after 1964, the planned level of employment increase
was very modest, just 2.3% per annum, less than half of that prevailing in 1953-61.[8] Industries and whole sectors of the economy
that had been favored by "political" investment now fell on hard
times as sterner economic criteria were applied. Mass firings
often occurred among the higher categories of the work force as
well as among the semiskilled and unskilled. The proportion of
qualified workers among registered unemployed in 1964 was one
sixth of the total; by 1968 it comprised one third (in absolute numbers, an increase from 32,000 to 95,000).[9] Graduates and school-
leavers were particularly hard hit. Thus it was that the regime
manufactured for itself a new stratum of underemployed, overedu-
cated youth, a stratum that was to occasion it a good deal of anxiety
in the late 1960s and early 1970s. The student disturbances at
Yugoslav universities in the northern summer of 1968 (particularly
those at Belgrade University) caused a minicrisis requiring the
personal intervention of President Tito. The ideology of the Belgrade movement had a marked New Left flavoring, which probably
reflected, among other things, the growing professional insecurity
of young graduates at the time. Again in the Croatian crisis of
1971, the role of university students was critical.[10]

Skilled planners and technocrats must have had their reservations
about the timing, if not the substance, of the 1965 reforms. Demographers and economists were certainly quick to point to the unfortunate link between lowered employment opportunities and increased
labor supplies.[11] The decision was, of course, a political one, the
outcome of a complex struggle in which various ideological and
ethnoregional orientations were heavily engaged.[12] It can at least
be asserted with confidence that on this occasion the top leadership
showed small regard, at least initially, for the demographic context
and demographic ramifications of their decisions.[13]

It was evidently felt that the problem could be solved by opening
the floodgates a little wider and allowing the surplus manpower to
seep out of the country. What in fact followed was a torrent. This
mass emigration (which will be discussed in the next chapter) did
not solve the problem of unemployment within the country, however.
Numbers registered as seeking jobs continued to increase,[14] even
when the employing capacity of the economy began to recover, after

1968. Since the defeat of the "liberal Westernizers" (for want of a better term) in 1971-72, there has been a marked reversion to labor-intensive growth, and annual employment increments have picked up, at the expense of productivity and real wages.[15] By now the annual increase in the 15-60 age group is diminishing and can be expected to go on doing so, thus raising the possibility that in the future some of the pressure will ease on the labor market. For this to happen it will be necessary for large numbers of the Yugoslav workers "temporarily abroad" to remain abroad. Since 1972-73, however, it has been official policy to "bring" them all back. More significantly, it has become official policy throughout Western Europe to favor indigenous workers over Gastarbeiter and to deport those of the latter who are unable to find work. The demographic strains on employment policy are thus likely to remain for some time yet.

In the official approach to employment problems, as intimated earlier, there has been a certain regression toward expanding employment, even at the risk of thereby lowering productivity and wages and adding to the inflationary and liquidity problems that have been dogging the economy since well before the post-1973 recession in Western Europe. But in labor policy, as in many other fields of government action, there are clear signs of a compromise between irreconcilable opposites, of gaping chasms thinly papered over. Though the "liberal Westernizers"[16] suffered something of an eclipse after 1971, their "technocratic" orientation continues to be influential. At the same time, the "Partisan" element, while reemerging strongly over the same period, did not achieve a fully dominant position. In employment policy the uneasy balance between these two conflicting tendencies seems to take the form of an incongruous mingling of sober "technocratic" employment plans with either swashbuckling "Partisan" rhetoric[17] or plain obfuscation.[18] Employment plans are set at relatively modest and realizable levels, but extravagant claims are sometimes made about the capacity of the economy (and, indeed, of those modest plans) to absorb Yugoslavia's various accumulations of surplus labor power. And there is evidence that many enterprises are subjected to extraeconomic pressures to take on more workers than they can effectively utilize. This practice of course contributes to swelling actual employment well above planned levels and depressing productivity.[19]

The current five-year plan to 1980 (srednjoročni plan) envisaged an increase in employment in the nonrural sector of almost one million, with an annual increase of employment in the socialized

sector of 3.5%, or about 180,000.[20] But the average annual incre-
ment in employment has in fact been above 4%. Productivity, by
contrast, has been increasing by only an average of 2.2%, instead
of the planned 3.9%.[21] Even with this kind of overfulfillment of the
plan, official unemployment figures have continued to rise.[22] This
is not really surprising, though at the outset of the five-year period,
commentators affected to believe that the planned development
would be sufficient to reduce existing unemployment, provide work
for large numbers of workers returning from abroad, soak up the
continuing inflow of peasants into the towns, and also absorb the
natural increase in the work-age population.[23]

This seems to have been a case either of misty and wishful thinking or disingenuous propaganda. To begin with, the Yugoslav economy then already had a pool of over 600,000 domestic unemployed
that had to be drained off. As was remarked earlier, this total has
been growing in recent years, despite the high employment increments. While the unemployment rate may be due in part to statistical anomalies,[24] the trend cannot be reassuring; nor are there
any obvious reasons why it should suddenly be reversed. Then
there is the pool of exported unemployment, the privremeno zapo-
sleni u inostranstvu (temporarily employed abroad), now becoming
more familiar by their new name of povratnici (returnees). While
there is evidence that only a surprisingly small proportion of the
returnees are at present seeking employment in the socialized sector,[25] this seems likely to change. Given the high unemployment
and (for them) the relatively low wages prevailing in their homeland, the possible prejudice against them on the part of employers,[26]
and their natural desire to enjoy a period of leisure financed by
their savings abroad, it is quite likely that some returnees will
choose to make a pause before seeking work in Yugoslavia. There
may be a delayed deluge awaiting Yugoslav employment offices.

Annual increments in the population of working age, while starting to diminish, are still quite high. Official estimates of the increase in the work force in the forthcoming period are, in the light
of this, surprisingly low and may be an underestimate.[27] Moreover,
given that the proportion of females in the urban labor force in
Yugoslavia is still a good deal lower than in other Socialist countries, and given that the existing trend is toward increase[28] (and
that official policy endorses this trend),[29] one can expect further
pressures to come from this source also. Estimates of the labor
surplus in Yugoslav agriculture vary. A figure of 2 million was
mentioned earlier for 1973. Another estimate, based on different

and more demand criteria, puts it at 5.5 million.[30] In any event, it is clear that with 38% of the active population still engaged in agriculture, the pressure of peasants on the urban labor market is not going to diminish for some decades yet. Puljiz has estimated that the agricultural population is "deruralizing" at the rate of a quarter of a million a year.[31] Even if only half of these people sought urban employment, that would have been sufficient, together with the natural increase in work-age population, to fully dispose of the planned increase in employment in the socialized sector to 1980. What then of the existing unemployed and the returnees? Or the existing labor surpluses in some enterprises?[32]

From these considerations it emerges clearly that official hopes notwithstanding, the next years will not bring any significant reduction in the Yugoslav reserve armies of unemployed — unless of course the present reorientation toward stabilization and greater productivity is reversed, and an all-out attempt is made to extend employment at the cost of everything else. Not only will unemployment not decline, it seems likely in fact that it will continue to increase, quite possibly alongside and despite above-plan employment increments. With the employment bubble of the mid-1960s returning to plague them, Yugoslav policy-makers have limited freedom of maneuver. The only way open to them to "solve" the unemployment problem comprehensively is to abolish it, or at least to radically redefine it. There are signs that some moves in that direction may be being longingly contemplated.[33] Other more substantive measures involving flirtation with private enterprise have been launched or are under consideration. As many of these latter closely relate to the position of the "returnees" in Yugoslav society, I shall defer fuller discussion of them to the next chapter.

The Yugoslav authorities are in an unenviable position. Their labor force embarrassment must be an important long-term factor disposing them toward seeking some kind of trading accommodation with the Comecon/Warsaw Pact countries: for investment funds to finance labor-soaking projects at home;[34] for secure markets for the products of their less viable industries and future extensive growth (which products are difficult to dispose of on competitive Western markets); and possibly even as alternative homes for Yugoslavia's inhospitably treated "guest workers." Large-scale employment of Yugoslav workers by Soviet-bloc firms does not seem imminent, however, though prospects for Yugoslav firms to take contracts in CMEA countries and import their own workers with them may be a little better.[35] The marked cooling of relations with Moscow since late 1975 will certainly not help to overcome the serious obstacles that stand in the path of increased coopera- tion in this field.

The labor surplus must also tend to favor reconciliation with the forces of state socialism at the domestic level. All the other European Socialist states, whatever periodic misgivings they may have about Soviet-style extensive development, with its high em- ployment and low efficiency, are at least spared the worry of high overt unemployment. Indeed, all are now afflicted in some mea- sure or other by labor shortages. Certain shortages of skills and regional shortages apart, Yugoslavia as a whole is unlikely to reach this luxurious stage for decades yet.[36] Until they do, they are bound to feel at least an occasional twinge of ambivalence about their neighbors' labor policies. During the reform period, from 1965 to 1971, their rejection of the state-socialist model was un- equivocal.[37] Even critics of the government's employment policies did not go so far as to laud the Soviet alternative. Economic ra- tionalism is still perhaps the dominant accent in the official posi- tion, despite the resurgence of political employment in the last four or five years. But an ambivalence is, at times, clearly de- tectable; and the reasons for it are not difficult to understand, particularly in the case of politicians from the less-developed southern republics.

For Yugoslavia's labor surplus is more than just a dilemma of economic management. It is a continuing threat to the stability, and indeed to the very survival, of the regime. Now that Western Europe has decisively closed its doors to new immigrant workers and is even seeking to rid itself of many of those it has already ac- cepted, Yugoslavia must solve the problem (made the worse by having been temporarily and partially shelved) with its own re- sources. There will be at least a nervous decade or two in which those resources are quite simply unequal to the task. This would be a testing time for any polity. But for the Yugoslav regime, fighting to maintain its independence between indifference and hos- tility, striving to maintain its own precarious unity and to placate the fissiparous passions of its turbulent nationalisms, and at the same time endeavoring to implement various ambitious social ex- periments, the task will be incomparably more difficult.

Reconciliation with Moscow and a relapse into state socialism would obviously be a defeat for any Yugoslav government. But it would be a defeat that would bring relief from external pressure and an opportunity to soak up (or more efficiently repress) pockets

169

of unemployed discontent at home. Perhaps, some Yugoslavs might argue, the defeat could be negotiated rather than imposed, in a way that would permit at least symbolic retention of national pride and independence and avoid any threat of imposed territorial revision. Such considerations as these may seem a far cry from a choice between annual employment increments of 2.5% and 5%. But the Yugoslav political economy is preeminently a system where tout se tient.

For the moment Yugoslavia is pursuing its usual policy of walking on both legs, placing rather less weight on the Western leg than in 1965-72, but favoring it nonetheless. While "struggling" to absorb its rationally unabsorbables and seeking, at the same time, to extend its trading contacts with the CMEA countries, it is also continuing its efforts to integrate its economy into the tougher league of non-Socialist trade. To do this Yugoslavia must maintain high standards of efficiency; neither its labor force, nor its markets, nor its currency are shielded by the protectionism of the CMEA system. The Soviet vices of "leveling" (uravnilovka),[38] slackness (nerad),[39] low wages, and low productivity make it more difficult for Yugoslavia to find a place in the international division of labor (uključiti se u medjunarodnu podelu rada). Unfortunately, however, not all Yugoslav industries and not all Yugoslav regions are ready for sharp international competition. Many could feel drawn by the relative tranquility and assured exchange of the CMEA. Some might prefer the relative comfort there as a long-term proposition. Among other things, it could provide them with a way of easing the growing burden of their labor surpluses.

Here, as in so many other respects, Yugoslavia is split asunder by a dilemma stemming ultimately from the fact that some parts of the country belong to the developed European West, while others belong more naturally to the European East, and others again to the Third World. Though the discussion thus far has been couched in overall, national terms, in fact the regional aspect of the manpower problem is one of the most sensitive and the most crucial, and one which is likely to linger on when, in the developed areas, the employment bubble caused by the high fertility of the postwar years has become no more than a distant memory. Slovenia, as we have said, is the only republic which, taken as a whole, can complain of a labor shortage. Elsewhere there is a surplus, though in the case of Croatia, Vojvodina, and part of Serbia, it is an accumulated surplus of rural overpopulation and urban unemployment (both hidden and overt, resident and exported), not one which is being further increased all the time by natural increase in the work force. In that sense it can be said that the urban economies of those regions are starting to gain on their objectives of full and rational employment, though the aggravation of returning economic emigrants may effectively conceal this for a good decade or more yet.

In the less-developed areas, however, natural increase is continuing to nullify the gains made by urban employment. Thus for the years 1971-76 it has been calculated that Bosnia and Hercegovina, Macedonia, and Kosovo, which comprise 32.4% of the total population, would contribute over two thirds of the natural growth in the economically active population.[40] In Bosnia and Hercegovina and Kosovo, in 1972, employment increments in the nonrural economy of 4.7 and 7.5%, respectively, were still not equivalent to the total increase in the able-bodied population (to say nothing of technological and accumulated labor surpluses of various kinds).[41] While in Bosnia and Hercegovina, Montenegro, and parts of Macedonia, some diminution of work-force growth rates is in sight, in the Albanian areas of Kosovo and Western Macedonia, no significant easing can be expected for at least two decades. And in all the less-developed regions, the accumulated gap between employment aspirations and possibilities is very serious. The urban unemployment rates of the less-developed republics are naturally higher than elsewhere, not only because of the greater demographic pressures, but also because of the modest dimensions of their nonrural economies, whose slender absorptive capacities can be the more easily overwhelmed. Thus in Albania and Macedonia registered unemployment has been running at around one third of the total[42] number of employed in the nonrural economy. Very rapid expansion of urban job opportunities is necessary if rural underemployment and these high levels of overt urban unemployment are to be relieved. The only alternative to this would be to facilitate mass emigration from the less-developed areas to the developed north of Yugoslavia or beyond.

While there has been some international emigration from the less-developed republics, the outflow from the more-developed regions, particularly in the earlier years, was proportionately much greater. The Albanians and Bosnian Moslems (like the Moslem peoples of Soviet Central Asia) seemed particularly reluctant to leave their homelands.[43] Just as this unfavorable regional distribution of emigration began to alter in the early 1970s,[44] external restraints were imposed on the process, first freezing it at a less than optimal stage in its evolution, and then reversing it. Since

Western European countries are seeking on the whole to shed their more recent and less-skilled immigrant workers, it is likely that the less-developed regions will bear a disproportionate burden of the return flow. Their slender economies, which needed the relief of emigration more in the first place, are correspondingly less able to deal with the remigration.

In the case of interregional migration within Yugoslavia, the barriers are less formal but not necessarily less formidable. Article 183 of the 1974 Constitution prescribes that the citizen's freedom of movement and settlement anywhere in Yugoslavia can be limited only in criminal cases, epidemic emergencies, and "in order to protect public order or in the interests of national defence."[45] And while, until recently, there appears not to have been an explicit policy on internal migration, the one that is emerging at the federal level favors movement of workers from labor-surplus to labor-deficit areas within the country.[46] There are in any case no regulations in Yugoslavia resembling the internal passport and restricted urban residence systems that have been maintained in the Soviet bloc countries. Despite all this, however, there are strong countervailing pressures against complete freedom of movement within Yugoslavia. Given that unemployment is endemic to most of the country, no republic or lower-level authorities will want to import other people's problems to compound their own. Ethnic resentments may operate to deter outsiders at every level, from administrative and enterprise decision-making to interpersonal relations. In the case of immigrants to Slovenia or emigrants from Kosovo, there may be linguistic problems. Published literature contains clear evidence of reluctance on the part of the more-developed republics to receive large numbers of workers from less-developed areas (where skills and general cultural levels are much lower)[47] and of resentment on the part of the authorities in high-fertility areas at the less than generous cooperation they receive from the better-off regions in their attempts to find work for their swelling labor forces.[48] Reliable sources suggest that behind the scenes, the Constitutional provisions about freedom of movement and settlement are apt at times to be sidestepped.[49]

It may be just as well from the regime's own point of view that they are. For while this may mean that labor surpluses get bottled up in the least-developed regions, leading to accentuated urban unemployment, rural overpopulation, a widening in the development gap between the regions, and possibly to acute local unrest — in other words, to a typical complex of Third World problems — any solution which sought to enforce mingling between peoples of such sharply divergent standards and traditions might well lead to a marked worsening of ethnic relations.

The development problem facing the less-developed regions of Yugoslavia is a daunting, if familiar, one. Their rapid population growth is, of course, a crucial factor impeding their efforts, forc- ing them to sprint desperately after an ever receding target. In the areas where population growth has fallen, by contrast, improve- ments in terms of per capita economic indicators are much more easily attained. Despite very considerable politically motivated capital flows from the more-developed to the less-developed re- gions in the postwar period, the development gap per capita has not narrowed, but widened. The Yugoslav press frequently dis- cusses and/or deplores this growing development gap between the different regions, and data relating to it (unlike in the USSR) are not scarce. Between 1947 and 1972 the ratio between highest and lowest income per head increased from 3.14:1 to 5.71:1 (in abso- lute terms from 1,986 dinars to 10,288 dinars). It was the four less-developed regions, Kosovo, Macedonia, Bosnia and Herce- govina, and Montenegro, which recorded the slowest per capita growth rates over that period.[50] It is a situation in which everyone tends to feel resentful: the poorer regions because they are falling behind, and the richer regions because they are required to pour money down a sink of low productivity, where advances are in any case nullified by excess population growth.[51]

The demogenic problems of Yugoslav labor, migration, and de- velopment policies have a certain similarity to those confronting the Soviet Union, and even to those confronting Poland in the 1960s and 1970s, with its high work-force increments and its occasional agonizing between the apparent alternatives of full or rational employment. But the constitutional and structural choices that the Yugoslav regime has made have caused the problems to present themselves in a much more overt and politically, perhaps, more acute form. The Yugoslav economic strategy makes it unlikely that a stage will be reached in the near future in which a pronatalist policy will seem to many an economic necessity. Nor is it likely that through systemic and systematic squandering, labor will become such a scarce resource that the temptation will be felt to bind it to its tasks by increasingly severe labor laws. Thus in Yugoslavia the two main threats to private autonomy posed by the political-

demographic dilemmas of state-socialism simply do not obtain.
Slovenia is the only area of Yugoslavia in which such problems
seem at all relevant. And Slovenia (as subsequent discussion
will illustrate) seems immune to the dangers.

CHAPTER 13

YUGOSLAVIA:
EMIGRATION

Yugoslavia is unique among Socialist states in tolerating emigration. Indeed, for a number of years it not only tolerated emigration but fostered it and planned its socioeconomic development on the implicit assumption that for the foreseeable future, the outflow of surplus labor might continue. Even before the economic reforms of the mid-1960s, the Yugoslav regime was relatively relaxed about admitting to some domestic unemployment and did not strain to sop it up by paternalistic employment policies. It also tolerated, though it did not actively encourage, a certain amount of both economic and noneconomic emigration.

There was some legal noneconomic emigration of national minorities (especially Turks) in the 1950s and early 1960s: between 1953 and 1961 (inclusive) a total of just under 300,000 people were officially recorded as leaving Yugoslavia. Since that time official emigration has topped 10,000 only in one year, and in recent years the registered numbers have been derisory.[1] Even before 1965, however, the official external migration figures were falling short of reality. An estimate for Yugoslavia as a whole gives the shortfall between official and actual net emigration between 1953 and 1961 as averaging somewhere between 12 and 17 thousand yearly.[2]

The vehemence of what was and still is officially termed the "temporary" economic emigration after 1965 appears to have taken the leadership by surprise, however. It had little in the way of a prepared policy to deal with the problem when it arose. At the beginning of 1965, the year after legal economic emigration began, Yugoslavia had still not signed agreements with any recipient countries concerning the legal status and social security of its citizens.[3] Supplementary schooling for migrant children abroad was not or-

175

ganized until 1970.[4] Only two fortnightly publications were being
produced for the emigrants as of 1969.[5] Improvement since has
been only relative, moreover, as later discussion will show.

The initial attitude seems to have been one of passive connivance
coupled with a slight, lingering disapproval of those who left.[6] In
the first years no attempt was made to gather adequate statistics
(and they are still not good). Similarly, little effort was expended
on maintaining contact with the emigrants and seeking to influence
their behavior in the interests of their former country.[7] It was
only after the phenomenon had already attained massive proportions
that official complaisance was disturbed. Even then the response
was lethargic, despite the energetic campaigns of alarm conducted
by scholars and publicists, often moved by fears for the survival
of their own ethnic communities.

The most emphatic public criticism came from the Croats (and
in lesser measure the Slovenes who contributed roughly one fifth
to one third of the total emigration in the earlier years).[8] At first
Croatian anxiety was thinly veiled in the form of a disinterested
concern about Croatia's capacity to contribute to overall Yugoslav
development. Later, in the climactic years 1970-71, it became
more and more openly nationalistic.[9] It should be emphasized
that there was a great deal of foundation for the Croats' anxiety.
The statistics on emigration were and are, as mentioned, quite
inadequate. But it was clear that Croatia's and the Croats' contribution to the outflow was disproportionate. While forming little
more than one fifth of the Yugoslav population, the Croats were
thought as of the late 1960s to be contributing somewhere between
40% and 65% of the emigrants.[10] Moreover, the great bulk of the
emigrants were under the age of 45,[11] so that the demographic effects of their departure, assuming that many of them would never
return, would be twofold. The loss of the workers themselves might
be compounded by the loss of their progeny or their reproductive
capacity.[12] And this was occurring at a time when Croatia's fertility had already dropped well below replacement levels.[13]

The emigration reached a crescendo in 1970-71 (simultaneously,
in other words, with the crescendo in strident nationalism), in which
two years 375,000 workers left the country. By that time, the emigration was ceasing to have any direct connection with employment
levels within Yugoslavia. In 1966-68, when the number employed
in the socialist sector had declined by 96,000, the number of departures for work abroad (as measured by the 1971 Census, admittedly
an underestimate) was 110,000. In 1969-71, while employment

increased by 460,000, the number of departures shot up to 535,000.[14] Altogether, as initial research revealed, the emigration was producing a host of unexpected consequences. Not only were too many leaving, it was the wrong people who were doing so. The more developed republics were, on the whole, supplying most of the emigrants. And increasingly workers were leaving posts in Yugoslavia to seek higher pay and better conditions abroad. One survey suggested that 77% of all emigrants had been employed in Yugoslavia before they left.[15] According to another enquiry, 60% of the emigrants were motivated principally by a desire for higher wages.[16] Skilled workers and specialists with higher education in deficit professions formed a growing proportion of those departing. Among those leaving directly from rural areas, many were abandoning good agricultural land and thereby placing a strain on Yugoslavia's capacity to feed itself. Over half the emigrants who left rural occupations to go abroad came from agriculturally developed areas rather than backward and overpopulated regions. Local agricultural labor shortages were so great that workers were even brought in from across the Romanian border to work farms in the rich agricultural province of Vojvodina.[17] Few seemed to be returning, and those who did seldom brought any new skills home with them[18] or put their accumulated funds to productive use in Yugoslavia. On the other hand, hard-currency remissions from those abroad, after modest beginnings, were forming a valuable and growing item in Yugoslavia's strained balance of payments;[19] and those who were abroad were at least not swelling domestic unemployment still further. There were, in other words, tangible economic benefits to offset the loss of young and expensively trained domestic manpower.

But the demographic, social, ideological, and political implications of the emigration seemed to be almost uniformly disastrous. Demographically, some parts of the country were being denuded. Owing to the separation of families, divorce was widespread among emigrants, and children were frequently neglected.[20] On the ideological plane the whole rationale of socialist self-management seemed called into question, if not positively mocked, by such an explicit and sincere acknowledgement of the superiority of other systems. Two decades of socialist education and upbringing were being abandoned to an onslaught of hostile ideological and political influences. And large numbers of the nation's potential defenders were being lost to the armed forces. Anywhere else in Socialist Europe, any one of these considerations might have been regarded as a decisive argument against further toleration of the emigration.

The remarkable thing is that the Yugoslav authorities remained unmoved by them for so long. Though there was some expansion of governmental activity among the migrants through the consular network and other agencies, such services have never been adequate.[21]

While the emigration continued to be described as "temporary," the leadership did not seem eager to precipitate any return flow. As late as 1971, President Tito was still defending the policy of organized emigration in terms which suggested he saw no prospects of its imminent revision.[22] Shortly thereafter, however, the line began to change,[23] apparently under strong pressure from (among other sources) military opinion. In the Gnjilano speech cited earlier, Tito had not found it necessary to regret the absence of young men of military age. In December 1972, however, he expressed grave concern that the equivalent of "three big armies" were abroad[24] and generally deplored the emigration. In the meantime, the Croatian crisis had come to a head, and the disarray in the Yugoslav party and state had been brought to order by Tito and a minority of senior associates, supported by the only truly federal institution in Yugoslavia, the army, and the organization of Partisan veterans. The inference seems clear that military opinion was strongly influential also in effecting the change in emigration policy that ensued (rather than, say, Croatian nationalist sentiment, which during the same period was being subjected to public obloquy). The army subsequently effected further changes in emigration policy to ensure that young men of military age did not evade service by going abroad.[25]

In addition reference began to be made to the economic losses involved in the emigration, and spokesmen began making statements to the effect that despite the serious employment situation at home, Yugoslavia should be making preparations to encourage its absentee work force to return. Given that there was no apparent way in which any such program could be carried out, or the returnees provided with jobs, the statements seemed more rhetorical than anything.[26] However, toward the end of 1973 Yugoslavia's resolve in the matter was given an unexpected jog by the slump in the Western European economy. Prompted by the oil crisis, successive Western European governments began introducing limitations on the inflow of foreign workers into their countries.[27] In time, as the recession deepened, they began to take measures to reduce the number of Gastarbeiter they already had. Thus without warning (and indeed without even so much as prior consultation) the Yugoslav government found itself suddenly confronted by a small flood of unemployed "returnees" (<u>povratnici</u>). Judging by the desperately reassuring tone of press articles at the time,[28] the alarm felt by both the government and the workers themselves must have been acute. Because of their rash earlier endorsement of a policy of "bringing back" the migrants, the authorities were even suspected by the workers in some instances of having themselves engineered the deportations.[29] Since the turn of 1974, thanks to the recession, the return flow of workers has far outweighed new employment abroad. It is difficult to say precisely how great the net inflow is. The Yugoslavs themselves do not really know, and the estimates given tend to vary. Perhaps the total net inflow for the five years after early 1974 is somewhere in the region of 300,000.[30] Whatever the number, it is certainly greater than even the accelerated expansion of employment of recent years can comfortably accommodate.

The initial remigration policy outlines formulated in 1972-73 were predicated on the assumption that there was no desperate urgency to the task. It was also hoped at that time that the Western governments involved could be induced to cooperate in the enterprise. Basically the intention was to lessen the outflow (and reduce the skill levels) of new emigrants and at the same time increase the inflow of returnees, in particular those with qualifications that were in short supply at home, thereby replacing what was essentially a one-way movement with a "circular flow" of migration.[31] Apart from the additional difficulties this policy would have created on the strained labor market (had it been successful), it is hard to imagine that Western governments and employers would have ever given the scheme their blessing. The Yugoslav authorities appeared to get "rather carried away by the illusion that the countries where most of our citizens were employed would accept our formula of a 'circular flow.'..."[32]

In the event, the recession rendered all these plans totally irrelevant. Once the restrictions had been abruptly and unilaterally imposed, the Yugoslav government was placed in the position of having to redeem its somewhat expansive promises according to a timetable imposed from without. They had now to find work for a potential total of returnees amounting to nearly one quarter of existing extrarural employment within the country. And they had virtually no control over the rate at which those returnees might be propelled back into the country to reclaim the right to work, which their new Constitution (like its predecessor) rashly guarantees them.[33] So far the remigration has been at times (especially in 1974-75) uncomfortably intense, without, however, reaching the torrential proportions of the earlier emigration peak. But it could of course suddenly intensify. The Yugoslav authorities must be continuing to watch Western economic barometers with quite as much anxiety as any of their Western counterparts.

However, the policy response to the emergency situation created by the recession has been surprisingly sluggish. Certain fairly obvious measures to deal with the returnees that have been proposed over and over again since the 1960s[34] have still not been implemented. The reassertion of party supremacy after 1972 notwithstanding, Yugoslavia remains much less monolithic than may sometimes appear to be the case. Though muffled by press controls and euphemism, the struggle between various ethnoregional and ideopolitical interests continues unabated, prolonging and sometimes even paralyzing the decision-making process. Policy regarding the returnees is one of the many areas of decision-making which have suffered in dispatch and coherence as a result. The constitutional upheavals of recent years have undoubtedly made their contribution to this same result. There is, in addition, the difficulty that some of the most effective means available to alleviate the returnee problem raise rather serious dilemmas for hard-line principle, and that at a time when hard-liners have been enjoying something of a renaissance.

The verbal efforts that have been made to absorb the returnees are (and have been for some years) extremely strenuous. One Yugoslav writer has revealed that at the Federal level alone, there had been produced the equivalent of sixty densely covered pages of resolutions on returnee policy between 1971 and 1974.[35] But some organizational steps have also been taken. Yugoslav enterprises are subjected to pressures to take on set quotas of returnees. Some customs and fiscal concessions have been offered to encourage emigrants to mechanize their agricultural holdings or set up tradesmen's establishments. On September 1, 1976, a new customs law came into effect in Yugoslavia which exempts returnees absent for at least two years from paying duty on household goods or tradesmen's equipment up to 15,000 or 25,000 dinars in value, respectively.[36] The taxation concessions under Yugoslav law are largely left to the initiative of local authorities. In consequence they have tended to be sporadic. Attempts to achieve national coordination of communal policies on taxation of private enterprise have evidently been going on for years.[37] But even where a paper unanimity is achieved in some matter affecting the returnees, not all local authorities are evidently ready to cooperate.[38]

What will purportedly be a comprehensive Federal law covering all aspects of economic emigration is currently in preparation.[39] On past performance one must be skeptical about the degree of national uniformity it will produce, even if it is passed.

There are a number of other policies that have been applied or at least canvassed by local or central authorities as means of absorbing the returnees. Thus, for example, emigrants from particular areas have been encouraged to invest through Yugoslav banks in the setting up of new enterprises in their home communes.[40] In exchange they are guaranteed interest on their capital upon its maturing after a certain period, and in the meantime they are offered work in the enterprise their funds have helped to create. It is also hoped that concessions to agriculture may induce more people to remain in that sector and returnees to go back to it rather than seek work in the towns.[41] It is frequently suggested that Yugoslavia's industrial capacity should be utilized more effectively, in particular, that the shift coefficient be raised to provide jobs without additional investment.[42] Proposals have also been voiced that the compulsory retirement age be lowered, and the widespread practice of part-time work for supplementary income be curbed. And there have been attempts made to expand the export of labor to the East and the Third World.[43]

Many of these measures or proposals seem to be at best problematical. Stopping the drift to the cities is difficult in any rapidly developing country, and not less so in Socialist countries, where rural incomes and living standards are well below those of the towns. Calls to increase the utilization of Yugoslavia's industrial capacity never explain why such an obvious step has not already been taken many times over. Part-time work is an endemic feature of Socialist economies. In the Yugoslav case it is a mass phenomenon with its own deeply entrenched vested interests (which, no doubt, have grown in symbiosis with the equally entrenched uravnilovka). It has been estimated that 3 million of the 5 million people employed in the Yugoslav (extrarural) economy take on part-time work to boost their incomes.[44] Overnight abolition of this widely enjoyed privilege scarcely seems practical. And of the proposal to lower the retirement age it has been well said that it would only lead to a different form of concealed unemployment.[45]

Unfortunately the more promising of the policies for economically absorbing the emigrants seem to be the very ones that have evoked the greatest controversy and ideological or other resistance. The tendency to disapprove of emigrants has never been quite ex-

punged from the psyches of Yugoslav decision-makers, and there
is continuing resistance to the idea that they should be given anything that might resemble preferential treatment. To the ideological hard-liner, or the self-made man who has climbed the bureaucratic ladder to success, it must seem particularly repugnant that
"deserters" to capitalism should return with hoards of accumulated
wealth and become "rentiers" in their Socialist homelands. And
some employers and rank-and-file workers may feel similar resentments.[46]

One Yugoslav questionnaire showed that 38% of all emigrants
were hoping to use their earnings to solve their housing problem.[47]
Accordingly, it would seem sensible to use this factor as a means
of drawing their funds back into the Yugoslav economy and providing employment in the construction industry. Yet housing construction continues to flag,[48] and plans to create special opportunities
for emigrants to spend their money on housing run into political
difficulties.[49] Another clearer example of this same kind of dog-
in-the-manger attitude is afforded by the proposals that were actually made in the Federal Assembly to discriminate in employment
policy against returnees who had jobs before leaving Yugoslavia.
This kind of retrospective punitive action may, of course, be a very
good way of ensuring that most of the best people remain abroad.[50]

These jealousies and animosities, both semiofficial and unofficial,
among the home population are reinforced and legitimized by the
circumstance that all proposals to utilize the wealth of the povratnici raise serious problems for the theory and practice of socialist
self-management. If small business undertakings are delivered
increasingly into private hands, individual farming extended and
strengthened, and such alien institutions as capital markets, private investment, etc., tolerated, is there not a danger that all this,
together with the continuing inflow of major Western credits, will
create a strong basis for the reemergence of capitalism? It is no
doubt considerations such as these that have helped to block the
large-scale replication of the Imotski experiment.[51] The new law
on customs has at last been passed, but only after prolonged resistance, it would seem.[52] The 1976 Basic Law on Associated Labor (the so-called "Workers' Constitution") contains provision for
the use of private funds in self-managing enterprises; but it still
remains to be seen to what extent it will succeed in drawing the
capital of returnees and other private citizens into expanding the
Yugoslav economy's employing capacity. So far it appears that
only Slovenia has taken any decisive legislative or other steps to

give full effect to these provisions of federal law.[53]

Thus while official policy is veering toward further exploitation of private initiative and private funds to overcome its medium-term employment difficulties, there appears to be strong and continuing opposition to such a strategy, especially in some regions. The medium-term (five-year) plan to 1980 envisaged an increase of 100,000 in employment in the private sector. This always seemed a utopianly optimistic assessment, recent and proposed reforms notwithstanding. Whatever formal legal provisions and government resolutions may say, for private enterprise to flourish, the mentality which has resisted the reforms for so long must be overcome. The Yugoslav press, however, contains innumerable proofs of its tenacity.[54] Actual employment trends in the private sector over recent years do not inspire confidence either. In 1971, 90,000 were employed there, in 1973, 93,000, and in 1974, 91,000.[55] This seemed scarcely the springboard for a leap forward of over 100% in the next five years. And indeed, by 1977 the figure had only crept up to 96,000.[56] In any case, even if such dramatic improvement is achieved, it will not be enough to avoid massive unemployment developing in at least some areas. The irony of the situation is that (as elsewhere in the Socialist world) the much-deplored stagnation of private trades and services is coupled with an acutely felt need for just such trades and services.[57]

Much of the emigrants' savings continue to stay out of the country in foreign banks. It is vital to Yugoslavia's chances of employing those emigrants at home that incentives be offered to draw their funds back into profitable investment within the country.[58] But the incentives must not only be offered, they must also be accepted and believed in by the emigrants themselves. Changes of political climate or economic strategy would have a disastrous effect on "business confidence." The emigrants thus have a kind of independent bargaining position, a potential pull over their Socialist masters. It would not be surprising if many Yugoslav politicians felt in these circumstances that it would be better if they simply washed their hands of the emigrants. Such sentiments are particularly likely to be felt in those regions which, under the new decentralized arrangements, are least likely to benefit from the influx of either hard currency or manpower.

In addition to expanding the socialist sector by policies of extensive growth and encouraging various forms of private initiative and finance, two other strategies for absorbing the returnees are sometimes advanced: increasing internal mobility of labor between

the less- and more-developed regions of Yugoslavia,[59] and encouraging further foreign investment (by which is usually meant
investment from Western sources, in particular, West Germany).[60]
Both of these may be sound policies in the long term. But in the
short term neither can be much more than palliative. And in each
case there are serious political problems. Internal migration
tends to be resisted by republican and local authorities and may
aggravate interethnic tensions.[61] And any further increase in the
volume of Western credits could endanger the policy of nonalignment, lead to excessive dependence on Western governments and
agencies, damage relations with the Soviet bloc countries, or
raise Yugoslav indebtedness to crippling levels.

Despite the difficulties it appears that the leadership will persist with both of these policies. There is increasing talk of re-
sponding to the growing Western European inclination to take capital to the workers rather than bring the workers to the capital.[62]
It might be sensible if similar thinking were to be applied within
Yugoslavia itself, and capital were to be encouraged to flow to the
areas where the returnees have the most aggravating effect on the
labor market, rather than redirecting workers en masse to the
more developed regions of the country. While it appears to be
felt that Kosovo must be treated as a special case in which outmigration is mandatory,[63] it is likely that official policy may come
in time to prefer flows of capital rather than manpower within
Yugoslavia as well as in Europe. It is now possible for enterprises
to invest directly in enterprises in other republics and thereby
contribute to discharging the quota obligations of its home republic toward the Federal Fund for the Undeveloped Republics and
Provinces. The Slovenian Chamber of Commerce has set up a
permanent delegation in Kosovo to facilitate such dealings. In an
article commenting on this event, it was pointed out that Slovenia
had run into a developmental limit in the form of a shortage of
human resources. "In large organizations one hears increasingly
of intentions to take investments to areas where there are more
people than jobs."[64]

It is not possible to produce either a current assessment of or
future projections for the demographic impact of the emigration.
It is still in a very volatile stage where economic movements in
the West might yet precipitate further landslides in at least one,
if not either, direction. For the moment the Western European
countries (especially Germany and Austria, the two most important
from Yugoslavia's point of view) are planning to further diminish

their migrant worker totals over the next few years.[65] If, on the other hand, a Western economic resurgence ever does take place, or the German "baby bust" of the 1970s starts to affect the labor market, fresh openings may appear. Despite its proclaimed policy of bringing its people back, the Yugoslav government would surely not be too distressed by such a development.

But a more serious obstacle to demographic assessment of the emigration is the fact that emigration statistics have always been and continue to be extremely sketchy. The authorities do not know exactly how many went, nor do they know how many have returned. The 1971 Census data on workers abroad[66] were widely criticized and in any case are now dated. Moreover, no one can predict how many would choose to return if they were given the luxury of a choice. Existing data on emigrant plans and preferences are conflicting and difficult to interpret. Similarly, the information available regarding the present demographic structure of the emigration is not very satisfactory. There is little precise quantitative knowledge about the assimilatory processes to which Yugoslavs abroad are subject. Vital statistics relating to Yugoslav families in emigration are not collected.[67] How many of them have contracted mixed marriages is evidently not known. Nor do there seem to be any overall statistics about knowledge of their native language among the children of the emigrants.

The fragmentary data that do exist on these matters, however, suggest that most of the present "temporary" losses will become permanent. Before the Western European countries adopted their discriminatory measures, actual rates of return were very low.[68] Most of those who have returned since 1974 had only been abroad for short periods. The proportion of long-term absentees is accordingly increasing. This can be strikingly illustrated by the statistics for West Germany, where more than half of all the economic emigrants are concentrated. As of September 1974 only 118,300 of the Yugoslav community in Germany had been there longer than six years, whereas in September 1977 the figure was 363,800.[69] The sex ratio among the emigrants is becoming more balanced, and all kinds of marriages, mixed and otherwise, are becoming more common. This kind of stabilization will obviously encourage people to stay on if they possibly can. Similarly, children born or living with their parents abroad will, with each passing year, become more firmly rooted in their immediate environment, quite possibly binding more reluctant parents in the process. As was remarked earlier, there seem to be no adequate statistics about these children's knowledge of their native languages. But in recent years there have been numerous pessimistic reports on the subject in the Yugoslav press.[70] It would appear that considerably less than one half of the children are reached by the "supplementary classes" (dopunska nastava) organized since 1970 by the Yugoslav authorities. In this, as in so many other spheres, action is greatly hampered by the inability of different republic bodies to reach an agreement. After more than five years of negotiations, a social compact (društveni dogovor) covering the financing of these activities has still to be signed.[71] Church organizations remain more active than official ones in most areas of sociocultural ethnic maintenance.[72] It seems likely, therefore, that as average stays abroad lengthen, the links of both parents and children with their homelands will either weaken or be directed along paths not acceptable to the Yugoslav regime. In either case the result may be a decision to stay abroad. Thus, all in all, as against the trend for some emigrants to return, there is a countervailing tendency for those who do not (and their families) to send down deeper roots in their "temporarily" adopted homelands.

With so many unknowns to deter him, it would be a rash observer who attempted any definitive judgments about the future ethnodemographic reverberations of the Yugoslav emigration. Two further comments can and should be made, however. The first is, paradoxically, that the total diaspora is shrinking only very slowly and, with the smallest change of circumstances, could begin to grow again.[73] For as against the returnees, there are also those dependent family members who are going abroad to join their breadearners. While tightening regulations regarding workers, Western countries have often made attempts to guarantee better living conditions for those of their migrants that they have been prepared to accept. And there has been a secular trend for some years toward increase in the numbers of family dependents joining migrant workers at their place of work.[74] To this factor must be added that of the ongoing fertility of the migrant families.

Given the age structure of the Yugoslav diaspora as revealed by the 1971 Census, it is inevitable that large and growing numbers of children must be being born to Yugoslavs abroad.[75] And as noted earlier, given the trend toward assimilation of these children so often deplored in the Yugoslav press, it is quite likely that the presence of the children abroad may in time deepen the alienation of the parents and strengthen their inclination to remain in their adopted countries.

The second point is that despite the tendency toward a more even ethnic distribution of the emigrants that set in in the last years before 1974, their national composition will never reflect the national composition of Yugoslavia; in other words, some Yugoslav nations will be demographically weakened by the emigration and others (relatively) strengthened. Since 1972 the Yugoslav press has been careful to avoid reference to the ethnic structure of the emigration. To my knowledge no official estimates of the position in this regard have appeared since the 1971 Census figures were published. Their accuracy then was questionable (and questioned).[76] Since that time the ethnic disproportions may have increased. For, as suggested earlier, the returnees, being rejects from sophisticated Western economies, are likely to contain large numbers of the least skilled. Also, residence permits and visas for family members are more readily given to the older, more established immigrants.[77] Again, it is the older migrants who are more likely to be living in family units abroad (with or without Yugoslav spouses). Conversely, it should be remembered that the Albanians and other less-developed ethnic groups had a particularly low rate of female emigration and therefore, presumably, of family formation abroad.[78] All these factors will tend to reinstate or reinforce the earlier trends of ethnic differentiation within the diaspora.

In summary, it seems inevitable that the economic emigration will leave a permanent (and recurring) indentation in the Yugoslav age pyramid; that the contributions of the various ethnic groups to that indentation will be generally speaking in inverse proportion to their employment rates within Yugoslavia; and that differential emigration will aggravate the impact of differential fertility on Yugoslavia's ethnic structure.

CHAPTER 14

YUGOSLAVIA:
ETHNIC RELATIONS

The following discussion will be based on two premises: first, that ethnic numbers in Yugoslav conditions can be to a significant extent converted into political power; and second, that ethnic harmony is unlikely to be achieved in the near or middle future by any process of homogenization or reconciliation. These propositions may need some prior elaboration.

Traditionally, Leninist Socialism[1] has recognized that ethnic groups have a right not only to exist but also to a position of equality in the state. While this principle is often honored in the breach,[2] it is never flatly disavowed. Efforts are usually made to solve the problem of ethnic antagonisms by removing their socioeconomic causes; that is to say, by attempting to iron out the inequalities of economic development or socioeconomic status that are believed to underlie them. Here again, while the socioeconomic equality may not always be in fact achieved, or even honestly striven for, it is usually legitimate for an underprivileged ethnic minority to demand action in that direction.

European Socialist states and societies are generally speaking organized in accordance with, among other principles, the "national key." Most party and government bodies on public display are given an elaborate balance of representatives of different ethnic groups. Great efforts are made to achieve proportionate representation in education, publishing, the professions, the arts, etc. The "socialist" content of the particular activity may betray the interests of the national group in question, but the form is national nonetheless.

Moreover, Socialist control systems, effective for most purposes, are nonetheless ill-equipped to deal with the pervasive, subtle, and extraordinarily tenacious sentiment of ethnic affinity. Georgian or Albanian nationalists may be condemned, but Georgians and Albanians cannot be abolished. Private farmers, craftsmen, traders, or liberal democrats can be prevented from organizing or even permanently erased from the scene; and they can certainly be excluded from joining the party ipso facto. But Georgians and Albanians cannot. Albanianism in itself is not an offense. Thus Socialism positively facilitates a degree of ethnic cohesion, on the one hand, and is powerless to eliminate it, on the other.

In Yugoslavia these factors are particularly relevant. Unlike the Soviet Union, the Yugoslav regime has sought to give genuine content to Marxist-Leninist traditions on nationality policy. Even before 1965, and certainly since, there has been no one dominant ethnic group that can succeed in bending the principles of nationalities policy to its own perceived advantage. The political significance of ethnic numbers in the USSR may well grow in the future, and it may be underestimated in the present. In Yugoslavia that significance has already become overwhelmingly evident. If economic equality, at least in per capita terms, has remained elusive (largely for demographic reasons),[3] political equality has been gaining in reality almost continuously. The main ethnic groups are now accorded almost a veto power over the activities of the federal political organs — certainly in theory and often too in practice.[4] And the "national key" (nacionalni ključ) is being progressively applied to more and more spheres of life.[5] The control system aspires to check only the more extreme chauvinist elements. But it does this at least in some degree in relation to all ethnic groups. Ethnic patriotism and consistent struggle for causes which are socialist in form and ethnic in content has been virtually legitimized through the federal system. The Yugoslav leadership has evidently arrived at the view that the only way to eliminate the perils of nationalist sentiment is to legitimize it and build it deep into the country's political structure. Perhaps, indeed, that "view" should not be seen as the conscious decision of a transcendent, ethnically unaffiliated elite, but rather as the resultant of conflicting ethnic forces both below and within the leadership.

Whatever the long-term success of the federal strategy may prove to be, in the short and medium term it can scarcely be expected to work miracles. For the Yugoslav regime is encumbered with a burdensome legacy of ethnic strife. Interethnic relations began on a sour note when the Yugoslav state was created after World War I and have been in a state of deterioration most of the time since. The Communist Party is virtually the only Yugoslav political party which has ever attracted anything like a nationwide and genuinely multiethnic following. To it too must go the credit for achieving the only period of relative ethnic tranquility in modern Yugoslav history, namely the first twenty years or so after the war — though even that interlude may have owed more to repression than to reconciliation. Be that as it may, in the last decade it has become clear that Yugoslavia has expunged none of its ethnic antagonisms, and that when Tito goes, or the Russians come, the League of Communists may be hard put to it to repeat its remarkable unificatory feat of World War II.

Unfortunately, demographic trends seem likely to inflame the general atmosphere of intolerance and suspicion still further, as well as leading to objectively destabilizing transformations in a number of specific directions. Reconciliation, if it comes at all, is unlikely to forestall the aggravation that demographic trends (together with other developments) are already producing.

Reconciliation is at least a possibility, if a long-term one. Homogenization, on the other hand, seems to be totally out of the question. Curiously, the leadership (unlike its Soviet counterpart) has set its face against developing any kind of supraethnic national identity. The ultimate reason for this difference in approach seems to be that the Russians are a dominant (if perilously maintained) majority, whereas the Serbs are not. While the non-Russian ethnic group in the USSR may see "Soviet man" and "the Soviet people" as Russian notions, there is not a great deal they can do to actively dethrone them. In Yugoslavia, on the other hand, the non-Serbs reached an agreement in effect to resist the notion of "Yugoslav" as a Serbian imposition. And they have succeeded very largely in officially discrediting it. Thus pressures toward homogenization of that kind have become largely a thing of the past. Ethnic particularisms are flourishing in Yugoslavia and, given existing conditions, are likely to go on doing so for a long time to come. They are increasing rather than diminishing.

This should not be taken as meaning that contacts between the ethnic groups are necessarily diminishing or hostility between them increasing. The contacts are increasing, and the hostility may not at the present moment be worsening. But while intermarriage has become a relatively more common phenomenon, intraethnic social interaction remains the norm; and the gulf between Christian and Moslem in particular remains very wide.[6] Quite apart from the possibility that greater social contacts may aggravate rather than relieve tension at a certain stage in development,[7] such contacts as exist are still and will long remain quite insufficient to bring about that ideal state identified by Soviet ideologists as sblizhenie. And in any case, though interethnic mingling is commended by official policy, sblizhenie is not a declared objective.

With these premises and considerations in mind, let us turn to briefly survey Yugoslavia's internal ethnodemographic landscape.

There is a pleasing symmetry about the vital statistics of the Orthodox Serbs and Catholic Croats in recent years.[8] So evenly are they matched, a religiously inclined observer might see in it an ecumenical intervention by extraterrestrial authority. The skeptic might say, on the other hand, that it would take more than absolute parity to satisfy the Serbs and the Croats, and he would, up to a point, be right. The nationalist solipsisms and the mutual antagonism are so deep-rooted that his own nation's low fertility seems far more important to the chauvinist than the fact that his adversaries are identically placed (even if he bothers to apprise himself of the latter circumstance — which he may not). In the heyday of Croatian nationalist demography in 1969-71, many commentators argued that Croatia's demographic problems were the result of machinations by "bureaucratic," "centralist," "statist," or "firm-handite" (čvrstorukaške) forces (for all of which read: Serbian).[9] There were at least two reasons why Croatian demographic comment up to 1971 tended to be more nationalistic than that of the Serbs. First, because their republican party authorities were supporting or at least tolerating spirited nationalistic utterances, whereas the Serbian party leadership was trying to hold its hotheads down. And second, because the Croats in some cases really did have a point. Though Serbian fertility had actually declined faster than Croatian to reach comparable levels, the Croatian emigration rate was much heavier.[10] Thus it seemed to Croats that their situation was much worse, and that if existing emigration patterns persisted, the Croatian population would be decimated, first by the direct loss of the emigrants themselves, and secondarily by the loss of their actual or potential progeny. As mentioned earlier, the 1971 Census came up with an official figure of 672,000 for the number of Yugoslavs "temporarily" working abroad. But all contemporary estimates from other sources suggested the real figure was nearer a million. The Census procedures for enumerating the emigrants and the resident population were severely and cogently criticized in Croatia.[11] The Census estimate of 261,000 ethnic Croats abroad was almost certainly an underestimate. Before the Census result was published, the Croatian media had been making free use of an estimate of half a million Croats abroad. If this were accurate, the number of Croats living and working abroad was approaching half the total number of people then employed in the nonrural economy of the Croatian republic.[12] It was at best uncertain whether very many of them would ever return. As the Croatian media often pointed out in 1969-71, Croatia had the highest emigration rate of any country in Europe.[13] Given its traditionally heavy emigration losses and the stagnation in its population over the 1930s-40s period, this further blow to national strength, pride, and prestige must indeed have seemed almost intolerable. And the indifference of Belgrade statistical and other authorities to this hemorrhaging of the national life blood must have seemed too gross to be without malice. The emigration rate from Serbia was, until the late 1960s, one of the lowest of any region in the country.[14] Had it been as high as Croatia's, it indeed seems unlikely that the policy of fostered emigration would have lasted as long as it did. When in fact the policy was reversed, Serbia's annual emigration rate had probably almost overtaken that of Croatia.

The Croats' main anxieties focus on their traditional adversaries, the Serbs. Their relations with the other two main groups with whom they live in geographical contact, the Moslems and the Slovenians, are rather better. Both have been in some measure allies against the "centralists" of Belgrade, and neither seems to be perceived as a major threat to Croatian interests. There were signs that the pre-1972 Croatian leadership supported the position of the ethnic Moslems who, demographically at least if not also politically, have now become the dominant ethnic group in Bosnia and Hercegovina, thereby supplanting the Serbs. Croats and Moslems in Bosnia and Hercegovina have both had a good deal of experience of pressures to become either Serbs or "Yugoslavs."[15]

An outside observer might suppose that Croat nationalists should be content to accept their own external migration on the basis that they could compensate for it economically and ethnodemographically by accepting migrants in turn from other parts of Yugoslavia and turning them into Croats. While there were strong assimilatory demands being made in Croatia during the height of the nationalist phase, it seems that most Croats would prefer to retain their own people rather than import substitutes.[16] Their attitude is the more understandable inasmuch as Yugoslav official policy stipulates that

all minorities within Yugoslavia should be entitled to special cultural and educational facilities. Thus in time immigrant communities might become a permanent and alien fixture within the Croatian Republic. Though Croatian strength within the Croatian Republic as measured by official statistics had remained unchanged
at about four fifths of the total in recent decades, the 1971 Census
assessment is to a significant extent fictional, since it includes all
Croats living "temporarily" abroad who could be traced by the
census clerks and does not include people from other republics
"temporarily" resident in Croatia. If Croatian emigrants were to
be replaced in a continuous process by peoples from the less-
developed regions, and if these latter peoples were guaranteed the
necessary facilities for maintaining their national identity, the
Croatian grasp on Croatia could be rapidly weakened, the more
rapidly inasmuch as the Croatian birthrate would be far below
that of its immigrant communities. In these circumstances any
Croatian republic authorities are likely to wish to maintain close
control on migratory movements in and out of their territory.

The Slovenians lack the keen anti-Serbian feelings or the tendency to grandiose nationalist illusions that are common among
the Croats. They do not live in close contiguity with any other
Yugoslav peoples apart from the Croats, with whom they share the
Catholic religion and an Austrian past, and with whom, also, their
relations have traditionally been tolerably good. Their tenacious
retention of a separate ethnic identity through long centuries of
Germanic rule, however, seems to have enhanced their national
anxieties as well as their national pride. In any case, despite the
fact that their age-specific fertility has been substantially higher
than Serb or Croat fertility in recent years,[17] they too have engaged latterly in considerable quantities of ethnodemographic soul-
searching. Newspaper stories with titles like "Are We Slovenians
Dying Out?" have been common, suggesting that there is a widespread fear that they may be.[18] Though the Slovenians do not have
any particular bête noire among the other Yugoslav nations, they
do not particularly like any of them either; and for reasons that
are apparent to any Western traveler of normal prejudices who
has taken a quick sampling of each of the Yugoslav regions, they
regard themselves as culturally superior to all of them. Autonomist and separatist sentiments are widespread in Slovenia,[19] and
what most of them would probably prefer would be to have as little
to do with the rest of Yugoslavia as possible.

Slovenian emigration to Europe, though not as heavy as the Croatian, was nonetheless substantial, particularly in the earlier years after 1964.[20] It was natural that the emigration should "begin" from Slovenia, given its greater geographical and cultural proximity to Central Europe. However, like the low natural increase rates that conceal a relatively healthy fertility, this trend was probably imperfectly understood by most Slovenians and, coupled with the very visible arrivals of migrant workers from other and less-developed regions, must have contributed to growing fears that Slovenia would be denuded of its own people and settled by the great unwashed from the remote and primitive hinterlands of Yugoslavia. Though "temporary" emigration from Slovenia was given as 48,000 by the 1971 Census, the real figure, as in the case of Croatia, was probably much higher. One estimate in 1974 placed it in excess of 80,000, while another in mid-1976 put it at 64,000 plus 3,000 in border regions.[21] Simultaneously there are in Slovenia somewhere between 100,000 and 150,000 migrants from elsewhere in Yugoslavia, and the number is presumably growing.[22] None of this, however, finds reflection in official Yugoslav demographic statistics.[23] Even the Slovenian authorities themselves, despite their efficient population registers, do not appear to know exactly how many domestic Gastarbeiter they are sheltering.[24] Whatever the precise figure, by European standards it is huge.[25] And as with Yugoslav workers abroad, it is not known how many of these immigrants want to stay or will stay permanently in Slovenia. It seems likely, however, that a large proportion of them will, if they can.[26] This being so, it is quite possible that Slovenia's ostensibly homogeneous ethnic structure (see Table 28, pp. 293-94) could be significantly altered: by Slovenians staying abroad; by Shiptars, Macedonians, and others remaining in Slovenia; and by second-generation effects in both cases.[27] While it would appear that most of the migrants in Slovenia are for the present single men or men whose families have remained at home, this pattern seems bound to alter in future. For social, ethical, and perhaps political reasons, it is desirable that it should.[28] Large numbers of single men of visibly different cultural standards are a threat to ethnic harmony anywhere. But admitting them to fuller socioeconomic status in Slovenia will offend the prejudiced and also have quite palpable effects on the ethnic composition of the republic's birthrate.

The present state of the Slovenian immigrant community is already a source of grave concern to many native Slovenians. No data have been published, to my knowledge, about the ethnic structure of the immigrants. But evidently many of them are Albanians, who form in most respects — demographically, economically, culturally — a diametrical antithesis to the Slovenians. Meanwhile, Slovenian ladies are locking themselves nervously into their flats,[29] and Slovenian economic analysts are stressing that Slovenia's capacity to take surplus labor from other regions is considerably less than it might appear.[30]

Much of the immigration in the past appears to have been "elemental" and unorganized. Now that the elements of a nationally coordinated internal migration policy are becoming visible, it is possible that Slovenia will be able to secure some restraints on further inflows. But official policy does appear to favor some degree of greater internal mobility at least. Moreover, Slovenia has a continuing and acute labor shortage.[31] And in any case, in Yugoslav conditions it is not always easy to control movements within the country. It is fortunate for the Slovenians that the word "elemental" is the pejorative antonym of "planned" in the Socialist vocabulary and Weltanschauung. This may enable them to devise some means of maintaining a degree of ethnic balance within their republic and to defend the means by which they achieve it.

The other key ethnodemographic problems emerging in Yugoslavia all concern the Moslems or the Shiptars. Accordingly, it will be useful to briefly consider the recent demographic development and future prospects of these two peoples.

Demographic statistics by nationality are very imperfect in Yugoslavia and always have been, particularly so in the case of the main Moslem groups. Census counts, both before and after World War II, have often striven or at least tended to conceal or diminish the presence of these groups, and as a result, it is difficult, if not impossible, to get any clear impression of their development over time.[32] The last census, however, was probably less imperfect than any of its predecessors in this respect. Indeed, it was probably the nearest thing to a free election that the Yugoslav peoples have experienced since the 1920s. Many Moslems who had previously felt it necessary to hide their ethnic affiliations behind one or other of the fig leaves that had been thrust upon them now felt able to display themselves.[33] In the result the Moslem nation suddenly emerged as the strongest single ethnic community in Bosnia and Hercegovina. Their registered numbers also showed a sharp increase in Montenegro[34] and may have done so in Macedonia, were it not for local political pressure against them to identify as anything other than Macedonians.[35] How much of their registered increase in Bosnia and Hercegovina in the postwar period has been due to a change in self-identification and how much to their more favorable fertility and migration patterns would be impossible to assess with precision. However, it can be asserted with confidence that the relative gains of the Moslems have been a real trend and not purely a statistical artefact.

Though the Moslem birthrate is now declining fairly rapidly, it is still substantially higher than that of either the Serbs or the Croats in Bosnia and Hercegovina, so that the relative advantage of the Moslems is bound to go on increasing in the future.[36] It is also, of course, quite likely that more of them remain concealed as "Yugoslavs," or even as Serbs, and that these people too may one day feel emboldened to declare themselves. Very large numbers of Serbs and Croats have left Bosnia and Hercegovina to settle in Serbia and Vojvodina and Croatia respectively in this century. The numbers involved could not be quantified with any worthwhile degree of precision but certainly run into the hundreds of thousands (without the recurring echo effects of transferred fertility).[37] The indications are that this trend is continuing, and that the relative strength of Serbs and Croats will be further diminished as a result. Moreover, while they are the largest of the three main ethnic groups, the Moslems made the smallest contribution to both inter-republic and external emigration from Bosnia and Hercegovina. At least until 1961, the net outflow of Moslems from Bosnia and Hercegovina seems to have been negligible (see Note 32). The 1971 Census results still suggest very modest net migratory outflows of Moslems from Bosnia and Hercegovina to Serbia, Croatia, and Slovenia.[38]

Given the combined effects of all these factors, it seems quite conceivable that at some stage in the future the Moslems will advance from their present 40% of the republic's population to become an absolute majority. In modern times the Serbs have tended to assume that they were the majority nation in Bosnia and Hercegovina. It is possible that this assumption contributed to the decision to colonize Vojvodina with (among other people) Bosnian Serbs after World War II. If so, a serious strategic miscalculation was involved. The hold on Vojvodina was strengthened, but at the cost of demographic dominance in Bosnia. Like the Russians the Serbs do not seem to have the numbers or the demographic or cultural dynamism to cement an empire. It really would appear that the republic of Bosnia and Hercegovina presents a case in which ethnically differentiated trends of fertility and migration have laid the foundations for a transfer of power from one ethnic group to another. Whether that transfer will take place remains, of course, to be seen. Certainly the one-time dominance of the Serb element in the republic party organization has been and is being greatly weakened; and presumably this process may go further yet, as the Serbs are still overrepresented in the party as a whole.[39]

In the late 1970s there has been a tendency for traditional Serb dominance to be reasserted in Bosnia and elsewhere, and for the Moslems' prominence in key political bodies to be reduced, particularly at the federal level. The Moslem premier Bijedić was replaced after his death by a Montenegrin, Djuranović, and a leading Moslem general, Džemil Šarac, was also replaced as secretary of the LCY in the army by a Montenegrin. Serbian-Montenegrin resurgence in top leadership positions in the party and army was strikingly exemplified in 1979 by the naming of Dušan Dragosavac, a Serb, as the ostensibly Croatian replacement for Stane Dolanc, the Slovenian secretary of the LCY Presidium. Even more startling, in some ways, was the move to put the Bosnian Serb Cvijetin Mijatović in the party Presidium as well as the state presidency (where he is the sole representative of his republic). This would have meant that the Bosnian Serbs would have had two representatives in the top party body, the Bosnian Croats one, and the Moslems none. One wonders what kind of political deals could have occurred within the federal leadership to make possible such a gross departure from the "national key." Could it be that the Serbs were being compensated by the tacit complaisance of other groups for their apparently confirmed defeat in Kosovo? Or was it some reckless assertion of sheer political weight and strength? In any event, shortly after Tito's return from a visit to four Arab states, it was announced that the Bosnian Moslem Hamdija Pozderac was to be coopted to the party Presidium. This will presumably involve Mijatović's withdrawal from the Bosnian contingent of three.[40] The Yugoslav Moslems are evidently not without influential friends abroad. Like recent reports that the Romanians are encouraging their tiny Moslem community to visit Mecca, and that an Iranian ayatollah told some Soviet reporters that more respect and freedom should be accorded the USSR's 45 million Moslems,[41] this Bosnian news item may be the first in a swelling dossier.

The position of Bosnia and Hercegovina in the Yugoslav state is crucial. Any partition of Yugoslavia or division of the country into Western "Catholic" and Eastern "Orthodox" (or "capitalist" and "communist") spheres of influence, whether carried out by internal or external agents, would have to find some way of solving the problem of Bosnia and Hercegovina. Both of the main antagonists, the Croats and the Serbs, would probably claim it all, and any division of the spoils would leave both sides aggrieved. Both the Croat and Serb populations of the republic are concentrated to a large extent far away from the heartlands of the metropolitan republic. Bosnia and Hercegovina is inoperable. The emergence of the Moslems as the dominant ethnodemographic group in the area represents a great threat to Serb and Croat chauvinists alike. However, for all that it will place a severe strain on interethnic relations in the republic itself, it does paradoxically at the same time represent a ray of hope for the Yugoslav Federation. Serb and Croat nationalists would never agree about Bosnia and Hercegovina and would be (and are) dissatisfied by any arrangement that is struck. With the Moslems the largest single community there, and possibly one day to become an absolute majority, both are thwarted and their claims to hegemony seem a little less justified and justifiable. Either side might, moreover, find it easier to reconcile itself to a common misfortune than one inflicted on it by the main adversary. Thus a Moslem majority in Bosnia and Hercegovina may strengthen the hand of moderate Serbs and Croats in the republic. And in a post-Tito setting the role of the Moslems as compromise or "neutral" custodians of positions of power at the federal level may also become more significant. Despite the recent decline in Moslem representation at the top, Bijedić's lengthy tenure in the premiership may yet prove to have been a harbinger of such a development.

Outside Bosnia and Hercegovina (apart from the Macedonian communities) the main concentrations of Moslems are in the Sandžak area of Serbia and the adjoining communes over the border in Montenegro, where, until the last census, their relative strength had been almost totally suppressed by official statistics. In several communes they are in a majority, and their overall strength is probably still greater than the most recent data suggest. Draža Mihajlović, the Četnik leader, was apparently planning to somehow dispose of this pocket of Moslem strength;[42] and its strategic significance has probably, for demographic reasons, increased since his time. The once ostensibly homogeneous Montenegrin republic, with its large and growing Moslem and Albanian minorities and its own considerable exodus of Montenegrins (despite their relatively high — though declining — fertility, the absolute number of Montenegrins actually decreased within Montenegro between the last two censuses, mainly due to changes in ethnic self-identification but also due to differential fertility and emigration to Serbia),[43] now

seems much less of an impenetrable fortress than it did formerly.
And any renewed elaboration of what might be described as the
Belgrade-Bar connection within Yugoslav politics could not rejoice
at having in its intestines a wide band of territory that was largely
peopled by an official Yugoslav nation with a republic stronghold
of its own and no particular sympathy for Serbo-Montenegrin interests. If the Moslems did acquire a controlling interest in Bosnia and Hercegovina, in the event of an ugly crisis threatening to
lead to Yugoslavia's disintegration, a humane population exchange
might then be possible that would, among other things, achieve
Mihajlović's objectives. It is a remote possibility, and one may
hope that the contingency should not arise; but it would be even
more remote were a Moslem Bosnia and Hercegovina never to
crystallize.

Albanian fertility is now beginning to fall but is still very high.
For some time now the differential population growth rates between
Shiptar and non-Shiptar populations have been enormous.[44] The
Albanians' share of the total population of Yugoslavia is increasing
rapidly and will continue to do so. In 1971 a group of researchers
published a remarkable set of population projections by republic
(province) and nationality to the year 2030.[45] According to these
projections, by 2030 the Albanians would constitute 16% of the total
population (compared with 4.9% in 1961); and according to one variant of their republican projections, the Kosovo Autonomous Province would number 6,769,000 in 2030, compared with 964,000 in
1961. As Kosovo is already the most densely populated region, the
pressures that would result from anything even remotely approaching such a buildup would obviously be enormous. As the authors
commented in their accompanying text: "What repercussions all
this will have had on earlier ethnic and republican borders, on the
living standards of individual ethnic groups, and on relations between those groups the future will reveal."[46]

The increase in the Moslem population projected by the group
was an unwitting underestimate.[47] Even so, they anticipated that
the combined strength of Moslems and (the largely Mohammedan)
Albanians by 2030 would be 25%. Clearly Yugoslav politics would
be transformed by such a development.

The methodology of the group was faulty and tendentious (no one
in the group appeared to be either an Albanian or a Moslem).[48]
The effect of their methodological procedures was undoubtedly to
inflate the estimated future number of Shiptars. The scientific
wisdom of taking any demographic projections more than thirty

years into the future is in any case extremely dubious. Nonetheless, the projections do serve to bring out the seriousness of the changes that are taking place: both their objective seriousness and the degree of anxiety felt about them by members of the "declining" ethnic groups.

Even without extending projections too far into the future, and even allowing for further and fairly rapid decline in Albanian fertility, it is certain that some major shifts will occur. In Yugoslavia as a whole, for example, it is obvious that the Albanians will overhaul the Slovenians (as the Moslems have already done) and distance their particular rivals, the Macedonians. These developments can be confidently expected within a decade. Let us, therefore, concentrate our attention on that closer perspective and consider the Albanian problem in its concrete regional setting.

First of all, the Albanian hold on the medieval center of Serbian civilization, Kosovo, has now been strengthened to the point where it can no longer really be in doubt. The Serbs have probably never been a majority there in modern times, despite the efforts to colonize the area in this century. And now the fertility scissors and the high emigration of Serbs from the area are ensuring that Albanian dominance will go on increasing by leaps and bounds. At the 1961 Census the Albanians were 69% and the Serbs 24% of the population. By 1971 their respective proportions had become 74% and 18% respectively. The absolute Serbian numbers are stagnating, despite a Serbian birthrate in Kosovo that is well in excess of the Serbian national average.[49] In May 1968 the prominent Serbian author Dobrica Ćosić and the historian Jovan Marjanović were criticized and later dropped from the Serbian Central Committee for raising, among other matters, the question of the Serbian exodus from Kosovo.[50] Both had prior "records" as Serbian nationalists, and it is possible that their expulsion was effectively for an accumulation of offenses, and not just for that particular episode.[51] However, it is easy to see their point of view in some measure, and hard to see, on the other hand, how a situation could have been long maintained in which the nationalist concerns of the largest national group were a grounds for excommunication, while elsewhere the party organs of the smaller republics were in some cases consecrating nationalist arguments as party orthodoxy.

The Serbian decline in Kosovo seems bound to continue until their proportion of the population falls below 10%. Not long ago they were a disproportionately influential one quarter, with much higher representation than that in the party and all other important spheres of life. Now the hold of ethnic Albanians over the local party organization is secure and likely to strengthen further with time. In 1953 Serbs and Albanians made up 38.5% and 46.8% of Kosovo's party membership respectively. In 1978 the figures had become 25.7% and 62.8% respectively.[52]

This remarkable transformation raises the question of how long Kosovo can be held to its present status of Autonomous Province within the Republic of Serbia, and the Albanians to their status of narodnost (as opposed to narod), in the face of local pressures for recognition as a republic and greater autonomy.[53] The reasons for denying them that status are being stripped of their plausibility all the time by the Shiptars' great demographic dynamism. Soon they will be the fourth most numerous ethnic group in Yugoslavia and their province the fourth most populous territorial unit. In this context it is relevant to ask what may be the long-term consequences of the Kosovo authorities' rapprochement with Tirana.[54] It is also highly apposite to the Kosovo question that the Albanians are making similar silent conquests in the adjoining Republic of Macedonia. Let us turn to review the situation there.

In 1961 the Albanians formed 13% of the Macedonian republic's population, while their total numbers in Yugoslavia as a whole were below that of the Macedonians. By 1971 there were 1,310,000 Albanians in Yugoslavia as compared with 1,195,000 Macedonians, and their percentage of the Macedonian republic's population had increased to 17%, while the Macedonian's had declined from 71% to 69%.[55] In the immediate postwar period Macedonian fertility was also very high, but it has now fallen very rapidly to something little above replacement level. Albanian fertility meanwhile remains high, and a period of sharply differential ethnic growth has thus been set in motion. In 1972 there were fewer than twice as many Macedonians born in Macedonia as Albanians: 20,751 Macedonians and 11,323 Albanians. By contrast, the 1971 Census revealed that there were more than five times as many Macedonians as Albanians in the 20-24 age group in the republic (110,746 as against 21,674). Thus within a generation a cohort ratio of more than 5 to 1 will be replaced by one of less than 2 to 1 in schools, on the labor market, and so on.[56] This raises a particularly disturbing prospect in the western communes, including the area around the capital of Skopje. In some of these communes the Albanians form a large majority. Their areas of settlement describe a kind of pincer formation threatening Skopje, in which city they already are a substantial minority.

The Turks of Macedonia, despite considerable emigration to Turkey up until the most recent period, are also displaying great demographic resilience. Over 57,000 of their total of 108,552 in Macedonia in 1971 were under the age of 20. The Turks' absolute numbers declined substantially during the intercensal period 1961-71, but it is likely that their total was overstated in 1961 as a result of Albanians giving their nationality as Turkish in order to facilitate emigration to Turkey. It is not clear how much emigration to Turkey is still going on, but probably not very much. In the period after 1965 Turks from Macedonia would have been more likely to emigrate to Western Europe. Between 1960 and 1966 (inclusive) 42,607 of the registered total of 73,291 official emigrants were headed for Turkey. Since the late 1960s, however, official emigration totals (as opposed to "temporary" departures) have declined. The Turkish government, troubled by its own labor surplus and already reluctantly accepting Turks from Bulgaria, would scarcely be eager to compound its difficulties by accepting more.[57] It seems quite likely that more of them could ultimately be assimilated by the Albanians than by the Macedonians, since they share with the former their Moslem faith and a similar socioeconomic pattern, as well as being concentrated geographically in the same areas.[58]

The Macedonians are thus faced with a serious and (literally) growing national minority problem,[59] one that is complicated by the fact that the "minority" is really an overwhelming majority in the area adjacent to the potentially irredentist country, Albania. Threatened by Bulgarian ambitions under possible Soviet sponsorship from one side, the Macedonians are exposed to an equal or possibly even greater potential pressure from the Albanians in the West. Albania has a somewhat comic-opera standing in the eyes of most students of world affairs. It should, therefore, be recalled, perhaps, that the total population of Albanians in the Balkans is now well in excess of 4 million; that that population is neatly concentrated in and just adjacent to the borders of the Albanian state; and that it can be confidently anticipated that by the end of this century, the total numbers of Albanians will be approaching the present numbers of Bulgarians, Greeks, or Serbs. Other factors may limit (or magnify) its strategic capacity, but the demographic factor seems to be laying the foundation for Albania's ultimate emergence on the Balkan scene as a country of a significance more comparable with that of its neighbors. Both Serbia (or Serbo-Montenegro) and Macedonia are threatened by this foreshadowed development. The Serbs will probably have to accept defeat in Kosovo, indeed perhaps have already done so, up to a point. But the Macedonians are exposed to a greater threat and can scarcely afford any such magnanimity. It is not accidental, to borrow a phrase, that the most resolutely and unapologetically Malthusian demographic commentators in Yugoslavia today are Macedonians.[60]

The distribution of the Albanian minority within the republic makes border adjustments an extremely painful prospect, and one that any Macedonian politician will probably always reject. With their own demographic resources they will be unable to counter the Albanian advance. They are doing all they can to draw emigrant Macedonians back from both East and West, but the numbers involved will be at best helpful, not decisive.[61] Even an effective differential population policy starting to work well immediately would not do more than mitigate the problem, and resettlement schemes could scarcely achieve more. Emigration of the remaining Turks might help slightly, but the numbers of Macedonians available for settlement in their place are necessarily limited. If in this situation Albanian agitation within the Yugoslav Federation for a readjustment of boundaries in favor of Kosovo were ever to gather strength, the Macedonians might conceivably feel pushed in the direction of a flirtation with the Bulgarians, who have a similar problem with Moslem minorities and a similar attitude toward them. Moreover, the Bulgarians have some spare Macedonians (though they are at present pretending not to have) and could in any case serve to provide a powerful counterweight to the Albanians. The only danger, from a Macedonian point of view, would be whether such a counterweight might not be positively crushing.[62] Here again we are looking rather a long way ahead. But that will be what many Macedonians are doing.

Meanwhile the Macedonians, in striking contrast to the seven-times more numerous Serbs, have been rather stern with their national minorities. Before the 1971 Census they announced firmly and repeatedly that none of their Macedonian-speaking Moslems felt any kinship with the newly emergent nation of Yugoslav Moslems; concurrently, the party line in Bosnia and Hercegovina was affirming that absolutely no restrictions were to be placed on the right of those of Moslem ethnocultural origins to so identify themselves.[63] The proportion of the 50,000 or so Macedonian Slavonic Moslems who would wish separate ethnic identity for themselves may or may not be very great.[64] But their repression by the Macedonian authorities is at the very least symptomatic of the latter's ethnodemographic anxieties.[65]

Thus recapitulating the overall picture, we have the Slovenians and Croats with low fertility and severe migratory imbalances and a consequent anxiety about national survival and the future ethnic composition of their republics; bloodless transformations in Bosnia and Hercegovina and the Autonomous Province of Kosovo, both at the expense of the largest Yugoslav nationality, the Serbs; the stirrings of what may some day become a more severe problem in Montenegro; and a crisis situation building in Macedonia. Serbia proper and the Province of the Vojvodina are the only areas in which demographic change — though acutely alarming to many Serbs (and Hungarians) — is not obviously a serious destabilizing influence on the tenuous local calm of ethnic relations.

At the level of the Federation also, serious adjustments will be necessary if conflict is to be avoided in the future. Several of the regional ethnodemographic problems have international implications of great potential gravity.[66] And it seems obvious that as time goes on, either the Moslems and Albanians will be accepted into progressively more equal partnership with the Slavonic "Christians," or trouble will brew. Should the Serbs (with or without Montenegrin cooperation) or the Croats ever choose to defend their threatened ethnonational interests by political or other coercion, the ultimate consequences for Yugoslavia and the world would indeed be difficult to foresee.

CHAPTER 15

YUGOSLAVIA:
IDEOLOGY

In the initial postwar years Yugoslavia took over the entire Soviet ideological corpus with virtually no modification. Even after the break with Stalin in 1948, the Yugoslavs strove for some time to be more doctrinally pure than their excommunicators. The subsequent growth of self-management, nonalignment, and other heresies in the 1950s, however, does not seem to have initially affected the official approach to population questions, which remained orthodoxly Stalinist. Thus in the late 1950s we still find newspaper articles with titles like "We're Living Six Years Longer,"[1] "A Land of Young People,"[2] or "The Dynamism of the Contemporary Yugoslav; Our Population Growing More Strongly All the Time":[3]

Data from the field of vital statistics are encouraging, for they prove that the postwar development and growth of our population are marked by a progressive upsurge.... Yugoslavia belongs to a group of countries of exceptionally high natality, occupying in this respect second place in Europe.[4]

In fact, in the year in which these words were written, three of Yugoslavia's eight republics and provinces already had net reproduction ratios below replacement level (Croatia, Serbia proper, and the Vojvodina).[5] But even when pockets of the "white plague" were perceived and acknowledged to exist, it was held nonetheless that there "diminution of natality and depopulation have remained as a grave legacy (teško nasledje) of the past."[6]

By the early 1960s, however, an awareness was beginning to grow that the old verities were of limited cognitive and practical value. Concern about demographic problems increased. In 1962 an Institute for Demographic Research was established in Belgrade, and early in 1963 there appeared the first issue of a quarterly dem-

205

ographic journal, Stanovništvo. Both of these developments were
explained in terms of "the seriousness and complexity of the present demographic situation."[7] As the old beliefs faded, a more
down-to-earth and empirical approach took their place. Similar
developments occurred at about the same time in some other European Socialist countries and later, to a considerable extent, in the
Soviet Union itself. But the Yugoslavs are probably justified in
claiming that "while the dogmatic approach to problems of population and employment did not bypass our country either, we did free
ourselves of it more quickly and radically than the other socialist
countries."[8]

This proposition needs to be qualified, however. A distinction
has to be drawn between the official approach to domestic and international population problems. Domestically, very little remains
of the old mercantilist and anti-Malthusian attitudes. For international consumption, however, after a phase of neo-Malthusianism
the Yugoslav line is again basically, if moderately, Marxist and
anti-Malthusian. Accordingly our discussion of Yugoslav demographic ideology shall differentiate between these two planes.

Domestically, since the repudiation of the Stalinist law of population under Socialism, it has been accepted that rapid population
growth is neither inevitable in Socialist countries in general nor
in fact actually happening in the Yugoslav case.[9] It is no longer
maintained or implied that there are any important and inherent
differences between demographic processes in socialist and non-
socialist countries. Insofar as pockets of high natural increase
still exist in Yugoslavia, or insofar as the echoes of past natality
booms continue to plague the labor market, it is conceded that this
is not an advantage. Socialism is not held to automatically ensure
full and efficient employment, and the potential conflict between
high employment and low efficiency is an issue that is always more
or less squarely faced. The old mercantilist hostility to emigration has largely vanished, though traces of it do appear at times
in the officially sponsored campaign to draw the economic emigrants of the 1960s and early 1970s back into the fold of Yugoslav
society. Stupendous or exceptional advances in life expectancy are
no longer claimed or expected, and public attention is just as likely
to be focused on increases in mortality in certain male age groups
or on the relatively high rates of infant mortality that still persist
in some parts of the country. In a word, myths have been supplant-
ed by pragmatic good sense.

Official interest in population theory at the domestic level re-

mains low, however. The Stalinist doctrine on population has not
been succeeded by anything either as primitive or as coherent.
And while some demographers seem prepared to explore the void
that has been left,[10] it would not appear that leading party figures
or theorists have any such ambitions. Rather than an official
theory of population, we now have official theories about various
matters pertaining to population. Received views on such questions
as the family, abortion and contraception, sex education, the role
of women in society and the home, or the administration of social
policy have all undergone considerable change in recent years,
but in no case does it appear that numerical demographic concerns
were a decisive factor in determining the direction of change.

Here emigration and employment policies constitute a partial
exception. The reversal on emigration policy after 1972 was to
some extent motivated by demographic concerns — the anxieties
of particular republics and ethnic groups about their shrinking
substance, and of the military about their declining manpower.
Similarly, employment policy in recent years has been more
closely geared to soaking up some of the labor surplus. But in
both cases such action was overdue and politically imperative. No
particular demographic insight or viewpoint was required on the
part of the decision-makers. Nor were their actions justified in
terms of any notions about "socialist" population trends or values.

As in the case of the Soviet Union, it is intriguing to speculate
on whether this relative reticence is due rather to a lack of demographic interest or understanding on the part of the authorities
(and a relegation of demographic matters to a relatively low level
of priority) or to their sense that these issues are so potentially
divisive that it is better to keep them out of ideological discussions and decision-making as far as possible. While demographic
trends and indeed a rubric known as "population policy" now figure
prominently in Yugoslav planning documents,[11] the demographic
element has been largely absent from current political debates
and press reporting on economic problems, regional development
and differentiation, etc. — at least since 1972. Given the density
and passion of the demographic reporting in 1971 (the year both
of the nationalities crisis focused in Croatia and the last census),
this seems to confirm that enforced self-restraint on these issues
is at least an implicit element in the compact struck between regional interests in the aftermath of Tito's crackdown on nationalism in September 1972. It is particularly significant that in recent
years the party daily and weekly, Borba and Kommunist, have con-

tained very few feature articles on demographic problems. Thus the vagueness and implicit nature of domestic population doctrine probably indicates above all a desire by the authorities to maintain an ideological stance broad enough to straddle all Yugoslavia's competing ethnic and regional particularisms. This conclusion is reinforced by a consideration of the official approach to global population problems, as we shall now see.[12]

At the international level, official doctrines on population have been rather more explicit and clear-cut.[13] By the 1960s Yugoslavia was following policies that were clearly divergent from those of Soviet bloc countries and rather more attuned to prevailing sentiment in the leading nonaligned nations, notably Egypt and India. Tito cultivated particularly close relations with Nehru and Nasser, together with whom he formed at one time a kind of Big Three of the nonaligned world. As both Egypt and India were particularly plagued by population pressures, and among the first Third World countries to recognize the fact, it seems likely that Tito and Yugoslavia's conversion to neo-Malthusianism in the 1960s stemmed partly from their influence.

While not sharing Third World neo-Malthusian alarms for domestic purposes, the Yugoslav government, and President Tito personally, became involved with Third World countries and leaders engaged in efforts to make the family planning movement fully respectable and to secure international financial and technical assistance for it. Tito was an original signatory (and the only Socialist signatory) of the Statement by Heads of State on Population issued by the UN Secretary U Thant on December 10, 1966. This document, prepared at the initiative of Mr. John D. Rockefeller of the Population Council, and also signed by, among others, Mrs. Ghandi and President Nasser, was markedly neo-Malthusian in vocabulary and sentiment. After first briefly characterizing the unique character of the modern population explosion, the statement declared, first, that population problems must be treated as "a principal element" in economic management; second, that the right to decide on numbers and spacing of children was a "basic human right"; third, that international peace depended on a solution being found to "the challenge of population growth"; and fourth, that the objective of family planning was the enrichment of human life, not its restriction.[14]

By the time of the Third UN World Population Conference, held in Bucharest in 1974, however, the official Yugoslav position had shifted. In official statements made in connection with the conference, the neo-Malthusian concern and emphasis on international cooperation of the 1966 statement are replaced by anti-Malthusianism and a clear orientation toward the more radical and confrontationist Third World countries.[15] Family planning, while still held to be an inalienable human right, is no longer regarded as having a "principal" role to play in economic development. The central problem, it is maintained, is to achieve a more equitable distribution of wealth within the international community. Population is scarcely mentioned at all, and then only in later paragraphs, in a fading, deprecating inflection. It is suggested that population problems will only be solved when "the root of all evil," the neocolonial system, is radically transformed.[16] There is even a slight tendency to treat the Third World population explosion as a kind of bargaining counter.

The reasons for this marked change of line are, of course, political rather than intellectual. At the time of the 1966 statement, relations between Western neo-Malthusians and Third World governments concerned about domestic population growth rates were just beginning to flourish. Governments and international agencies everywhere seemed to be overcoming their past resistance to the idea of worldwide fertility-control campaigns.[17] Since that time, however, the climate has changed markedly. The Soviet bloc countries, for example, after initially softening their traditional anti-Malthusian stance in the mid-1960s, have tended to revert again toward their hard-line position of the 1950s. China, despite its domestic antinatalism of recent years, vigorously opposes international initiatives in the area of fertility control. And many of the more radical nonaligned Third World countries, including some that are domestically strongly antinatalist, have come increasingly to resent what they see as excessive Western concentration on this issue. These countries prefer to direct their efforts in the international arena toward securing a reordering of priorities away from population programs. Their growing voting strength in international forums is devoted first and foremost to the establishment of a new economic order, to which objective all others are increasingly subordinated. By the time of the Bucharest Population Conference in 1974, many Third World countries were maintaining that the population issue was a red herring, a minor irrelevancy, and should be so regarded even at a conference expressly devoted to population.[18]

A Yugoslav writer has suggested that the reason for the growing discord on international population problems after 1967 lay in changes of policy on the Western side — the increasing insistence by the United States and the World Bank on the preeminent importance of fertility control.[19] Certainly Third World resistance to international initiatives in this area seems to have increased in direct proportion to growing governmental commitment to them in the West. And the attitude of the World Bank and its president, Robert Macnamara, was at least the occasion for sharp debates on the subject in the UN in 1970.[20] But given the relatively small proportion of international aid made available in the form of population programs,[21] and given the strongly Malthusian attitudes taken by many of the resisting governments domestically,[22] it is unlikely that for the international fraternity of "anti-Malthusians," the decisive argument against expanding international population programs is skepticism as to their efficacy. Rather they seem to be motivated by an emotional reaction to "genocidal" pressures, coupled with a shrewd insight that the issue is one that can be converted into political and therefore, perhaps, economic capital in the overall North-South struggle.

Thus it seems very likely that Yugoslavia, long a pillar of the nonaligned movement and still eager to play a leading role in it, was tugged along by the trend of opinion among its Third World associates. And indeed, the interview with the head of the Yugoslav delegation to Bucharest cited above makes it clear that political rather than substantive considerations were paramount. Vratuša speaks with satisfaction of the prestige accruing to Yugoslavia from its participation in the conference[23] and points out that thanks to skilled organization and caucusing, the nonaligned countries were able to "impose"[24] their will on the developed nations. The intellectual disingenuousness of the official line emerged rather clearly in two articles published on the occasion of the Bucharest Conference in the party daily, Borba. The first of them, significantly entitled "Population — a Worry for the World," reproduced a number of statistics on world population growth, food production, etc., and while not neglecting the injustices of the international economic order altogether, emphasized the sui generis nature of the population problem and the gravity of its implications.[25] The second of them, which appeared just a fortnight later, during the conference, was entitled, equally significantly, "A Battle between Rich and Poor" and presented the population problem as being basically a minor aspect and by-product of the unjust international economic order. The tone and vocabulary of the article were martial; the content was oversimplified, political, sloganizing, and quite bereft of any demographic content whatsoever.[26]

It might appear from the foregoing that the Yugoslav ideological position on international population problems has edged back very close to that of the Soviet Union.[27] This is in a sense true. While this trend may reflect in some degree the general shift toward Moscow in the year or two after 1972 (a movement since arrested), it should be emphasized that differences between the Yugoslav and Soviet views on world population problems remain. Yugoslav spokesmen tend to be more moderate in their formulations, more insistent on family planning as a basic human right, and more prepared to give qualified support to international fertility-control programs.[28]

Notwithstanding the gulf that has grown up between their domestic and international ideological attitudes to population problems, one feels reluctant to castigate the Yugoslavs for their opportunism. Given their special political circumstances, cast adrift between the mercies of the Brezhnev and Sonnenfeldt doctrines, they can scarcely be reproached for seeking to maintain those of their international links which seem to offer them some measure of security. Moreover, there is a level at which their domestic and international doctrines are in unity. Both at home and abroad, they maintain that it is the obligation of the more developed to further the growth of the less developed. The new international economic order has its domestic counterpart in the ideological principle of solidarity and the practice of redirecting funds toward the backward regions of the country. At home, as well as abroad, the Yugoslavs proclaim family planning and the knowledge and means essential for its implementation to be basic human rights. And most important of all, both internationally and domestically they consistently adhere to the principle that no pressure should be put on countries or republics (or provinces) with high population growth rates to reduce their natality as a precondition for receiving aid from those better off. This, of course, is a principle which reflects credit on their political prudence as well as on their generosity of spirit. If the federal authorities in Yugoslavia were to put pressure on the Kosovo leadership to slow down the Albanian birthrate or forfeit aid from the Fund for Undeveloped Republics and Regions, the most likely result would be a tidal wave of irredentism quite possibly reaching even the high land of the province's central party organs. But whatever their motives, the Yugoslav counsel of respecting sovereignty, supplying generous development funds, and also supplying the means to fertility control without obtrusive advice on whether, why, or how to use it may still be the wisest available, both for their own purposes and for the world beyond.

Insofar as Yugoslav population doctrines are schizophrenic, they are in any case a faithful reflection of the national makeup. Yugoslavia, as the cliches always have it, is a bridge between East and West, between state-socialism and democracy, between Europe and Asia, between Christendom and Islam, between developed and undeveloped, between rich and poor, between the haves and have-nots. These contrasts have their embodiment within Yugoslavia in the form of sharp regional differentiation. They also find reflection within the loose orthodoxy of the ruling League of Communists and even, at times, within the minds of individual Yugoslav theorists and activists. It is not in the least surprising that while on the one hand struggling to gain admission to the affluent economic elite of Western Europe and North America, Yugoslavia also feels a strong bond of sympathy with the downtrodden and dispossessed of the world. The summary manner in which, for example, Yugoslavia's vital exports of anything ranging from meat to manpower are abruptly curtailed by Western European nations whose economies and polities are infinitely stronger would be quite sufficient explanation on its own for any inconsistencies of self-identification on her part. The needs and problems of the nonaligned and Third World countries seem to make little enough impression on the Western powers. Accordingly, when something arises which does seem to seize their imaginations and make them anxious — namely the population explosion — it is not surprising that the exploders rejoice in the fact, even if the negative consequences of the detonation will be mainly theirs to bear. In this respect one sometimes has the feeling that Yugoslav commentators are almost sorry they do not themselves have a population explosion large enough to excite the apprehension of their more opulent neighbors to the West.[29]

This brief review of Yugoslav ideological pronouncements and attitudes on population questions would be incomplete without some reference to less official strands of thought that obtrude from time to time. It was said earlier that official thinking, particularly at the domestic level, is unsystematic, less than fully coherent, and given only limited prominence in official pronouncements and the media. In any case, despite the greater restrictions of recent years, Yugoslavia is, of course, far more tolerant of heterodoxy than any of the Soviet bloc countries.

The usual theoretical framework of demographic writing in Yugoslavia is vaguely Marxist. But sometimes the Marxist element is totally lacking,[30] and at other times it is a critical Marxism which displays little patience with such of the old orthodoxies as still linger in the Soviet bloc[31] and is equally severe about the inadequacies of official Yugoslav thinking. [32]

But more significantly, there are periodic manifestations of an at times virulent Malthusianism. Since 1972 these outbursts have been relatively infrequent in the popular press, but they are still to be found quite often in scholarly comment and conference proceedings. Predictably, they seem to be concentrated in areas where a dominant ethnic group feels its place threatened by a more fecund minority. As a Macedonian observer (himself somewhat Malthusian) has put it:

The causes of unemployment and underemployment are known. They should be sought simultaneously in inadequate investment and in demographic expansion. In this country, however, a one-sided approach is common which seeks the cause exclusively in either inadequate investment or demographic expansion, depending on whether the researcher comes from our developed or insufficiently developed regions.[33]

The most elaborate and thorough-going Malthusian analysis I have encountered comes from the pen of a Serbian professor of medicine (and former high official) from Bosnia and Hercegovina, where the erstwhile Serb majority has recently melted away.[34] The Malthusians often speak from lofty forums. Thus a Slovenian Malthusian, writing in the party newspaper, draws explicit comparisons between the perils of the world population explosion and the situation in Yugoslavia and issues a transparent warning that diligent and tidy peoples with small families cannot be expected to go on paying for the "irresponsibility" of the overfecund.[35]

Perhaps the most consistently Malthusian of all are the Macedonians, threatened by the demographic and national upsurge of their large Albanian minority.[36] Few Macedonian contributors to demographic discussions fail to make the point in some form or other that high natality is a severe economic burden, and one which can and must be reduced by a vigorous program of enlightenment in the field of fertility control. Thus virtually all of the Macedonian contributors to the Belgrade Conference on Population Policy in 1973 placed great stress on the desirability of checking fertility in order to promote the economic growth of their republic. They seemed to believe that great strides could be taken by educational and propaganda campaigns (contrary to the hard-line Marxist doctrine that development is a prerequisite for fertility control, and that the role of "subjective" factors like family-planning programs can only be at most ancillary). One contributor, for example, wrote that: "Factor analysis has shown that in most cases, natality is independent of the majority of factors associated with social development. This suggests the conclusion that natality is mainly affected by habits, customs and traditions.... Communes with the highest and lowest natality can have the same socioeconomic conditions...."[37]

* * *

Some of the most contentious and divisive issues in the global population debate are reproduced almost exactly within the Yugoslav microcosm. This being so, the task of maintaining some kind of unity of theory and practice is a formidable one. So far the regime is still maintaining its footing on the ideological tightrope.

CHAPTER 16

YUGOSLAVIA:
INTERNATIONAL POLITICS

It has been demonstrated in earlier chapters that the demographic factor is for the most part working to aggravate rather than alleviate Yugoslavia's domestic security problems. Unemployment is continuing to grow and seems likely to go on doing so. Substantial numbers of emigrants are now returning from Western Europe to their homeland, where they may significantly swell the numbers of the unemployed. They may also be returning with some form of political contamination acquired abroad, while beyond the reach and influence of the Yugoslav media and control mechanisms.[1] Above all, the crisscrossing ethnic antagonisms that have bedeviled Yugoslavia's short history are almost all being accentuated or likely to be accentuated by demographic trends.

Yugoslavia's internal security problems are closely bound up with its external problems. In consequence, any discussion of the influence of demographic factors on Yugoslavia's foreign relations is bound to seem rather like a reprise of her domestic population difficulties seen from a slightly different perspective. This is all the more difficult to avoid inasmuch as Yugoslavia's relations with other countries, though often bad, have seldom been quite as bad as her relations with herself. However, the two perspectives are vital complements to one another. The perilous and intractable complexity of Yugoslavia's political-demographic problems only emerges fully when the two are juxtaposed.

At the most general level Yugoslavia's overall economic and political strength might not seem threatened by the course of its demographic development in recent decades. For many years after the war it had one of the highest natural increase rates in Europe, and despite the very low fertility prevailing in some regions of the

country, it still belongs to the upper bracket. With the exception
of Albania, most of its neighbors are growing more slowly, or at
any rate no faster. Romania, a country of comparable size, has
in recent years overtaken Yugoslavia in population, and thanks to
its pronatalist exertions and restrictions on emigration, is now
forging steadily ahead; but Romania is perhaps Yugoslavia's strongest ally in the region, and it is unlikely that many Yugoslavs would
give the matter a second thought.

Economically Yugoslavia has firmly renounced Soviet employment policies, with their depressed wages and productivity, and
there seems little likelihood that she will return to them in the
foreseeable future (though some concessions in the direction of
"excessive" employment may be made during the present phase
of acute unemployment). Its economic performance (unlike that
of many of the other Socialist countries) has not depended crucially
on incremental labor inputs for more than a decade past. Given
this economic development strategy and the problems it entails,
the slump in fertility in most parts of the country after the early
1950s must be seen more as a blessing than a bugbear. In any
case, it is unlikely to affect Yugoslavia's economic strength vis-à-
vis its neighbors.

The massive outflow of young emigrants in the 1960s and 1970s,
on the other hand, must have at least temporarily weakened the
country's defense capabilities. Yet for many years there seems to
have been remarkably little public concern about the matter, not
even among the defense forces. Independent critics of government
policy sometimes referred to the military disadvantages of the emigration, but usually only fleetingly or to complain that no serious
study had yet been made of the problem from that point of view.
The military may have been making representations privately, but
in public they seem to have been remarkably poker-faced until
after 1972. Thus, for example, a 1971 article on the census by an
army colonel scrupulously avoids commenting on either the emigration or the sharp decline in the birthrate that had been occurring
in the years before.[2] When the military did press the issue, in the
early 1970s, their wishes were acceded to, and restrictions were
introduced on young men leaving the country.[3] Now the recession
in Western Europe has eliminated any element of policy option in
the matter. Presumably, with time (if they are given it), the Yugoslav defense forces will be able to progressively repair the numerical indentations they must have suffered through emigration, although as they do so, they will be slightly harassed by dimin-

ishing cohorts of 18-20 year-olds.

It seems curious that the drain of emigration on the country's defense potential was tolerated for so long. It is all the more curious, given the Yugoslav strategic doctrine of total or general national defense (opštenarodna odbrana).[4] This doctrine, which seeks to apply updated lessons from the successful Partisan resistance of World War II to contemporary conditions, postulates that the broadest possible strata of the population should be drawn into active defense operations. This being so, it is all the more desirable that not only those of prime military age but also all adults up to the age of 40 or 45 should be on hand and in training ready for an emergency. Yet it was precisely these groups which were most depleted by the emigration. According to the 1971 Census results, 92% of all workers abroad were under 45, and 53% were under 30. Sixty-nine percent were men. The census undoubtedly underestimates the numbers of older emigrants; but suppose nonetheless we were to take the figures 90% and 50% for under 45 and under 30, respectively, and apply them to the estimated maximum number of "temporary" emigrants of 1.1 million. We then get 990,000 under 45 and 550,000 under 30, of whom some 685,000 and 380,000 respectively would have been men. In 1971 there were 1,950,000 and 4,250,000 men in the age groups 18-29 and 18-44 respectively in Yugoslavia (including those emigrants who were recorded by the census). On this very rough reckoning, as of circa 1973, nearly one sixth of all potential soldiers under 45 and nearly one fifth of all those under 30 must have been out of the country. In the light of this estimate, Tito's comments about "three big armies" (Note 24, Chapter 13) seem to be very restrained.[5]

The doctrine of opštenarodna odbrana also lays great stress on the role of the civilian population in defense against peace-time subversion and in organized and coordinated sabotage activities against any invading forces.[6] This being so it is clearly of crucial importance that the dangers of fifth column operations should be kept to a minimum. The importance of morale is all the greater, given the prominent role assigned by opštenarodna odbrana to territorial defense units manned by nonregular personnel and subject in the first instance to communal and republic political authority. The territorial defense forces, whose institution was a response to republican demands as well as to national strategic considerations, have been assessed by some skeptical outside observers as being a way of equipping the country for future civil war.[7] The task of reabsorbing the returnees into these defense arrangements certainly must be a delicate one.

If, moreover, the Yugoslavs really believe their own intermittent suggestions that aggressive initiatives are to be expected from a Western power, then it is all the stranger that they displayed such equanimity to vast numbers of their citizens being exposed to moral and political danger in West Germany and elsewhere. While their potential ideological backsliders in the West could succumb to political views of either a left- or right-wing type, it is of course possible that both left-wingers and right-wingers and ethnic partisans of all descriptions could be organized to participate in a plan directed from one center. This is a possibility of which the Yugoslavs are very conscious and to which it will be necessary to revert a little later.

Having made these general observations about the demographic factor in Yugoslavia's external relations, let us now look more closely at some of the specific national minority questions involving Yugoslavia and her different neighbors, beginning with the three nonsocialist states among them.

Though there has been a long history of dispute between Yugoslavia and Italy over ethnodemographic issues in the past, most notably and most recently over the question of Trieste, the issue seems, for the time being at least, to have been effectively buried by the Osimo Agreement of 1975.[8] In any case the ethnic minorities remaining on either side are already small and are continuing to decline rapidly thanks to emigration and assimilation.[9] Though Slovenians betray at times a sense of regret about the might-have-beens of the Trieste area, the question seems headed for oblivion, and Slovenian interests are unlikely to persuade future Belgrade governments that it ought to be pursued all out for its own sake.

Relations with Greece have been relatively good, though there is a fundamental conflict in relation to the Slavic Macedonians of Greek Macedonia. Greek governments, the present one included, have never recognized this ethnic group as being in any way distinct, much less as affiliated in any way with Yugoslav Macedonians. The Yugoslav government has not been prepared to accept this view and continues to press gently for acknowledgement of the existence of a Macedonian national minority.[10] Their fervor vis-à-vis Greece, however, is much less than that they display toward Bulgaria on the same question. While the Yugoslavs undoubtedly have ethnographic truth on their side, the political wisdom of their pursuing this issue with Athens is open to question. Given their perilous rivalry with Bulgaria over Macedonia (of which more in a moment),

they can ill afford to alienate the Greeks as well, for in doing so
they may well create a strong common bond between Greece, Bulgaria, and any other interested parties hostile to the further expansion of the Macedonian national idea. If Belgrade is under
pressure from Skopje to recruit reinforcements for that cause (as
seems likely given, among other things, the demographic upheavals
that are occurring), they would probably be well advised to be selective in their support of it. The indications are that they are
conscious of a need to tread warily.

In Austria, according to the 1971 Austrian Census, there were
22,000 Slovenians and 25,000 Croats. The Yugoslav press has been
recalling, however, that in 1846 there were 103,000 Slovenians, and
in 1910 some 44,000 Croats.[11] The continuing decline of Slav numbers and the somewhat heavy-handed assimilationism of the Austrian authorities have been a regular subject for vehement condemnation in the Yugoslav media in recent years.[12] Both the vehemence and the regularity seem rather surprising. Given that the
numbers involved are not great, that some of the assimilation is
probably not artifically induced, and that Yugoslavia has gained
considerable expanses of Austrian territory and rid itself of well
over a million Volksdeutsche as a result of World War II, the
strong reactions of the Yugoslavs seem disproportionate. No doubt
the bitter memories of Germanic occupation are an important element in the situation. Certainly Yugoslav press reporting has given
prominence to the Germanic nationalist excesses involved on the
Austrian side.[13] Prominence has also been given in official comment to what is seen as Austrian backsliding from the 1955 Austrian State Treaty.[14] But perhaps an even better clue to understanding the Yugoslav attitude was provided by a front-page story
in the Belgrade daily Politika, which reported on an obscure and
unofficial UN committee meeting in New York at which there were
signs of cooperation, not to say collusion, between the Austrian,
Bulgarian, and Soviet representatives. The UN committee meeting
in question was concerned with the implementation of the Covenant
on Racial Discrimination. The Austrian and Bulgarian delegates
supported one another against Yugoslavia, and the Soviet delegate
agreed with them both that conducting a census is an internal matter.[15] The Austrian problem is in any case not more than a quasidemographic one. The numbers involved and the apparent direction
of demographic trends must tend to diminish it as time goes on.

Yugoslavia's relations with her Socialist neighbors vary from
sharp hostility, in the case of Bulgaria, through mitigated hostility

(Albania) and mitigated cordiality (Hungary) to more or less whole-hearted cooperation (Romania). The two main factors involved in each case are ethnic entanglements and the relationship with Moscow.

In the case of Yugoslav-Romanian relations, the respective minorities on each side are small (about 0.2 or 0.3% of the population), stagnant or declining, and quite insufficient to form an adequate basis for serious dispute. But in any event, this and other potential causes of tension are submerged beneath the common fear of Soviet intervention. Romania is developing its own strategy of total national defence, and cooperation between her and Yugoslavia will probably continue to grow, at least while the Ceausescu leadership remains in control.

Hungary, despite the keen nationalist and revisionist sentiments of its population, maintains for the most part an outwardly modest demeanor in regard to nationality problems, both within its borders and beyond them. This is true also of the official Hungarian attitude to the large Magyar population in the Yugoslav Vojvodina. A Hungarian census taken during World War II while part of the Vojvodina was under the Horthy regime's administration still managed to suggest that the Hungarians were the largest single ethnic group in the Vojvodina as a whole.[16] Since then Hungarian strength has slipped badly on paper (Yugoslav paper) and undoubtedly has done so also in fact. The large Hungarian minorities in Czechoslovakia and Romania have also, relatively speaking, lost ground since before the war.[17] The current Budapest policy is to accept these discouraging trends in its neighbor states with such overt good grace as it can muster. But there are reasons for supposing that this policy could change in the case of Yugoslavia. It has been noticeable in the past that Moscow sometimes permits Hungary a good deal of leeway in relation to the Hungarian minority in Romania.[18] A similar right may be extended to them in the case of Yugoslavia as well, should Moscow's interests so dictate. Cominformists on trial in Yugoslavia have been accused of maintaining contacts with émigrés in "Moscow, Kiev and Budapest."[19] The Hungarian media have at times been apparently entrusted with special missions that may well be anti-Yugoslav in their implications.[20] And a Belgrade paper has expressed certain reservations and suspicions about the activities of some of its Soviet bloc neighbors (including Hungary) in recruiting students for higher education among the Yugoslav nationalities, often at bargain rates.[21]

But for the most part Hungary (unlike Bulgaria) still seems committed to a policy of maintaining its links with its potential irredenta

by cultivating a conspicuously correct nationalities policy in relation to its own minorities and seeking reciprocity from its neighbors. Given the steady relative decline of the Hungarian population
in the Vojvodina (marked, like Hungarian populations elsewhere,
by low fertility and also inclined to assimilatory losses), it seems
likely that the Vojvodinian problem will continue to diminish naturally. There have been reports that nationalist elements in Serbia
would like to accelerate the Hungarian decline by strengthening
their control over Vojvodina. If they do attempt anything of the
kind, the effects may be counterproductive. But in any case, demographic trends as such are unlikely to aggravate the situation on
either side.

This leaves the two most difficult external ethnodemographic
problems facing the Yugoslav government: the Macedonians and
Bulgarian-Yugoslav relations, and the Shiptars and Yugoslav-
Albanian relations.

The Macedonian problem is not demonstrably demographic inasmuch as there is no way of knowing whether population trends in
the area are ripening the apple of discord. But it does assume
quasidemographic forms and interlocks with related problems
which are strongly demographic in character.

Basically the conflict rests on the fact that the Bulgarians maintain that the Macedonians in Yugoslavia are really Bulgarians,
whereas the Yugoslavs assert the contrary and claim that there
may be anything between 200,000 and 500,000 people in Bulgaria
who would want to identify themselves as Macedonians also.[22] Even
the closest outside observers of these matters feel reluctant to
give unequivocal judgments on the inherent justice of these two
positions.[23] The Bulgarian view at least must be regarded as overstated, however. The Macedonian Republic has been in existence
for thirty years, has developed its own literary language distinct
from Bulgarian (in which language Macedonian nationalists once
wrote), and has presumably succeeded therefore in greatly strengthening such distinct identification as existed before. Power structures develop their own raison d'être and ideological accretions at
the worst of times. There is already a small army of people in the
Macedonian Republic who are in a sense committed and professional
Macedonians, and who would find life difficult and no doubt hazardous in any Bulgarian Macedonia.

There are undoubtedly, at the same time, some Macedonians who
still feel a loyalty to a broader identification with Bulgaria as well
as Macedonia. However, even these people are scarcely likely to

be greatly enamored of Bulgaria's current policy toward its Macedonians. In the immediate postwar period the new Bulgarian communist regime initially recognized a Macedonian national minority
within its borders (at a time when they believed long term cooperation, if not indeed a federal merger with Yugoslavia, was a realistic future possibility). After relations with Yugoslavia deteriorated,
however, they came to regret this decision and have over the past
two decades sought progressively to undo their mistake. This is
in line with their general policy toward their other main national
minorities (the Turks and the Pomaks, or Bulgarian Moslems),
which in recent years has become increasingly oppressive and assimilationist.[24] This is not likely to recommend itself to more
than a minority of Yugoslav Macedonians. The vigor of Bulgarian
policies seems to suggest that they are heedless of whether or not
Yugoslav Macedonians will be alienated by their actions. Presumably, therefore, they believe it will be possible one day to take over
the Yugoslav Macedonians and convert the stubborn among them
into Bulgarians in the same way as they are attempting to deal with
their own recalcitrant Macedonians. The only possible scenario
that seems to make sense of such a policy is a disintegration or
partition of Yugoslavia in which Macedonia were divided between
Bulgaria and a Greater Serbia or other such rump state. This
would evidently have to be under Soviet sponsorship and adjudication. In this context it is interesting that the Skopje party newspaper has referred explicitly to talk in Bulgaria about the forthcoming "falling apart" of Yugoslavia, linking these assertions directly with Bulgaria's Macedonian policy.[25] There is evidently a
Serbian element which would welcome such a resolution, as the
Kekec incident, perhaps, illustrates.[26] After the illegal pro-Soviet
Yugoslav Communist Party held its countercongress in late 1975,
there was a spate of articles in the Yugoslav press hinting very
strongly that an "Informbureauist" underground existed within the
party in many areas of the country, and that too great a liberalism
had been displayed toward it in the past.[27] These strictures were
certainly applicable to, among others, Montenegro and Serbia.

While the Macedonian question is a demographic one in the sense
that successive Bulgarian censuses are an important factor in ostensibly "solving" it from the Bulgarian point of view, while simultaneously aggravating it from the Yugoslav (and no doubt the
Bulgarian Macedonian) point of view, there is no way of determining
in what measure demographic trends in the area are tending to alleviate or exacerbate the conflict. The Bulgarian authorities are

evidently seeking to disperse as well as forcibly assimilate those of their citizens who refuse to renounce their Macedonian identity. What success they are having is something that can only be guessed at, although it is perhaps relevant that the Yugoslav media have been claiming that numerous arrests of Macedonian patriots are still being made in the Pirin Macedonia area.[28] Measures like these suggest that the Bulgarians have a considerable problem on their hands, and that in the event of a conflict, the Yugoslavs would be capable of taking effective subversive countermeasures behind the Bulgarian lines, if time permitted.

Though the demographic factor in the Macedonian question is of uncertain status, there is no mistaking the crucial importance of demographic trends in the area of Albanian settlement in and beyond Albania's borders. Relations between Shiptars and Serbs and Shiptars and Macedonians are like a time bomb placed at the central point of gravity in the Yugoslav structure. If differential fertility trends do indeed light the fuse, the destruction is almost bound to involve other parts of the building.

If, for example, the Albanians were to determinedly seek full republic status (as they have already evinced a desire to do), thus converting the Serbs into a mere ethnic minority in their historic heartlands, or if they were to seek to alter further the balance of linguistic privilege in their area (as they are also showing signs of wanting to do),[29] Serb resistance both within and beyond the province might create acute tension, if not open conflict. It is an issue which would serve eminently to fully unite the Serbs with the Montenegrins. Any such crisis would greatly favor the plans of an aggressor or aggressors from the East. Given the growing numerical strength of Albanians in all walks of life in their own province, however, such conflicts seem difficult to avoid. Kosovo Albanian politicians must maintain their credibility with their constituents, and so they must to some degree reflect the pressure for further change that the steeply mounting cohorts of young educated Albanians are bound to exert on language policy, cadre policy, university admissions policy, etc., etc.

Simultaneously, the Albanians are entering into a parallel stage of development in Western Macedonia. But there they do not yet have any such position of power as they enjoy in Kosovo. Kosovo Albanians may realize that they do not have the strength within the Yugoslav Federation to represent too actively the interests of the Macedonian Albanians. But given the imbalance between demographic and other forms of strength in Western Macedonia,[30] an imbalance which must be resolved by some form of compromise or growing repression in the future, it may not be easy for the Kosovo Albanians (including ranking politicians) to avoid their "responsibilities" in the area. If they were to be involved, the crisis would worsen markedly, as the Serbs and Montenegrins would then almost inevitably be implicated as well. The Federal Yugoslav authorities could not afford to offend any of the key participants in such a dispute. They need to maintain Macedonian loyalties because of the Bulgarian threat (though the Bulgarians' hard-line tactics may give them some leeway there). At the same time, they need to maintain the loyalty of the Yugoslav Albanians, particularly so in view of the danger of a possible Soviet-Albanian rapprochement.[31] And finally, of course, they cannot afford to alienate the sympathies of their largest national group, the Serbs, or the Serbs' better fifteenth, the Montenegrins.

Here again, the Yugoslav regime is balanced on a tightrope, a tightrope that is being tugged at from all directions, in some cases deliberately and maliciously. If the federal authorities recognize the claims of one group, they must antagonize the others. Their general policy is, of course, to support the republic or provincial majorities while seeking to safeguard the interests of the minorities. But how is this policy to be applied to a situation like that in Western Macedonia, where the minority is a local majority of rapidly increasing dimensions, with potential revisionist support both from another unit within Yugoslavia and also from beyond its borders? If the Yugoslavs were to try to appease their Albanian minority by making border adjustments between Kosovo and Macedonia, this would greatly embitter the Macedonians (not to put it any more strongly). Macedonians could hardly fail to see any such adjustments as being the thin edge of the wedge. Having seen the way successive concessions to the Albanians had led to the decline of Serbo-Montenegrin influence in Kosovo, they would be all the more reluctant to contemplate any in their own domain.

Apart from enraging the Macedonians, any such border adjustments would also have the effect of substantially extending the border area between Yugoslavia and Albania that was not only under heavily Albanian settlement but also under (Yugoslav) Albanian control. There is already a considerable degree of rapport between Priština and Tirana. Thus, for example, Kosovo Albanian is being standardized to norms based on southern dialects. This involves considerable difficulties for the northern Albanians of Kosovo. It also involves elimination of many Turkish and Serbian words in northern usage, something which the Kosovo authorities are evidently only too happy to endorse.[32] There has also been a good deal of cooperation in education (provision of textbooks, teacher exchanges, etc.) and economic matters,[33] at times brought to fruition simultaneously with intensified ideological cannonades aimed by Tirana at a forbearing Belgrade. In the light of this asymmetrical pattern of rapprochement, any intervention by the Yugoslav leadership to bring the Macedonian-Kosovo border more in line with ethnic realities might seem like an open invitation to irredentism.[34] The present Yugoslav policy of minimal change in external forms, coupled with flexibility in matters of national rights and local autonomy, is possibly the best available. Nonetheless, one wonders whether it can hold out in a situation where demographic and related socioeconomic forces seem likely to make fundamental change almost inevitable.

In all the circumstances it seems that Yugoslavia has a vested interest in maintaining bad relations with Bulgaria and especially good relations with Albania. Their efforts in this latter direction, however, have not seemed to achieve very much so far. To many Serbs and Montenegrins the hard-line alternative of national repression of the Albanians must seem more attractive, both emotionally and politically, even if it does logically involve better relations with Bulgaria and the USSR.

The Yugoslav nightmare is, of course, diplomatic equivocations notwithstanding, that the Soviet Union will coordinate a three- or four-pronged[35] attack on her national integrity, utilizing Hungarian, Bulgarian, and Albanian territorial revisionism in the process and rewarding them all in some way with the spoils. To do this, it seems to be accepted,[36] some internal crisis in Yugoslavia would have to be precipitated. Unfortunately, the potential causes of such a crisis are present in abundance. In my view the destabilizing demographic growth of the Albanians may be the spark that sets the bonfire ablaze. Since late 1975 Yugoslav anxieties about Kosovo have been particularly apparent. The various enemies of the Yugoslav state and their coordinators may have felt that the moment was propitious: Tito's advanced years, the recent nationalities crisis in Yugoslavia and its precarious solution, the peculiar course of détente, the exceptional dithering of presidential election years, the signs of Western complaisance intimated in the so-called Sonnenfeldt doctrine,[37] etc. Perhaps they are right. Western policy, which seems wedded to defending the indefensible until its indefensibility is proven beyond all doubt, and to repeatedly selling the last scraps of independence of countries that really could benefit from its aid for an undisclosed but apparently modest figure, is unlikely to play any very imposing role in future dénouements, although it may seek to preserve the Adriatic littoral or part of it for its own purposes.[38] These being, apparently, the facts of life, it will be up to Yugoslavia itself to prove its stability and viability under great external and internal pressures.

CHAPTER 17

YUGOSLAVIA:
POPULATION POLICIES[1]

Development of Population Policies
at the Federal Level

It is only in the last fifteen years or so that "population policy" has slowly begun to make its appearance on the Yugoslav scene as an independent area of government concern. The course of development of social and economic policy in the earlier period was often of great relevance to demographic development. But demographic considerations do not appear to have been prominent among the decision-makers' motives.

Indeed, in the first decade and a half of Socialist Yugoslavia, the régime seems to have paid little or no attention to demographic questions. It was mentioned earlier that the factor of population increase was apparently completely overlooked or ignored by the drafters of the First Five-Year Plan in 1948, and that it was only after 1957 that demographic considerations began to be taken into account by planners.[2] For many years the general attitude of authority seems to have been one of blithe confidence that socialism produced high natality, low mortality, and rapid natural increase, that this was a good thing, and that a Socialist state could certainly cope with any temporary difficulties that might arise as a result.[3]

Some Yugoslav commentators still maintain that Yugoslavia does not have a population policy or policies as such. This view is particularly common among family planning activists, who are always at pains to disassociate their movement from any connection with or responsibility for the demographic situation in Yugoslavia. But it is not confined to them. And in fact, in what follows we shall often be considering trends in demographically relevant social policy, irrespective to some extent of whether the decisions in question were made with explicitly demographic objectives in view.

Though the postwar baby boom in Yugoslavia was basically the result of a concentration in time of long-delayed nuptiality and natality, it seems very likely that the social and economic reforms introduced by the new communist authorities made some contribution to it. Postwar reconstruction and the orchestrated euphoria surrounding it, rising employment, land redistribution and resettlement, the provision of basic social welfare benefits, and family allowances in particular[4] — policies such as these were bound to enhance the pronatalist atmosphere, just as they did elsewhere in Eastern Europe. If, however, Socialist socioeconomic programs tended at first to stimulate fertility, their long-term effect seems to have been, in Yugoslavia as elsewhere, to produce fertility decline of a rapidity and scope scarcely equaled in the demographic history of Europe. The summary list of causes of fertility decline in Yugoslavia proposed in Chapter 11 contains several items peculiar to the European Socialist countries, or at least particularly marked in their case, and the effect of these seems to have been far greater in the long term than the pronatalist impact of welfare legislation or the increasingly empty and celebratory anti-Malthusianism of the first two decades or so after the war.

In fact, if actions rather than words are made the basis of one's assessment, it could be argued that by the late 1950s or early 1960s, the régime was beginning to display some antinatalist leanings. After the first postwar years, child allowance benefits stagnated in relation to incomes[5] and were graded regressively by birth order. As of the mid-1960s Yugoslavia was the only country in Europe with a degressive scale of payments for family allowances.[6] Programs for building child-care centers were allowed to lapse. In 1952 the first liberalization of the abortion laws took place, and liberalization of practice followed, culminating in 1960 in further legislative reforms.[7] In the 1950s efforts to popularize contraception began to win official toleration, and by the early 1960s that toleration was starting to grow into approval. The usual view of Yugoslav commentators is that these developments occurred for basically nondemographic reasons.[8] However, presumably by that time the pronatalist ideological predispositions of the authorities must at least have weakened for such things to have been possible. No doubt general attitudes in party and society were changing also. Before the war both abortion and contraceptives had been totally banned in Yugoslavia, and the initial postwar official attitudes un-

doubtedly owed a good deal to general conservative inertia on sexual questions as well as to Marxist doctrines on population.

With the exception of the abortion reforms, it is unlikely that
any of these trends in official policies and attitudes exerted a very
major influence on fertility. Most of the fertility decline was concentrated in the 1950s and was due rather more to the overall socioeconomic modernization that Yugoslav society was undergoing,
the demographic effects of which were sharply silhouetted by the
sudden exhaustion of the postwar compensatory phase. After the
1950s, though some fertility indicators continued to show a decline,
the trend was markedly slower and more differentiated by region.
In fact, by the time the fertility decline began to be generally noticed, it had already almost, if temporarily, arrested itself. It was
not until the early 1960s that alarms began to be publicly expressed
about the demographic situation, and even then, most came from
nonofficial or only semiofficial sources. The first explicit demands
that the government should adopt a population policy seem not to
have been made until the early 1960s.[9] Many of those who made
these demands were particularly concerned about trends in differential fertility and sought action from the authorities that would
even these differences out.[10] But at this stage there was little of
the acerbic and explicit nationalism that later became characteristic of such writing.

During the 1960s the concern of ethnic nationalists about demographic trends grew rapidly. The group which had the greatest
impact on the course of official policy, however, was the family
planners.[11] These were the people who had secured the reforms
of the abortion legislation and the initiation of contraceptive services in the 1950s. In 1963 a Coordinating Committee for Family
Planning was set up within the official Yugoslav women's organization. The rising influence of this body soon became apparent. In
1966, as mentioned earlier in another context, President Tito
signed the Declaration of Heads of State on World Population.[12]
This document asserted that family planning was a basic human
right. As suggested earlier, Tito may have been pushed in this
direction by his association with Nehru and Nasser and other Third
World leaders concerned about population programs. He was undoubtedly under considerable pressure in the same direction domestically. In 1967 the Coordinating Committee for Family Planning became the Federal Council for Family Planning, with participation from bodies outside the women's movement. And in 1968 a
public debate was initiated on the role of family planning in Yugoslav

society. The outcome of the debate, which became at times quite acrimonious, was a victory for the family planners.[13] In 1969 the Yugoslav Federal Assembly enacted a new law on abortion, reconfirming the liberal stance taken by the 1960 legislation.[14] At the same time, it passed a Resolution on Family Planning,[15] which completed the legitimization of the movement and the liberal, humanist philosophy which it espoused.

The resolution reaffirmed the proposition put forward in the 1966 statement that it is a basic human right to be able to plan the size of one's family and the spacing between births. It went on to declare that "society should make it possible for married couples to get information about modern methods of birth control and provide them with adequate means to plan their families."[16] Abortion, though deplored, was given a place in the scheme of things as a method of last resort. And in fact, it was suggested that abortion administration procedures should be made simpler and more humane. The resolution also stressed the importance of proper sex education for the young.

With the swelling emigration of the late 1960s and early 1970s, concern about demographic trends grew even greater, particularly among nationalists anxious about the future of their own peoples. In early 1971, in response to these developments, a Croatian conference on emigration, employment, and population was held in Zagreb, which was described by a reviewer as the first of its kind to have taken place in Yugoslavia.[17] In 1973 a much larger, national conference was held in Belgrade, whose express purpose was said to be to contribute toward the "building of views" about population policy at the federal level. A second major republic conference was held in Slovenia in 1974,[18] and there have since been a number of other meetings of a similar kind dealing with a variety of demographically related topics.

Since 1969 the federal authorities have altered their position on emigration policy and begun to formulate an approach to internal migration policy. They have also given increasing prominence to demographic considerations in official planning documents[19] while maintaining, as it would seem, some restraints on public and parliamentary discussions of population problems. The basic orientation set by the 1969 Resolution on Family Planning, however, has so far not been altered. In 1973, at the initiative of the Federal Council for Family Planning, the Federal Assembly considered the implementation of the 1969 resolution and reaffirmed its general principles, while at the same time calling on all parties involved to im-

prove their performance.[20] In 1974 the family planners scored
another triumph when the new Federal Constitution and all the republic constitutions incorporated a guarantee that "it is a human
right to freely decide about the birth of children."[21] While the final
formulation was less detailed and explicit than some family planners may have hoped[22] (and does contain a proviso about limitations
in the interest of health), it seems to be clear confirmation that in
this area, an official about-face would be difficult to engineer.

In recent years responsibility for most health and social welfare
policies of demographic relevance has passed to the republics and
provinces, and more recently even lower to the communes and other
local agencies. It remains to be seen what patterns of development
will evolve at these levels in the future. The federal authorities,
however, will continue to lay down general principles in most areas
of governmental responsibility. On present indications it seems
likely that republic practice will vary in a multitude of relatively
minor ways, but that sharp divergences on matters of principle
will somehow be prevented. Accordingly, it may be helpful at this
point to spell out in slightly greater detail the federal approach to
population policy as it has emerged since the 1960s.

Federal Population Policy:
The Present Official View

Despite my use of a singular connoting the existence of a unified
and coherent population policy, it is still questionable whether Yugoslavia has a population policy at all. The 1973 Belgrade Conference,
it will be recalled, was devoted explicitly to the creation of such a
policy, and many of the contributors commented on the fact of its
continuing absence.[23] And while the Draft Long-Term Plan published
in 1974 spoke of "population policy" as of a known and established
policy area, the Tenth Congress of the League of Communists held
in the same year did not devote any of its resolutions or documents
to such an entity. In fact the author was told by a reliable source
that an attempt at the congress to establish a party body concerned
specifically with population problems had failed. The Eleventh
Party Congress in 1978 was similarly silent on the subject. Nor
is there any government population commission like the ones now
in existence almost throughout Eastern Europe. Nonetheless I feel
that enough official statements of one kind and another have accumulated for the use of the singular "policy" to be justified, if only to

characterize a certain kind of approach to matters of demographic relevance.

The first point to make about Yugoslav population policy at the federal level is that unlike those of all other European Socialist governments, it is not pronatalist. In fact it explicitly declares itself to be not concerned with the quantitative but rather with the qualitative aspects of human reproduction and demographic development. The central aim of population policy is said to be the humanization of all aspects of reproductive processes. Responsibility for decisions about new life is firmly vested in the parents. In some interpretations even propaganda aimed at encouraging families of a particular size is seen as improper.[24] And quite emphatically there must be no limitation placed on the availability of any reasonably safe means of family limitation, including abortion, though abuse of the latter must be reduced. Moreover, every effort should be made to ensure not only that the means of fertility control are made available, but also that the population is fully informed about all the possibilities that exist. Contraception should be propagated and fully incorporated into the socialized health system.

While the family should be accorded the fullest freedom to make its own procreatory decisions, it should also receive assistance and support from society. Society itself, in any case, has a vital interest in the matter. While laws and regulations providing benefits for the family are latterly a matter for republic and local authorities to determine, the lead given by federal authorities is toward favoring their increase, though again without any apparent demographic motivation.[25]

But while society should provide optimal conditions for family life, it has no right to force people to live together against their wills, either for demographic or any other reasons. Unlike Romania, in other words, Yugoslavia is moving toward further liberalization of its divorce laws. This again is a republic/provincial responsibility; but while there has been significant regional variation in recent family legislation,[26] it does not seem to be open to any republic or province to, for example, formulate restrictive divorce criteria in the hope thereby of encouraging fertility.

Federal documents invariably emphasize the principle of the equality of the sexes. Women are entitled to the fullest participation in social, economic, and political life, and social and population policy must be designed to implement and further their rights. Society must strive to equalize the roles of the sexes and also to humanize the relations between them. Patriarchal dominance and exploitation must be eliminated both in the home and at work. To this end children should be educated to an acceptance of their roles in the new egalitarian family. They should also be given adequate sexual education in school to be able to conduct themselves with decency and responsibility in adult life.

It will have been noticed that the principles outlined so far are not in a sense principles of population policy at all. They might rather be termed "metaprinciples," normative principles within the limits of which population policy objectives must be pursued. As far as demographic objectives in the narrower sense are concerned, federal policy is rather more reticent. It is conceded that very high and very low fertility are not desirable, and that the sharp regional differences that exist at present are not desirable either. The confidence is usually expressed that these differences will be ironed out in due course. No sense of urgency about the matter is ever betrayed, however. This is a development which is to be expected in the next "decades."[27] It is in any case not a matter over which the federal authorities claim direct jurisdiction. Just as decisions concerning family size are left to the parents, decisions about what economic or other measures might be taken to affect demographic indices are left to the republics and lower-level authorities.

As suggested earlier, the effect of the 1974 constitutional reforms was to extend the process of decentralization beyond the republics to the commune, the "interest community" or SIZ (Socijalistička interesna zajednica), the enterprise, and even the Basic Organization of Associated Labor — BOAL (Osnovna organizacija udruženog rada — OOUR). In essence the new system purports to increase the role of the individual worker in all aspects of social life affecting him. Elaborate multitiered representative structures (the SIZ or interesne zajednice) have been established to administer social policy.[28] Most fields of demographic relevance — health, social security, preschool education, housing, and so on — fall under this new system. What the de facto power relations between these new structures and the existing federal, republic, and local party and administrative authorities are remains unclear. However, first indications suggest that as far as efficiency is concerned, they have not wrought an instantaneous revolution: some at least of the areas in question, housing and child-care institutions, for example, continue to suffer relative neglect. There has also been a good deal of criticism of the SIZ for having increased the size and expense of the welfare bureaucracy without achieving any com-

233

pensatory gains. The tone of some of this criticism almost suggests a tax revolt may be brewing.[29] It seems also that the decentralization at which the reforms were ostensibly aimed is to be partially neutralized by the reaching (under centralized party or governmental direction in many cases) of "social compacts" on unified policy guidelines. Nonetheless, decentralization, local diversity, and fissiparation of policy continue to mark the Yugoslav social policy scene, just as they did before the creation of the interest communities.

Lest the above exposition of theory should have inadvertently suggested that Yugoslavia is a humanist paradise, a few additional words should be said about the practice of population policy. Despite the lengthening history and considerable political influence of the family-planning movement in Yugoslavia, fertility control services are in fact still generally on a very low level, particularly in the less-developed republics.[30] Knowledge about contraceptive procedures is weak; apart from coitus interruptus, they are generally not used at all.[31] And the overall level of what the Yugoslavs call "sexual culture" is in most regions rather low. There is an excessive dependence on abortion, especially in the areas of Serbian settlement.[32] Despite the relative ease with which legal abortion is made available, illegal abortion remains widespread, and substantial numbers of deaths from abortions have been reported.[33] Propaganda of less damaging means of fertility control has been quite inadequate, especially in those areas of the country where fertility is highest.[34] It was only after the 1969 Resolution on Family Planning that contraceptives were formally incorporated into public health programs (though they had been introduced in fact in some regions earlier); and even after the legal requirement was passed, practice often lagged far behind.[35] The medical profession has frequently taken a negative, conservative attitude to fertility control;[36] they almost invariably have no training in the field and are often hostile to it, making the experience of women seeking abortion, for example, so unpleasant that many still prefer the lethal attentions of illegal practitioners.

In other spheres of demographically relevant social policy, outside Slovenia at least, the record of the Yugoslav system is not very much more favorable. The housing problems of the country, for example, are in many ways like those of Poland or Czechoslovakia: a chronically acute shortage of urban housing, ineffective deployment of funds that are made available, underfulfillment of housing plans, slow construction,[37] long waiting lists, widespread

incidence of one-room subtenancies,[38] irrational rent and allocation policies in the "socialized" sector,[39] innumerable bureaucratic
restrictions on any self-help initiatives in the area,[40] and so on.
In addition Yugoslavia has some rather distinctive problems of its
own, including spiraling costs and prices in the housing industry,[41]
colossal price variations from commune to commune,[42] and illegal
and often substandard housing in outer city suburbs.[43]

Preschool child-care institutions are also totally inadequate despite female work-force participation rates that are higher than
most in Western Europe (if not as high as some in Eastern Europe).
For a long time this area was entirely neglected. As President
Tito has put it: "We'd started well after the war. Then suddenly
money took over, and everything was looked at purely in terms of
the dinar. The few kindergartens there were were disbanded...."[44]
Since the late 1960s some fresh initiatives are again being taken.
But the starting point is very low, and progress, seemingly, not
always satisfactory.[45] Sexual education has been introduced in
schools in several republics, but in the largest, Serbia, resistance
is evidently continuing.[46] Child allowances and related social service benefits have been increased in recent years, but they are
certainly not on anything like the level that is being maintained in
some of the more emphatically pronatalist countries of Europe.

Yugoslavia's approach to population policy differs sharply from
that of other Socialist countries in several respects. Poland and
the Soviet Union, though markedly less pronatalist than the other
Socialist countries, at least declare themselves to be pronatalist
and are becoming gradually more so. Even by contrast with them,
Yugoslavia is emphatically not pronatalist or mercantilist. There
is far less of what I have termed "econocentrism" in Yugoslav population policy than elsewhere in Socialist Europe. The unequivocal
emphasis on human rights and freedom from administrative restrictions or oppressive propaganda campaigns about "proper" family
models also mark Yugoslavia off from counterpart regimes elsewhere. And the decentralization of population policy-making is,
of course, a feature quite unique among Socialist states.[47]

While the relative liberalism of Soviet population policy seems
curious given the attitude of the present Soviet leadership to other
matters, and seems thereby to suggest that no clear parallel need
necessarily obtain between the overall orientation of a Socialist
regime and its population policy, the Yugoslav case, on the other
hand (like the Hungarian, Romanian, and Polish cases), seems to
confirm that such a parallel indeed does exist, and that the excep-

tional liberalism of Yugoslav population policy is a reflection of the exceptional liberalism of the regime itself (when judged by Socialist standards). Its sustained tolerance of emigration and legal abortion, despite their apparent threat both to the national interest and to powerful ethnic interests within the country, seems to point to a high degree of principled devotion to man-centered ends and means. In population policy Yugoslav protestations of antietatism seem genuinely borne out by the facts on record.

But there are other influences at work, not all of which may be quite so lofty. First and foremost, it is undoubtedly the case that the federal authorities are bound to be resistant to pronatalist and mercantilist arguments as long as they are confronted by labor surpluses and a severe unemployment problem. Though the logical connection between the two policy areas may not be very close, the leadership is likely to react instinctively along the lines of "We don't want more people — we've got more than we can handle already." Thus the draft Long-Term Plan speaks with satisfaction of the projected decline in the rate of population growth over the next decade, saying that it will bring Yugoslav reproduction closer to the type prevailing in "developed countries." The passage in question betrays no sensitivity to the fact that, judged by more analytical measures, Croatia and Serbia had already far outdone "developed countries" in fertility limitation by the end of the 1950s. The plan goes on to declare that this "calming down" of population growth would favor economic and social development.[48]

Moreover, it seems probable (as in the Soviet Union) that top-level interest in and understanding of Yugoslavia's true demographic situation are still not very great. Highly placed politicians do not betray any of the keen awareness of population trends displayed by their colleagues in Hungary, Bulgaria, or Czechoslovakia, for example. And again as in the Soviet case, it seems more than likely that the leadership is hamstrung by the nationalities issue: even if the "Christian" element could agree on the need for vigorous pronatalism (and Serbs and Croats would be likely to suspect one another's motives), they would not wish to exacerbate the already very delicate interrepublic and interethnic relations in the party and the country by taking any strongly centralist and strongly quantitative population policy line. Liberalism and decentralization are, in a sense, the line of least resistance, the only resolution of otherwise irreconcilable contending interests.

The exceptional vigor and strength of the Yugoslav family-planning movement may be in large measure a consequence of some of the factors already mentioned. But it seems that it should also be accorded the status of an independent influence on events. Most of the successive developments in official policy have occurred in response to initiatives stemming from the family planners. As one of the leading Yugoslav demographers has written:

The initiative did not flow from governmental or planning bodies, whom the complexity of demographic-socioeconomic trends completely eluded. . . . Nor were sociopolitical organizations (i.e., the party, the Socialist Alliance, the trade unions, etc.) ready to take up the initiative to seek political solutions for existing demographic problems. In this respect the activities of the Conference for Social Action among Women represented an exception. They made a major contribution to bringing about abortion reform and the attainment of a political attitude to family planning.[49]

As this passage indicates, among the family planners there has been a strong feminist influence. Population policy is regarded in many countries as being a feminine preserve, and this is substantially true in the Yugoslav case as well. Feminine pressures everywhere in the Socialist world (and outside it) tend to be in the direction of humanizing reproduction rather than increasing it, and in Yugoslavia the social and political standing of women may be marginally higher than elsewhere in Eastern Europe. This proposition is undoubtedly less applicable to the less-developed southern regions of the country. But official population policy seems to reflect northern liberalism disproportionately. Perhaps at the grass roots the position of women in the north is not much better than it is in some other parts of Socialist Europe. Certainly press reports of inequality between the sexes and weak participation in social and political life by women are frequent. But at the top, at least, women have been relatively prominent in recent years. Two women have been successively president of the League of Communists of Croatia (Savka Dabčević-Kučar and Milka Planinc), and a woman was for some time secretary of the Serbian party (Latinka Perović).[50] Perhaps all in all it could be said that in Yugoslavia women enjoy sufficient standing in some spheres of the sociopolitical elite to be able to strongly influence certain issues.

It has been suggested that the Yugoslav theory of population policy is both liberally humane and ingeniously well adapted to the country's very difficult political-demographic situation. But quite apart from the deficiencies of practice, there are some serious lacunae and ill-concealed dilemmas in the policy itself. They may be inevitable, but they are there.

To begin with, there is the crucial question of whether and how

decentralization of demographic goal-fixing will achieve the reduction of regional differences to which federal policy is committed.
The Federation has effectively delegated responsibility for this
task to the lower tiers of government while at the same time placing limits on the means they might use to set about it. It has not,
on the other hand, proposed any system for coordinating emergent
republic and provincial policies to achieve the harmonious results
sought. What if the regions with rapidly growing populations, for
example, made no effort to reduce their fertility? What if they
were to decide for tacitly nationalist reasons to pursue pronatalist
policies? And how should the Federation respond if all the regional
authorities do adopt appropriate population policies, but the fertility
scissors still do not close? Federal policy has set a leisurely
timetable for achieving "moderately low" growth everywhere. But
with or without regional cooperation, they may find they have a
problem on their hands that seems to require adjudication impera-
tively and without delay.

In addition to being forced to reconcile conflicting regional trends
or conflicting regional policies, the Federation may also find itself
confronted with the cognate task of reconciling its own or republic
perceptions of the country's socioeconomic and political needs with
wayward macrotrends in parental decision-making. If, for example,
parental sovereignty results in further aggravation of ethnic imbalances, will the Federation continue to defend complete freedom
of choice? Alternatively, if overall fertility were to fall to a level
where it is held to be manifestly too low to sustain further economic
development or the most elementary national defense, should the
Federation then intervene?

Yugoslav theorists have proposed at least two solutions to dilemmas of this kind. One suggestion emphasizes the "happy circumstance" that, as fertility surveys have shown, parents in high fertility areas wish to have fewer children than they in fact have,
whereas those in low-fertility areas wish to have more.[51] But it
is an unstable theoretical structure that rests on a "happy circumstance." What if patterns of parental preference were to alter in
directions adjudged unsuitable by the authorities? In any case
Macura's happy circumstance is not entirely felicitous, since there
remain considerable differences between notions of ideal family
size in different regions and among different ethnic groups.[52]

Another suggestion that has been made is that any potential conflict between national needs and individual decisions will be averted
by the fullest development of self-management. The individual citi-

238

zen will be drawn fully into the making of population policy through
local authorities and "interest communities" and will thereby be
enabled to see how private and public responsibilities should be
matched. In this version the right to family planning should also
be seen as a duty.[53] It is not explained, however, how all individual citizens will gain such a grasp of economic and macrodemographic trends as to be able to judiciously blend their procreatory aspirations with the needs and possibilities of the nation in any given
epoch. What if the economic and educational measures sanctioned
prove unequal to the task of guiding the individual's conscience?
This is, or will be, everywhere a difficult moral problem. In Yugoslavia it is even more difficult than elsewhere because of the ethnic
complication. The glosses of Macura and Tŏmsič do not really provide a solution. But given the problem's quite exceptional delicacy
in Yugoslav conditions, it is understandable that official and even
semiofficial thinking should hold back from trying to solve it until
the last possible moment.

It has been suggested that one of the reasons why federal population policy assumed its present liberal form in Yugoslavia was that
this made it possible to at least shelve if not solve certain intractable domestic political problems. It will, however, be a continuing
problem for federal population policy to contain the different cross-
currents that threaten it. Ethnoregional particularisms are the
most prominent among them.[54] But there are others. The debate
over legal abortion is probably not fully settled. There is likely
to be continuing, if cautiously expressed, opposition to the present
dispensation. The Catholic Church in Croatia and Slovenia has
been a fierce opponent of the legislation. There has been dissatis-
faction expressed in other quarters as well.[55] Obviously it would
be impractical as well as undesirable to have sharply different
criteria in different republics, as women reluctant to avail themselves of the services of nonprofessionals could simply travel to
another region. Reversal of the present liberal policy in all areas
might also fail in its purpose, if that purpose were to strengthen
the relative position of the less fertile majority. Eastern European
experience may suggest that in the early phase of fertility limitation, if abortion is available, it will be preferred to other methods.
Accordingly, reversal of the abortion legislation might have only
slight effects in the north while seriously checking a growing trend
toward family planning in the less-developed regions. Despite the
thorniness of abortion reform and counterreform as population policy, pressures of that kind are probably not easily contained. There

is also an ongoing struggle between defenders of the official orientation, which sees population policy as firmly integrated in social policy and principles, and those who would like to make it an independent and autonomous area of policy with its own objectives and priorities.[56] Finally, mention might be made of those who favor migration as a solution to population pressures and those who believe family planning should be made the answer,[57] and relatedly, the Malthusians and the anti-Malthusians. All of these (and other) issues of principle tend to become tangled up with the existing ethnoregional lines of division so that each reinforces the other. None of them have really been permanently solved by the present federal policy.

Population Policy below the Federal Level

While the federal authorities have to some extent simplified the task of republic authorities in the field of population policy by laying down guidelines that remove certain elements of agonizing choice, they have not solved all their problems for them. As the administration of social and population policy is now decentralized virtually to the level of the BOAL, republic authorities may well encounter many of the problems of coordination and reconciliation that have previously been outlined as facing the Federation, the more so since most of the republics, like the Federation itself, are torn by their own internal regional and ethnic divisions. As in the case of Yugoslavia as a whole, there is generally a strong correlation between regional, ethnic, and developmental factors within the republics. All the republics now have their own regional policies aimed at reducing the economic gap between their more- and less-developed communes. The problems are perhaps most acute in Serbia proper, Montenegro, and Macedonia, though even within Kosovo there are marked regional variations. Leading party officials in Serbia and Montenegro have described the regional development question as "politically very sensitive" and "very complex."[58] From the context it is clear that each had in mind the strongly Moslem Sandžak area that spans the Serbo-Montenegrin border.[59]

In fobbing the more strictly demographic aspects of policy-formation off onto the lower levels, the Federation has freed itself from the difficult task of finding population policies that will be capable of achieving numerical aims. At the same time, of course, it has restricted the lower authorities' range of choice. The republics that would like to increase their fertility are virtually limited to offering various kinds of economic inducements to achieve their objective. While they may approve of the kinds of policies involved as a matter of principle (generous child allowances, maternity leave and benefits, extensive networks of child-care centers, etc.), it may not be within their economic means to provide all these things within the foreseeable future. Slovenia is the only republic that is sufficiently well placed to easily afford extensive programs of this kind, and its fertility is in fact well above that of Serbia or Croatia and has been for many years. Serbs and Croats may, therefore, feel that the ethical guidelines laid down by the Federation discriminate against them.

Numerous policy problems and dilemmas await the republic authorities, some of them strongly ethnoregional in coloration, and some of them more universal. For example, should child-care centers be built to enable mothers to participate fully in public life, or is it economically, socially, and educationally preferable that women should rear their children themselves for at least the first years of their life?[60] If pronatalist inducements are offered for higher-order children, how steeply progressive should they be? Should a means test be applied for family benefits, and if so from what level? Should special efforts be made to encourage the fertility of any particular categories of the population (say, those whose fertility is lowest, or those whose rearing performance seems best)? It will not be possible to go into all of these questions here. Rather I shall restrict myself to saying something about republic and provincial differentiation of natalist policy.

Decentralization of child allowance payments has been in force in Yugoslavia since 1967 in the case of republics and 1969 in the case of the autonomous provinces.[61] In that time there has emerged a definite tendency toward the payment of higher benefits in the wealthier and less fertile regions and lower benefits in the poorer and more fertile regions.[62] However, the differences are still not spectacular and appear, if anything, to be in relative decline. They may reflect relative capacities to pay more than differences in degree of pronatalist ambition. There is a tendency for child allowance increases to follow inflation in a fairly automatic fashion in one republic after another, and there are, in fact, signs of central policy direction in this area.[63] Moreover, a means test is applied, and payments are graduated by parental income and also (degressively) by birth order. This latter feature is virtually unique among the Socialist countries. All of this suggests that the orientation is more to social policy than to pronatalist population policy. This impression is borne out by the language of the sparse press reports on the subject, which very seldom contain pronatalist accents.[64]

Income tax concessions for dependent family members are also granted in varying amounts by the different republic and provincial authorities (and may be varied by communal authorities as well). But it would seem that differences by republic are not as great as those between communes,[65] and therefore that they do not reflect any obvious division between pro- and antinatalist regional authorities.[66] In any case, only a relatively small proportion of income earners are involved, since the taxable minimum even before concessions are allowed for dependents is customarily twice the average annual income for that republic or province.

The more basic income tax (or "contribution" — doprinos — as the jargon of self-management euphemistically terms it) paid by Yugoslav wage earners is now fissiparated into a multitude of republic, communal, and other local or special deductions which vary in bewildering fashion from one commune to another. Thus in Titovo Užice workers pay twenty-six (sic) different "contributions," in Belgrade twenty-four, in Zagreb sixteen and in Skopje thirteen.[67] These deductions may even vary quite substantially from one enterprise to another. While enterprises are usually bound by higher authority to observe certain principles when determining their own allocatory procedures in such matters, reports of evasion are not infrequent. Thus, for example, a Belgrade enterprise was said to have introduced a system of housing allocation that would have required an Albanian worker with the firm to have either 800 children or, alternatively, only 224 children but 100 years' service to qualify for a flat.[68]

It is the doprinosi which finance the various spheres of social activity and social security that are potentially of the greatest demographic relevance: housing, health, child-care, social security, etc. The politics of these allocations under the new constitutional arrangements are still somewhat obscure. But given the immense local variation that exists, it would probably be safe to say that there are few signs of the emergence of clearly and systematically elaborated republic fiscal policies, much less programs of action aimed at achieving palpable, numerical demographic goals. Advocates of vigorous republic population policies, though less prominent than in the period before 1972, still make their voices heard from time to time in the press. But for the most part they seem to be back in the political wilderness. As at the federal level, the

family planners and the social policy lobby seem to have relatively
better access to authority.

And again as at the federal level, this is probably due to some
extent to continuing noncomprehension of demographic facts by
political elites and a reluctance to grasp sharp ethnic nettles. It
may also have something to do with disapproval by the center of
vociferously nationalist population policies being pursued by the
republics or provinces.

By making family planning a national dogma and by specifying
that abortion is to be regarded as a legitimate (if highly undesirable) form of fertility control, the federal authorities have, as
noted earlier, largely precluded the republics and provinces from
manipulating either as tools of population policy. There are some
variations in the republic abortion laws that have been drafted since
the constitutional amendments made this an area of exclusive republic responsibility. However, the same amendments included
the enshrining of the right to family planning. The variations have
accordingly been inevitably limited in scope and do not have any
demographic significance.[69] Levels of contraceptive practice differ greatly from republic to republic,[70] and there is some room
therefore for the less-developed regions to apply antinatalist policies by vigorously pursuing family planning campaigns. Calls for
such action have certainly been made, notably in Macedonia,[71] and
there is evidence that differentiated republic family-planning policies have begun to be applied.[72] Of course, some republic authorities would like to pursue antinatalist policies in some parts of their
territory and pronatalist policies elsewhere.[73] The decentralization of the Yugoslav system seems to give them a way of doing so.
However, to achieve this they might have to secure the cooperation
of the local populations concerned or, alternatively, succeed in
manipulating ostensibly autonomous self-managing decisions by
local agencies. Neither course of action would be without its difficulties. All the major national groups have centers of power
either within Yugoslavia or beyond its borders. Virtually the only
significant minority group that could be proceeded against with
relative impunity in such matters would be the Gypsies.[74]

The development of republic and provincial population policies
has been little studied either in or outside of Yugoslavia to date.
To do so would be a formidable task, given the complexity, obscu-
rity, and at times inscrutability of the material. I have not made
any systematic attempt to do so myself. It may, however, be worth
offering one's impressions of how overall policy trends are shaping

in the different units, simply on the basis of the evidence that is
more or less readily available. The task is all the more difficult
in that at the republic as at the federal level, "Yugoslav legislation...has been consistently neutral toward demographic phenomena. No direct population policy, either pronatalist or antinatalist,
has so far been made explicit in law or statutory regulations."[75]

   Slovenia and Croatia seem to be talking most about the need for
a pronatalist policy[76] and also taking the most vigorous steps toward implementing one. Croatia was the first republic to introduce the extended maternity leave for working mothers, for example,[77] and Slovenia is paying more generous child allowances
than any other republic. While in both republics there are Catholics and nationalists who would be only too happy to adopt "administrative measures" to increase the birthrate, the liberal, economic
approach to population policy seems more securely established
there than anywhere else.

   Serbia, despite the fact that its ethnodemographic interests are
as much threatened as those of either the Slovenians or the Croa-
tians, seems strangely sluggish in its response. Child welfare
services in Serbia proper are not apparently advancing very rapidly, and the press virtually never reports on the need for an active population policy, despite the fact that Serbian fertility is the
lowest in the country.[78]

   Serbia is well behind Slovenia and even Croatia in the provision
of preschool care centers. As of 1970 only 5.3% of children aged
3-6 in Serbia proper were in kindergartens, compared with 8.5%
in Croatia, 15.2% in Slovenia, and 24.7% in Vojvodina.[79] Since then
there has been improvement, but probably not in relative terms.
Of Serbia's 212 child-care institutions in 1975, 163 were in Belgrade; thirty communes had none at all.[80] A press article in 1973
suggested that at that time, family allowances were in many cases
simply not being paid in Serbia.[81] In 1976 a rapporteur to the Serbian parliament declared that "the average rate of taxation for
child welfare (in Serbia) has been falling since 1971. Only last
year a large number of communal child welfare communities in
our republic reduced their rates...." The speaker went on to say
that more would do so in 1976, and that plans for the next five years
revealed a further expected relative decline.[82] The Serbian lag
continues. Despite it the authorities are still reluctant to accept
the Slovenian system of private crèches run by varuške.[83] There
are signs that illiberal solutions to the fertility problem have special appeal in Serbia; but since they are not at present an available

option, Serbian inactivity in other respects is all the more strange.

There seem to be more traces of pronatalist thinking in official circles in the Vojvodina than in Serbia proper.[84] Because of its age structure, Vojvodina's crude birthrate is markedly lower than Serbia's, and this may help to explain the greater alarms there. Among the less-developed regions there seems to be a general disposition to limit expenditures that might have a pronatalist impact; but with the possible exception of Macedonia, no very vigorous antinatalist campaigns seem to be conducted. It would be interesting to know just exactly to what extent and in what ways the Macedonian authorities are seeking to implement the innumerable demands made by ethnic Macedonians that a differentiated population policy be put into effect within the republic. There is some evidence to suggest that they are doing so in the sphere of family planning at least, and that the program is meeting with hostility on the part of the Albanian population.[85]

The Kosovo authorities, on the other hand, are not to my knowledge vigorously pursuing antinatalism. The more recent increases in the child allowance there are quite generous (more so, at times, than concurrent increases elsewhere).[86] It is possible that the Kosovo leadership shares the belief of its compatriots in Tirana that vigorous population growth is essential to national (ethnic) security.[87]

The Montenegrins also need to conduct a differentiated policy; and it is possible that they are now trying to do so, though as of 1973 little was being done in the field of fertility control, at least.[88] The decline in child allowance payments in Montenegro after 1970 (see Table 32, p. 301) may conceivably have reflected a punitive policy aimed against high fertility, but it seems unlikely. Like most other republics, Montenegro has a means test for child allowances and pays higher sums to lower-income families.[89] This would presumably favor the most fertile Albanians and Moslems in the less-developed communes.

But irrespective of the present or future direction of republic and provincial policies, the political problems, dilemmas, and conflicts inherent in the Yugoslav demographic situation are unlikely to be rapidly alleviated in the decades that lie ahead. They will rather become worse.

The efficacy of population policies in either increasing or reducing fertility is in itself somewhat uncertain. Some Eastern European countries, it is true, are currently achieving considerable apparent success with their pronatalist policies. In Czechoslovakia, Hungary, and Romania, both natality and fertility have undoubtedly been raised. But it remains to be seen to what extent these are long-term or short-term effects. And in any case they have been achieved by a combination of measures most of which are not open to Yugoslav republic authorities. Thus Romania, for example, abruptly delegalized abortion and banned the import and free sale of contraceptives. Czechoslovakia, being a relatively advanced economy, has been able to afford to introduce generous economic inducements to motherhood. And all are able to mount elaborate and orchestrated propaganda campaigns on behalf of the family model they deem nationally desirable. Virtually none of these approaches seem open to the Yugoslav republics at present.

But even if Croatia, Serbia, Vojvodina, and Slovenia were to institute successful pronatalist policies, Macedonia, Montenegro, and Bosnia and Hercegovina appropriately differentiated programs, and Kosovo a family-planning campaign of unprecedented intensity, it is unlikely that this in itself would mitigate the ethnodemographic confrontations already in gestation. The age structures of the different ethnic populations have been so sharply differentiated by their recent demographic histories that even if inherent fertility levels were to be relatively quickly brought to parity, differences in natural growth rates would persevere for some decades beyond that time. As in the case of the Soviet Union, the time when the dominant ethnic groups could have sought by policy measures to significantly modify the trends we are now witnessing is buried well in the past. Present actions cannot undo present trends. They can only serve — perhaps — to alleviate future trends and, more probably, to ease present neuroses. The only real solutions (short of political or other violence) lie in accommodation and compromise, acceptance of change, and imaginative response to it.

PART FIVE

SOME GENERALIZATIONS AND CONCLUSIONS

CHAPTER 18

SOME GENERALIZATIONS
AND CONCLUSIONS

In some important respects, it was pointed out earlier, the cases
of the USSR, Poland, and Yugoslavia deviate from the general pattern of demographic politics in Socialist Europe. They are, perhaps, if we exclude the anomalous Albania, the three least "typical"
of all. The USSR and Yugoslavia are far more ethnically diverse
than any other country in the group; Poland is now far less so. All
three are markedly less pronatalist than the others. Yugoslavia,
with its labor surplus, its toleration of mass emigration, its decentralized social policy administration, and its strong commitment to nonmercantilist values, is altogether an exceptional case.
While pragmatic considerations preclude even the most cursory
of discussions of the political-demographic problems of the other
Socialist countries, individually an overall survey of the entire
area may help to identify and locate the positions of our three case
studies more precisely.

Generally speaking, in the present work five main spheres of
interaction between demographic trends and politics have been
distinguished: (a) labor supply and economic policy; (b) ethnic relations; (c) ideology; (d) international politics; and (e) population
policies and policy-making. More prominence has been accorded
domestic than international implications, and particular attention
has been devoted to (b) and (e). The same pattern of emphasis will
be repeated again in these concluding remarks.

Economic Policy

In the area of economic policy, the crucial problem raised (or
apparently raised) by population trends is that of labor supply.

249

Some Generalizations and Conclusions

Soviet-style economies are extremely profligate with resources, human resources included. Labor (like capital) has traditionally been cheap and, relatively speaking, still is. There are also strong reasons inherent in the annual and five-year planning systems for hoarding materials, human materials again included. Enterprises thus have a vested interest in maintaining more people on their staff than they need. And since till recently there has always been an abundant supply of labor (based more on mobilization of women and peasants than on high birthrates in the preceding generation but on the latter also, to some extent), there have been few pressures at the macroeconomic level to strive for efficient and sparing use of labor. Now, suddenly, the situation has changed or is changing almost everywhere. Planners and governments are finding themselves having to apportion carefully what they have traditionally tended to treat as one of nature's limitless bounties. Although the causes of this situation are not primarily demographic, the dramatic "disappearance" of labor reserves has the effect of concentrating the minds of the authorities on demographic issues.

In East Germany and the Czech lands, labor reserves have been virtually exhausted for some time past. In both cases earlier trends in natality and postwar migration played an important role in bringing this situation about. In the USSR and Poland the stage of exhaustion has not yet quite been reached, but labor shortages are widespread and will become more so in the future. Hungary's labor reserves are apparently now on the verge of exhaustion. Even in less-developed countries like Romania and Bulgaria, concern about diminishing labor resources has become very marked, forcing the regime to adopt such expedients as thinning out white-collar personnel, imposing labor discipline on school-leavers and graduates, inducing pensioners to remain at work, etc.

The labor situation in agriculture is usually worse than that in industry. Though considerable proportions of the population are still engaged in agriculture in the less-advanced countries (i.e., all those other than East Germany and Czechoslovakia), in most cases the labor force is heavily feminized and ageing and lacking in skills and modern equipment, so that it is often necessary to draft urban labor or the army during seasonal peaks. At the same time, many regimes are taking measures to limit further rural-urban migration.

Although the overall trend is toward increasing scarcity of labor, there have also been periods and regions in which demographic fluctuations (as well as other causes) have brought about a certain embarrassment of riches. Soviet ideology holds, it will be recalled, that unemployment is a purely capitalist phenomenon. Stalin abolished it by proclamation in the 1930s, and unlike some of his other victims, it has not yet been rehabilitated. But there are times when Socialist states could make good use of some respectable notion of unemployment. In Yugoslavia in the last decade and a half (particularly after the efficiency-oriented reforms of 1965), unemployment and permitted economic emigration have been rife simultaneously, and Stalinist employment doctrines have long since been jettisoned. Elsewhere unemployment is denied to exist and often quite effectively concealed by inefficient production. But in the areas of rapid population growth, concealment is not always possible and will become less so as ever larger cohorts of school-leavers of increasingly urban training and orientation add to the accumulated clogging of the labor market. This is particularly true of those parts of the USSR and Yugoslavia where natural increase rates have been running at Third World levels over the last two or three decades.

The prominence of economic, particularly labor force, considerations in demographic debate and policy-making reflects certain characteristic features of Socialist society: its econocentrism, its increasingly technocratic outlook and values, its similarity to a gigantic corporation (unfettered by company law), and its strong orientation to the objectives of physical economic growth. The significance of the growing labor shortages in the population policy context is that pronatalist views are thereby reinforced. As the labor shortages increase and are sharply aggravated by the fertility decline of the late fifties and early sixties, it is possible that they may become the catalyst of Eastern Europe's long-awaited and long-shelved or only partially implemented economic reforms. These reforms, it is often suggested, could lead to a decentralization of decision-making in Socialist societies generally and a steady growth of structural pluralism and private, individual autonomy, with the worker becoming the focal point in economic processes rather than a minor cog in the machinery. However, the alternative possibility also exists that the demographically aggravated labor shortages will lead rather to increasingly mercantilist population policies and to elaborate labor controls of the type introduced by Stalin in 1940 (but this time writ technologically large).[1] At present the latter possibility seems if anything the more likely.

In the case of the areas with demographically aggravated labor surpluses, it is quite possible that serious local unrest may develop,

not perhaps due so much to economic hardship consequent on unemployment (Socialist economies are quite efficient at swallowing
labor surpluses — though in Yugoslavia the unemployment problem
may well play a crucial role) as to the complications introduced
into the situation by the ethnic factor, to a brief discussion of which
I shall now turn.

Ethnic Relations

Of the countries in the area, only Poland and East Germany can
be said to be more or less free of ethnic problems, problems
which, it will be recalled, bedeviled East European politics before
World War II. Frequently, ethnic tensions remain key elements in
national politics (for all that during periods of calm they may be
kept largely hidden from view). And in many cases demographic
trends threaten to make ethnic relations more and not less volatile.

The Socialist countries can be divided according to their ethnodemographic structure into four groups: the first and most important group includes the Soviet Union and Yugoslavia. Both have a
large and dominant or formerly dominant group forming roughly
50% of the total population and considerable numbers of larger
and smaller ethnic minorities, many of which present the regimes
with serious political and social problems. The differential growth
rates of the various ethnic populations range to wide extremes and
are in some cases of great political significance.

Czechoslovakia forms a group on its own. Here we have a formerly overwhelmingly dominant majority which is gradually being
overtaken demographically, economically, and politically by a substantial minority (the Slovaks now form close to 30% of the population; in 1921 they made up scarcely more than 15%).[2] This improvement in the relative position of the Slovaks owes more to the
expulsion of the German minority after the war and the annexation
of Ruthenia by the USSR than to national birthrate trends. Nonetheless the differentiation in fertility and natural increase (though not
comparable with that prevailing in the USSR and Yugoslavia) has
been and continues to be significant.

In addition to the Czech-Slovak ethnodemographic problem,[3]
Czechoslovakia is also faced by the rapid growth of a highly fertile
pariah minority in its Gypsy community. As elsewhere in Eastern
Europe, data on the Gypsies in Czechoslovakia are not very satisfactory. During the later 1960s some rather startling estimates

252

and projections concerning the size of the Gypsy population reached
the pages of the Czechoslovak press. More than one writer offered
forward estimates of 300,000 for 1970 and one million by the year
2000. The 1970 Czechoslovak Census, however, managed to produce the rather low result of 203,000, later adjusted to 220,000.
The latter figure is almost certainly still an underestimate. Gypsy
fertility is extremely high, and the projection of one million for the
year 2000 may not prove to have been entirely fanciful.[4] There is
also a substantial though demographically stagnant Hungarian minority (4% of the total population) and small and rapidly disappearing German and Jewish communities.

Romania, Hungary, Bulgaria, and Albania all have significant
ethnic minorities, but none of comparable weight to that of the Slovaks. Little is known about Albania's minorities, which will accordingly be excluded from the discussion. Romania has a culturally
and politically formidable minority in its Transylvanian Hungarians,
who formed 7.9% of the population according to the 1977 Census.
This figure, which has been in a prolonged decline, may well be an
underestimate. There is also a significant German minority (2%)
and a Gypsy population which is being progressively defined out of
existence. However, the natural increase of the minorities appears
to be modest, and they are in relative decline. While this may be
a fictional trend in the case of the Gypsies, it is likely to represent
reality in the case of the other ethnic groups. Thus population developments seem to be working for the assimilatory ambitions of
the Romanian regime (ambitions which have been to some extent
softened recently, partly under pressure from Moscow).[5] Indeed,
the Romanians are sufficiently confident about their ethnic dominance as to oppose any emigration of their discontented German
minority.[6]

Hungary has a number of minority groups which it treats with
elaborate respect, apparently in the hope thereby of securing better
conditions for its own large minorities in surrounding countries.
Of these the only one representing a serious demographic-political
problem is the Gypsy minority, which, like that in Czechoslovakia,
is increasing rapidly and may already form close to 5% of the total
population. The Gypsies are likely to present severe social, if not
also directly political, problems in the future.[7] Bulgaria too has a
rapidly growing minority in its Turks, whose fertility appears to
far outstrip that of the Bulgars themselves, and whose relative
strength (currently about 10% of the total population) continues to
be considerable and to increase despite the effects of intermittent

emigration. There are also substantial (2 to 3%) Macedonian and Bulgarian Moslem (Pomak) minorities and a sizable (over 5%) Gypsy population.[8] Thus in one country within this group (Romania) we have a very significant minority, which is, however, in demographic decline, and two groups where the minorities are less formidable in political terms (and in demographic terms in the case of Hungary) but are, on the other hand, growing much faster than the host nation.

Finally we have East Germany, with its small and dwindling Lusatian Sorb communities,[9] and Poland, with its rather larger but also dwindling East Slav, German, and Jewish minorities.[10] While some of the Polish minorities are extremely important politically, it is not their demographic strength or growth which makes them so.

Basically I would suggest that countries in the bloc are faced by ethnodemographic problems of two or perhaps three types: racial or quasiracial and nonracial.[11] By racial conflict I mean those in which ingroup and outgroup are socially identified on the basis of visible physical differences that are believed to be and in some measure actually are more or less immutable. Quasiracial conflicts are those in which there is a strong subjective conviction of recognizable physical differences (believed to be more or less immutable), but in which this conviction is in fact demonstrably based rather on cultural stigmata (dress, hair arrangement, etc.). Nonracial ethnic tensions are those based on cultural differences not lending themselves to immediate physical identification. Racial feelings, in addition to creating and maintaining greater intergroup distance, tend both to be more severe and more resistant to ameliorative social trends or policies than nonracial ethnic tensions. The different types are not, however, clearly distinguished and mutually exclusive: quasiracial conflicts form a kind of extended and diffuse border area between the two poles of racial and nonracial. In the European Socialist countries there are examples of all three: relations between Russians (and other Europeans) and the Moslem peoples of Central Asia, for example, or more debatably, between Eastern Europeans and their Gypsy communities could, I believe, be classified as racial. Relations between certain Christian Slav groups in Yugoslavia and the Shiptars or between the Russians and Ukrainians and Soviet Jews may represent instances of quasiracialism. And relations between Czechs and Slovaks, Romanians and Hungarians, and Russians and Ukrainians or Latvians seem typical instances of nonracial ethnic conflicts. It should perhaps be stressed that no East European country appears to have racial divisions quite so sharp and intractable as those currently afflicting Britain or the United States. To say this, however, is not to say that ethnic harmony in the Socialist countries is any greater, merely that the physical bases for prejudice are not nearly so evident, and that therefore the prejudice itself may prove to be less deep-rooted.

From the demographic-political point of view, the distinction between racial and nonracial, though somewhat furry and based in the twilight areas of transition on erratic, subjective, and irrational social definitions of what "race" is, has a considerable significance. Whereas in the case of national or nonracial conflicts, the tension appears to stem from perceptions (however distorted) concerning the division of wealth, power, and prestige in the community, in the case of racial tensions, while these factors may also be present, we are confronted in addition with a more volatile and unpredictable element of disinterested loathing and disgust. Whereas in the first case there may be a certain mutual respect between the two communities (if not a great deal of love), in the second, tolerant contempt is the best that can be hoped for. In demographic-political terms one is in the first case dealing basically with a "fifty-fifty" problem; that is to say, only when one side's effective dominance is challenged by demographic trends will violence be likely to be precipitated by those trends. In the case of racial conflicts, on the other hand, any demographic change may be regarded as intolerable, no matter how slight. It is sufficient for one black to move into the neighborhood for the local bigots to organize. In other words, with racial tensions a modest redistribution of numbers may be sufficient to touch off violence.

But there is a further reason why the demographic factor may accentuate the already greater volatility of racial tensions. For it is an empirical demographic fact that racial (and, to a lesser degree, quasiracial) differences are more frequently associated with sharp divergences in fertility levels than other kinds of ethnic differences.[12]

If these judgments about the nature of ethnic tensions in the European Socialist countries are correct, it seems to follow that the USSR is exposed to a particularly dangerous situation. For there racial distance is more marked, and the racial tensions are between major population groups. Elsewhere racial distance is physically less apparent and may therefore prove more amenable to social or political management. Gypsy communities, like Jewish ones, could conceivably be sufficiently suffused into their surroundings by socioeconomic development (and intermarriage) for the cultural stig-

mata to disappear and the physical differences to lose all their
subjective salience (though even that may not eliminate the incidence of "racialist" attitudes among the host populations). More
importantly, however, it needs to be emphasized that the racial
and quasiracial tensions outside the USSR almost all involve overwhelming majorities and relatively modest (if rapidly expanding)
minorities. In other words, the problems that arise are likely to
be social rather than political in the first instance, though they do
perhaps contain the danger of scapegoating civil disorders and social and political degeneration of the kind that has been observed
in many other parts of the world. The one quasiracial conflict
that seems to involve two groups of politically significant size is
that between the Albanians and some of the Christian Slavic nations
of Yugoslavia. Should social distance and conventions coupled with
political hostility maintain subjective perceptions of "inherent" differences in this case (where the differentiating stigmata are very
largely cultural in reality), an already extremely delicate problem
may degenerate into something far worse.

It is, of course, quite possible that it will be nonracial ethnic
tensions that prove to be politically the most troublesome in the
area. There the demographic factor will be less relevant in objective terms, as differences in demographic behavior between different "European" groups are no longer very great. But in some
cases they are still of significance (Moldavians and Russians;
Czechs and Slovaks; Moslem Serbo-Croat-speakers and others).
And in many others they may be felt to be of significance. In interethnic relations the wildest fantasies sometimes acquire a particularly virulent and destructive reification.

While differences in demographic behavior are frequently inflated
in the minds of their observers, one cannot help feeling also that
in some cases the full implications of population trends in Socialist
Europe have not yet been grasped by those most directly involved.
As one contemplates the trends in sociodemographic development
of the Shiptars and their neighbors, or the Soviet Central Asians
and their neighbors, it is difficult to avoid feeling a kind of awe and
dread at the magnitude of the forces at work and the violent and
contradictory momenta they are either creating or whipping on.
The ethnodemographic advance of some communities and the retreat of others calls to mind the movement of large land masses
on plates headed in opposing directions. The existing sociopolitical
forms seem too rigid (especially in the Soviet case) to permit these
masses free movement but, at the same time, too brittle to withstand

forever the increasing pressures that are building. Without some
skilled and timely subterranean lubrication, major ruptures in the
crust of society seem inevitable.

Ideology

The ideological impact of rapid population growth in the world
and rapid population decline within the Socialist countries themselves has dealt a severe blow to anti-Malthusian self-confidence
at home and slightly modified the erstwhile rigor of anti-Malthusian
doctrines abroad. The Stalinist "law" of socialist population has
been more or less dethroned, the science of demography rehabilitated, and tentative first steps toward a total ideological reappraisal of the situation taken. It seems unlikely, however, that demography will now be ever "reideologized." The regimes have basically pragmatic and (with the exception of Yugoslavia) mercantilist
attitudes toward population. They want more subjects, and they
would like to solve demographic problems as they become aware
of them, on the basis of informed and expert advice. Western analyses and techniques are not necessarily eschewed because they are
Western. Contacts between Eastern and Western demographers
are growing and in many ways may be closer than those prevailing
in any other social science. The anti-Malthusian tradition remains
influential, but rather more as a normative than an empirical orientation for domestic purposes. Internationally anti-Malthusianism,
after a period of partial eclipse after 1965, seems to be growing in
favor again, as the Soviet Union perceives a resurgence of anti-
Malthusian attitudes among Third World countries (particularly
those in Africa and Latin America) and seeks to capitalize upon it,
or at least not to be left behind by it. The Soviet bloc countries
naturally follow Moscow's lead (whatever views their demographers
or other private citizens may have), and Romania and Yugoslavia,
while acting independently, are moved by analogous considerations.

In the other relevant sphere of Marxist-Leninist ideology, that
concerning relations between the sexes, the family, and the role of
women in the home and society, there has been a good deal of discussion recently in most of the Socialist countries but little decisive
deviation from the Soviet pattern described in Chapter 3. In most
of the countries, especially Yugoslavia, but also in East Germany,
Poland, and elsewhere, there has been since the midfifties a certain
revival of the sexual liberalism of traditional Marxism. But in

Czechoslovakia, Bulgaria, and Hungary, this revival has come under some threat in recent years from a new pronatalist patriarchalism justified in terms of the "biological future of the nation." And in Romania in 1966 there was a total about-face on all such issues simultaneously, in a concerted attempt to revive the nation's drooping birthrate. In this and other ways there is a tendency for practical or extraneous policy considerations to dilute implementation of the ideological teachings of the classics on demographically relevant matters. Even where the position of women is rather more advanced at the verbal or theoretical level (as in Yugoslavia), it may well be worse in practical terms.

Nonetheless it should be emphasized that the relative socioeconomic strength and importance of women in Socialist society have undoubtedly grown in recent decades (as elsewhere in areas of European culture, and possibly a little faster), and that the liberal element in the Marxist-Leninist tradition on sexual and family matters has not been by any means wholly eliminated, despite the reverses it has suffered in Stalinist Russia and contemporary Romania. The doctrinal tenets remain alive and available to be utilized by defenders of such causes as women's rights, the autonomy of family life, and some freedom of choice in fertility control and other sexual matters.

International Politics

Given the stability, not to say the immobilism, of international relations among the European Socialist countries since the war, the importance of any factors, the demographic included, seems slight when compared with the overwhelming diplomatic and military superiority of the Soviet Union. The highly complex pattern of affinities and antagonisms that existed in Central and Eastern Europe before World War II has been largely obliterated by Soviet hegemony. As far as more global concerns go, it is perhaps worth noting that demographic trends on either side of the Warsaw Pact-NATO line more or less parallel one another, and that Soviet fertility decline is more than balanced by that occurring in Eastern Europe itself (so that its hegemony over the area is not being reduced by the demographic factor). Turning to consider what I have referred to as the latent geopolitics of the area, it is presumably not without significance that, for example, the Ukrainian population is growing only very slowly compared to that of Poland; that Poland,

from being scarcely more than 30% larger than East Germany in
population in 1946, is now almost twice as large; that the difference
between the Polish and the combined East and West German populations is currently diminishing by about half a million a year; that
the indigenous Moldavian population, owing to its higher fertility,
is maintaining its relative ethnic superiority in the Moldavian Republic of the USSR, despite extensive and presumably "not accidental" Slav immigration. The true significance of developments like
these will probably only become apparent when Soviet Russian influence in the area declines. Nonetheless, despite their limited
practical relevance for the present, they quite certainly engage the
intellectual interest and, even more, the emotions of demographic
commentators in the area, whatever their overt political persuasion.
Debates about national population policy (of which more in the next
section) invariably raise the subject of what is usually referred to
vaguely and euphemistically as "the national interest." It is clear
that those who think in these terms are intimately looking forward
to, or in any case not left irresolute and inconsolable by, the prospect of Soviet withdrawal from the area.

The two spheres in which demographic trends are of the keenest
contemporary relevance are Sino-Soviet relations and Yugoslavia's
relations with its Socialist neighbors, especially Albania. China's
population is so vast and its absolute rate of increase so far in excess of that of the Soviet Union (and its European element in particular), that whatever view might be taken of the notion of demographic
"lateral pressures" or of the strategic significance of manpower
in the nuclear age, it seems clear that the Soviet Union must regard
the trends with a good deal of apprehension.

The Yugoslav-Albanian case involves a different and rather less
problematical kind of demographic factor. The Albanians in Albania
are obviously not going to multiply to the point where they will
thereby achieve some early ascendancy in national military or economic power (though their growth is certainly not strategically irrelevant). The demographic triggering mechanism is located inside
Yugoslavia itself, in its large and rapidly growing Shiptar minority,
whose growing strength and ambitions seem likely sooner or later
to precipitate some kind of structural transformation. This the
Yugoslav state may be hard put to accommodate, particularly if the
internal mechanism touches off some kind of external intervention
as well as a domestic crisis.

Despite the drastic slaughter, migrations, and deportations of the
World War II period, many of Eastern Europe's traditional ethnic

entanglements have remained in dimensions sufficient to cause trouble. Many of these have an external aspect of some importance. In some cases that external aspect is quasidemographic in the sense that disputes about censuses or population trends in the ethnic group in question seem to lie at the heart of the matter. But probably in no case, other than the two mentioned, will differential growth rates play a crucial role in igniting or seriously exacerbating conflict.

Population Policy and Policy-making

Domestic population policies, it has been pointed out, are difficult to appraise inasmuch as many social policies may be adopted for nondemographic reasons and yet appear to have considerable impact on demographic development. Moreover, governments with populationist intentions have often chosen to conceal those intentions behind a smokescreen of more lofty humanist aspirations. In this work I have in general used the term population policy in the sense of programs or measures aimed deliberately and consciously at affecting population growth rates, though attention has also been devoted to certain demographically relevant social policies whose status as population policy would be difficult to establish.

The first point that needs to be made about the Socialist countries from this point of view is that most of them do have population policies in the sense of conscious and deliberate attitudes and programs. In the USSR, Poland, and Yugoslavia governmental concern is less pronounced than elsewhere (though public concern, in the first two at least, is very great). But in general throughout the European Socialist world, official interest in population issues is high and growing. Politicians in Czechoslovakia, Hungary, Romania, and Bulgaria often refer to population statistics with the same kind of tender regard that company directors might devote to key items in their annual report. And in the USSR and Yugoslavia it is possible that much more concern would be expressed were the issue not quite so politically sensitive.

The next general point to note is that virtually throughout the entire area, both in official and nonofficial circles, there is a strongly pronatalist orientation that contrasts sharply with the influence of movements like Zero Population Growth in the West. There are probably several different reasons for this.

1. The continuing influence of the anti-Malthusian tradition and

the extreme rationalist optimism with which it has been associated
ever since Marx and Engels's time.

2. The mercantilist attitude of Socialist governments to the accumulation of national wealth of all kinds. Socialist governments
are composed of men who in a much more meaningful sense than
their bourgeois counterparts in the West own their countries.
Their power and their sphere of competence are much greater.
And since the bureaucratic stabilization of the post-Stalin years,
their tenure of (some) office is much more secure than that in virtually any other system anywhere else in the world. Accordingly
they have a natural and long-term interest in seeing their ranches
expand. And relatedly,

3. The unself-conscious etatism and nationalism of the Socialist
regimes. Governments that emphasize the glory or importance of
the state, be they right-wing or left-wing, seem disposed to adopt
pronatalist policies. (Compare the well-known cases of Fascist
Italy and Nazi Germany.)

4. The prominence of economic planners and planning considerations in governmental decision-making. When planners encounter
labor shortages (as they have been doing increasingly in the last
decade or so), it is natural that they should feel an impulse to
"solve" the problem by planning for higher production of labor
power. These labor shortages are not necessarily related to past
trends in the birthrate, and the policy inference may be fallacious.
But it seems to be often made. (Again this is a point related to
point 2.)

5. The sharp drop in fertility that occurred in the Socialist countries in the 1950s and 1960s, and the slightly delayed echo it has
produced in the minds of many Socialist politicians and publicists.
The even sharper fertility declines that have occurred in many
Western countries in the later 1960s and the 1970s have not so far
given rise to anything quite like the national anxieties felt by both
governments (in many cases) and wide sections of the general public (in virtually all cases) in Eastern Europe. What we are probably dealing with here is thus a combination of sharp demographic
stimulus and extreme nationalist sensitivity.

The European Socialist countries can be divided according to the
degree of their pronatalism and also according to the methods by
which they are pursuing their objectives.

In degree of pronatalism they can be subdivided into three groups:

i) the more emphatically pronatalist, as judged both by the
saliency of this issue in official statements and by the programs

adopted: Czechoslovakia, Hungary, Bulgaria, and Romania;

ii) the more mildly pronatalist, who declare themselves to be so oriented, but less often, and have a more modest program of positive and negative inducements to childbirth: Poland and the USSR; East Germany is probably suspended between this group and the first one;

iii) Yugoslavia, which is formally neutral and declares that its population policy, at the federal level at least, is concerned with purely nonnumerical values, and also that decisions as to the desirability of changing vital rates are best decentralized.

Socialist commentators on population policy usually distinguish three types of policies that can be used to further the state's objectives: (a) economic (by which they have in mind such measures as maternity and child-care leave, family benefits and maternity grants, child-care allowances, taxes on the single and childless, subsidies for children's goods, etc.); (b) moral (by which they mean propaganda campaigns in public entertainment and the media, mobilization of mass organizations, etc.); and (c) legal-administrative (by which they mean prohibiting or permitting abortion and contraceptives, raising or lowering the minimum age for marriage, administrative regulations affecting housing allocations, etc.).

It will be apparent that of these three categories, only the first and third are in any marked degree available to most Western governments; and in the case of the third, the idea of their being manipulated as a policy weapon in order to affect the birthrate (especially in an upward direction) has begun to seem remote (though of course in some countries limitations on abortion and contraception still exist for "moral" reasons).

In Socialist Europe, however, all three types of measures are widely used, and each can serve as a rough classificatory principle. In the four more pronatalist states, use is made of all three types, though in varying degree. Czechoslovakia, Bulgaria, and Hungary all make use of legal-administrative measures, but in moderation, placing much greater emphasis on economic and "moral" inducements and penalties. In fact there were periods in the late 1950s and the 1960s when none of them had recourse to restrictive legislation to increase the birthrate. Hungary[13] in particular long followed a markedly liberal policy in regard to both abortions and contraceptives, while Czechoslovakia[14] applied only some mild and intermittent restrictions on the availability of abortion. In Bulgaria unrestricted abortion was maintained for over a decade from 1956, though it appears that contraceptives were not made very accessible.[15]

Now all three have populationist restrictions on the availability of
legal abortion. Romania, after a period of tolerance toward divorce, abortion, and contraception, suddenly greatly restricted all
three in 1966 in an attempt to increase its birthrate.[16] These restrictive measures have been maintained to the present and, in
the case of abortion at least, regularly reaffirmed. However, the
population has naturally developed methods of bypassing them, so
that the 100% increase in the birthrate registered in the first year
(200% in the first months) has since been dwindling; moreover, illegal abortion is evidently rising, and so again is divorce. Romania's relative stress on economic inducements is less than that
of the other three states, though some have been introduced, notably at the time of the illiberal administrative package of 1966.
As to propaganda, it would probably be fair to say that of all the
pronatalist states, Czechoslovakia is maintaining the most elaborate, all-pervasive, and obtrusive media campaign on behalf of
fecundity.

East Germany for a long time formed a group on its own. While
it had a number of strongly pronatalist measures on its books[17]
and a very great, indeed a notorious, need for a pronatalist policy
to make up for its large emigratory losses in the pre-Wall era and
its low fertility and even lower birthrate, it did not pursue any very
emphatic propaganda campaign on behalf of motherhood. Then in
1972, despite its low fertility, legal abortion was made uncondition-
ally available on demand. (Earlier it had shared with Albania and,
after 1966, Romania the position of being the only Socialist states
with strongly restrictive legislation on abortion.) Since 1976, however, it has veered much closer to the strongly pronatalist states,
but exclusively by dint of economic inducements rather than administrative sanctions.[18]

Albania also forms a group on its own. Abortion is illegal and
contraceptives largely unknown. The birthrate, though declining
quite rapidly, is still by far the highest in Europe, and the official
view is that this is an extremely good thing and symptomatic of the
vibrant, life-affirming strength of the Albanian people. The decline
in the birthrate is not evidently due to the spread of family planning
services, which remain primitive or nonexistent.[19] It is difficult
to describe government policy as pronatalist in the usual sense,
however, since specifically pronatalist inducements are not offered
and would anyway be superfluous.

Yugoslavia is the only country among the nine which is not explicitly or at least ostensibly pronatalist. Officially Yugoslavia is

committed to a purely social, humane, and nonquantitative view of
population policy. It is stated as an immutable constitutional principle that parents have the right to plan their families by any means
they see fit, including abortion (which is, however, viewed officially
as a dangerous and unsatisfactory means of fertility control).[20] It
is, moreover, held that parents have a right to information about
all methods of family planning, and encouragement is given to organizations engaged in spreading knowledge about these matters.
At the republic level, and indeed at the communal level, policies
of encouraging or discouraging population growth may be followed
within these guidelines.

Poland and the USSR are in many ways similar to one another.
Each maintains some economic inducements to having children.
Their respective policies, however, may be largely inspired by
social motivations at this stage (whatever the original intention of
the legislation — in the Soviet case it was, at the outset, clearly
pronatalist). Each also maintains liberal legislation on abortion,
contraception, and divorce (despite the fact that there have been
pressures within the regimes and within the respective populations
for more "administrative" pronatalist policies to be adopted —
from Catholics and nationalists in Poland and from Russian and
other nationalists in the USSR). Neither has any more than a mild
and relatively unobtrusive propaganda campaign in favor of motherhood (for a time in the late 1950s, Poland actually had a very active
campaign against the high birthrate that then still prevailed).

In the more decisively pronatalist Socialist countries, debate
over population policy issues has to some extent been narrowed.
A definite policy line has been adopted, and it remains principally
to implement and applaud (though criticism of implementation may
sometimes create an opening for more normative evaluation of
existing policy). Nonetheless, when questions of demographically
relevant social policy or population policy in general are broached
in the Socialist countries, a wide variety of matters tend to rise to
the surface. It is indeed remarkable with what candor and vehemence these issues have at times been discussed. This having been
said, it needs to be added at once that the areas we have identified
as ethnic relations and international politics are normally not al-
luded to in explicit form. It is considerations of that kind lurking
in the background, however, which appear to give the whole subject
the special piquancy it has in the East European context. Where
most overt political discussion is taboo, demographic commentary
forms a splendid surrogate. But the emotional energy invested in

demographic debate is not wholly misplaced or wholly symbolic. The differential trends in fertility that are perceived are not always the figments of inflamed nationalist imaginations (though Eastern Europe has plenty of those), and it is not surprising that many Socialist observers are keenly if discreetly absorbed by them. Apart from ethnic and national rivalries, however, there are a number of important problems which Socialist demographic commentators do discuss quite explicitly. Particularly prominent among them are such issues as living standards and consumption priorities; public versus private expenditure; egalitarian versus demographic considerations; the role of population growth in long-term economic development and planning; the place of women in society and the home; the future of the family and of relations between the sexes; sexual education for the young; eugenics and the rights of the individual; abortion and contraception; divorce; the mechanics of social and population policy-making; the role of social scientists in the Socialist polity, and so on. Within the confines of this brief summary, it would be impossible to convey very much of the variety of opinion that finds expression on any of these matters. Something of that variety can be gleaned from the discussion in Chapter 10 of Poland's population debate in recent years. Many of the Polish themes are prominent elsewhere; few are peculiar to Poland alone.

Perhaps the most significant thing about the Socialist population debate latterly has been the persistent assertiveness with which nonofficial people of one kind and another have sought to present their views. Among them those working in demography and related disciplines have been particularly prominent. Whatever views they espoused (and there has often been a diversity of views among them), they have almost invariably made an explicit or implicit claim that on all matters (including the normative and the politically sensitive) they should at least be consulted. At times their claims are even carried to the point of suggesting that demographic policy-making might best be left in their hands more or less entirely. Most of them (whether employed by government departments or universities) seem to accept the principle of bureaucratic decision-making in these as in other matters. But they certainly demand a say and in some cases virtually imply that they should become the bureaucracy for these purposes. It ought not to be inferred from this, however, that these experts are necessarily illiberal or manipulatively "technocratic" in outlook. They are often, in fact, the main advocates of parental sovereignty and economic rather than "ad-

ministrative" solutions. And if they sometimes declare a preference for the former over the latter on the stated grounds that economic solutions are more effective, it may well be that they are
merely speaking to their superiors in a manner they know will be
more readily understood.

There has been a good deal of formalization of decision-making
about population problems in recent years. Czechoslovakia, Bulgaria, Romania, East Germany, and Poland have all established
central government commissions that are charged with coordinating research into population problems and recommending possible
solutions to their governments. The Czech Population Commission
is particularly powerful. There is also a similar body located in
a ministry in Hungary, and there have been some signs that a pres-
tigious demographic center in Moscow University may ultimately
emerge with similar responsibilities in the Soviet Union. While
this reflects to some extent a general trend throughout the world,
one nonetheless gets the impression that in this, as in other respects, the concern of Socialist governments about population development runs well ahead of that of their Western counterparts.

Given the single-minded pronatalism of the Socialist countries,
it might be asked whether this development is wholly desirable.
Despite the fact that the policies being adopted by Socialist governments are more or less liberal and the advice being tendered them
is in general more liberal still, and despite the fact that eugenics
has for four decades received an almost uniformly bad press in
the Socialist countries and that no eugenic experiments are, to my
knowledge, being legislated for or otherwise permitted, one is still
left with a slight feeling of unease that states with a tradition em-
bracing the Gulag Archipelago and the Serbskii Institute are taking
a keen and increasingly active interest in their subjects' reproductive behavior. If all this is not to end in 1984 and Brave New World,
what will stop it? Will the humanist ideals of would-be demogra-
pher-kings be sufficient? Would they themselves survive the temp-
tations of Socialist bureaucratic power with those ideals intact if
their claims to rule were recognized? How much of the original
liberalism of Marx and Engels has survived to the present generation of Socialist bureaucratic decision-makers?

There is another rather disturbing aspect of the Socialist approach to population policy. At a time when the considered opinion
of many experts is that population and economic growth must be
halted and redirected if the world is to survive, it is not particularly reassuring that the Socialist countries (Yugoslavia excepted)

are set determinedly on a course of pronatalism at home and demagogic "anti-Malthusianism" abroad. If some kind of demographic disarmament ever becomes an issue of world politics, Socialist attitudes are likely to make the negotiations hard and protracted. Ehrlichites and family planners in the West might well take more careful note than they have done so far that there is a large part of the world where their ideas are almost completely shut out.

APPENDIX TABLES

Table 1

Crude Birth and Natural Increase Rates in Socialist and Selected Non-Socialist European Countries
(per thousand of population)

Country	Total population midyear 1976 (in thousands)	1950 births	1950 nat. inc.	1960 births	1960 nat. inc.	1965 births	1965 nat. inc.	1970 births	1970 nat. inc.	1976 births	1976 nat. inc.
Albania	2,500	38.5	24.5	43.3	32.9	35.2	26.2	32.6	23.3	NA	NA
Austria	7,510	15.6	3.2	17.9	5.2	17.9	4.9	15.2	1.8	11.6	-1.0
Bulgaria	8,760	25.2	15.0	17.8	9.7	15.3	7.2	16.3	7.2	16.5	6.4
Czechoslovakia	14,920	23.3	11.8	15.9	6.7	16.4	6.4	15.9	4.4	19.2	7.8
Finland	4,730	24.5	14.4	18.5	9.5	16.9	7.2	14.0	4.4	14.1	4.7
France	52,920	20.7	7.9	17.9	6.5	17.8	6.7	16.8	6.1	13.6	3.1
East Germany	16,790	16.5	4.6	17.0	3.4	16.5	3.0	13.9	-0.2	11.6	-2.4
West Germany	61,510	16.5	6.0	17.8	6.4	17.9	6.4	13.4	1.3	9.8	-2.1
Great Britain	55,930	16.3	4.5	17.5	6.0	18.3	6.7	16.3	4.5	12.1	-2.1
Hungary	10,560	20.9	9.5	14.7	4.5	13.1	2.5	14.7	3.1	17.6	5.1
Poland	34,362	30.7	19.1	22.6	15.0	17.4	10.0	16.6	8.5	19.5	10.7
Romania	21,450	26.2	13.8	19.1	10.4	14.6	6.0	21.1	11.6	19.5	10.0
Spain	35,970	20.2	9.3	21.8	13.0	21.3	12.7	19.6	11.1	17.7	9.7
USA	215,120	23.5	13.9	23.7	14.2	19.4	10.0	18.3	8.9	14.7	5.8
USSR	256,670	26.7	17.0	24.9	17.8	18.4	11.1	17.4	9.2	18.5	9.0
Yugoslavia	21,560	30.2	17.2	23.5	13.6	20.9	12.1	17.8	8.9	18.0	9.8

Source: Główny Urząd Statystyczny (Warsaw), Rocznik Demograficzny 1972, Warsaw, 1972, and Rocznik Demograficzny 1977, Warsaw, 1978. Crude death rates per thousand can of course be obtained by subtracting natural increase from the birthrate for any given year.

Table 2

Net Reproduction Rates in Socialist and
Selected Non-Socialist Countries of
Europe, 1950-73

Country	1950	1955	1960	1965	1970	1973
Albania	NA	NA	NA	NA	NA	2.20
Austria	0.91 (1947)	1.00 (1957)	1.19	1.25	1.07	0.92
Bulgaria	1.11	1.01	1.01	0.95	1.01	1.01
Czechoslovakia	1.31	1.31	1.12	1.11	0.98	1.13
Finland	1.38	1.35	1.27	1.14	0.87	0.71
France	1.33	1.24	1.29	1.34	1.17	1.16
East Germany	NA	1.08	1.07	1.16	1.04	0.73
West Germany	0.93	0.95	1.11	1.16	0.94	0.72
Great Britain (England and Wales)	1.02	1.04	1.25	1.33	1.13	0.96
Hungary	1.08	1.26	0.91	0.83	0.91	0.91
Poland	1.49	1.52 (1956)	1.34	1.15	1.01	1.06
Romania*	NA	1.41	1.13	0.93	1.40	1.18
Spain	NA	NA	NA	NA	1.35	1.32 (1974)
USA	1.44	1.68	1.72 (1958-59)	1.38 (1964-65)	1.17	0.88
USSR	NA	NA	1.26	1.13	1.13	1.13
Yugoslavia	1.45	1.24	1.12	1.08	1.02	1.03

Sources: UN Demographic Yearbook 1975, New York, 1976; Rocznik Demograficzny 1972 and Rocznik Demograficzny 1977; V. V. Bodrova, Narodonaselenie evropeiskikh sotsialisticheskikh stran, Prilozhenie tablitsy 2-8. A Net
Reproduction Ratio of 1.00 is regarded as replacement level. Lower values indicate that the present fertile age groups are producing a generation smaller
than their own.

*Romanian figures are Gross Reproduction Rates. The corresponding NRRs
would be likely to be from 0.07 to 0.15 lower. Where different years are indicated, the dates relate to the entry immediately below.

Table 3

USSR Population, 1970 and 1979

1. By Republic

Republic	Population in thousands		1979 as a percentage of 1970
	January 15, 1970	January 17, 1979	
USSR, total	241,720	262,442	109
RSFSR	130,079	137,552	106
Ukrainian SSR	47,126	49,757	106
Belorussian SSR	9,002	9,559	106
Uzbek SSR	11,799	15,391	130
Kazakh SSR	13,009	14,685	113
Georgian SSR	4,686	5,016	107
Azerbaidzhan SSR	5,117	6,028	118
Lithuanian SSR	3,128	3,399	109
Moldavian SSR	3,569	3,948	111
Latvian SSR	2,364	2,521	107
Kirgiz SSR	2,934	3,529	120
Tadzhik SSR	2,900	3,801	131
Armenian SSR	2,492	3,031	122
Turkmen SSR	2,159	2,759	128
Estonian SSR	1,356	1,466	108

Source: Izvestia, April 22, 1979, p. 1.

Table 3 Continued

2. By Nationality

Nationality	Population in thousands		1979 as a percentage of 1970
	1970	1979	
USSR	241,720	262,685	8.43
Russians	129,015	137,397	6.50
Ukrainians	40,753	42,347	3.91
Uzbeks	9,195	12,456	35.46
Belorussians	9,052	9,463	4.54
Kazakhs	5,299	6,556	23.72
Tatars	5,931	6,317	6.51
Azerbaidzhani	4,380	5,477	25.05
Armenians	3,559	4,151	16.63
Georgians	3,245	3,571	10.05
Moldavians	2,698	2,968	10.01
Tadzhiks	2,136	2,898	35.67
Lithuanians	2,665	2,851	7.06
Turkmen	1,525	2,028	32.98
Germans	1,846	1,936	4.88
Kirgiz	1,452	1,906	31.27
Jews	2,151	1,811	−15.87
Chuvash	1,694	1,751	3.36
Dagestani peoples	1,365	1,657	21.40
Latvians	1,430	1,439	0.63
Bashkirs	1,240	1,371	10.56
Mordva	1,263	1,192	−5.62
Poles	1,167	1,151	−1.38
Estonians	1,007	1,020	1.30
Chechens	613	756	23.33
Udmurts	701	714	1.42
Mari	599	622	3.84
Ossetians	488	542	11.07
Komi and Komi- Permiaks	475	478	0.63
Koreans	357	389	8.96

Source: Naseleniia SSSR po dannym Vsesoiuznoi Perepisi: Naseleniia 1979 goda, Moscow, Politizdat, 1980. Percentage computations by the author.

Table 4

USSR Crude Birth, Death, and Natural
Increase Rates, 1926-76 (in ‰)
(within present borders)

	Births	Deaths	Natural Increase
1926	44.0	20.3	23.7
1928	44.3	23.3	21.0
1937	38.7	18.9	19.8
1938	37.5	17.5	20.0
1939	36.5	17.3	19.2
1940	31.2	18.0	13.2
1950	26.7	9.7	17.0
1955	25.7	8.2	17.5
1956	25.2	7.6	17.6
1957	25.4	7.8	17.6
1958	25.3	7.2	18.1
1959	25.0	7.6	17.4
1960	24.9	7.1	17.8
1961	23.8	7.2	16.6
1962	22.4	7.5	14.9
1963	21.1	7.2	13.9
1964	19.5	6.9	12.6
1965	18.4	7.3	11.1
1966	18.2	7.3	10.9
1967	17.3	7.6	9.7
1968	17.2	7.7	9.5
1969	17.0	8.1	8.9
1970	17.4	8.2	9.2
1971	17.8	8.2	9.6
1972	17.8	8.5	9.3
1973	17.6	8.6	9.0
1974	18.0	8.7	9.3
1975	18.1	9.3	8.8
1976	18.4	9.5	8.9

Source: Naselenie SSSR: Spravochnik, Moscow, 1974, p. 9; Narodnoe khozia-istvo SSSR za 60 let, Moscow, 1977, p. 69.

Table 5

USSR Crude Birth, Death, and Natural Increase Rates by Republic
in Selected Years, 1940-76 (in ‰)

	1940			1950			1960			1965			1971			1976		
	B	D	N.I.	B	D	N.I.	B	D	N.I.	B	D	N.I.	B	D	N.I.	B	D	N.I.
USSR	31.2	18.0	13.2	26.7	9.7	17.0	24.9	7.1	17.8	18.4	7.3	11.1	17.8	8.2	9.6	18.4	9.5	8.9
RSFSR	33.0	20.6	12.4	26.9	10.1	16.8	23.2	7.4	15.8	15.7	7.6	8.1	15.1	8.7	6.4	15.9	10.0	5.9
Ukraine	27.3	14.3	13.0	22.8	8.5	14.3	20.5	6.9	13.6	15.3	7.6	7.7	15.4	8.9	6.5	15.2	10.2	5.0
Belorussia	26.8	13.1	13.7	25.5	8.0	17.5	24.4	6.6	17.8	17.9	6.8	11.1	16.4	7.5	8.9	15.7	8.8	6.9
Uzbekistan	33.8	13.2	20.6	30.8	8.7	22.1	39.8	6.0	33.8	34.7	5.9	28.8	34.5	5.4	29.1	35.3	7.1	28.2
Kazakhstan	40.8	21.4	19.4	37.6	11.7	25.9	37.2	6.6	30.6	26.9	5.9	21.0	23.8	6.0	17.8	24.3	7.2	17.1
Georgia	27.4	8.8	18.6	23.5	7.6	15.9	24.7	6.5	18.2	21.2	7.0	14.2	19.0	7.4	11.6	18.2	7.8	10.4
Azerbaidzhan	29.4	14.7	14.7	31.2	9.6	21.6	42.6	6.7	35.9	36.6	6.4	30.2	27.7	6.5	21.2	25.7	6.6	19.1
Lithuania	23.0	13.0	10.0	23.6	12.0	11.6	22.5	7.8	14.7	18.1	7.9	10.2	17.6	8.5	9.1	15.7	9.6	6.1
Moldavia	26.6	16.9	9.7	38.9	11.2	27.7	29.3	6.4	22.9	20.4	6.2	14.2	20.2	7.7	12.5	20.6	9.0	11.6
Latvia	19.3	15.7	3.6	17.0	12.4	4.6	16.7	10.0	6.7	13.8	10.0	3.8	14.7	11.0	3.7	13.8	12.1	1.7
Kirghizistan	33.0	16.3	16.7	32.4	8.5	23.9	36.9	6.1	30.8	31.4	6.5	24.9	31.6	7.0	24.6	31.3	8.2	23.1
Tadzhikistan	30.6	14.1	16.5	30.4	8.2	22.2	33.5	5.1	28.4	36.8	6.6	30.2	36.8	5.7	31.1	38.2	8.5	29.7
Armenia	41.2	13.8	27.4	32.1	8.5	23.6	40.1	6.8	33.3	28.6	5.7	22.9	22.6	4.9	17.7	22.7	5.5	17.2
Turkmenistan	36.9	19.5	17.4	38.2	10.2	28.0	42.4	6.5	35.9	37.2	7.0	30.2	34.7	6.7	28.0	34.7	7.7	27.0
Estonia	16.1	17.0	-0.9	18.4	14.4	4.0	16.6	10.5	6.1	14.6	10.5	4.1	16.0	10.9	5.1	15.1	12.0	3.1

Source: Narodnoe khoziaistvo SSSR 1922-1972: Iubileinyi statisticheskii ezhegodnik, Moscow, 1972, p. 42; Narodnoe khoziaistvo SSSR za 60 let: Iubileinyi statisticheskii ezhegodnik, Moscow, 1977, p. 73.

276

Table 6

USSR General Fertility Rates and
Total Fertility Rates, by Republics

	1958-59		1969-70		1973-74	
	GFR	TFR	GFR	TFR	GFR	TFR
USSR	88.7	2.81	65.7	2.39	66.8	2.41
RSFSR	82.9	2.63	53.4	1.97	55.3	2.00
Ukraine	70.7	2.30	55.3	2.04	55.7	2.04
Belorussia	91.0	2.80	61.3	2.30	58.9	2.33
Uzbekistan	158.8	5.04	158.5	5.64	156.8	5.71
Kazakhstan	143.0	4.46	96.1	3.31	94.1	3.31
Georgia	85.0	2.59	73.3	2.62	69.4	2.58
Azerbaidzhan	163.3	5.01	134.6	4.63	108.0	4.04
Lithuania	82.8	2.63	67.2	2.35	60.9	2.23
Moldavia	111.7	3.57	71.6	2.56	75.1	2.59
Latvia	59.2	1.94	53.5	1.93	53.4	1.97
Kirghizistan	140.1	4.32	134.7	4.85	131.6	4.81
Tadzhikistan	123.5	3.93	166.4	5.90	170.6	6.20
Armenia	159.2	4.73	92.9	3.20	84.7	2.91
Turkmenistan	161.6	5.12	165.6	5.93	158.6	5.85
Estonia	59.9	1.95	59.3	2.14	57.9	2.11

Source: V. A. Borisov, Perspektivy rozhdaemosti, Moscow, 1976, pp. 238-40.
The general fertility rate is the number of live births per 1,000 women aged
15-49. The total fertility rate is the summation of age-specific rates. A TFR
of roughly 2.15 corresponds to replacement level.

Table 7

Numerical Trends in Soviet Ethnic Groupings

1. Nations Forming Their Own Republics

	Numbers (in thousands)			Number in 1970 as percent of:	
Peoples	1926	1959	1970	1926	1959
Russians	77,791	114,114	129,015	165.8	113.1
Ukrainians	31,195	37,253	40,753	...	109.4
Uzbeks	3,928	6,015	9,195	234.1	152.9
Belorussians	4,739	7,913	9,052	...	114.4
Kazakhs	3,968	3,622	5,299	133.5	146.3
Azerbaidzhanis	1,715	2,940	4,380	255.4	149.0
Armenians	1,568	2,787	3,559	227.0	127.7
Georgians	1,821	2,692	3,245	178.2	120.6
Moldavians	279	2,214	2,698	...	121.9
Lithuanians	42	2,326	2,665	...	114.6
Tadzhiks	980	1,397	2,136	218.0	152.9
Turkmens	764	1,002	1,525	199.6	152.2
Kirgiz	763	969	1,452	190.3	149.9
Latvians	151	1,400	1,430	...	102.2
Estonians	155	989	1,007	...	101.9

Table 7 Continued

2. Peoples Having Some Degree of Formal Autonomy

Peoples	Numbers (in thousands)			Number in 1970 as percent of:	
	1926	1959	1970	1926	1959
Tatars	3,311	4,968	5,931	179.1	119.4
Jews	2,666	2,268	2,151	...	94.8
Chuvashes	1,117	1,470	1,694	151.7	115.3
Peoples of Daghestan	698	945	1,365	195.6	144.5
Mordvinians	1,340	1,285	1,263	94.3	98.3
Bashkirs	714	989	1,240	173.7	125.4
Udmurts	514	625	704	137.0	112.7
Chechens	319	419	613	192.2	146.3
Maris	428	504	599	140.0	118.8
Ossetes	272	413	488	179.4	118.2
Komis and Komi-Permiaks	376	431	475	126.3	110.2
Buriats	238	253	315	132.4	124.5
Iakuts	241	233	296	122.8	127.0
Kabardinians	140	204	280	200.0	137.3
Karakalpaks	146	173	236	161.6	136.4
Ingushes	74	106	158	213.5	149.0
Peoples of the North, Siberia, and Far East	131	130	151	115.3	116.2
Karelians	248	167	146	58.9	87.4
Tuvinians	...	100	139	...	139.0
Kalmyks	132	106	137	103.8	129.3
Karachais	55	81	113	205.5	139.5
Adyghe	65	80	100	215.4	125.0
Abkhazians	57	65	83	145.6	127.7
Khakasses	46	57	67	145.7	117.6
Balkars	33	42	60	181.8	142.9
Altaians	51	45	56	109.8	124.5
Circassians	...	30	40	...	133.3

Appendix Tables

Table 7 Continued

3. Peoples Not Having Territorial Unit of Their Own

Peoples	Numbers (in thousands)			Number in 1970 as percent of:	
	1926	1959	1970	1926	1959
Germans	1,239	1,620	1,846	149.0	114.0
Poles	782	1,380	1,167	...	84.6
Koreans	87	314	357	...	113.7
Bulgarians	111	324	351	...	108.3
Greeks	214	309	337	157.5	109.1
Gypsies	61	132	175	...	132.6
Uighurs	66	95	173	262.1	182.1
Hungarians	6	155	166	...	107.1
Gagauz	1	124	157	...	126.6
Romanians	5	106	119	...	112.3
Kurds	69	59	89	129.0	150.8
Finns	135	93	85	...	91.4
Turks	9	35	79	...	225.7
Dungans	15	22	39	260.0	177.3
Iranians (Persians)	53	21	28	52.8	133.3
Abazinians	14	20	25	178.6	125.0
Assyrians	10	22	24	240.0	109.1
Czechs	17	25	21	123.5	84.0
Tats	29	11	17	58.6	154.5
Shors	13	15	16	123.1	106.7
Slovaks	10	15	12	120.0	80.0

Source: S. I. Bruk, "Population of the USSR — Changes in its Demographic, Social and Ethnic Structure," Geoforum, 1972, no. 9, pp. 16-17. (The author's name has been retransliterated into the form that will be more familiar to readers of this kind of material. The stylings of the three subgroups have also been altered in an attempt at greater clarity.)

Table 8

Changes in Percentages of Soviet Ethnic Populations
Using Their Own Mother Tongue

	1926	1959			1970		
	total	total	urban	rural	inside own republic	outside own republic	total
Russians	99.7	99.8	99.9	99.8	100.0	99.3	99.8
Ukrainians	87.1	87.7	77.2	94.5	93.5	51.2	85.7
Belorussians	71.9	84.2	63.5	94.2	93.2	41.9	80.6
Lithuanians	46.9	97.8	96.6	98.4	99.2	80.3	97.9
Latvians	79.0	95.1	93.1	96.9	98.4	53.2	95.2
Estonians	88.4	95.2	93.1	97.0	99.3	56.6	95.5
Moldavians	92.3	95.2	78.4	97.7	98.2	77.7	95.0
Georgians	96.5	98.6	96.8	99.7	99.5	73.4	98.4
Armenians	92.4	89.9	84.4	97.1	99.2	78.1	91.4
Azerbaidzhanis	93.8	97.6	96.4	98.2	98.1	95.1	98.2
Kazakhs	99.6	98.4	96.7	98.9	99.2	95.6	98.0
Uzbeks	99.1	98.4	96.7	98.9	98.6	97.4	98.6
Turkmens	97.3	98.9	97.3	99.4	99.5	92.0	98.9
Kirgiz	99.0	98.7	97.4	98.9	99.7	92.3	98.8
Tadzhiks	98.3	98.1	96.4	98.6	99.3	94.6	98.5
Tatars	98.9	92.1	87.5	96.1	98.9	89.3	89.2
Bashkirs	53.8	61.9	73.3	59.1	57.6	75.1	66.2
Chuvashes	98.7	90.8	71.2	95.6	97.5	83.2	86.9
Mordvinians	94.0	78.1	52.2	88.8	97.3	70.9	77.8
Maris	99.3	95.1	75.8	97.8	97.8	92.6	91.2
Udmurts	98.9	89.1	69.7	94.7	93.2	75.9	82.6
Komis	96.5	88.7	74.3	93.4	93.8	60.9	83.7
Karelians	95.5	71.3	51.7	80.0	80.9	61.3	63.0
Kabardinians	99.3	97.9	90.8	91.1	99.2	79.2	98.0
Ossetes	97.9	89.1	82.0	93.0	98.0	73.1	88.6
Chechens	99.7	98.9	97.0	99.4	99.7	97.8	98.7
Avars	99.3	97.2	91.2	97.2	99.2	80.6	97.2
Kalmyks	99.3	91.0	83.8	93.2	98.2	79.6	91.7
Buriats	98.1	94.9	81.5	97.6	96.8	93.1	92.6
Iakuts	99.7	97.5	90.7	98.9	98.2	82.8	96.3
Jews	71.9	21.5	21.5	31.1	-	-	17.7
Germans	94.9	75.0	66.3	80.6	-	-	66.8
Poles	42.9	45.2	38.6	48.6	-	-	32.5

Source: V. I. Kozlov, "Ethnic Processes in the USSR," Geoforum, 1972, no. 9, p. 50.

Table 9

Differential Growth Rates by Soviet Nationality
(Average Percentage Increases Per Annum), 1959-70

Estonian	0.2	Armenian	2.3
Latvian	0.2	Kazakh	3.5
Ukrainian	0.8	Azerbaidzhan	3.7
Russian	1.1	Kirgiz	3.7
Belorussian	1.2	Tadzhik	3.9
Lithuanian	1.2	Turkmen	3.9
Georgian	1.7	Uzbek	3.9
Moldavian	1.8		

Source: F. A. Leedy, "Demographic Trends in the USSR," in U.S. Congress Joint Economic Committee, Soviet Economic Prospects for the Seventies, Washington, 1973, p. 450.

Table 10

USSR Average Number of Children Planned* by
Nationality of Mother (results of
fertility survey of September 1972)

Nationality	Average number of children planned
Uzbeks	6.26
Kirgiz	6.04
Karakalpak	5.98
Tadzhik	5.97
Turkmen	5.93
Kazakh	5.01
Azerbaidzhani	4.89
Armenian	3.43
Tatar	2.86
Georgian	2.83
Moldavian	2.62
Belorussian	2.31
Lithuanian	2.23
Estonian	2.18
Ukrainian	2.08
Russian	2.00
Latvian	1.99
Jewish	1.71

Source: V. A. Belova et al., Skol'ko detei budet v sovetskoi sem'e, Moscow, 1977, p. 23.

*"Skol'ko detei vsego sobiraetes' imet' ?"

Table 11

Estimated Increments to the Population in the Able-Bodied Ages in the USSR, Central Asia and Kazakhstan, and the Transcaucasus, by Plan Period: 1959 to 2000
(Based on data as of January 1, in thousands)

Plan period	USSR		Central Asia and Kazakhstan		Transcaucasus	
	total increase	average annual increase	total increase	as a percent of national increase	total increase	as a percent of national increase
1959-65	5,173	739	NA	*	NA	*
1966-70	7,808	1,562	NA	*	NA	*
1971-75	12,726	2,545	3,551	27.9	1,231	9.7
1976-80	10,408	2,082	3,495	33.6	1,148	11.0
1981-85	2,687	537	2,823	105.1	701	26.1
1986-90	2,830	566	2,938	103.8	531	18.8
1991-95	4,020	804	3,565	88.7	628	15.6
1996-2000	9,012	1,802	4,999	55.5	1,082	12.0

Source and methodology: Estimates of the Foreign Demographic Analysis Division, March 1974. The projections for the years 1973-2000 were based on the assumptions that fertility will remain constant at the estimated 1972 level, that mortality will decline by an amount equivalent to an increase in life expectancy at birth of approximately 2.5 years, and that net migration will be insignificant. Taken from Feshbach and Rapawy, "Soviet Population and Manpower Trends and Policies," in U.S. Congress Joint Economic Committee, Soviet Economy in a New Perspective, Washington, 1976, p. 129.

NA—Not available.
*—Not applicable.

283

Appendix Tables

Table 12

USSR Proportion of Population in Able-Bodied Age Groups
by Republic in 1970 (in %)

RSFSR	56.2	Moldavia	53.3
Ukraine	55.6	Latvia	56.3
Belorussia	53.0	Kirgizistan	45.2
Uzbekistan	42.2	Tadzhikistan	42.3
Kazakhstan	50.0	Armenia	48.4
Georgia	52.8	Turkmenia	43.9
Azerbaidzhan	43.9	Estonia	56.3
Lithuania	53.7		

Source: Naselenie SSSR: Spravochnik, Moscow, 1974, p. 26.

Appendix Tables

Table 13

Basic Demographic Rates in Postwar Poland
(per thousand)

	Marriages	Divorces	Live births	Deaths	Natural increase	Infantile mortality*
1950	10.8	0.4	30.7	11.6	19.1	111.2
1955	9.5	0.5	29.1	9.6	19.5	82.2
1960	8.2	0.5	22.6	7.6	15.0	54.8
1965	6.3	0.8	17.4	7.4	10.0	41.4
1970	8.5	1.1	16.6	8.1	8.5	33.4
1973	9.4	1.2	17.9	8.3	9.6	26.1
1976	9.5	1.1	19.5	8.8	10.7	24.0

Source: Rocznik Demograficzny 1974, pp. XX-XXI; Rocznik Demograficzny 1977, pp. XVI-XVII.
*Infantile mortality rates per 1,000 live births.

Table 14

Urban and Rural Net Reproduction Ratios in Poland

	Overall	Urban	Rural
1950	1.491	1.300	1.610
1955	1.519	1.366	1.675
1960	1.339	1.098	1.601
1965	1.149	0.879	1.487
1970	1.011	0.794	1.315
1973	1.055	0.805	1.449
1976	1.074	0.857	1.494

Source: Rocznik Demograficzny 1974, p. 107; Rocznik Demograficzny 1977, p. 99.

Table 15

Officially Registered Abortions in Poland*
(in thousands)

1961	230
1963	260
1965	235
1968	220
1970	213
1971	204

Sources: Polityka ludnościowa: współczesne problemy, Warsaw, 1973, p. 129; S. Klonowicz, "Legalizacja sztucznych poronień a dynamika rozrodczości w Polsce," Studia Demograficzne, vol. 36 (1974), p. 101.
*It is generally agreed that in Poland the official statistics on abortions are very incomplete (though there is some disagreement about how incomplete they are — see second source quoted above, p. 101). The figures include abortions, presumably mostly illegal, that were begun outside hospitals.

Appendix Tables

Table 16

Polish Net Increases in Working-Age Population

	Net increase (in thousands)
1951-55	1,130
1956-60	660
1961-65	790
1966-70	1,560
1971-75	1,800
1976-80	1,260
1981-85	430
1986-90	160

Sources: A. Rajkiewicz, Ekonomista 2, 1971, p. 198, cited in H. Trend, "Arbeitsmarkt und Vollbeschäftigung in Polen," Osteuropäische Rundschau, 1972, no. 9, p. 1; M. Kabaj, Nowe Drogi, 1978, no. 2, p. 123.

Table 17

Official Polish Labor Market Statistics 1955-75*

	Seeking work (in thousands)		Vacancies		Number of vacancies per individual seeking work	
	men	women	men	women	men	women
1955	10.7	19.9	39.2	7.2	3.7	0.4
1960	7.4	29.9	39.7	6.8	5.4	0.2
1965	7.5	54.5	40.8	12.1	5.4	0.2
1970	8.1	71.3	31.0	8.5	3.9	0.1
1973	1.3	26.8	105.7	41.2	81.3	1.5
1975	3.4	15.6	98.0	48.6	28.8	3.1

Source: M. Kabaj, "Bariera zatrudnienia," ŻG, October 12, 1975. A misprint in the source has been corrected after reference to the original.

*These figures should not be taken as giving an accurate picture of unemployment in Poland (see Note 46). However, they do reflect certain general trends, e.g., the unemployment among women in Gomułka's last year (1970) or the overemployment of men (despite the enormous cohorts of school-leavers coming onto the labor market) under Gierek.

Table 18

The Population of Yugoslavia 1921-71
by Republic and Province (in thousands)

Year	Yugo-slavia	Bosnia and Herce-govina	Monte-negro	Croatia	Macedonia	Slovenia	Serbia (total)	Serbia (proper)	Vojvodina	Kosovo
1921	12,544	1,890	311	3,427	809	1,288	4,819	2,843	1,537	439
1931	14,534	2,324	360	3,789	950	1,386	5,726	3,550	1,624	552
1948	15,842	2,564	377	3,780	1,153	1,440	6,528	4,154	1,641	733
1953	16,991	2,843	420	3,936	1,305	1,504	6,979	4,464	1,699	816
1961	18,549	3,278	472	4,160	1,406	1,592	7,642	4,823	1,855	964
1971	20,523	3,746	530	4,426	1,647	1,727	8,447	5,250	1,953	1,244
Indices for 1971/1921	163.6	198.2	170.4	129.2	203.6	134.1	175.3	184.7	127.1	283.4

Source: Razvitak stanovništva Jugoslavije u posleratnom periodu, p. 5. The data refer to the present territory of the various units.

Table 19

Republic and Provincial Populations as Percentage of
Yugoslav Total in Census Years

Year	Yugo-slavia	Bosnia and Herce-govina	Monte-negro	Croatia	Macedonia	Slovenia	Serbia (total)	Serbia (proper)	Vojvodina	Kosovo
1921	100	15.1	2.5	27.3	6.4	10.3	38.4	22.7	12.4	3.5
1931	100	16.0	2.5	26.1	6.5	9.5	39.4	24.4	11.2	3.8
1948	100	16.2	2.4	23.9	7.2	9.1	41.2	26.2	10.4	4.6
1953	100	16.8	2.5	23.2	7.7	8.9	41.1	26.3	10.0	4.8
1961	100	17.7	2.5	22.4	7.6	8.6	41.1	26.0	10.0	5.2
1971	100	18.3	2.6	21.6	8.0	8.4	41.2	25.6	9.5	6.1

Source: V. Simeunović, Stanovništvo Jugoslavije i socijalističkih republika 1921-1961, p. 35. The computation for 1971 has been added. All data refer to the present area of the territorial units.

Table 20

Yugoslav Live Births and Natural Increase Rates by Republic/Province

	Year	Yugo-slavia	Bosnia and Herce-govina	Monte-negro	Croatia	Macedonia	Slovenia	Serbia (total)	Serbia (proper)	Vojvodina	Kosovo
Births per 1,000 population	1950-54	28.8	38.2	32.7	23.2	38.4	22.8	27.4	26.1	23.2	43.5
	1955-59	24.8	35.4	30.1	20.8	34.0	19.4	22.0	19.6	18.4	42.2
	1960-64	22.0	31.4	26.7	17.2	29.4	18.0	19.8	16.6	16.2	41.5
	1965-69	19.5	25.0	22.1	15.7	26.5	17.8	18.3	15.2	14.4	38.3
	1970-73	18.0	21.1	19.4	14.6	22.8	16.7	17.7	15.0	13.0	36.4
	1975	18.2	19.8	18.8	14.8	22.5	16.8	18.5	15.6	14.5	35.1
	1977*	17.7	18.1	18.6	14.7	21.8	17.6	18.1	15.3	14.0	33.9
Natural increase per 1,000 population	1950-54	17.0	26.2	22.7	11.5	22.9	11.9	15.0	14.7	10.8	25.5
	1955-59	14.2	23.8	21.6	10.7	22.3	9.7	11.7	10.3	6.1	26.6
	1960-64	12.0	22.4	19.4	7.5	19.6	8.4	10.3	7.0	6.5	28.5
	1965-69	10.0	18.0	15.8	6.0	18.3	7.7	9.5	6.7	4.8	28.9
	1970-73	9.1	14.4	13.3	4.2	15.2	6.3	8.4	5.8	2.7	28.2
	1975	9.5	13.4	13.0	4.7	15.3	6.6	9.4	6.7	3.7	28.0
	1977*	9.3	12.3	12.5	4.7	14.5	7.6	9.3	6.3	3.7	27.6

Source: Razvitak stanovništva Jugoslavije u posleratnom periodu, p. 8; Statistički Godišnjak 1978, pp. 408-9.
*The figures for 1977 were only provisional.

Table 21

Yugoslav Net Reproduction Ratios by Republic and Province

Year	Yugo-slavia	Bosnia and Herce-govina	Monte-negro	Croatia	Macedonia	Slovenia	Serbia (total)	Serbia (proper)	Vojvodina	Kosovo
1950	1.54	1.93	1.67	1.27	2.13	1.36	1.49	1.44	1.31	2.28
1955	1.24	1.64	1.56	1.05	1.82	1.12	1.10	0.98	0.99	2.01
1960	1.12	1.48	1.39	0.92	1.52	0.98	1.02	0.87	0.91	2.07
1965	1.17	1.47	1.34	0.99	1.50	1.16	1.06	0.90	0.95	2.26
1970	0.98	1.12	1.12	0.81	1.21	1.00	0.97	0.82	0.75	2.02
1972	1.01	1.14	1.11	0.89	1.16	1.00	0.98	0.82	0.77	2.07
1975	1.02	1.06	1.10	0.89	1.16	1.02	1.04	0.87	0.84	2.18

Sources: Demografska statistika 1972, p. 57; Demografska statistika 1975, p. 56; and Fertilitet ženskog stanovništva 1950-1967, p. 18.

Appendix Tables

Table 22

Yugoslav Net Interrepublic Migratory Balance 1961
(in thousands)*

Bosnia and Hercegovina	-259
Montenegro	- 75
Croatia	- 45
Macedonia	- 5
Slovenia	- 1
Serbia	+358

Source: Migracije stanovništva Jugoslavije, p. 102.
*This table, which is based on the results of the 1961 Census, should not be taken to be an accurate indicator of the precise net result of interrepublic migratory movements in the decades preceding 1961. Nor does it convey any impression of the indirect demographic effects of those movements.

Table 23

Yugoslav Net Interregional Migration 1961-71
(in thousands)*

Bosnia and Hercegovina	-187
Montenegro	- 14
Croatia	+ 59
Macedonia	- 21
Slovenia	+ 34
Serbia proper	+148
Vojvodina	+ 27
Kosovo	- 47

Source: Stariha Mladen, "Notranje neto migracije SFRJ v razdobju med popisoma 1961 in 1971 po republikah in pokrajinah, po spolu in po starosti," paper presented to the Slovenian Demographic Symposium (Slovenski demografski simpozij), held in Ljubljana, 1974, p. 4.
*These calculations, though a more accurate measure than those in Table 22 (having a more limited time reference and being based on a more sophisticated methodology), also suffer from a serious drawback in that they do not take account of workers "temporarily" employed or resident in republics or regions outside that in which they have their permanent residence.

Table 24

Yugoslav Workers Temporarily Abroad at 1971 Census
(by Republic and Province and by Major Nationality)*

	Yugo-slavia	Bosnia and Herce-govina	Monte-negro	Croatia	Macedonia	Slovenia	Serbia (total)	Serbia (proper)	Vojvo-dina	Kosovo
								Serbia		
Total	671,908	137,351	7,829	224,722	54,433	48,086	199,487	114,581	60,545	24,361
Montenegrins	5,260	101	3,278	204	44	28	1,605	556	655	394
Croats	261,721	58,236	83	195,353	115	1,101	6,833	1,189	5,501	143
Macedonians	38,298	60	29	161	36,915	41	1,092	603	451	38
Moslems	40,565	35,687	1,323	462	404	34	2,655	2,088	102	465
Slovenians	46,856	121	17	1,059	22	45,066	571	241	322	8
Serbs	191,342	40,921	325	19,048	805	312	129,931	101,374	24,733	3,824
Albanians	34,748	69	1,990	55	11,692	15	20,927	1,932	28	18,967

Source: Savezni zavod za statistiku, "Lica na privremenom radu u inostranstvu," Statistički Bilten, no. 679, Belgrade, 1971, p. 13.
*These data were very severely criticized as inadequate at the time of their publication. Whatever their merit then, they have be-come unquestionably dated since. They are offered, faute de mieux, as official confirmation of some of the trends discussed in Chapter 13.

Table 25

Age Structure of the Yugoslav Population by Republic/Province, 1971

Age group	Bosnia and Hercegovina	Montenegro	Croatia	Macedonia	Slovenia	Serbia (total)	Serbia (proper)	Vojvodina	Kosovo	Yugoslavia
Total	100.0	100.0	100.0	100.0	100.0	100.0	100.0	100.0	100.0	100.0
0-19	45.4	42.8	31.5	43.0	33.2	34.2	31.3	30.0	52.8	36.5
20-39	29.8	29.0	30.0	30.2	30.1	30.2	31.0	30.6	26.2	30.1
40-59	16.7	16.7	23.0	17.7	21.9	22.2	23.6	24.2	13.1	20.8
60 and over	7.7	11.0	14.9	8.8	14.8	12.9	13.6	14.8	7.1	12.3

Source: Razvitak stanovništva Jugoslavije u posleratnom periodu, p. 31.

Table 26

Percentage of Yugoslav Population Economically Active,
by Republic/Province

	Yugo-slavia total	Bosnia and Herce-govina	Monte-negro	Croatia	Macedonia	Slovenia	Serbia	Serbia (proper)	Vojvodina	Kosovo
1948	49.1									
1953	46.2	42.5	36.4	47.7	40.8	48.0	48.4	52.4	45.4	33.2
1961	45.0	39.2	34.3	47.0	39.4	48.2	47.3	51.1	44.0	34.8
1971	43.3	36.7	32.7	45.5	38.3	48.4	45.7	51.5	42.7	26.0

Source: "Economically Active Population," Yugoslav Survey, 1975, no. 3, p. 4.

Table 27

National Structure of Yugoslavia in 1961 and 1971

	In thousands		Percentage structure		% increase 1971 over 1961
	1961	1971	1961	1971	
Total respondents who stated their nationality	18,549.2	20,522.9	100.0	100.0	
Croats	4,293.8	4,526.7	23.2	22.1	5.4
Macedonians	1,045.5	1,194.5	5.6	5.8	14.2
Montenegrins	513.8	508.8	2.8	2.5	-1.0
Moslems	972.9	1,729.9	5.2	8.4	77.8
Serbs	7,806.1	8,143.2	42.1	39.7	4.3
Slovenes	1,589.2	1,678.0	8.6	8.2	5.3
Albanians	914.7	1,309.5	4.9	6.4	43.1

Source: "National Structure of the Yugoslav Population," Yugoslav Survey, 1973, no. 1, p. 12.

Table 28

Yugoslav Ethnic Demographic Strength by Republic and Province
(thousands of population and % of total)

	1961		1971	
	thousands	%	thousands	%
Bosnia and Hercegovina				
Moslems	842	25.7	1,482	39.6
Serbs	1,406	42.9	1,393	37.2
Croats	712	21.7	772	20.6
Montenegro				
Montenegrins	384	81.4	356	67.1
Moslems	31	6.5	70	13.3
Albanians	26	5.5	36	6.7
Serbs	14	3.0	40	7.5
Croatia				
Croats	3,334	80.3	3,514	79.4
Serbs	625	15.0	627	14.2
Macedonia				
Macedonians	1,001	71.2	1,142	69.3
Albanians	183	13.0	280	17.0
Turks	131	9.4	109	6.6
Serbs	43	3.1	46	2.8
Slovenia				
Slovenians	1,522	95.6	1,624	94.0
Serbia (total)				
Serbs	5,705	74.6	6,017	71.2
Albanians	700	9.2	985	11.7
Hungarians	450	5.9	430	5.1
Croats	196	2.6	186	2.2
Moslems	93	1.2	154	1.8
Montenegrins	105	1.4	125	1.5
Serbia proper				
Serbs	4,459	92.6	4,699	89.5
Moslems	84	1.7	124	2.4
Albanians	51	1.1	66	1.2
Bulgarians	54	1.1	50	0.9
Montenegrins	32	0.7	57	1.1
Croats	44	0.9	39	0.7

Table 28 Continued

	1961		1971	
	thousands	%	thousands	%
Vojvodina				
Serbs	1,018	54.9	1,089	55.8
Hungarians	443	23.9	424	21.7
Croats	145	7.8	139	7.1
Slovaks	74	4.0	73	3.7
Romanians	57	3.1	53	2.7
Montenegrins	35	1.9	36	1.9
Kosovo				
Albanians	647	67.2	916	73.7
Serbs	227	23.6	228	18.4
Montenegrins	38	3.9	32	2.5
Moslems	8	0.8	26	2.1
Turks	26	2.7	12	1.0

Source: Savezni zavod za statistiku, Statistički bilten, no. 727 (plus Aneks uz Statistički Bilten 727), "Nacionalni sastav stanovništva po opštinama," Belgrade, 1972.

Table 29

Yugoslav Employment in Social and Private (nonrural) Sectors
by Republic/Province
(in thousands)

Year	Yugo- slavia	Bosnia and Herce- govina	Monte- negro	Croatia	Macedonia	Slovenia	Serbia (total)	Serbia (proper)	Kosovo	Vojvodina
1965	3,662	500	73	959	237	520	1,373	856	90	427
1967	3,561	485	71	913	233	504	1,355	865	91	399
1969	3,706	497	75	931	247	526	1,430	935	96	399
1972	4,210	572	91	1,047	292	594	1,614	1,061	116	437
1974	4,514	631	96	1,101	318	645	1,723	1,135	128	460
1977	5,161	737	113	1,271	370	723	1,947	1,285	150	512

Source: _Statistički godišnjak Jugoslavije 1975 and 1978_, pp. 381 and 420, respectively.

298

Table 30

Yugoslav Registered Unemployed, by Republic/Province

Year	Yugo-slavia	Bosnia and Herce-govina	Montenegro	Croatia	Macedonia	Slovenia	Serbia (total)	Serbia (proper)	Kosovo	Vojvodina
1965	266,901	26,998	4,932	64,096	47,078	13,252	110,545	64,952	23,968	21,625
1967	291,530	32,408	5,863	66,375	51,644	19,044	116,196	66,746	24,266	25,184
1969	315,572	35,290	6,464	52,824	57,573	17,570	145,851	89,642	26,950	29,259
1972	333,544	41,175	7,179	50,083	64,595	12,561	157,951	99,535	26,532	31,884
1974	478,460	69,769	15,367	59,415	86,070	9,462	238,377	155,106	35,977	47,294
1977	716,698	112,340	20,996	88,054	97,841	11,973	385,494	252,085	53,812	79,647

Source: Statisticki godisnjak Jugoslavije 1975 and 1978, pp. 396 and 431.

Table 31

Official Yugoslav Projections of Population for 1985 and 2000, by Republic/Province,
(in thousands; migration excluded; medium variant)

	Yugo-slavia	Bosnia and Herce-govina	Montenegro	Croatia	Macedonia	Slovenia	Serbia (total)	Serbia proper	Vojvodina	Kosovo
1985	23,236	4,523	630	4,662	2,053	1,876	9,492	5,645	2,031	1,816
2000	25,653	5,258	725	4,829	2,413	2,015	10,414	5,830	2,055	2,529

Source: Savezni zavod za statistiku, Projekcije stanovništva Jugoslavije 1970–2000 godine po polu i petogodišnjim grupama starosti, Belgrade, 1973, data reproduced in Demografska statistika 1972, pp. 25 ff.

These projections are not to be confused with those cited in Note 45 to Chapter 14.

Table 32

Family Allowances in Yugoslavia

	1964	1965	1966	1967	1968	1969	1970	1971	1972	1973	1976
Number of recipients (in thousands)	1,412	1,476	1,506	1,110	895	874	809	762	858	753	951
Number of children involved (in thousands)	2,862	2,961	2,976	2,304	1,933	1,910	1,779	1,702	1,750	1,668	2,059
Total expenditure on endowment (in millions of dinars)	1,042	1,313	1,554	1,244	1,100	1,000	966	1,205	1,822	2,321	5,078

Source: Statistički godišnjak Jugoslavije 1975 and 1978, pp. 310 and 391, respectively. It should be noted that the figures for ex-penditure are not standardized to allow for the steep inflation that has been occurring in Yugoslavia over the relevant period.

Table 33

Yugoslav Family Allowances by Republic/Province

	Bosnia and Herce-govina	Monte-negro	Croatia	Macedonia	Slovenia	Serbia proper	Vojvodina	Kosovo
1970								
Number of children (thousands)	335	147	288	242	199	319	164	160
Sum expended (millions of dinars)	141	65	250	228	183	512	132	152
1972								
Number of children (thousands)	315	76	275	234	247	313	132	158
Sum expended (millions of dinars)	284	63	416	168	410	295	97	89
1973								
Number of children (thousands)	305	62	289	207	241	296	158	109
Sum expended (millions of dinars)	338	69	496	210	475	489	153	NA
1976								
Number of children (thousands)	409	68	329	221	320	415	130	167
Sum expended (millions of dinars)	899	136	1,081	480	945	946	310	281

Source: Statistički godišnjak Jugoslavije for 1971, 1974, 1975, and 1978, pp. 490, 526, 521, and 590, respectively. Expenditures are given in current terms without allowance for inflation.

NOTES

Preface

1. Here and elsewhere I wish to use Socialism with a capital "S" to denote all those states of Eastern Europe which profess allegiance to Marxism-Leninism, if not always to Moscow.

2. See his "Reflections on Demophobia," Intercom, September 1978, pp. 6-7.

3. On internal population distribution policies, see, e.g., R. Fuchs and G. Demko, "Spatial Population Policies in the Socialist Countries of East Europe," in Social Science Quarterly, vol. 58 (1977), no. 1, p. 60; and on international distribution policies, Friedrich Levcik, "Migration and Employment of Foreign Workers in the CMEA Countries and their Problems," in U.S. Congress Joint Economic Committee, East European Economies Post-Helsinki, Washington, 1977, p. 458.

4. See, e.g., J. Berent, "Causes of Fertility Decline in Eastern Europe and the Soviet Union," Population Studies, vol. 24 (1970), pp. 35-58 and 247-92; C. Tietze, "The Demographic Significance of Legal Abortion in Eastern Europe," Demography, vol. 1 (1964), p. 119; A. Klinger, "Demographic Aspects of Abortion," IUSSP International Conference London 1969, vol. 2, p. 1153; Robert J. McIntyre, "The Effects of Liberalized Abortion Laws in Eastern Europe," in R. Clinton and R. Godwin, Research in the Politics of Population, Lexington, 1972; J. van der Tak, Abortion, Fertility and Changing Legislation, Lexington, 1974, pp. 13-30; C. Tietze and M. C. Murstein, "Induced Abortion: 1975 Factbook," Reports on Population/Family Planning, December, 1975; S. Klonowicz, "Legalizacja sztucznych poronień a dynamika rozrodczości w Polsce," Studia Demograficzne, no. 36 (1974), p. 85.

5. See, e.g., Henry P. David, Abortion and Family Planning in Socialist Countries of Eastern Europe, New York, 1970; V. Bodrova, "La politique démographique dans les Républiques Populaires d'Europe," Population, 1973, p. 1001; G. Acsadi, "Recent Problems on Population Policies in the European Region of

Socialist Countries," IUSSP International Conference, London 1969, vol. 2, p. 1381; M. Macura, "Population Policies in Socialist Countries of Europe," Population Studies, vol. 28 (1974), no. 3, p. 369; R. McIntyre, "Pronatalist Programmes in Eastern Europe," Soviet Studies, vol. 27 (1975), no. 3, p. 366; K. Dzienio, "Doświadczenia europejskich krajów socjalistycznych w zakresie kształtowania polityki ludnościowej" (paper presented at a conference on population policy held in Jadwisin, near Warsaw, March 1972); B. Berelson, Population Policy in Developed Countries, New York, 1974, chaps. 6, 9, 12, 13, 17, and 25; M. Kirk, M. Livi-Bacci, and E. Szabady, Law and Fertility in Europe, 2 vols., Dolhain (Belgium), 1975, chaps. 3, 4, 8, 11, 15, 16, and 21. K. Dzienio, "Wnioski wynikające z doświadczeń w zakresie realizacji polityki ludnościowej w wybranych europejskich krajach socjalistycznych," Biuletyn Instytutu Gospodarstwa Społecznego, vol. 20 (1977), no. 2, pp. 47-85.

6. Within this area special attention will be devoted to the demographic aspects of labor supply; it is this aspect which engages the greatest degree of official concern in Socialist countries.

7. The question of international population policy (i.e., the attitude adopted by governments toward world population problems and attempts made by the UN and other international organizations to solve them) will be considered, where applicable, under the heading of "Ideology." In fact the USSR and Yugoslavia appear to be the only two states which pursue fully sovereign policies in this regard.

8. This inherently important subject will for practical reasons be passed over lightly. It is a vast topic and at the same time one concerning which data is perhaps unusually elusive. Moreover, in the case of international migration at least, it has been of limited relevance to Socialist countries other than Yugoslavia.

9. The term "interest groups" should, of course, be understood here in the sense appropriate to the Socialist states. The whole question of group influences on the making of policy in the area of population problems is one worthy of more than the incidental treatment I give it. As the issues involved in population policy are usually seen officially as less than of the first importance, group participation tends to be more active and (or?) more visible than is usually the case. One is thus afforded a better glimpse than is customary of the policy-making process (see in this connection the unusually informative study of Soviet family reforms in the 1950s and 1960s by Peter Juviler in P. Juviler and H. Morton, Soviet Policy-Making: Studies of Communism in Transition).

10. For a most interesting (and rare) glimpse of Albanian demographic developments, see E. Hofsten, "Demographic Transition and Economic Development in Albania," European Demographic Information Bulletin, vol. 6 (1975), no. 3, p. 147.

Chapter 1

1. The term "political studies" has been used here as one broad enough to embrace both Western social science and what is known in the Socialist countries as (the field of) "population policy" (Russian: politika narodonaseleniia; Polish: polityka ludnościowa; Serbo-Croat: populaciona politika).

2. A. E. Keir Nash, "Pollution, Population and the Cowboy Economy," Journal of Comparative Administration (1970), no. 1, pp. 119-20, quoted in Richard L. Clinton, William S. Flash, and R. Kenneth Godwin, Political Science in Population Studies, Lexington, 1972, p. 147.

3. Report of the Commission on Population Growth and the American Future,

vol. 4, Governance and Population, Washington, 1972, p. 13.

4. B. Berelson, "Population Policy: Personal Notes," Population Studies, vol. 25 (1971), p. 173.

5. For a discussion of the frustrations suffered by the "international population community" at the UN Population Conference held in Bucharest in 1974 (resulting to some extent from their neglect of some of these matters), see J. Finkle and B. Crane, "The Politics of Bucharest: Population, Development and the New International Economic Order," Population and Development Review, vol. 1 (1975), no. 1, p. 87. For two typical neo-Malthusian pieces which almost wholly ignore the Socialist world while purporting to deal with world population problems, see S. Kaplan and R. McCormick, Innovative Organization for Population Research, Springfield, Ill., 1971 (the index of which contains one reference to the USSR and none to Karl Marx), and M. Endres, On Defusing the Population Bomb, New York, 1975 (which does briefly discuss Marx's views but does not appear to offer any advice on how to defuse Socialist opposition to defusing the population bomb).

6. Compare the works by Bodrova, Acsadi, Macura, and Berelson cited in the Preface, Note 4.

7. In some ways it is even harder for them to be fully candid when they are invited to contribute to international volumes, where willy-nilly they find themselves forced into the role of flying the national flag.

8. W. Petersen, Population, London, 1969, p. 633. On the continuing gaps in our knowledge of vital statistics during the Soviet period, see David M. Heer, "The Demographic Transition in the Russian Empire and the Soviet Union," Journal of Social History, vol. 1 (1967), p. 206.

9. The policy of concealing population losses from the West was successful. "...while Western analysts in 1950 accepted the Soviet statement that the USSR's population was about 200,000,000 — the Soviet authorities had direct data showing the population to be only about 180,000,000." M. Roof, "Soviet Population Trends," Survey, no. 37 (July-September 1961), p. 35.

10. To my knowledge there is no satisfactory account of the history of Soviet demography through the dark decades of the '30s, '40s, and '50s. Soviet bloc scholars are naturally cautious of even drawing attention to the large gap in the history of their discipline. In the earlier Brezhnev years some allusions could be made to past disasters. See, for example, G. Gerasimov, "Demograficheskie neozhidannosti," Novy mir, 1967, no. 2, p. 267; B. Ts. Urlanis, "The Problem of Demography and Planning," in E. Szabady, ed., World Views of Population Problems, Budapest, 1968, p. 349. Gerasimov quotes Oscar Wilde as having declared that if people don't speak of something, this must mean that the thing doesn't exist. "For a long time we didn't speak about demography," comments Gerasimov. "To many people it seemed that it didn't exist." Since Gerasimov's time the situation has changed in that now it would appear to be no longer possible to talk about the fact that it was once impossible to talk about demography.

11. By 1963, a year when Soviet publications on demographic themes were just beginning to appear systematically, Czechoslovakia, Hungary, and Poland all had flourishing demographic journals. Despite innumerable pleas from members of the demographic community, there is still no specialist demographic journal in the USSR.

12. The papers presented at the conference were published (with some omissions) in Polityka ludnościowa: współczesne problemy, Warsaw, 1973.

13. "Savetovanje o izgradnji društvenih stavova o populacionoj politici u

Jugoslaviji." Some of the papers presented at this conference were published in the Zagreb journal Naše teme, 1974, no. 4.

14. V. S. Steshenko and V. P. Piskunov, Demograficheskaia politika, Moscow, 1974.

15. B. Berelson, ed., Population Policies in Developed Countries, New York, 1974.

16. In 1959 the then President Eisenhower said: "I cannot imagine anything more emphatically a subject that is not a proper political or governmental activity or function or responsibility...as long as I am here this government will not have a positive political doctrine on birth control." In 1968 he said: "Once as President of the United States I thought and said that birth control was not the business of the Federal Government. The facts changed my mind...I have come to believe that the population explosion is the world's most critical problem" (Quoted in R. Symonds and M. Carder, The United Nations and the Population Question, London, 1973, pp. 95, 133). In the Socialist countries (with the exception of Yugoslavia) a similar evolution has occurred, if for diametrically opposed reasons. Virtually all countries (with the notable exception of the USSR and also Yugoslavia) have some kind of central coordinating state body responsible for monitoring demographic development and proposing policies relevant to it. There has been a rapid multiplication of similar bodies in Western and developing nations as well. See Berelson, Population Policy in Developed Countries, pp. 775-77.

17. Thus in a Czech textbook on demography, in a brief definitional passage on population policy, we find the following characterization: "Population policy is a collection of measures (mostly of a long-term character) intended to regulate population development according to the established state doctrine of the society in question. Population policy is usually pronatalist" (V. Srb, M. Kučera, and L. Růžička, Demografie, Prague, 1971, p. 575, emphasis added).

Chapter 2

1. For a discussion of this point, see H. Kent Geiger, The Family in Soviet Russia, Cambridge, Mass., 1968, pp. 28 ff.

2. F. Engels, The Origin of the Family, Private Property and the State, Moscow, FLPH, n.d., p. 6.

3. F. Engels, op. cit., pp. 5-6.

4. Scholars writing in the Soviet Marxist tradition have tended to blame Engels for this "aberration" insofar as they have acknowledged it at all. See Geiger, op. cit., pp. 31-32; M. Sawer, "The Question of the Asiatic Mode of Production: Towards a New Marxist Historiography," unpublished Ph.D. thesis, Australian National University, 1974, pp. 151 ff. and 252 ff. For an apparent attempt to restore the demographic factor to a more important role in historical materialism, see A. Vishnevskii, "Demograficheskaia revoliutsiia," Voprosy filosofii, 1973, no. 2, p. 53.

5. Anthony Flew, "Introduction" to the Pelican edition of Malthus's An Essay on the Principle of Population, Penguin, 1970, p. 51.

6. For the foregoing list of expletives and further instances of Marx and Engels's vigorous style in disputation with Malthus, see Ronald L. Meek, ed., Marx and Engels on Malthus, London, 1953, pp. 59-60, 81, 83, 116-17, 118-19, 121, 123, 126, 138-39, and 158.

7. Malthus, An Essay on the Principle of Population, 1970, p. 69.

8. Ibid.

9. See W. Petersen, "Marx versus Malthus: The Symbols and the Men," in The Politics of Population, London, 1965, pp. 72-89.

10. W. Petersen, "Malthusian Theory: A Commentary and Critique," in Petersen op. cit., p. 39. See also J. Overbeek, History of Population Theories, Rotterdam, 1974, pp. 44-48.

11. See the passage from Capital reproduced in Meek, op. cit., pp. 98-99.

12. See the section headed "Ideology" in the chapter devoted to the Soviet Union, pp. 95-103. The traditional antagonism between Marxist and Malthusian approaches to population questions is a most regrettable historical millstone around humanity's neck, but one which has been and is very seldom regretted. For an interesting attempt to reconcile and conjoin the two, see H. E. Daly, "A Marxian-Malthusian View of Poverty and Development," Population Studies, 1971, no. 1, p. 25.

13. Engels, Outlines of a Critique of Political Economy, quoted in Meek, op. cit., p. 63.

14. Letter to Lange, March 29, 1865, quoted in Meek, op. cit., pp. 62 and 82.

15. Letter to Kautsky, February 1, 1881, quoted in Meek, op. cit., p. 108.

16. Engels's letter to Kautsky of February 1, 1881, Meek, op. cit., p. 109.

17. W. Petersen, "Notes on the Socialist Position on Birth Control," in Petersen, op. cit., p. 90.

18. The Engels's quotation has, however, been put to very good use by liberal Socialist demographic commentators who have been seeking to break down Stalinist orthodoxy on population growth.

19. This boundless confidence about the possibilities of nature as harnessed by man survived virtually unscathed in the Soviet period until well into the 1960s. As late as the Belgrade World Population Conference in 1965, some Soviet delegates were still making extravagant claims — for example, that "our planet could provide the food for four million million people." For some instances of this kind of thinking, see Robert C. Cook, "Soviet Population Theory from Marx to Kosygin," Population Bulletin, vol. 23 (1967), no. 4, pp. 91-92 and 97-99.

20. R. Meek, "Malthus — Yesterday and Today: An Introductory Essay," in Meek, op. cit., p. 26.

21. See the passages from Das Kapital, translated in Meek, op. cit., pp. 85-105.

22. For a discussion of this point, see Petersen, op. cit., p. 84.

23. Das Kapital, vol. 1, translated in Meek, op. cit., p. 100.

24. Ibid., p. 99.

25. Engels, The Condition of the Working Class in England, in Marx and Engels on Britain, Moscow, FLPH, 1953, pp. 159 ff. and 181 ff.

26. This is the kind of embarrassment of riches which teleological, historicist theories tend to fall into. On the one hand, the onward march of history or its agents requires something to happen, and therefore it happens; and on the other hand there are good positivist, factological reasons why that something should be so, which may indeed be quite sturdy enough to maintain the full weight of causal explanation without any assistance from the historicist theory. And if the two levels of explanation seem in ill accord, the historicist is left saying a little lamely that History sometimes moves in mysterious ways its wonders to perform.

27. Petersen, op. cit., pp. 91 ff.

28. See, for example, W. Przelaskowski, "Problematyka demograficzna w

pracach W. Lenina," Studia Demograficzne (1970), no. 24, pp. 3-31. This is a purely exegetical essay which in fact concentrates on Lenin's writings on the social structure of prerevolutionary Russia. Many demographers might feel there was virtually no demographic content in the article at all — merely a few pedestrian details of economic and social statistics. For a vain struggle to find something to say about Lenin's contribution to demographic theory (a struggle sustained over several pages), see D. I. Valentei, ed., Marksistsko-leninskaia teoriia narodonaseleniia, 2nd ed., Moscow, 1974, pp. 5 ff.

29. Engels, The Origins, pp. 71 ff.

30. Ibid., pp. 123 ff.

31. Ibid., p. 134.

32. But compare the somewhat different view he took earlier of situations in which the wife went out to work and the husband was reduced to the humiliating role of performing the housework. "Can anyone imagine a more insane state of things than that described in this letter? And yet this condition, which unsexes the man and takes from the woman all womanliness without being able to bestow upon the man true womanliness, or woman true manliness — this condition which degrades, in the most shameful way, both sexes, and through them, Humanity, is the last result of our much-praised civilization...." Engels, The Condition of the Working Class, in Marx and Engels on Britain, p. 179.

33. Engels, The Origins, p. 119.

34. Ibid., p. 123.

35. Ibid., p. 135. It will be noticed that here, as with the population question, Engels is eager to avoid commitment. One might be forgiven for suspecting that in both cases he was reluctant to propose solutions partly because the problems were too hard.

36. Geiger, op. cit., p. 43.

37. V. I. Lenin, Polnoe sobranie sochinenii, vol. 49, Moscow, 1964, pp. 51-52 and 54-57.

38. Klara Zetkin, Reminiscences of Lenin, London, 1929, excerpted in Women and Communism, London, 1950. Though Lenin's remarks to Zetkin have acquired a good deal of posthumous fame, it needs of course to be borne in mind that neither they nor any similar airing of his views was published during his lifetime.

39. Women and Communism, p. 92.

40. Ibid., p. 96.

41. Ibid., p. 97.

42. Ibid., p. 98.

43. V. I. Lenin, "O karikature na marksizm," Polnoe sobranie sochinenii, vol. 30, Moscow, 1962, p. 125.

44. Women and Communism, p. 97.

45. W. Petersen, "Notes on the Socialist Position on Birth Control," in Petersen, op. cit., p. 90.

46. On first principles, of course, it seems quite inconceivable that Marx and Engels could have ever opposed the distribution of contraceptive devices (as some of their modern followers have done). Presumably Engels's reference to the "spontaneous" decline in fertility in France and Lower Austria (see Note 16), despite the unfortunate use of the term "without planning" (by which, it is clear from the context, Engels meant "without planning by the state"), can be taken to indicate that he had no objection to any methods that might have been used to achieve such a state of affairs.

47. Published in Pravda, June 16, 1913. V. I. Lenin Polnoe sobranie sochinenii, vol. 23, Moscow, 1961, pp. 255-57. The quotations in the text follow the translation contained in Women and Communism, pp. 81-82 (the semantic content of the original has been checked).

48. "Most speakers...raised the question of so-called Neo-Malthusianism (artificial measures seeking to prevent conception), and in the process touched on the social aspect of the matter as well." "It would be hard to find a more graphic illustration of the reactionariness and impoverishment of 'social Neo-Malthusianism,'" Polnoe sobranie sochinenii, pp. 255, 256 (author's translation).

Chapter 3

1. For a Soviet exposition of the evolution of social policy in this general area, with citations of original legal sources, etc., see A. M. Beliakova and E. M. Vorozheikin, Sovetskoe semeinoe pravo, Moscow, 1974, chap. 3.

2. For a description of this legislation, see Beliakova and Vorozheikin, op. cit., pp. 63 ff.

3. The law did not amount to an expression of enthusiastic support for the practice of abortion, however. The preamble to the decree described abortion repeatedly as an evil. For an English text, see R. Schlesinger, The Family in the USSR, London, 1949, p. 44. For comment on the decree and a description of its subsequent implementation, see Mark G. Field, "The Re-Legalization of Abortion in Soviet Russia," New England Journal of Medicine, vol. 255, no. 9, pp. 421 ff.

4. The most radical aspects of this legislation were not extended to the Central Asian republics: Schlesinger, op. cit., p. 349. For a text of the code, see ibid., pp. 154-68.

5. See on these points V. Gsovski, "Family and Inheritance in Soviet Law," The Russian Review, vol. 7 (1947), p. 71.

6. Geiger, op. cit., p. 43.

7. See the entries for Armand and Kollontai in Sovetskaia istoricheskaia entsiklopediia, vol. 1, Moscow, 1961, p. 739, and vol. 7, Moscow, 1965, p. 502.

8. See the lively discussion of the code that took place in the RSFSR Central Executive Committee, in Schlesinger, op. cit., pp. 81-153.

9. The critics included Trotsky, Bukharin, and the minister for health, Semashko. See E. H. Carr, Socialism in One Country, vol. 1, London, 1958, pp. 31-34.

10. See Geiger, op. cit., pp. 61, 62, 68.

11. Significantly, no move was made contemporaneously to increase the availability of contraceptive devices, the distribution of which has never in fact received more than qualified official approval. See, for example, David and Vera Mace, The Soviet Family, London, 1964, p. 224; W. Petersen, "The Evolution of Soviet Family Policy," in Petersen, op. cit., p. 106; H. P. David, "Abortion and Family Planning in the Soviet Union: Public Policies and Private Behaviour," Journal of Biosocial Science, vol. 6 (1974), pp. 424-25.

12. J. Dreijmanis, "The Soviet Pro-Natalist Policy," Population Review, 1972, p. 20.

13. For an English text of the 1944 Family Law, see Schlesinger, op. cit., p. 367.

14. The new approach found very clear reflection in Soviet literary production. See Vera S. Dunham, "Sex in the Soviet Union," The Russian Review, vol. 10 (1951), pp. 199-209; Louise E. Luke, "Marxian Woman; Soviet Variants," in

Ernest J. Simmons, Through the Glass of Soviet Literature, New York, 1961, p. 27.

15. The phrase is that of the prominent Soviet expert on family matters, G. M. Sverdlov, quoted in A. Inkeles, Social Change in Soviet Russia, Cambridge, Mass., 1968, p. 217.

16. S. Wolffson, "Socialism and the Family," Pod znamenem marksizma, 1936, translated in Schlesinger, op. cit., p. 302. Wolffson had once been a radical on family policy. The article cited was a desperate attempt by him to erase his own life's work: "In my book, The Sociology of Marriage and the Family, published in 1929, the entirely erroneous thesis is developed that socialism entails the extinction of the family. Considering these ideas harmful I have completely disowned them," ibid., p. 315.

17. "The roots of any looseness of sex relations must consequently be sought in the existence of survivals of capitalism in family life, in the tenacity of the old bourgeois attitude to women...." V. Svetlov, "Socialist Society and the Family," Pod znamenem marksizma, 1936, translated in Schlesinger, op. cit., p. 343.

18. H. P. David estimates that for families having a fifth child while the fourth was still eligible for monthly payments, the total family allowance in 1944 amounted to 51% of the average annual wage, only 19% in 1948, and 12% in 1964. David, Abortion and Family Planning, p. 50.

19. Dreijmanis, op. cit., p. 21.

20. P. Juviler, "Family Reforms on the Road to Communism," in Morton and Juviler, op. cit., p. 33.

21. Dreijmanis, loc. cit.

22. Field, op. cit., p. 426.

23. Juviler, op. cit., p. 36.

24. Field, loc. cit.

25. For an assessment of the 1968 Code (from the standpoint of a Western feminist), see B. Jančar, "Women and Soviet Politics," in H. Morton and R. Tőkés, Soviet Politics and Society in the 1970's, New York, 1974, pp. 134-35.

26. Juviler, op. cit., p. 32.

27. D. and V. Mace, op. cit., p. 224. The Maces are charitable enough to be inclined to accept this versatile explanation.

28. Schlesinger, op. cit., pp. 310-11.

29. Ibid., pp. 330-31 and 338.

30. Juviler, op. cit., pp. 48-52.

31. See David M. Heer, "The Demographic Transition," Journal of Social History, vol. 1 (1967), pp. 210-11.

32. For an account of the evolution of family welfare legislation and activities in the Soviet Union, see Bernice Q. Madison, Social Welfare in the Soviet Union, Stanford, 1968, chaps. 3-5.

33. R. Schlesinger, "Introduction" to op. cit., p. 7 (emphasis added).

34. See, for example, the Central Executive Committee discussion of 1926 referred to earlier, in Schlesinger, op. cit., pp. 81-153, and Geiger, op. cit., chaps. 3 and 4.

35. Quoted in Geiger, op. cit., p. 56.

36. Krupskaya reported in 1923 that there were seven million children on the official register of the homeless. The institutions entrusted with caring for these children had, at their peak in 1922, an accommodation capacity of 600,000 (Madison, op. cit., pp. 39 and 41). Improvements were claimed in the late 1920s and early 1930s; but given the public and private chaos of the period, this seems

scarcely credible. In any case, qualitatively, if not quantitatively, the problem evidently became a critical one again by the early 1930s, leading to the decree of 1935 rendering children of 12 years of age and older criminally responsible in full degree and subject to all measures of punishment. (For the text of the decree, see James H. Meisel and Edward S. Kozera, Materials for the Study of the Soviet System, Ann Arbor, 1953, pp. 219-20.) Rauch comments on the results of this decree as follows: "Some landed up in prisons and camps, and the rest were accommodated in reformatory colonies. From the age of twelve on children could also be condemned to capital punishment. Die 'Besprizornye' verschwanden damit aus der Öffentlichkeit." G. von Rauch, Geschichte der Sowjetunion, Stuttgart, 1969, p. 267.

37. Geiger, op. cit., pp. 57-60, contains an account of some of the shortcomings of the domestic services sector of that period.

38. There is a fuller discussion of current trends and issues in Soviet population policy in Chapter 9.

39. Though the problems of eugenic controls and genetic engineering will not be systematically discussed in this book, their inherent importance and their relevance to any consideration of what Driver calls the "philosophy" of population policy are obviously great.

40. T. H. Rigby, "Stalinism and the Mono-organizational Society," typescript 1975, p. 12. For an interesting literary reflection of wariness on the part of Soviet women about the prospect of state intervention in procreatory matters, see Natalia Baranskaia, "Nedelia kak nedelia," Novy mir, 1969, no. 11, especially pp. 25 ff.

41. On the population policy of the Third Reich, see, for example, H. P. Bleuel, Sex and Society in Nazi Germany, Philadelphia, 1973, chap. 5 and passim; Richard Grunberger, A Social History of the Third Reich, Penguin, 1974, chaps. 15-17 and passim; David V. Glass, Population Policies and Movements in Europe, London, 1967, chap. 6 (for domestic policy in the period before 1939); and Robert L. Koehl, RKFDV: German Resettlement and Population Policy 1939-1945, Cambridge, Mass., 1957 (for the colonial and genocidal aspects of the later phase).

Chapter 4

1. For more detailed general discussions of demographic developments in the Soviet Union and Eastern Europe, see, for example, F. Lorimer, The Population of the Soviet Union, Geneva, 1946; J. N. Biraben, "Essai sur l'évolution démographique de l'U.R.S.S.," Population, vol. 13 (June 1958), p. 29; W. Petersen, Population, 2nd ed., New York, 1969, pp. 630 ff; David M. Heer, "The Demographic Transition in the Soviet Union," Journal of Social History, vol. 1 (1967), p. 193; Milbank Memorial Fund, Population Trends in Eastern Europe, USSR and Mainland China, New York, 1960; Paul F. Myers, "Demographic Trends in Eastern Europe," in U.S. Congress Joint Economic Committee, Economic Developments in Countries of Eastern Europe, Washington, 1970; "La population des pays socialistes Européens," Population, vol. 21 (1966), p. 939; F. A. Leedy, "Demographic Trends in the USSR," in U.S. Congress Joint Economic Committee, Soviet Economic Prospects for the Seventies, Washington, 1973; M. Feshbach and Stephen Rapawy, "Soviet Population and Manpower Trends and Policies," in U.S. Congress Joint Economic Committee, Soviet Economy in a New Perspective, Washington, 1976, p. 113; Godfrey Baldwin, "Population Estimates

and Projections for Eastern Europe: 1950 to 2001," in U.S. Congress Joint Economic Committee, East European Economies Post-Helsinki, Washington, 1977, p. 420; V. V. Bodrova, Narodonaselenie evropeiskikh sotsialisticheskikh stran, Moscow, 1976; T. B. Riabushkin, ed., Naselenie soiuznykh respublik, Moscow, 1977; Robert A. Lewis, Richard H. Rowland, and Ralph S. Clem, Nationality and Population Change in Russia and the USSR, New York, 1976; Leszek A. Kosiński, ed., Demographic Developments in Eastern Europe, New York, 1977; United Nations Economic Commission for Europe, The European Economy in 1968, New York, 1969, pp. 182-216; and Economic Survey of Europe in 1974, New York, 1975, part 2, "Post-war demographic trends in Europe and the outlook until the year 2000"; J. Berent, "Causes of Fertility Decline in Eastern Europe and the Soviet Union," Population Studies, vol. 24 (1970), p. 35 (part 1) and p. 247 (part 2); Vasile Ghetau, "L'Évolution de la fécondite en Roumanie, Population, vol. 33 (1978), no. 2, p. 426; Heinrich Vogel, "Les tendances démographiques en Bulgarie," Revue de l'Est, vol. 9 (1978), no. 2, p. 89; E. Csocsan de Varallja, "La population de la Hongrie au XXe siècle," Revue de l'Est, 1974, no. 3 (chap. 1), no. 4 (chap. 2), and 1977, no. 3 (chap. 3), see especially chap. 1; Paul E. Lydolph et al., "Recent Population Trends in the USSR," Soviet Geography: Review and Translation, October 1978, p. 505; V. Srb, "Obyvatelstvo Československa v letech 1918-68," Demografie, vol. 10 (1968), no. 4, p. 289; Razvitak stanovništva Jugoslavije u posleratnom periodu, Belgrade, 1974 (for World Population Conference, Bucharest, 1974); K. Dziewoński and L. Kosiński, Rozwój i rozmieszczenie ludności Polski w XX wieku, vol. 1, Warsaw, 1967; E. Rosset, Demografia Polski, 2 vols., Warsaw, 1975; A. Maryański, Problemy ludnościowe krajów socjalistycznych, Warsaw, 1974. See also the respective demographic journals of Poland, Czechoslovakia, Hungary, and Yugoslavia: Studia Demograficzne (Warsaw), Demografie (Prague), Demográfia (Budapest), and Stanovništvo (Belgrade).

2. See Appendix Table 3, pp. 273-74.

3. See Petersen, op. cit., pp. 660-64.

4. The estimate of Michael Roof, another leading expert on Soviet demography (for the period 1913-59 and including net emigration), is "70 to 80 million." See Robert C. Cook, "Soviet Population Theory from Marx to Kosygin," Population Bulletin, vol. 23 (October 1967), no. 4, p. 93.

5. See Paul F. Myers, op. cit., p. 71.

6. For a discussion, see Kosiński, op. cit.

7. See J. W. Brackett, "Demographic Trends and Population Policy in the Soviet Union," in U.S. Congress Joint Economic Committee, Dimensions of Soviet Economic Power, Washington, 1962, pp. 529-30.

8. David, op. cit., p. 232.

9. Ibid., p. 20.

10. The Romanian government greatly restricted their abortion legislation in 1966. Since the introduction of more restricted indications for legal abortion in 1974, Hungary's abortion rate appears to have fallen below its birthrate.

11. Substantial increases in the birthrate have been achieved in Hungary and Czechoslovakia in particular and (though with a subsequent decline setting in) in Romania. See Appendix Tables 1 and 2, pp. 271-72.

12. See Appendix Tables 2, 5, and 20, pp. 272, 276, and 289.

13. The Romanian figure is from Anuarul demografic al Republicii Socialiste Romania 1974, p. 133, and the East German and Albanian ones from Rocznik

demograficzny 1977, Warsaw, 1978, p. 194. The Albanian statistic actually refers to 1969.

14. Narodnoe khoziaistvo SSSR v 1972 godu, pp. 48-49. The range in 1976
was even greater: see Appendix Table 4, p. 275.

15. Statistical Pocket-Book of Yugoslavia 1974, p. 34.

16. Naselenie SSSR, Spravochnik, Moscow, 1974, p. 96.

17. R. Szporluk, "The Nations of the USSR in 1970," in Survey, vol. 17 (1971),
no. 4 (81), p. 98.

18. "National Structure of the Yugoslav Population," Yugoslav Survey, vol.
14, no. 1, p. 13. The percentage increase of the Serbs is somewhat deflated by
changed self-identification of Bosnian Moslems (who at the 1961 census had declared themselves as Serbs).

19. For a wide-ranging discussion of the fertility decline in Western coun-
tries, see F. Marchal and O. Rabut, "Evolution récente de la fécondité en
Europe occidentale," Population, vol. 27 (1973), p. 838. See also J. Bourgeois-
Pichat, "La deuxième conférence démographique européenne de Strasbourg,"
Population, vol. 27 (1972), pp. 422-32. For the earlier postwar phase, see D. V.
Glass, "Fertility Trends in Europe since the Second World War," Population
Studies, vol. 22 (1968), p. 103.

20. See J. Lindgren, "Finland's Declining Fertility," Yearbook of Population
Research in Finland, vol. 22 (1971), p. 21. In the last two or three years Finland's birthrate has increased slightly. See Appendix Tables 1 and 2, pp. 271-72.

21. See K. Schwarz, "Ursachen und Folgen des Geburtenrückgangs in der
BRD," European Demographic Information Bulletin, vol. 2, no. 1-2, pp. 1-11.
See Appendix Tables 1 and 2, pp. 271-72.

22. See Appendix Tables 1 and 2, pp. 271-72. President Giscard himself has
recently called on his fellow-countrymen to have larger families and foreshadowed further economic inducements to them to do so. Canberra Times (AAP-
AP Despatch), December 27, 1978.

23. See Lydolph et al., pp. 507-8.

24. See A. Elias, "Magnitude and Distribution of the Labour Force in Eastern
Europe," in Economic Developments in Countries of Eastern Europe, p. 155;
Baldwin, 1977, p. 424.

25. See The European Economy in 1968, 1969, p. 209.

26. See A. Elias, op. cit., pp. 196-200, and P. F. Myers, op. cit., pp. 101-8.

27. Finding reported by K.-H. Mehlan, "The Socialist Countries of Europe,"
in B. Berelson, ed., Family Planning and Population Programs, Chicago, 1966,
p. 223. Such remarkable results almost invite paraphrase of Lenin's celebrated
aphorism about voting with the feet. Small wonder, perhaps, that Ceausescu
shortly afterward embarked on the Great Demographic Leap Forward of 1966.

28. The rural net reproduction ratio has been some 70 to 75% higher than the
urban one for the last decade or so. See Appendix Table 14, p. 285.

29. See Economic Survey of Europe in 1974, 1975, p. 117.

30. On permanent migration movements, see Kosinski, 1977, and on temporary, Levcik, op. cit.

31. T. Vais, "Sotrudnichestvo stran SEV v ispol'zovanii trudovykh resursov,"
Voprosy ekonomiki, 1975, no. 9, p. 106.

32. Economist, January 18, 1975.

33. Vjesnik, August 13, 1979, cited by S. Stanković in RFE RAD Background Report 199 (Yugoslavia), September 19, 1979.

34. These matters will be discussed in greater detail in Chapter 5.

Chapter 5

1. For a discussion by a socialist economist of the reasons for this, see M. Kabaj, Elementy pełnego i racjonalnego zatrudnienia w gospodarce socjalistycznej, Warsaw, 1972, chap. 6.

2. The Shchekino experiment has been given little chance to spread its wings and has not, accordingly, obviated pressures on managers to maintain excessive levels of manpower. See M. Feshbach and S. Rapawy, "Labor Constraints in the Five-Year Plan," in U.S. Congress Joint Economic Committee, Soviet Economic Prospects for the Seventies, Washington, 1973, p. 489. See also the article by E. Manevich in Ekonomika i organizatsiia promyshlennogo proizvodstva, 1978, no. 2, p. 75.

3. See Appendix Table 11, p. 283.

4. In recent years there has been a flood of articles and monographs dealing with the growing problem of labor shortage and proposing means of overcoming it (better utilization of existing reserves, activation of pensioners and invalids, increasing the birthrate, etc.). See, for example, the articles by K. A. Novikov in Kommunist, 1969, no. 13; V. Guseinov and V. Korchagin in Voprosy ekonomiki, 1971, no. 2, p. 45; R. Ivanova in Voprosy ekonomiki, 1973, no. 1, p. 40; R. Galetskaia in Voprosy ekonomiki, 1973, no. 10, p. 155; N. Novitskii and M. Babkina in Voprosy ekonomiki, 1975, no. 8, p. 57; L. Danilov in Kommunist, 1977, no. 9, p. 39; V. Perevedentsev in Zhurnalist, 1978, no. 5, p. 20; and by Bachurin, Manevich, and Maslova in Voprosy ekonomiki, 1978, pp. 3, 38, and 49. See also the collective volume entitled Demograficheskie aspekty zaniatosti, Moscow, 1975. For excellent Western reviews of the problems, see Feshbach and Rapawy, op. cit., 1973 and 1976.

5. See, for example, his article in Ekonomika i organizatsiia promyshlennogo proizvodstva, 1972, no. 1, p. 74.

6. In addition to the literature previously cited, see, for example, P. P. Litviakov, ed., Demograficheskie problemy zaniatosti, Moscow, 1969; Osnovnye problemy ratsional'nogo ispol'zovania trudovykh resursov v SSSR, Moscow, 1971; Naselenie, trudovye resursy SSSR, Moscow, 1971; Narodonaselenie: Naselenie i trudovye resursy, Moscow, 1973. Numerous monographs have also been published on the labor reserves of particular regions of the USSR.

7. See, for example, Literaturnaia gazeta, August 8, 1973, p. 10. There is, in fact, a vast literature in both West and East on this subject alone.

8. For some candid reporting on evasion of migration and labor controls, see the article by D. Ivanov and V. Trifonov in Krokodil, June 16, 1971, p. 2.

9. The Soviet economist L. Chizhova has said of the indigenous populations of Central Asia, Kazakhstan, and the Caucasus area that "Practice has shown that some of them still adapt badly to industrial labor," "Regional'nye aspekty ispol'zovaniia trudovykh resursov," in D. Valentei, ed., Narodonaselenie: Naselenie i ekonomika, Moscow, 1973, p. 25.

10. T. Khachaturov in Voprosy ekonomiki, 1971, no. 3, p. 8.

11. According to A. Kvasha in Literaturnaia gazeta, March 22, 1972, p. 10, the female work-force participation rate had increased from 78% in 1959 to 92% "now."

12. According to computations presented in Feshbach and Rapawy, op. cit., 1976, by the quinquennium 1986-90, Central Asia and Kazakhstan will be providing annual labor force increments greater than the net national figure. See Appendix Table 11, p. 283.

13. See, for example, D. I. Valentei, Osnovy teorii narodonaseleniia, Moscow, 1973, p. 65.

14. See table of interregional migratory flows 1959-70 in V. Perevedentsev, "Population Distribution and Migration," translated in Soviet Law and Government, vol. 13 (1974), no. 2, p. 88.

15. See Itogi Vsesoiuznoi perepisi naseleniia 1970 goda, vol. 7, Moscow, 1974, pp. 6-7.

16. Note, for example, the remarkable lack of facts and figures in "Tendentsii migratsionnykh protsessov i nekotorye voprosy upravleniia imi," in Upravlenie razvitiia narodonaseleniia v SSSR (collective volume), Moscow, 1977. There is a good discussion of the statistical paradox apparently presented by the results of the Census enquiry into migration patterns in 1968-69 in T. Shabad, "Soviet Migration Patterns based on 1970 Census Data," in Kosiński, op. cit., 1977, p. 173.

17. See, for example, the articles by T. Arbuzova and L. Evdokimova in Voprosy ekonomiki, 1972, no. 6, p. 156; Beketov and Latifi in Pravda, November 14 and 15, 1976; and Perevedentsev in Zhurnalist, 1978, no. 5, p. 21; see also V. Zorza in The Guardian, January 7, 1970.

18. See the table in Naselenie SSSR: Spravochnik, pp. 84-88. The term "Central Asian" is used here in the narrow sense, excluding the Kazakhs. Generally, however, throughout this book "Central Asians" and "Central Asian" are used in the wider sense including Kazakhstan and the Kazakhs.

19. N. Pankrat'eva, Naselenie i sotsialisticheskoe vosproizvodstvo, Moscow, 1977, p. 182.

20. The experimental system of labor controls introduced in Leningrad, Moscow, Ufa, and Kaluga (see Feshbach and Rapawy, op. cit., 1973, pp. 541-43 for a description) seemed to herald a return to Stalinist norms of labor law. However, these agencies were subsequently shorn of their powers. See A. Tenson, "The Curtailment of the Powers of Public Employment Agencies," Radio Liberty Research, 210/73, July 9, 1973.

21. Data cited by L. Danilov in Kommunist, 1977, no. 9, translated in CDSP, vol. 29, no. 32, p. 4.

22. Bachurin, op. cit.

Chapter 6

1. The terms "plural," "pluralism," and "pluralist" are themselves a good illustration of this. See L. Kuper and M. G. Smith, Pluralism in Africa, Berkeley, 1969, chap. 1, and R. A. Schermerhorn, Comparative Ethnic Relations, New York, 1970, chap. 4.

2. Partial exceptions will be made in the case of Soviet Moslems and Eastern European Gypsies. Because of their strong cultural and linguistic links (and also because of the attempts made in the past to bring about their unification), the Soviet Moslems and the "Central Asians" — Uzbeks, Kirgiz, Karakalpaks, Tadzhiks, Turkmen, and Kazakhs — are for certain purposes treated as entities. This procedure, however, could be justified on "ethnic" as well as on religious grounds. In the case of the Gypsies, who tend not to be treated as an ethnic minority for national statistical purposes by East European states, a conscious decision has been made to reject the official classification.

3. Kuper and Smith, op. cit., pp. 139-40.

4. For an excellent historical perspective on the spread of "ethnonational-

ism," see Walker Connor, "The Politics of Ethnonationalism," Journal of International Affairs, vol. 27 (1973), no. 1, p. 1.

5. N. Choucri, Population Dynamics and International Violence, Lexington, 1974, p. 76.

6. A South African clergyman named M. Steyn was reported in Die Zeit (June 1, 1973, p. 2) as proposing that the pill be banned to the white population and given to the blacks (whose morals were in any case so low that even the pill could do them no further damage). And a Dr. Van Rensburg has been reported (Canberra Times, January 1, 1975) as warning a South African sociological conference of "annihilating chaos" unless a birth-control campaign for blacks were introduced. Compare the following, unequivocal conclusion of two specialist analysts of multiethnic politics: "In the case of the dominant minority situation, one consideration especially stands out: the overriding fear held by the minority, whether rightly or wrongly, that they stand to be overwhelmed by a vastly larger majority," A. Rabushka and K. A. Shepsle, Politics in Plural Societies: A Theory of Democratic Instability, Columbus, Ohio, 1972, p. 158.

7. Pierre van den Berghe, for example, has declared that the distinction between multiracial and multiethnic societies is an important one, for all that they have much in common (P. L. van den Berghe, Race and Ethnicity, New York, 1970, p. 10). Many writers who do not draw the distinction explicitly nonetheless show that they implicitly accept it by using expressions like "ethnic and racial" or "ethnic or racial" over and over again. One gains the impression at times that the distinction between racial and nonracial would have even more adherents were it not for the disrepute that all forms of "racialism" have fallen into in the intellectual community in recent decades and the desire felt by representatives of problem-solving social science to define some part of their problem out of existence.

8. As, for example, by G. Franklin Edwards in "Race Relations," in International Encyclopaedia of the Social Sciences, New York, 1968, vol. 13, p. 269.

9. See Michael Banton, "The Concept of Racism," in S. Zubaida, ed., Race and Racism, London, 1970.

10. Sexual prowess may be an exception here. See, for example, Calvin C. Hernton's Sex and Racism, London, 1970.

11. In this connection it is interesting that John Barron, in his book on the KGB (KGB, London, 1975, especially pp. 45 and 61), cites instances of Soviet employees in Middle Eastern countries describing Arabs variously as "yellows" and "blackasses" (chernozhopy) and declaring them to be "subhuman." Barron rather undermines his own credibility as a witness by elsewhere in the book describing FBI agents in terms of a comicstrip lyricism, but the passages referred to have a strong flavor of authenticity nonetheless.

12. See Ernest Krausz, Ethnic Minorities in Britain, London, 1972, p. 10: "Two Government White Papers in 1964 emphasized that in the case of Commonwealth immigrants 'the evidence laid more stress on the hostility towards [them] stemming directly from colour prejudice' "; and, p. 58: "The amount of discrimination and prejudice immigrants have to endure seems to vary even by the shade of their skin colour" (evidence cited).

13. See Pettigrew and Cramer's interesting finding that in the southern United States, the incidence of lynching is inversely related to the relative size of the Negro population. Thomas F. Pettigrew and M. Richard Cramer, "The Demography of Desegregation," Journal of Social Issues, 1959, no. 4, pp. 62-63.

14. For a contrary view, see, for example, D. Horowitz, "Three Dimensions of Ethnic Politics," World Politics, vol. 23 (1971), no. 2, p. 232; J. Rex, "The Concept of Race in Sociological Theory," in S. Zubaida, ed., op. cit.; and N. Choucri, op. cit., p. 77.

15. For a remorseless critique of the fragilities of Marxist theory in the face of ethnic facts, see L. Kuper, "Race, Class and Power: Some Comments on Revolutionary Change," in Comparative Studies in Society and History, vol. 14 (1972), p. 400. There is a rather less than lethal riposte to Kuper's article in D. Lane, "Ethnic and Class Stratification in Soviet Kazakhstan 1917-1939," in Comparative Studies in Society and History, vol. 17 (1975), p. 165.

16. Edward D. Sokol, The Revolt of 1916 in Russian Central Asia, Baltimore, 1954, p. 33; G. Wheeler, The Modern History of Soviet Central Asia, London, 1964, p. 50.

17. G. Wheeler, Racial Problems in Soviet Muslim Asia, London, 1962, p. 8.

18. Richard A. Pierce, Russian Central Asia 1867-1917, Berkeley, 1960, pp. 203-24 and 249.

19. E. Bacon, Central Asians under Soviet Rule, Ithaca, 1966, p. 215.

20. A. Bennigsen and C. Lemercier-Quelquejay, Islam in the Soviet Union, London, 1967, p. 197. Compare the discussion in the section on ethnic assimilation in this chapter.

21. For an account of the Tatar role in the Muslim revival in Tsarist Russia, see Hans Bräker, "The Muslim Revival in Russia," in G. Katkov, E. Oberländer, N. Poppe, and G. von Rauch, eds., Russia Enters the Twentieth Century 1894-1917, London, 1971. "Pan-Islamic" activity need not be taken in the strictly religious sense, though in this context it is interesting that Bräker cites a Soviet source according to which religion has more adherents in the "Eastern" republics than elsewhere in the Soviet Union (p. 182). If there is to be some fresh pan-Moslem or pan-Turkic movement in the USSR, the role of the astoundingly resolute and solid Crimean Tatars could again become crucial, just as it was in the pre-Revolutionary Moslem revival. In this connection see the extremely interesting Crimean Tatar samizdat documents translated in Osteuropa, vol. 25 (1976), no. 1, pp. A10-31. Despite the emphatic (though at times somewhat pro-Peking) Marxism-Leninism that the Crimean Tatar protesters profess, it is noticeable that they do not hesitate to speak of the Moslem peoples of the USSR as forming an emergent national group (p. A22) or to accuse their adversaries explicitly of "racism" (e.g., pp. A30-31).

22. The majority of Tatar dialects are to greater or lesser degree mutually comprehensible with the Turkic languages of Central Asia.

23. A Soviet anthropologist has said of the Volga Tatars and Russians that they cannot be reliably distinguished on the basis of physical appearance. Yet 25% of her respondents claimed to be able to tell their own people on the street "easily," and a further 38% said that they could do so sometimes. G. V. Starovoitova, "K issledovaniiu etnopsikhologii gorodskikh zhitelei," Sovetskaia etnografiia, 1976, no. 3, p. 45.

24. There is no very precise information on the state of ethnic relations in Russian Central Asia before the revolution either. See G. Wheeler, Racial Problems, p. 8.

25. The following discussion will assume rather than expound the basic patterns of interethnic relations in the USSR and the main lines of official policy on nationality questions. Among the more significant Western expositions, see, for example, Problems of Communism, September-October 1967 (special issue on

"Nationalities and Nationalism"); B. Lewytzkyj, Die Sowjetische Nationalitätenpolitik nach Stalins Tod 1953-70, Munich, 1970; E. Goldhagen, ed., Ethnic Minorities in the Soviet Union, New York, 1968; E. Glyn Lewis, Multilingualism in
the Soviet Union, The Hague, 1972; Edward Allworth, ed., Soviet Nationality Problems, New York, 1971; Z. Katz et al., eds., Handbook of Major Soviet Nationalities,
New York, 1975; E. Allworth, ed., Nationality Group Survival in Multi-ethnic States:
Shifting Support Patterns in the Soviet Baltic Region, New York, 1977; the symposium
in Canadian Slavonic Papers, 1975, no. 2-3; Grey Hodnett, "The Debate over Soviet
Federalism," Soviet Studies, vol. 18 (1967), p. 458; V. S. Vardys, "Verschmelzung
der Nationen ?" Osteuropa, vol. 18 (1968), p. 524; E. Oberländer, "Der Sowjetische
Nationsbegriff heute," Osteuropa, vol. 21 (1971), p. 273; D. Pospielovsky, "Einige
Aspekte nationaler Spannungen in der UdSSR," Osteuropa, vol. 27 (1977), no. 3, p. 210;
A. Shtromas, "The Legal Position of Soviet Nationalities and their Territorial Units
According to the 1977 Constitution of the USSR," The Russian Review, vol. 37 (1978),
p. 265. Semiofficial expositions of current Soviet doctrine can be found in E. Bagra-
mov, "Razvitie KPSS Marksistsko-Leninskogo ucheniia o natsional'nykh otnosheni-
iakh," Kommunist, 1973, no. 4, p. 34, and N. Tarasenko, "Sblizhenie natsii — zakono-
mernost' kommunisticheskogo stroitel'stva," Kommunist, 1978, no. 13.

26. M. Feshbach, "Population," in U.S. Congress Joint Economic Committee,
Economic Performance and the Military Burden in the Soviet Union, Washington,
1970, p. 61. The 1977 figure is calculated from estimates given (for January 1)
for the populations of the USSR and RSFSR in Narodnoe khoziaistvo SSSR za 60
let, Moscow, 1977, p. 49.

27. It is possible that such projections do not in fact exist, at least for the
nationalities. G. A. Bondarskaia, in Rozhdaemost' v SSSR, Moscow, 1977, dis-
cusses the problems of projecting population statistics in abstract terms that
rather suggest such analyses are still at the planning stage. Characteristically
the discussion is cloaked in euphemism and qualification, and no estimates of
likely numbers are offered (though some extrapolations possibly meant to
startle are deployed). See especially chap. 3.

28. See A. Bohmann, "Russen und Russisch in der UdSSR," Aussenpolitik,
1971, p. 757. Bohmann's figures include Poles, Bulgarians, Czechs, and Slovaks
as well as the larger Slavic groups.

29. See Appendix Tables 4 and 5, pp. 275-76.

30. All the earlier percentages refer to 1926, except for Lithuania and Moldavia (both 1936), Latvia (1935), and Estonia (1941). The figures have been
taken from F. Lorimer, op. cit., pp. 63-64, and B. Lewickyj, "Sowiecka polityka
narodowościowa," Kultura, Paris, 1960, no. 152, pp. 80-82.

31. Pravda, April 17, 1971.

32. Iunost', 1967, no. 10, p. 90.

33. T. B. Riabushkin, ed., Naselenie soiuznykh respublik, Moscow, 1977, p. 209.

34. T. Parming, "Soziale Konsequenzen der Bevölkerungsveränderungen in
Estland seit 1939," in Acta Baltica, vol. 11 (1971), p. 21.

35. Compare tables 1 and 2 in Naselenie soiuznykh respublik, pp. 303 and 305.

36. See Appendix Table 5, p. 276.

37. Naselenie soiuznykh respublik, p. 177.

38. See Appendix Tables 4 and 5, pp. 275-76.

39. The initial census results published in the various republic newspapers
in April, May, June, and July of 1971 contained interesting differences in the
amount of detail presented on national composition. Where the trends favored
the indigenous nationality (as in Georgia and Kazakhstan, for example), more

information was made available. Where the trends were less favorable, a policy of least said soonest mended was usually followed; thus the only republic paper not to provide nationality structure data in percentage form for its own republic for 1959 and 1970 was Sovetskaia Estoniia (May 18, 1971). Those reports which included ethnic breakdowns for the capital city in 1959 and 1970 were invariably able to record a relative improvement in the position of the republic nationality. This group, a surprisingly large nine of the fifteen, includes Kiev but does not include Tallin, Riga (where there is now a Russian majority), Kishinev, Dushanbe, or Frunze.

40. In putting the case in these terms, I am not, it should perhaps be emphasized, implying that economic and other factors are of little or lesser relevance, merely that demostrategic considerations must always be present, at least as an important arrière-pensée.

41. For the basis for these generalizations, see Appendix Tables 4, 5, and 9.

42. Lewickyj, op. cit., p. 82.

43. See Lorimer, op. cit., p. 138.

44. See Appendix Tables 8 and 9, pp. 281-82.

45. See Shabad, op. cit., in Kosinski, 1977, pp. 186 ff, where evidence for these trends is adduced. See also M. Rywkin, "Central Asia and Soviet Manpower," Problems of Communism, Jan.-Feb. 1979, pp. 10-11.

46. This and the immediately following statistics are taken from Pravda, April 4, 1971.

47. Szporluk, op. cit., p. 98.

48. The Karelian SSR, which was established in 1940, was demoted to ASSR status in 1956, presumably partly in consequence of the small and diminishing proportion of representatives of the titular nationality.

49. Kazakhstanskaia Pravda, June 9, 1971.

50. Pravda, April 4, 1971.

51. Sovetskaia Rossiia, May 20, 1970, p. 3.

52. N. Baskakov in Iazyki narodov SSSR, vol. 2, Tiurkskie iazyki, reviewed by G. K. Dulling in Central Asian Review, vol. 25 (1967), p. 160. Dulling expresses some skepticism about this claim. The more dubious it is linguistically, however, the more significant it is from other points of view. Bennigsen and Lemercier-Quelquejay (op. cit., p. 207) assert that "Linguistic kinship is still very much alive — an Uzbek has little difficulty in understanding a Kazakh, a Turkmen or an Azeri." A leading world authority on Turkic languages, Professor S. Wurm of the Australian National University, suggests that in fact there are significant differences in degree of mutual comprehensibility, Turkmen, Azeri, and Turkish, for example, being very close, and Kazakh and Kirgiz a good deal closer to one another than either is to Uzbek or Turkmen. An Uzbek would have relatively little difficulty in understanding a Turkmen, but much greater difficulty in communicating with a Kazakh, or more especially, an Azeri — Turkmen constituting a kind of link between the Turkmen-Azeri-Turkish group and the one to which Uzbek belongs (personal communication).

53. See, for example, the evidence cited by G. Sultan, "Demographic and Cultural Trends Among Turkic Peoples of the Soviet Union," in E. Goldhagen, ed., Ethnic Minorities in the Soviet Union, New York, 1968, p. 268.

54. G. Baldwin, Estimates and Projections of the Population of the USSR by Age and Sex 1950 to 2000, Washington, D.C., 1973, reproduced in Leedy, op. cit., p. 473. The C series is based on the assumption of a mild decline in fertility over the period (GRR from 114 in 1972 to 108 in 2000).

55. G. Jukes, The Soviet Union in Asia, Sydney, 1973, p. 56.

56. "Greetings to you, my Uzbek, our thoughts and reveries are one, you are the closest kin, the right hand of a Kirgiz, and Tashkent is the capital of Central Asia." Baydilda Sarnogoev, "Salat saga," in Ala Too, 1970, no. 2, quoted in A. Procyk, "The Search for a Heritage and the Nationality Question in Central Asia," in E. Allworth, ed., The Nationality Question in Soviet Central Asia, New York, 1973, p. 130.

57. Compare Notes 21 and 56.

58. "In the competitive case, prejudice against groups seems to build up to a point of dangerous tension in response to such conditions as rapid influx of lower-caste migrants or rising unemployment." P. van den Berghe, op. cit., p. 30.

59. L. Kuper, "Race, Class and Power," p. 414.

60. Robert A. Lewis, et al., "Modernization, Population Change and Nationality," Canadian Slavonic Papers, 1975, no. 2-3, p. 286; see especially pp. 294-98.

61. Iu. Arutiunian, "Konkretno-sotsiologicheskoe issledovanie natsional'nykh otnoshenii," in Voprosy filosofii, 1969, no. 12, p. 129.

62. For most illuminating discussions of instances of the latter type occurring in the Socialist bloc, see Grey Hodnett and Peter Potichnyj, The Ukraine and the Czechoslovak Crisis, Canberra, 1970, and Robert R. King, Minorities under Communism: Nationalities as a Source of Tension among Balkan Communist States, Cambridge, Mass., 1973, especially chaps. 4 and 6.

63. Their only rivals in this respect are the indigenous peoples of the Transcaucasian area. See, for example, E. Manevich "Vosproizvodstvo naseleniia i ispol'zovanie trudovykh resursov," Voprosy ekonomiki, 1978, no. 8, p. 39.

64. For a closer discussion of these problems, see the third section of this chapter, pp. 78-83.

65. The special status of the main Transcaucasian peoples in their republics was nicely illustrated by the republic constitutions adopted in 1978. Only in Armenia, Georgia, and Azerbaidzhan were the republic languages officially designated as state languages. See Ann Sheehy, "The National Languages and the New Constitutions of the Transcaucasian Republics," Radio Liberty Research Report, no. 97, May 3, 1978.

66. The Kosovo case will be discussed in detail in Part IV.

67. For a different view on this and related issues, see Rein Taagepera, "The 1970 Soviet Census: Fusion or Crystallization of Nationalities?" in Soviet Studies, vol. 23 (1971), no. 2, p. 216. For another analysis, see R. Szporluk, op. cit.

68. "The Politics of Ethnonationalism," p. 20.

69. See the national composition by republic, ASSR, and oblast of the relevant regions in Itogi, vol. 4.

70. Between 1959 and 1970, thanks in substantial measure to the return of Kalmucks from Central Asia following their rehabilitation, the Kalmuck percentage of the republic's population rose from 35 to 41% while the Russian component fell from 56 to 46%. Even if few of the remaining 27,000 Kalmucks outside the Kalmuck ASSR were to succeed in returning, the greater demographic dynamism of those already there should make them a simple majority at least by the early 1980s. Recent estimates of population for the republic, however, suggest that this is not happening. According to Narodnoe khoziaistvo SSSR za 60 let (p. 45), the increase between 1970 and 1977 was only 6,000, or about 0.3% a year. Given that Kalmuck fertility is twice that of the Slav population, this is a surprising statistic. What the reasons behind it are must for the moment remain a matter for speculation.

71. The example has been chosen because of its capacity to stimulate the imagination. The conditions stated are quite unreal. Fertility differentials between white and black in the United States are actually much less than those between European and Moslem in the USSR and on present indications appear likely to diminish further. See "Family Size and the Black American," Population Bulletin, vol. 30, no. 4.

72. There has been a tendency recently for per capita GNP differentials between the republics to increase, and less emphasis is placed in official statements on equalization and more on rational utilization of productive forces. Nonetheless capital redistribution continues on the whole to favor the poorer republics, and were it not for their more rapid population growth and lower productivity, this would find greater reflection in relative per capita growth rates. For further discussion of these problems, see H.-J. Wagener, "Die RSFSR und die nichtrussischen Republiken: Ein ökonomischer Vergleich," Osteuropa Wirtschaft, vol. 2 (1969), p. 113; V. Bandera and Z. Melnyk, The Soviet Economy in Regional Perspective, New York, 1973, especially chap. 7, "Regional Differences in Incomes and Levels of Living in the USSR," by Gertrude E. Schroeder; P. Wiles, "Recent Data on Soviet Income Distribution," Survey, vol. 21, no. 3, pp. 36-37; V. Holubnychy, "Some Economic Aspects of Relations among the Soviet Republics," in E. Goldhagen, op. cit., pp. 50-120.

73. Competition for jobs (particularly in industry) and discrimination against Central Asians on linguistic or other grounds have already been frequently commented on. See the evidence cited, for example, in Teresa Rakowska-Harmstone, Russia and Nationalism in Central Asia: The Case of Tadzhikistan, Baltimore, 1970, pp. 286-88, and V. Holubnychy, "Spatial Efficiency in the Soviet Economy," in Bandera and Melnyk, op. cit., p. 6. Rywkin has challenged this view, emphasizing that Central Asians are often in fact given preferential treatment to maintain nationality quotas in particular spheres of activity. This practice, however, does not appear to apply to industrial labor; nor probably does it benefit the vast proportion of Central Asians who do not know Russian. M. Rywkin, "Religion, Nationalism and Political Power," Canadian Slavonic Papers, 1975, no. 2-3, pp. 278-79. See also Note 9 to Chapter 5.

74. Instances are quoted, for example, by P. Berton in "The Border Issue: China and the Soviet Union," Studies in Comparative Communism, July-October 1969, p. 137. The Chinese appear to have been the first to set this particular fuse alight: see H. Brahm, "Pekings Spiel mit der Rassenfrage," Osteuropa, vol. 15 (1965), p. 813. See also H. Salisbury, The Coming War between Russia and China, London, 1969, passim. It would appear that the blanket definition of "Asian" to include Soviet Central Asian peoples as well as Chinese is something with which Soviet Asians are prepared to identify. Shafarevich writes: "More than once — and it has happened to more people than me — I have had occasion in our Central Asian cities to hear the cry 'Just wait till the Chinese come — they'll show you!'" I. Shafarevich, "Obosoblenie ili sblizhenie?" in A. I. Solzhenitsyn et al., Iz-pod glyb, Paris, 1974, p. 97.

75. Developments in Soviet Russian culture and literature since about the mid-1960s would certainly seem to suggest this. See, for example, the discussions in Slavic Review, vol. 32 (1973), nos. 1 and 4.

76. Given the growing demographic pressures on arable land and the labor market in the area, it is of course quite possible that indigenous outmigration could occur in the future irrespective of what the European settlers should choose to do.

77. Furthering intermingling between the different ethnic groups — though often proposed as a palliative or cure for racial tensions — seems at best a hazardous treatment. If it succeeds, it of course succeeds; but if it does not succeed, it must inevitably make things worse. Connor says, "Intergroup contacts are at least as apt to lead to increased discord as they are to mutual understanding: a review of ethnopolitical history strongly suggests discord is the more likely." "The Politics of Ethnonationalism," p. 20.

78. According to reports (Newsweek, September 3, 1973, p. 24), the sweat-suited vigilantes who threw their weight around at the Israel-Cuba basketball match were supplied by the army. Also see M. Agurskii, "Neonatsistskaia opasnost' v Sovetskom Soiuze," samizdat article published in Novyi zhurnal, no. 118 (March 1975), p. 199.

79. It would appear that there is not a great deal of ethnic intermingling in the residential areas of Central Asian cities, though unequivocal evidence on the point is not available. See Robert J. Osborn, Soviet Social Policies: Welfare Equality and Community, Homewood, Ill., 1970, pp. 261-62. See also T. Rakowska-Harmstone, op. cit., p. 275; Olaf Caroe, Soviet Empire: The Turks of Central Asia and Stalinism, 2nd ed., New York, 1967, p. xxiii. The existence of national language schools, moreover, has the effect of reinforcing segregation patterns.

80. See Osteuropa, vol. 21 (1971), no. 12, pp. A749-53, for excerpts from three most interesting articles about the Uighurs which appeared in the Soviet German-language paper Freundschaft. See also R. Šilde-Karklins, "The Uighurs between China and the USSR," Canadian Slavonic Papers, 1975, no. 2-3, p. 346.

81. See Current Scene, vol. 11 (1973), no. 12, pp. 19-20.

82. For a thorough discussion of assimilation trends in the USSR (not updated to embrace the 1970 census results, however), see B. Silver, "Social Mobilization and the Russification of Soviet Nationalities," American Political Science Review, vol. 68 (March 1974), p. 45. See also Robert A. Lewis et al., op. cit., 1976, chap. 7.

83. Rywkin, however, reports an increase in circulation of Central Asian language newspapers. "Religion, Nationalism and Political Power," p. 275.

84. For a discussion of the relative position of Russian and the minority languages in Soviet education, see B. Silver, "The Status of National Minority Languages in Soviet Education," Soviet Studies, vol. 26 (1974), no. 1, p. 28.

85. Sovetskaiia pedagogika, 1972, no. 6, pp. 40-46.

86. Istoriia SSSR, 1970, no. 1, p. 222.

87. Among recent examples, see V. I. Kozlov, Etnicheskaia demografiia, Moscow, 1977; G. A. Bondarskaia, Rozhdaemost' v SSSR (Etnodemograficheskii aspekt), Moscow, 1977; Skol'ko detei budet v sovetskoi sem'e (collective volume), Moscow, 1977; V. A. Borisov, Perspektivy rozhdaemosti, Moscow, 1976.

88. Most of the mixed marriage studies and statistics that have been published relate to Caucasian or Central Asian areas, where high indices are bound to be recorded. While there are obviously good scientific reasons why this should be so, the strong official interest in the subject makes one wonder whether it is entirely accidental. See, for example, Trud, October 22, 1965; Sovetskaia etnografiia, 1971, no. 4, p. 80, and no. 6, p. 112; Izvestiia AN Turkmenskoi SSR, Seria obshchestvennykh nauk, 1969, no. 5, p. 16; Sovetskaia etnografiia, 1967, no. 4, p. 137.

89. In a speech in celebration of the fiftieth anniversary of the establishment of the USSR, Kommunist, 1972, no. 18 (December), p. 15.

90. See Lorimer, op. cit., pp. 138-39.

91. Itogi, vol. 4, p. 9. See Appendix Table 7, pp. 278-80.

92. For a detailed analysis of assimilation trends among Belorussians, see Steven L. Guthier, "The Belorussians: National Identification and Assimilation, 1897-1970," Soviet Studies, vol. 29 (1977), no. 1, p. 37 (part 1), and no. 2, p. 270 (part 2).

93. See Appendix Table 7, pp. 278-80.

94. Itogi, vol. 4, pp. 152-53 and 192-93. See the discussion of the Soviet Polish minority in Chapter 14.

95. See Appendix Table 7, pp. 278-80.

96. For an excellent discussion of the whole problem, see Ethel and Stephen P. Dunn, "Ethnic Intermarriage as an Indicator of 'Cultural Convergence' in Soviet Central Asia," in E. Allworth, op. cit., p. 45. See also Wesley Fisher, "Ethnic Consciousness and Intermarriage Correlates of Endogamy among the Major Soviet Nationalities," Soviet Studies, vol. 29 (1977), no. 3, p. 395.

97. Izvestiia AN Turkmenskoi SSR. Seriia obshch. nauk, 1969, no. 5, p. 16.

98. According to an article by Iu. Bromlei in Istoriia SSSR, 1977, no. 3, p. 19 (translated in CDSP, vol. 29, no. 28, p. 1), 98% of all teenagers in Russian-Chuvash families opt for Russian citizenship.

99. L. F. Monogarova, "Statisticheskoe izuchenie pokazatelei odnonatsio-nal'noi i smeshannoi brachnosti v Dushanbe," Sovetskaia etnografiia, 1971, no. 6, p. 112.

100. Bromlei, op. cit.

101. Well over one third of the Koreans in Kazakhstan gave Russian as their native language (and only a negligible proportion Kazakh) in the 1970 Census. Itogi, vol. 4, p. 223.

102. Marvin Harris, "Race," International Encyclopaedia of the Social Sciences, vol. 13, New York, 1968.

103. Connor, "The Politics of Ethnonationalism," p. 21.

104. Itogi, vol. 4, pp. 273, 280, and 317; the arithmetic is mine.

105. Bromlei, op. cit.

106. See Appendix Table 7, pp. 278-80.

107. R. Chernikov, "Natsional'naia shkola segodnia i zavtra," Nauka i religiia, 1976, no. 6, p. 6.

108. R. Kaiser, Russia: The People and the Power, London, 1977, p. 75; Pravda, June 22, 1977, cited in Ann Sheehy, Radio Liberty Research, RL 226/77, October 3, 1977.

Chapter 7

1. From an account by a Western observer of the Soviet participation in the 1954 United Nations Population Conference in Rome. Soviet Studies, vol. 7 (1955-56), pp. 220-21.

2. For a good review of that literature, see N. Choucri, Population Dynamics and International Violence, Lexington, Mass., 1974.

3. Compare the table presented in Feshbach and Rapawy, op. cit., pp. 520-21.

4. E. Brubaker, "The Opportunity Costs of Soviet Military Conscripts," in Soviet Economic Prospects for the Seventies, p. 167.

5. Feshbach and Rapawy, op. cit., 1976, p. 151.

6. Ibid., p. 148.

7. On this point see also Anne Sheehy, "Language Problems in the So-

viet Armed Forces," Radio Liberty Research, RL 196/78, September 11, 1978.

8. A ZPG advocate might say a more appropriate word than "languishing" would be "flourishing." Here as elsewhere in this essay, however, I would prefer to avoid discussion or criticism in terms of the possible effects of population growth of current East European dimensions on pollution, resource exhaustion, etc. I am doing so partly because these arguments remain for the present somewhat problematical, and partly because they are virtually never raised by Socialist economic or political demography.

9. President Geisel appears to be gradually redirecting Brazilian population policy away from its traditional mercantilist orientation. See M. de Mello Moreira et al., "Brazil," in Population Council, Country Profiles, May, 1978.

10. E. Stuart Kirby, The Soviet Far East, London, 1971, p. xiv.

11. See N. Keyfitz, "Migration as a Means of Population Control," Population Studies, vol. 25 (1971), p. 63.

12. See, for example, J. Brackett and J. De Pauw, "Population Policy and Demographic Trends in the Soviet Union," in U.S. Congress Joint Economic Committee, New Directions in the Soviet Economy, Washington, 1966, pp. 607-10.

13. Itogi vsesoiuznoi perepisi naseleniia 1959 goda: svodny tom SSSR, Moscow, 1962, p. 280.

14. See O. Caroe, Soviet Empire, p. xxii.

15. Lucian Pye, "China: Ethnic Minorities and National Security," Current Scene, vol. 14 (1976), no. 12, pp. 6-7. See also M. Freeberne, "Demographic and Economic Changes in the Sinkiang Uighur Autonomous Region," Population Studies, vol. 20 (1966-67), p. 103.

16. See Jukes, op. cit., Foreword.

17. For the text of the decree, see Sobranie postanovlenii, 1973, no. 13.

18. See Current Scene, vol. 12 (1974), no. 10, p. 19. This is only the latest of a long series of outdated or misleading statements made by high-level Chinese spokesmen. See, for example, John S. Aird, "Population Policy and Demographic Prospects in the People's Republic of China," in U.S. Congress Joint Economic Committee, People's Republic of China: An Economic Assessment, Washington, 1972, pp. 238, 276, 288, and passim.

19. John Shaw, formerly Time correspondent in Moscow (personal communication).

20. Current Scene, vol. 12, no. 3, p. 15; Aird, op. cit., p. 326.

21. See also P. Paillot and A. Sauvy, "La Population de la Chine," Population, May-June 1974, p. 535.

22. Planet was the unofficial newspaper of the 1974 Bucharest World Population Conference.

23. For comprehensive accounts of the evidence available, see Aird, op. cit., and Leo Orleans, Every Fifth Child, London, 1972. For a shorter general survey, see, for example, "China: Population in the People's Republic," Population Bulletin, vol. 27 (1971), no. 6.

24. Sydney Morning Herald, September 20, 1973, p. 4.

25. Canberra Times (Reuters), January 23, 1979.

26. For discussions of the reliability of recent Chinese reports on population trends, see Leo Orleans, "Chinese Population Figures: Can the Contradictions be Resolved?" Studies in Family Planning, vol. 7, February 1976, no. 2, p. 52, and "China's Population Growth: Another Perspective," Current Scene, vol. 16 (1978), no. 2-3, pp. 1-24. Orleans seems inclined on the whole to give credence

where he possibly can. For a more skeptical view (putting the 1976 total at about 950 million), see John Aird, "Recent Provincial Population Figures," China Quarterly, March 1978, pp. 1-44.

27. See the juxtaposition in Population Bulletin, vol. 27 (1971), no. 6, p. 23.

28. For more detailed surveys of that context, see E. Stuart Kirby, op. cit., and W. A. Douglas Jackson, Russo-Chinese Borderlands, New York, 1962 (a work the more remarkable in that it antedates clear evidence of the Split).

29. Robert C. North and Nazli Choucri, "Population and the International System: Some Implications for United States Policy and Planning," in Governance and Population, vol. 4 of the Report of the U.S. Commission on Population Growth and the American Future, p. 266.

30. "Prodolzhenie spora," Literaturnaia gazeta, 1968, no. 12.

31. Ia. A. Guzevatyi, "Population and World Politics," Mezhdunarodnaia zhizhn', October 1967, translated in Studies in Family Planning, no. 49, January 1970, p. 6.

32. B. Urlanis, Problemy dinamiki naseleniia SSSR, Moscow, 1974, p. 27.

33. Sovetskoe gosudarstvo i pravo, 1975, no. 1, pp. 34-35.

34. Iu. A. Levada, "Lektsii po sotsiologii," Informatsionnyi biulleten', no. 2 (Moscow, 1969), pp. 123-24. See Note 24, Chapter 13, and Note 2, Chapter 16.

Chapter 8

1. A Soviet delegate to the UN Population Commission in 1947, quoted by Petersen, Population, p. 635.

2. The word is Khrushchev's: Pravda, January 8, 1955.

3. Richard N. Gardner, "The Politics of Population," in S. Mudd et al., The Population Crisis and the Use of World Resources, The Hague, 1964, p. 355. For other evidence of waverings and second thoughts before 1965, see, e.g., P. Mouches, Demographie, Paris, 1964, p. 208; D. Morison, "Recent Soviet Interest in Population Problems of the Developing Countries," Mizan, vol. 7 (1967), pp. 183-84.

4. See the statement attributed to him in Filosofskaia entsiklopediia, Moscow, 1964, vol. 3, p. 549.

5. See J. Brackett, "The Evolution of Marxist Theories of Population: Marxism Recognizes the Population Problem," Demography, vol. 5 (1968), no. 1, pp. 167 and 171-72.

6. See Literaturnaia gazeta, nos. 133, 139, 142, and 152 for 1965, and nos. 23, 27, 62, and 68 for 1966.

7. So much so, in fact, that repetition here would probably be superfluous. See, for example, the article by Brackett cited in Note 5. See also Robert C. Cook, "Soviet Population Theory from Marx to Kosygin: A Demographic Turning Point?" Population Bulletin, vol. 23 (1967), no. 4. S. Krašovec, "Stihijnost ili kontrola kretanja stanovništva," Stanovništvo, vol. 8 (1970), p. 5, provides an interesting Yugoslav view.

8. For a comprehensive account of trends in world opinion as reflected in politicking and debates at the UN and its agencies, see R. Symonds and G. Carder, The United Nations and the Population Question 1945-1970, Sussex University Press, 1973.

9. See B. Ia. Smulevich, "Demografiia i politika," in A. G. Volkov, ed., Voprosy demografii, Moscow, 1970, pp. 29-31. Though it is clear from the context that Smulevich is thinking principally about the international arena, it is perhaps significant that he should also have found it necessary to remind his readers in this same context that the traditional line, in citing Soviet experience

as a model for emulation, ignored "the inappropriateness of using average data for the Soviet Union as a whole" — a delicate allusion to the way in which international and domestic political considerations in this area support one another.

10. See Symons and Carder, op. cit., pp. 136-37.

11. United Nations World Population Conference 1965, vol. 2, p. 61.

12. See, for example, Narodnoe khoziaistvo SSSR v 1972 g., p. 84.

13. "Ugroza! No komu?" Literaturnaia gazeta, March 13, 1965, and "Sushche-stvuiut li problemy narodonaseleniia?" Literaturnaia gazeta, November 23, 1965.

14. On the evolution of official U.S. policy, see Symons and Carder, op. cit., especially pp. 92-96 and chaps. 10-12.

15. The Azerbaidzhanis, the Armenians, the Ossetians, and the Dagestani peoples (the latter regarded for convenience as one ethnic unit). See the table in Lorimer, op. cit., pp. 138-39. It will be recalled that by contrast, between 1959 and 1970, of the twenty-three most numerous nationalities, only six registered smaller increases than the Russians.

16. See, for example, B. Ts. Urlanis, Problemy dinamiki naseleniia, Moscow, 1974, p. 302-3; D. Valentei, Teoriia i politika narodonaseleniia, Moscow, 1967, pp. 163-64. See Note 9 above.

17. P. G. Pod''iachikh, "Statistika naseleniia, nauka o narodonaselenii i nauka demografiia (o novykh popytkakh likvidatsii statistiki, kak obshchestve-nnoi nauki)," Moscow, 1969, mimeograph.

18. See "Nas 250 millionov," Sovety deputatov, 1973, no. 9, pp. 20-21.

19. Though compare the suggestion by Gardner cited earlier that Khrushchev may have been converted to a concern about rapid population growth (population growth where, one wonders) late in life.

20. For a brief but evocative description of the development of sociology under the new post-Khrushchev leadership, see L. Churchward, The Soviet Intelligentsia, London, 1973, pp. 119-21.

21. Compare the Central Committee resolution "On Measures for the Further Development of the Social Sciences and Increasing their Role in Socialist Construction," Pravda, August 14, 1967.

22. Ekonomika Sovetskoi Ukrainy, 1973, no. 3, pp. 95-96.

23. See G. Gerasimov's most interesting observations on this perhaps very important semantic detail in Literaturnaia gazeta, 1966, no. 27. Anyone who spent any part of his postpubertal years in Stalin's Russia might be forgiven for harboring great suspicion of "kontrol' nad rozhdaemost'iu."

24. For excellent accounts of the political divisions between different groups of countries on demographic issues, see Jason L. Finkle and Barbara B. Crane, "The Politics of Bucharest: Population, Development, and the New International Economic Order," Population and Development Review, vol. 1 (September 1975), no. 1, p. 87, and W. Parker Mauldin et al., "A Report on Bucharest," Studies in Family Planning, vol. 5 (December 1974), no. 12. On the specific question of Soviet-Chinese tactical maneuvers before and during the conference, see H. Desfos-ses, "The USSR and the World Population Crisis," in L. Kosinski, op. cit., 1977.

25. See, for example, the theoretical work of A. G. Vishnevskii, Demografi-cheskaia revoliutsiia, Moscow, 1976; "Sotsial'noe upravlenie rozhdaemost'iu," in Voprosy filosofii, 1978, no. 6, p. 85.

Chapter 9

1. Chapter 3 gives a historical account of the evolution of Soviet population

policies. A good deal has been written on recent trends and dilemmas in Soviet population policy. In addition to works previously cited, see Helen Desfosses Cohn, "Population Policy in the USSR," Problems of Communism, July-August 1973, p. 41; D. Heer, "Three Issues in Soviet Population Policy," Population and Development Review, vol. 3 (1977), no. 3, p. 229.

2. Pravda, February 28, 1976, p. 8.

3. In Hungary, where generous child-care allowances were introduced, leading to the withdrawal from the work force of 80% of those eligible to receive it, pressure from industry led to further measures meant to encourage the women to return to work. In such a situation, of course, where a concession has already been made, the only politically and economically acceptable way to right the damage is to make a further concession; and this appears to have been the course the Hungarian government took — giving women the added incentive of working for wages and receiving the allowance. See Radio Free Europe [RFE], Hungarian Situation Report, 1976, no. 2, pp. 9-10.

4. See Chapter 8, Note 17.

5. V. Boldyrev, "Dvesti piat'desiat millionov," Kommunist, 1973, no. 12, pp. 85-87.

6. See Boldyrev's contribution to the round-table discussion, "Sotsial'no-filosofskie problemy demografii," in Voprosy filosofii, 1974, no. 11.

7. Examples of this could be multiplied almost at will. See, for example, "Nas — 250,000,000!" Sotsialisticheskaia industriia, August 8, 1973, p. 4. See also Brezhnev's attribution of the impending labor shortages to the demographic consequences of the war in Politicheskoe samoobrazovanie, 1976, no. 11, p. 13.

8. Sobranie postanovlenii, 1973, no. 18, item 102.

9. Sobranie postanovlenii, 1974, no. 21, item 121. For a detailed commentary on this legislation (which, incidentally, describes and evaluates it purely in terms of social, and not demographic, policy), see V. A. Acharkan, "Sotsial'-no-pravovaia priroda posobiia na detei maloobespechennym sem'iam," Sovetskoe gosudarstvo i pravo, 1975, no. 10, p. 34.

10. For Brezhnev's speech, see Pravda, February 28, 1976, p. 8; for the plan guidelines, see Izvestia, March 7, 1976, p. 7.

11. Significantly, the new child allowance is only for children under the age of eight. Ibid., p. 39.

12. See, for example, Henry P. David, "Abortion and Family Planning in the Soviet Union: Public Policies and Private Behaviour," Journal of Biosocial Science, vol. 6, pp. 423-25.

13. V. S. Tadevosian, "Demograficheskaia politika i pravo," Sovetskoe gosudarstvo i pravo, 1975, no. 8, p. 24.

14. See the statements made by B. Petrovskii, the Soviet minister of health, and representatives of the pharmaceutical industries in Literaturnaia gazeta, 1968, no. 50 (December 11), p. 10.

15. A. G. Vishnevskii, "Demograficheskie protsessy v SSSR," Voprosy filosofii, 1973, no. 9, p. 125.

16. See Appendix Table 1, p. 271. These matters will be discussed again in the concluding chapter of this book.

17. B. Urlanis, "Demograficheskaia politika v sovremennom mire," Mirovaia ekonomika i mezhdunarodnye otnosheniia, May 1975, p. 111. See Note 13.

18. A. Kruczek, "W sowieckiej prasie," Kultura (Paris), 1973, no. 7-8, p. 122.

19. See M. Agurskii, "Neonatsistskaia opasnost' v Sovetskom Soiuze," Novyi zhurnal, no. 118 (March 1975), pp. 202-3.

20. Sovetskoe gosudarstvo i pravo, 1975, no. 1, p. 28.

21. Nedelia, December 26, 1977 — January 1, 1978.

22. D. I. Valentei, Teoriia i politika narodonaseleniia, Moscow, 1967, p. 163. See also, e.g., the recommendations of a symposium held to discuss "Women in Productive Work and the Family" in Minsk in June 1969 (reproduced in Soviet Sociology, vol. 12 [1973], no. 2; R. Kallistratova, "'Rozhdaemost' i pravo," Sovetskaia iustitsiia, 1971, no. 2, p. 16: K. Vermishev, "Stimulirovanie rosta naseleniia," Planovoe khoziaistvo, 1972, no. 12, p. 102 and especially p. 105; "Demograficheskaia politika: ee napravleniia. Problemy narodonaseleniia," Voprosy ekonomiki, 1975, no. 8, pp. 148-52; G. I. Litvinova, "Vozdeistvie gosudarstva i prava na demograficheskie protsessy," Sovetskoe gosudarstvo i pravo, 1978, no. 1, p. 132. The list could be expanded almost indefinitely.

23. "Vstrecha s iugoslavskim uchenym," Voprosy ekonomiki 1973, no. 5, p. 159. For other decentralizing proposals, see R. Kallistratova, op. cit., and G. A. Zlobin, Sovetskoe gosudarstvo i pravo, 1975, no. 1, p. 33.

24. "The Soviet society has a vested interest in (zainteresovano v) increased fertility, normal population growth, reduced mortality." V. S. Tadevosian in Sovetskoe gosudarstvo i pravo, 1975, no. 8, p. 22. The linking in apposition of these three very different notions, as though they were virtually synonymous, is characteristic.

25. "Chelovek i sreda ego obitaniia," Voprosy filosofii, 1973, no. 2, p. 46.

26. Iu. Riurikov, "Pochemu detei stanovitsia men'she?" Literaturnaia gazeta, November 17, 1976.

27. Literaturnaia gazeta, March 16, 1977.

28. Zhurnalist, 1978, no. 5, pp. 21-22.

29. D. I. Valentei, "Problemy upravleniia protsessami razvitiia narodonaseleniia," Problemy filosofii, 1978, no. 2, p. 3.

30. Izvestia, June 16, 1977, p. 1. The quotation follows the translation in CDSP, vol. 39, no. 24, p. 18.

31. A recent article by a leading labor economist quotes Brezhnev's reply to Le Monde and explicitly condemns advocacy of a differential population policy. A. Manevich, "Vosproizvodstvo naseleniia i ispol'zovanie trudovykh resursov," Voprosy ekonomiki, 1978, no. 8, p. 38.

Chapter 10

1. A separate section is set aside for this because of the special interest of Poland's Malthusian phase in the late 1950s.

2. See Edward Rosset, Demografia Polski, two vols., Warsaw 1975; L. Kosiński, "Population Trends in Poland after World War II," in Kosiński, ed., Demographic Developments in Eastern Europe, New York, 1977, pp. 309-38; Z. Smoliński, "Procesy demograficzne w XXX-leciu PRL," in Aktualne problemy demograficzne kraju, Warsaw, 1974; K. Kersten, Repatriacja ludności polskiej po II wojnie światowej, Wrocław, 1974.

3. During the thaw period of 1957-58 in Poland, voices were sometimes raised proposing emigration as a means of dealing with the country's manpower surplus. For a brief discussion, see Besemeres, "Population Politics in Poland," East Central Europe, vol. 3 (1976), no. 2, pp. 127-76, fn. 4.

4. Rocznik Demograficzny 1974, Warsaw, 1974, p. xxi.

5. Ibid., p. 107.

6. Z. Krzyżanowska, "Niecierpliwość — zły doradca," Trybuna Ludu

(hereinafter TL), December 3, 1972.

7. See Appendix Table 14, p. 285.

8. A view based, in the case of the more sophisticated, on assumptions about growing urbanization and increasing educational standards (given the very strong correlation of both with lower fertility in Poland), and also on investigations of intended family size which show planned fertility as steadily declining by cohort. See, e.g., Z. Smoliński, "Perspektywy dzietności," Życie Gospododarcze (hereinafter ŻG), March 11, 1974.

9. See Appendix Table 14, p. 285.

10. Rocznik Demograficzny, 1974, p. XX.

11. Rocznik Statystyczny, 1971, p. 68.

12. A. Józefowicz, "Polityka ludnościowa i zatrudnienia w Polsce," Biuletyn Instytutu Gospodarstwa Społecznego (hereinafter BIGS), vol. 5 (1962), no. 4, p. 13.

13. For a review of the more important ones from the point of view of population policy, see M. Latuch, "Elementy polityki ludnościowej w Polsce," in Polityka ludnościowa: współczesne problemy (hereinafter Polityka ludnościowa), Warsaw, 1973, p. 106, especially pp. 116-24.

14. The legislation on abortion was taken over directly from prewar Poland. It would appear that by the midfifties, however, evasion of the restriction had become widespread and prosecution infrequent. See M. Parzyńska, "Po dyskusji — projekt ustawy," Życie Warszawy (hereinafter ŻW), April 13, 1956.

15. See "Rok działalności Towarzystwa Świadomego Macierzyństwa," TL, 1958, no. 12. For further details on the shift in policy, see Besemeres, op. cit., fns. 17-19.

16. W. Bieda, "Uwagi o niektórych ekonomicznych stronach zjawisk ludnościowych," Myśl Gospodarcza (hereinafter MG), 1957, no. 5; S. Wyrobisz, "Fatalizm populacyjny czy interwencja," MG, 1957, no. 8; J. Czarkowski, "Przyrost ludności a stopa życiowa," MG, 1957, no. 9; A. Józefowicz, "Ekonomika i ludność," ŻG, 1957, no. 17. These articles developed the idea that rapid population growth was economically disadvantageous, placing as it did excessive strain on both current consumption and current future investment. While the authors of these more scholarly articles were fully aware of, and indeed emphasized, the unfamiliar and taboo nature of their subject matter, they tried to some extent to avoid being identified as Malthusians. Certain journalists of similar views, on the other hand, were much less cautious. A. Szypulski, for example, writing in the Democratic Party weekly Tygodnik Demokratyczny (May 7, 1957, "Przyrost naturalny a środki spożycia") urged radical and antiegalitarian measures to check population growth, which policy he described as the only way out of the clutches of poverty: "Let us cry out 'People' for God's sake: you're not rabbits!' If we don't, we'll be sorry."

17. TL, October 18, 1959. After the events of 1970 and the major disturbances of early 1976, the time would appear to be ripe for someone to undertake a special study of the historiopoeic role of the meat shop in postwar Poland.

18. "Zmiany w sposobie udzielania orzeczeń o przerywaniu ciąży," TL, January 12, 1960.

19. See, for example, TL, July 26-27, 1975, p. 3, where a peasant from Bydgoszcz Province remarks, "I even feel ashamed these days that I come from a family of eleven children." One legacy of the Gomułka antinatalist phase to the Polish language is the contemptuous neologism "dzieciorób" (roughly: "Kidmaker"), which immediately suggests associations with the word "brakorób," meaning "poor workman," "producer of worthless goods," in other words, one of the perennial villain figures in the exhortatory industrial literature of socialism.

20. E.g., TL, August 1, 1961. Even in 1964, by which time Poland's age-specific fertility was already drawing close to replacement levels and was well below it in the cities, the latest reported decline in the birthrate was greeted as representing a tendency "which is naturally advantageous." ŻG, August 2, 1964.

21. For a brief discussion of the signs of growing dissent in unofficial circles, see Besemeres, op. cit., p. 135, fn. 28.

22. A. Marek, "School organization problems in connection with demographic law," Radio Free Europe Research Poland, November 30, 1970. See also Słowo Powszechne (hereinafter SP), April 10, 1970.

23. See Besemeres, op. cit., p. 157.

24. The literature on labor and employment policy in Poland is particularly abundant. See, for example, A. Rajkiewicz, Zatrudnienie w Polsce Ludowej w latach 1950-1970, Warsaw, 1965; H. Jędruszczak, Zatrudnienie a przemiany społeczne w Polsce w latach 1944-1960, Wrocław, 1972; L. Sobczak, Rynek pracy w Polsce ludowej, Warsaw, 1971; K. Dzienio and M. Gołacka, Bilanse siły roboczej, Warsaw, 1971; M. Olędzki, Polityka zatrudnienia, Warsaw, 1974; E. Kozłowska and J. Wojtyła, Ludność, zatrudnienie, prawo, Katowice, 1975; S. Klonowicz, Zdolność do pracy a wiek człowieka, Warsaw, 1973; M. Kabaj, Elementy pełnego i racjonalnego zatrudnienia w gospodarce socjalistycznej, Warsaw, 1972; W. Ratyński, Problemy polityki zatrudnienia, Warsaw, 1972.

25. See Rajkiewicz, op. cit., pp. 135-36.

26. A. Józefowicz suggests ("Z zagadnień dynamiki ludnościowej w Polsce," Nowe Drogi [hereinafter ND], 1959, no. 2, p. 56) that the period of 1950-56 had been one in which demographic considerations were accorded little attention by planners, and that work on the long-term plan for 1960-75 was associated with a considerably enhanced degree of emphasis on the demographic factor.

27. The jednostki inicjujące entrusted with the experimental introduction of Gierek's economic reforms in fact increased their employment levels appreciably faster than other sectors of the economy, thereby making a disproportionate contribution to the growing labor shortage of recent years. See the article by B. Fick in ŻG, December 15, 1974, and the comment on it by W. Laskowski in ŻG, June 8, 1975. See also M. Kabaj, "Doskonalenie gospodarowania zasobami pracy," in ND, 1978, no. 2, p. 122.

28. In 1958, 1963, and again in the late 1960s. See Rajkiewicz, op. cit., pp. 139 ff. and 220 ff.; and Ratyński, op. cit., chap. 5, in which Gomułka's policy of attempting to force up productivity by forcing down employment increments is severely criticized. See also U. Fox, "Versteckte Arbeitslosigkeit in Polen," Osteuropa Wirtschaft, March 1977, pp. 1-20.

29. See, e.g., L. Zacher, Problemy strategii rozwoju gospodarczego Polski Ludowej, Warsaw, 1974, pp. 102, 124-25; K. Dzienio, "Demograficzne uwarunkowania strategii zatrudnienia," in Demografia społeczna, Warsaw, 1974, p. 293.

30. This obviously applies only to the pre-Gierek period. See Olędzki, op. cit., pp. 264 and 309. See also Zacher, op. cit., pp. 133-34.

31. See, e.g., K. Dzienio in Demografia Społeczna, Warsaw, 1974, p. 295.

32. See, e.g., M. Kabaj, "Bariera zatrudnienia," ŻG, October 12, 1975.

33. Ibid. See also Olędzki, op. cit., p. 112. In this respect Gierek's period has not been exceptional.

34. For unusually candid airings of this line of argument, see the contributions by K. Toeplitz, J. Bocheński, W. Górnicki, and A. Micewski to the collective volume Polski problem Nr 1, Warsaw, 1972. Under Gierek alcohol consumption has risen sharply.

35. See Ratyński, op. cit., pp. 10 and 76; Dzienio and Gołacka, op. cit., p. 108.

H. Król, the prominent labor economist, revealed in an article in TL, February 15, 1971, that the Gomułka version of the 1971-75 plan was contemplating an unemployment figure of 200,000 by 1975, and this on the basis of certain quite unreal premises about female and peasant employment. Król's estimate was that the figure unemployed by 1975 would in fact have been about half a million. He also asserts that influential party economists were urging this on the basis that the demographic situation demanded it. If this is not an oversimplification or distortion of their position, it would certainly seem, as Król suggests, that these people timed the introduction of their measures very badly, given the enormous increases in the work force in the late 1960s and early 1970s. (See Appendix Table 16, p. 286.) Król also revealed that the old suggestion of economic emigration had again been raised, presumably in camera. See Note 3.

36. For a discussion, see H. Trend, "Arbeitsmarkt und Vollbeschäftigung in Polen," Osteuropa Rundschau, 1972, no. 9, p. 1.

37. For statistics showing the state of employment as measured by state employment agencies (and here Rajkiewicz's caveat of 1957 — ŻG, March 3, 1957 — that "No one believes the official data, not even the state agency that gathers them," may still be of some relevance); see Appendix Table 17, p. 286. For instances of administrative restrictions on employment levels, see, e.g., ŻG, February 10, June 23, and December 15, 1974, and June 8, 1975, all at p. 15, and TL, November 28, 1974. See also Nowe drogi, 1979, no. 2, p. 43.

38. The use of the word "reforma" fairly quickly became taboo after Gierek's accession, and the form "udoskonalanie (udoskonalenie) systemu zarządzania gospodarką narodową" or similar became mandatory.

39. Estimates of the numbers involved vary. For a review of the evidence, see J. L. Kerr, "Gastarbeiter in Eastern Europe," Radio Free Europe RAD Background Report, 169 (Eastern Europe), December 4, 1975, pp. 10-12.

40. See ZW, March 3, 1975, p. 3, and TL, August 1, 1975, p. 8.

41. See Gierek's speech to the Sixth Congress, VI Zjazd PZPR Stenogram, Warsaw, 1972, pp. 156-57; Polityka, March 15, 1975, p. 2.

42. The total increase in the work force in 1981-85 will be less than a quarter and that in 1986-90 less than one tenth what it was in 1971-75. See Appendix Table 16, p. 286.

43. See A. Elias, Manpower Trends in Czechoslovakia, Washington, 1972, p. 5. For an interesting and less than approbatory Polish glimpse of these measures, see W. Grochola, "Jak polubić dzieci," in Polityka, January 5, 1974, p. 11.

44. Dziewoński and Kosiński, op. cit., p. 157.

45. In 1968 a trial run for the 1970 census was held, the questionnaires for which included a question about nationality. Ostensibly for reasons of economy, this question was dropped from the 1970 census papers. "Cechy demograficzne ludności," ŻG, September 6, 1970. The author of this article noted, however, that the question had proved a very "sensitive" one. See also A. Kwilecki, "National Minorities in Poland," Polish Round Table Yearbook 1968, p. 146.

46. ŻW, December 12, 1963. The 31,000 Jews have since declined to 10,000 to 15,000 in the wake of the "events" of 1968 and the resulting emigration (New York Times Magazine, April 15, 1973). The German figure of 3,000 was evidently something of an underestimate, since an agreement has since been signed which provides for the emigration of a further 120,000 to 125,000 (The Australian, October 11, 1975). Most of the 125,000 have now left Poland. See The Economist, August 25, 1979, p. 36.

47. The ŻW article previously cited mentions euphemistically that two thirds

of the Ukrainians had "settled" in the west and north. Dziewónski and Kosiński cite two different estimates of the numbers of Ukrainians thus resettled: 120,000 and 150,000. Dziewónski and Kosiński, Rozwój i rozmieszczenie ludności Polski w XX wieku, p. 82.

48. For a sampling of the tone of official comment on the East Slav nationalities, see the article by B. Porowski in Argumenty, September 14, 1969 (translated in Osteuropa, 1971, no. 1, p. A41).

49. For some appreciation of the remarkable inflammatory capacity of sparks of liberalism near totalitarian tinder, see the excellent discussion of the role of the Ukrainian minority in Czechoslovakia in the period circa 1968 in G. Hodnett and P. Potichny, The Ukraine and the Czechoslovak Crisis, Canberra, 1970 (Occasional Paper no. 6 of the Department of Political Science, R.S.S.S., Australian National University).

50. "Abbau der Illusionen," Die Zeit, October 26, 1973.

51. Their numbers declined from about 110,000 in 1921 to 72,000 in 1950 (V. Srb, "Obyvatelstvo Československa v letech 1918-1968," Demografie, vol. 10 [1968], no. 4, p. 302) and 67,000 in the 1970 Census.

52. See, for example, W. Sworakowski, "The Poles in the Soviet Union," Polish Review, vol. 19 (1974), no. 3-4, pp. 143 and 145.

53. Kultura (Paris), 1975, no. 1-2, p. 230.

54. The population in the productive age groups in Poland increased by 25% over the period 1951-70 (and has increased much further since), while that of East Germany declined over the same period by 18%. W. Iskra, Czynnik ludzki w rozwoju gospodarczym krajów socjalistycznych, Warsaw, 1974, p. 114.

55. By 7.2% per annum 1951-73, compared to 6.9% (East Germany) and 5.9% (Czechoslovakia).

56. Few truly Polish hearts can fail to beat faster at the thought that for some years now the difference between the population of Poland and that of the two Germanies combined has been reduced annually by between half and three quarters of a million.

57. Compare the respective tables for the RSFSR in Naselenie SSSR 1973: statisticheskii sbornik, Moscow, 1975, p. 70, and for Poland in Rocznik Demograficzny, 1977, p. XVII.

58. Wyszyński's sermon is quoted in H. J. Stehle, The Independent Satellite, London, 1963, p. 121.

59. See, for example, "Niepokojący sygnał," SP, February 14, 1973, where the author refers merely to "Poland's future place in the great family of nations of the world." See also the similar tone and similar formulations in the following articles: "Ile dzieci," Kultura, October 22, 1972; "Zaproszenie do myślenia," Kultura, November 12, 1972; "Lata 1973-78 zadecydują o przyszłości Polski," Kierunki, December 10, 1972; "Quid pro quo," Życie Warszawy, November 25, 1976.

60. See Note 16.

61. The theme of "unreasonable burdens" on the state budget was one of the standard features of Gomułkaist journalism. It was still prominent in the official justifications given for the ill-fated price rises of December 1970. For a sampling of this style of journalism in the neo-Malthusian context, see "W odpowiedzi matkom-Polkom," TL, August 25, 1958.

62. See, for example, "Niepokojący rekord," ŻW, April 26, 1958.

63. Polityka, September 11, 1971.

64. Thus in, of all places, a Soviet collective volume including contributions

from the bloc countries, Edward Rosset expresses his conviction that stationary population is both a near prospect and a necessary and desirable objective. "Since the population of the earth cannot continue to grow to infinity, since population growth must come to an end somewhere, I would favor some solution which would not require that humanity should be bathed in a sea of blood." V. S. Steshenko and V. P. Piskunov, eds., Demograficheskaia politika, Moscow, 1974, p. 63. See also the contribution by A. Jagielski to Demografia Społeczna, especially pp. 71-73 ff. and pp. 82-83, and A. Lubowski, "Widmo przeludnienia krąży nad światem," ŻG, November 3, 1974. The contents of Lubowski's article are unequivocally Malthusian. The use of the "specter haunting" from the Communist Manifesto is evidently deliberate. Lubowski is either unaware of or unconcerned by the fact that Soviet orthodoxy would regard his use of a Marxian tag in this context as virtually sacrilegious.

65. For polemics by bloc demographers with the old Stalinist approach, see, e.g., Materiały międzynarodowego sympozjum demograficznego w Zakopanem 1964, Warsaw, 1966, especially pp. 13-60 and 252 ff. Most of the more stubborn demographic hardliners at this symposium were from the USSR.

66. See Besemeres, op. cit., fns. 17 and 77.

67. See Besemeres, op. cit., fn. 78.

68. See, for example, "Zabobon i życie," TL, June 1, 1959; "W obronie życia," Polityka, August 8, 1959; "Propaganda kleru a prawda o przyroście naturalnym w Polsce," Fakty i Myśli, December 15, 1959; "O ograniczaniu przyrostu ludności," ŻG, January 3, 1960.

69. The best general source on this subject is the volume Polityka ludnościowa: współczesne problemy, Warsaw, 1973, which is a selection from the proceedings of a conference on population policy held near Warsaw in March 1972. The remaining papers are mostly published in BIGS, vol. 16 (1973), no. 1, and the discussions in BIGS (1973), nos. 3-4. See too Socjalne i prawne środki ochrony macierzyństwa, Warsaw, 1976 (also the proceedings of a conference on social and population policy); Aktualne problemy demograficzne kraju, Warsaw, 1974. For a well-balanced and critical survey of the whole area of population policy in Poland written in English by a Polish scholar, see J. Ziółkowski's chapter in B. Berelson, ed., Population Policy in Developed Countries, New York, 1974.

70. J. Rolicki, Kultura, October 1, 1972.

71. See, e.g., S. Klonowicz, "Dwunasty model reprodukcji," Polityka, January 1, 1973; 2. Smoliński, "Zasiłek nie na czasie," Polityka, December 10, 1977.

72. See Besemeres, op. cit., p. 135. For retrospective criticisms of the Gomułka regime's "voluntaristic" refusal to accept demographic advice, see "Ku czemu zmierzamy," Polityka, November 6, 1971, and (less emphatically and more obliquely) "Międzynarodowa dyskusja demografów," TL, March 17, 1972.

73. See, e.g., "Jak sterować rozwojem ludności," SP, July 14-15, 1973. Z. Smoliński has declared baldly (Kultura, October 22, 1972) that an economy not based in the long term on expanding labor resources is "sick." See also A. Wielowieyski, Przed trzecim przyspieszeniem, Cracow, 1968, pp. 242 ff; T. Wołynowicz, "2 + 4," Życie Warszawy, September 9, 1976.

74. M. Macura, "Komponente populacione politike saobrazne sadašnjim i budućim potrebama Jugoslavije," Naše teme, 1974, no. 4, p. 568.

75. One exception to this among demographers is Edward Rosset, who has a special academic (and by now a strong personal) interest in the question of the proper utilization of the skills of the old.

76. There may be good political reasons for the reticence on this point, given the party's commitment to earlier retirement and the unpopularity of any suggestion that a promised social reform might be withdrawn. See Besemeres, op. cit., pp. 154-55.

77. For an interesting critique of the economic pronatalist position, see S. Klonowicz, Zdolność do pracy a wiek człowieka, pp. 411 ff.

78. "A short resumé: family bonds are disintegrating, more and more marriages are ending in divorce, more and more are admitting to conflicts, many are childless, and one third of all families have only one child." A. Kantowicz, "Polska rodzinna," Kultura, March 12, 1972.

79. For a selection of views of this kind, see, e.g., the round-table discussion "Rodzina współczesna — tendencje, perspektywy," Argumenty April 16, 1972.

80. The pro-régime PAX organization and its press were very active in the campaign to restore the standing of the family, as were the ecclesiastically authorized Catholic publications.

81. TL, March 7, 1975, p. 3.

82. Polityka, July 1, 1978, p. 2.

83. Kantowicz commented in 1972: "The past years have not been the happiest for family life. The main reason for that was the semiofficial theory of the fifties that many families were bastions of political and social reaction." Kultura, March 12, 1972.

84. The tables for crèches (p. 550) and kindergartens (p. 469) in Rocznik Statystyczny, 1971, suggest virtual stagnation for both after about 1955. (Gomułka, it will be recalled, came to power in 1956.) This was not due to any decline in demand consequent on the decline that occurred over this period in the birthrate. See Besemeres, op. cit., pp. 156-57, fn. 96.

85. See Besemeres, op. cit., fns. 97 and 98, p. 157, and Appendix Table 6, p. 277.

86. Ibid.

87. This fact emerges to some extent from the tables given in the statistical volume Kraje RWPG: ludność, gospodarka, kultura, pp. 88-90, despite some attempt at cosmetic presentation.

88. Sometimes the argument seemed almost to take the form of "we (or "they," depending on the writer's perspective) will stop our Geburtenstreik if you (or "we") build us (or them) more flats." This kind of approach was detectable both among pronatalists (build more flats so that the birthrate will rise) and anti-pro-natalists (build more flats or the birthrate certainly won't rise).

89. See Kultura, October 1, 1972. The following schema has been outlined many times. A young couple are both working (the overwhelmingly typical case) and earning, say, 3,000 zlotys each. Their first child is born. No crèche place is available (there are far fewer places in crèches than in kindergartens), so the wife stops working. The family income falls from 6,000 divided among two to 3,000 divided among three. Per capita income in the family falls to virtually a third of its former level. Social services and subsidies for children's goods (in Poland, as opposed to certain other Socialist countries) make up little of the difference.

90. L. Sobczak, Rynek pracy w Polsce Ludowej, pp. 192-93. Though it would appear that once they have joined the work force they are in fact reluctant to leave it. See Note 95.

91. Although many male ideologues since Lenin have echoed his injunctions to the men of Socialist societies to give their wives more assistance in the home, most wives in Poland and elsewhere are effectively "na dwóch etatach"

(have two full-time jobs). Trybuna Ludu in its regular family rubric periodically calls on men to be more helpful, but the issue is not apparently a top priority among the all-male upper echelons of the party-state apparatus.

92. "Family life is burdened by the nightmare of everyday life, in other words, by the lamentable state of the service industries in the country." A. Kantowicz, loc. cit. This area is another that has been given great prominence since Gierek's accession, and great improvements have been promised. But progress has been slow. See, e.g., "Dla czego w usługach niewiele sie zmienia," TL, November 3, 1975.

93. An interview-article with Germaine Greer published in the (usually) sophisticated weekly Polityka concluded with the interviewer confiding to the reader reflections that occurred to her as she drove with Ms. Greer in the vicinity of Stratford at the conclusion of their talk: "Who had cast such a spell on Titania as to leave her so angry"; and "would she one day find her Oberon?" A. Osiecka, "Rozmowy z Tytanią," Polityka, November 11, 1972.

94. See Besemeres, op. cit., fn. 106, for some examples of Polish-style male chauvinism and feminism.

95. See B. Łobodzińska, Rodzina w Polsce, Warsaw, 1974, pp. 91 ff.

96. "It is recognized now that a man can be just as good at looking after children. The idea that there is some biological link between a mother and her child for the first three years of its life is a fairy tale." A. Wróblewska, "Trzy lata z głowy," Polityka, December 24, 1977.

97. The non-Catholic antiabortionists were for the most part concentrated in and around the journal Kultura. The fact that Wilhelmi, the editor-in-chief, personally identified himself with this view of abortion would suggest that some highly placed people other than Wilhelmi himself felt that the indications for legal abortion should be restricted.

98. For more details, see Besemeres, op. cit., fn. 110, p. 161.

99. M. Latuch, "Elementy polityki ludnościowej w Polsce," in Polityka ludnościowa, p. 139.

100. Czechoslovakia's success in increasing its fertility after (among other measures) certain restrictions on the availability of abortion had been introduced may also contribute to producing some waverers. K. Romaniuk, an economic pronatalist, had declared in TL on February 21, 1971, that "It can be said with complete certainty that decisions of an administrative character have produced meager and in general short-term effects..." and described parental decisions in these matters as their "personal concern," and the state's role as limited. In his contribution to the volume Demografia społeczna in 1974, on the other hand, the same author said: "The experience of countries...like Czechoslovakia or Hungary (Hungary also introduced restrictions on abortion some months before the publication of Demografia społeczna — J.F.B.) suggests that both economic and legal-administrative measures are necessary..." (p. 249).

101. "I'm not calling for the papers and television to be filled with hurrah-family items, and stupid ones at that, as is usually the case with mass propaganda occasions." J. Rolicki, Kultura, October 1, 1972.

102. "Proponuję państwu troje dzieci," Kultura, October 8, 1972.

103. See, e.g., M. Klimczyk, "Przynależność do grup społeczno-zawodowych a dzietność biologiczna kobiet w Polsce," in Polityka ludnościowa, p. 250.

104. D. V. Glass, "Fertility Trends in Europe since the Second World War," Population Studies, 1968, pp. 118 ff.

105. This implicit assumption is everywhere apparent but only rarely explicitly

defended. There is an example of such a defence in Mikołaj Kozakiewicz's contribution to the Argumenty debate cited earlier (April 16, 1972). Having first protested his support for the then prevailing educational policies giving preference to the children of workers and peasants (which were in fact widely resented by the intelligentsia, including those more recently recruited to it), Kozakiewicz says: "In a dynastic intelligentsia, or 'elite,' there are virtues as well as defects ... such a dynastic intelligentsia makes a very important contribution to progress."

106. See, e.g., Smoliński in BIGS, 1972, no. 3-4, p. 114; A. Rajkiewicz in Socjalne i prawne środki, vol. 2, pp. 16-17 (where he suggests that rather than follow a generally pronatalist policy, attention should be concentrated on "certain groups," in particular "women with higher education"); J. Wilhelmi in Kultura, November 12, 1972.

107. This theme has been broached many times since the abortion debates of 1956, and examples could be cited at great length. "In the present phase we should oppose elemental reproduction in groups belonging to the social margin and in pathological milieus, or at least not adopt measures which might have a stimulating effect on them." BIGS, 1973, no. 3-4, p. 82. See also "Linia życia," Polityka, January 21, 1978.

108. See Besemeres, op. cit., fn. 121, pp. 164-65.

109. See Hagmajer's modest proposals for modifications in the abortion law presented during the discussion cited earlier in the Sejm Commission on Health and Physical Culture, Biuletyn Wydziału prasowego Sejmu, no. 243, VI Kad., March 27, 1973.

110. In the words of a critic. BIGS, 1973, no. 3-4, p. 96.

111. See the contribution by A. Józefowicz to Polityka ludnościowa, pp. 88 ff.

112. J. Rolicki in Kultura, October 1, 1972.

113. Two prominent and forceful representatives of this discipline and its characteristic orientation are Antoni Rajkiewicz and Jan Rosner: see, e.g., their contributions in BIGS, 1973, no. 3-4. Generally speaking, the contributors to the main demographic conferences can be divided into pronatalists (usually demographers) and anti-pro-natalists (usually concerned with the theory or practice of polityka społeczna). On polityka społeczna as a science and as a vocation, see, e.g., A. Rajkiewicz (ed.), Polityka społeczna, Warsaw, 1972, and the two interesting articles in ŻG, January 27, 1974, p. 10.

114. The 1963 version of Jerzy Holzer's textbook on demography (Podstawy analizy demograficznej) does not contain a section on population policy. The 1970 version (Demografia), whose structure is otherwise very similar, does contain one. Mikołaj Latuch, writing in TL, March 17, 1972, recorded the formation of a Section for Population Policy within the Academy of Sciences' Committee for Demographic Sciences.

115. In addition to publishing the fire-eating anti-pro-natalism of Urban ("Who Wants to Live Standing Up," September 9, 1971, and January 21, 1978) and Grochola (October 10, 1972, and January 5, 1974), Polityka also published an item with a title and style strongly reminiscent of the antinatalist campaign of 1960: "Łatwiej płodzić niż myśleć" (the pungency of which is rather inadequately rendered by "Impregnation Is Easier than Cogitation"), Polityka, November 11, 1972.

116. See, e.g., BIGS, 1973, no. 3-4, pp. 76 and 111.

117. Characteristically the authorities solved the problem by permitting both bodies to be established.

118. Radio Warsaw II, November 13, 1972.

119. M. Kozakiewicz, "Population Policy," Polish Perspectives (in English), 1975, no. 4, p. 13.

120. D. Graniewska, "Urlopy opiekuńcze matek — cele i uwarunkowania," Nowe Drogi, 1978, no. 4, p. 120.

121. The increases brought the monthly amounts paid to 160, 250, 340, and 360 zl. for the first, second, third, and fourth children, with 360 for each subsequent child; however, only families with an income of less than 1,400 zlotys per head monthly were eligible, and the graduation was in any case a good deal less steep than that prevailing in Hungary, Bulgaria, or Czechoslovakia. The average monthly wage in the socialized sector in 1974 was 3,185 zlotys. For a full description of the benefits, see M. Piątkowski, Zasiłki rodzinne, Warsaw, 1974.

122. For an official catalogue of the new benefits granted to women under the Gierek administration, see, e.g., I. Sroczyńska, "W trosce o rodzinę," ND, 1978, no. 1, pp. 78-89. Characteristically, the article strikes no pronatalist notes. For a summary of pronatalist measures taken elsewhere in the bloc, see R. McIntyre, "Pro-natalist programmes in Eastern Europe," Soviet Studies, July 1975.

123. For an account of these measures, see TL, March 8-9, 1975, and March 12, 1975 (J. Sieradziński, "Dla młodych małżeństw"). The credits carry an interest rate of 6%, which is substantial and points up the contrast between this measure and the much more generous ones in Hungary or Czechoslovakia, where the debts are also partly or wholly remitted according to the number of children the young couple produce. In general the costs of housing for Polish young marrieds in the 1970s have increased sharply. See D. Fikus, "Małżeństwo — sprawa nie tylko prywatna," Polityka, May 30, 1978.

124. See Fikus, op. cit., compare Notes 84 and 85 on the Gomułka legacy and the Gierek leadership's attempts to overcome it. Reports in late 1978 suggest that the priority that Gierek has sought to give housing is losing ground in the face of the other pressures generated by the overheated economy. The 1978 housing plan seemed likely to be underfulfilled by a wide margin despite desperate "storming" tactics in the last months of the year — which themselves will doubtless leave many an unpleasant surprise for the fortunate who do receive a flat. See "Mieszkaniowy finisz," ŻG, December 3, 1978. This in turn suggests that the ambitious plans to build a "second Poland" in the 1980s are unlikely to be achieved.

125. P. Stecko, "Pomyślność rodziny — celem polityki społecznej partii i państwa," ND, 1978, no. 7, p. 42.

126. For a brief account of this development, see BIGS, 1974, no. 2, pp. 89-97. See also Nowe drogi, 1979, no. 2, p. 91.

127. TL, March 7, 1975.

128. ŻW, November 10, 1976.

129. Stecko, op. cit., p. 46. On the Sejm meeting, see RFE, Polish Situation Report 15, June 30, 1978, pp. 10 ff.

130. RFE, op. cit. More pronatalist is B. Porowski, "Młoda rodzina i jej problemy," ND, June 1979, p. 111.

131. See A. Bromke, "The Opposition in Poland," Problems of Communism, September-October 1978, p. 43.

132. The text of the letter was published in Tygodnik Powszechny, January 9, 1979.

133. For a fuller discussion of the recent politics of the abortion question in Poland, see Besemeres, op. cit., pp. 171-72.

Chapter 11

1. Perhaps because of the great diversity of Yugoslavia's subpopulations, there are relatively few general works covering broad areas of its demographic development. The quarterly Stanovništvo (appearing somewhat irregularly of late) has published many scholarly articles on Yugoslavian demography since its first appearance in 1963, but most are synchronic studies and regionally or thematically specialized. Monographs, particularly those of a general character, have not been plentiful. See Centar za demografska istraživanja, Razvitak stanovništva Jugoslavije u posleratnom periodu, Belgrade, 1974; D. Breznik, Demografski metodi i modeli, Belgrade, 1972, chap. 8 and prilog 1; V. Simeunović, Stanovništvo Jugoslavije i socijalistickih republika 1921-1961, Belgrade, 1964; Centar za demografska istraživanja, Fertilitet stanovništva u Jugoslaviji, Belgrade, 1972, and Migracije stanovništva Jugoslavije, Belgrade, 1971; M. Rašević, Determinante fertiliteta stanovništva u Jugoslaviji, Belgrade, 1971. The publications of the Savezni zavod za statistiku (Federal Institute for Statistics), in particular the demographic annual, Demografska statistika, also contain some retrospective data. The English-language journal Yugoslav Survey regularly carries demographic articles of good quality.

2. Razvitak stanovništva u posleratnom periodu, p. 5.

3. For vital rates by republics, see Simeunović, op. cit., pp. 43 and 46, and Savezni zavod za statistiku, Demografska statistika 1975, Belgrade, 1977, pp. 33-35. For birth and natural increase rates only, see Appendix Table 20, p. 289.

4. The 1921 census figure for Hungarians and Albanians (based on linguistic affiliation) is from S. Clissold, ed., A Short History of Yugoslavia, Cambridge, 1966, p. 165. In 1972 in Yugoslavia there were 54,334 and 5,717 live births to Albanian and Hungarian mothers respectively. Demografska statistika 1972, p. 146.

5. Statistički godišnjak 1978, p. 79 (preliminary data).

6. Ibid.

7. Savezni zavod za statistiku, Fertilitet ženskog stanovništva 1950-1967, Belgrade, 1971, p. 22.

8. Ibid.

9. See Appendix Table 21, p. 290.

10. The Yugoslav calculations are from Fertilitet ženskog stanovništva 1950-1967, p. 22. My own calculations are based on the official Census results for population in Macedonia by age, sex, and nationality (as of March 31, 1971) and total births by nationality of mother in Macedonia during 1970. No allowance was made for the slight time discrepancy, as the main objective was simply to render an impression of the current state of differential fertility in the republic. See Savezni zavod za statistiku, Popis stanovništva i stanova 1971, vol. 1, Belgrade, 1974, p. 28, and Savezni savod za statistiku, Demografska statistika 1970, Belgrade, 1973, p. 144.

11. See Fertilitet ženskog stanovništva 1950-1967, p. 22.

12. The procedure adopted was the same as that for the Albanians and Macedonians in Macedonia and utilized the same statistical sources: Popis stanovništva i stanova 1971, vol. 1, p. 16, and Demografska statistika 1970, p. 143.

13. Fertilitet ženskog stanovništva 1950-1967, p. 22. Here the discrepancy in computation procedures between the Yugoslav source and me is probably negligible, though there are problems with ethnic self-identification, particularly in the case of the Moslems. There is reason to believe that there was a substantial undercount of Moslems in 1953 and 1961 because of the pressure on them to

identify themselves as "Yugoslavs." As the GFRs were based on this Census undercount on the one hand and vital statistics on the other, they may have the effect of inflating Moslem fertility in the earlier years. Moslem women in childbirth seem less likely to have been identified as "Yugoslavs" or even Serbs or Croats than households being visited by officials at the time of a national undertaking like a census.

14. The Serbs, Croats, Slovenes, and Montegrins are all sufficiently concentrated and dominant in their own republics (in the case of the Serbs, in Serbia Proper) for the republic NRRs to be a fair guide to ethnic fertility trends. The figures for Kosovo are also a reasonable indicator of Albanian trends (though the presence of a substantial Serbian minority of lower and, in recent years, sharply falling fertility would cause some slight downward distortion).

15. It has been calculated (on the basis of 1971 Census data) that for the female cohorts of 50-54 years of age, employed urban women had an average of 1.70 children and unemployed urban women an average of 3.55. In the same cohorts women without education had an average of 4.46 children, women with completed basic schooling an average of 2.43 children, and women with higher education 1.04 children. Razvitak stanovništva Jugoslavije u posleratnom periodu, p. 17. In 1961 the General Fertility Rate for the urban population of Yugoslavia was 73.3, and for the rural population 98.1. Fertilitet stanovništva u Jugoslaviji, p. 95.

16. The Yugoslav Statistical Yearbook does not appear to supply any information on the numbers or proportions of children in preschool child-care institutions, but from fragmentary data for parts of the country appearing in the press, it is clear that the coverage is a good deal weaker than in any of the European Socialist countries. These matters are discussed further in Chapter 17.

17. Razvitak stanovništva Jugoslavije u posleratnom periodu, pp. 1 and 41.

18. V. Puljiz, "Oblici i posljedice deagrarizacije u Jugoslaviji," paper presented to the Belgrade Conference on Population Policy, 1973 (Savetovanje o izgradnji društvenih stavova o populacionoj politici), mimeograph, p. 16.

19. Razvitak stanovništva Jugoslavije u posleratnom periodu, p. 24.

20. In sharp contrast to other Socialist countries, the Yugoslav press seldom comments on this problem, except in the specific context of agriculture. For an exception, see M. Nikolić, "Fenomen starenja aktivnog stanovništva u nas," Borba, July 14, 1974.

21. See Appendix Tables 25 and 26, pp. 293-94.

22. B. Mujović, "O problemu nezaposlenosti i realnim mogucnostima za njegovo rješenje," Naše teme, 1973, no. 4, p. 758.

23. M. Karan, "Zapošljavanje radnika sa Kosova u inostranstvu," Socijalna politika, 1971, no. 1-2, p. 13.

24. Z. Ančić, "Population Changes in Yugoslavia," Yugoslav Survey, vol. 12 (1971), no. 3, p. 4. By 1971 Kosovo's population density was 114/sq. km. (compare 70/sq. km. in Albania and 80/sq. km. in Yugoslavia as a whole).

25. I.e., not including the Balkan Wars of 1912-13. See Clissold, op. cit., p. 159. This devastating loss effectively put paid to Serbian imperial aspirations, though not all Serbs have yet realized it.

26. Total Yugoslav casualties are usually put at 1.7 million, or 11% of the then population. As can be seen from Appendix Table 18, p. 287, the casualties were concentrated in Croatia (whose population actually declined between 1931 and 1948), Bosnia and Hercegovina, and Montenegro. (The stagnation of Vojvodina's population over the same period was due more to migratory factors.)

Croatian commentators sometimes draw attention to their particularly heavy losses in World War II, though without detailing how they came to pass. See, e.g., A. Wertheimer-Baletić, Stanovništvo SR Hrvatske, Zagreb, 1971, p. 25, where a figure of 661,500 is cited for Croatia's war dead. Serbs in Croatia were undoubtedly well represented in this total.

27. Razvitak stanovništva Jugoslavije u posleratnom periodu, p. 11.

28. For an overall picture of interregional migratory trends, see Tables 22 and 23 in the Appendix, p. 291. At the 1971 Census Serbia proper and the Vojvodina had a net inflow of Serb residents from Kosovo of 48,935 and a net inflow of Montenegrins from Montenegro and Kosovo of 23,041 and 6,147 respectively. These figures, it should be emphasized, do not convey the full demographic effects of the migratory patterns in question, since they fail to record past immigrants deceased at the time of the 1971 Census and, of course, those children of immigrants who are born in the new area of settlement. The figures are probably further affected by changes in ethnic identification, e.g., from Montenegrin to Serb, after settlement in Serbia. And finally it needs to be remembered that the criterion of permanent residence employed in censuses (see Note 32) may also lead to underregistration of southern migrants (notably Albanians) in the northern regions. The figures have been computed from Popis stanovništva i stanova 1971, pp. 76, 78, 82, and 84. The net inflow of Serbs from Bosnia and Hercegovina to Serbia as of 1971 was 161,052 (again by my computation), op. cit., pp. 76 and 82.

29. The 1971 Census reveals a net inflow of 94,455 Croats from Bosnia and Hercegovina into Croatia. The same strictures apply to this result as to the computations presented in the previous note. A calculation of net migratory flows in and out of Bosnia and Hercegovina by nationality based on the 1961 Census results showed that of a total deficit of 211,000 for the republic as a whole, 132,000 were Serbs and 66,000 Croats. The total deficit for Moslems and Yugoslavs (undetermined) was only 4,000. Again, it must be stressed that these figures do not near adequately render the demographic consequences of interregional migratory flows in recent decades. See Migracije stanovništva Jugoslavije, table 28, pp. 210-11.

30. Ibid., pp. 5-9 and 328-30.

31. Popis stanovništva i stanova 1971, vol. 1, p. vi.

32. The only figures I have seen are for Slovenia, where estimates range between 100,000 and 150,000. Occasionally fragmentary data are published for other republics or regions, but they too are said to be unreliable. "Statistical registration of these movements is inadequate.... Permanent migration is much greater than that which is officially recorded and is often spontaneous (stihijske) and unorganized." M. Bekić, a member of the Federal Committee for Labor, quoted in Vjesnik u srijedu (VUS), May 1, 1976, p. 18.

33. One estimate (among many) gives the figure of 1,122,000 workers abroad (including overseas countries) as of late 1974. M. Mišović, "Sedma republika," Nedeljne informativne novine (NIN), October 19, 1975, p. 10. Neither this nor the estimate cited in the following note includes nonemployed dependents residing abroad.

34. "Vratiti se ili ostati," Politika, March 25, 1979, p. 10.

35. On the recent economic emigration, see I. Baučić "Some Economic Consequences of Yugoslav External Migrations," in Leszek A. Kosiński, ed., Demographic Developments in Eastern Europe, New York, 1977, pp. 266-83. For a useful survey of Yugoslav international migration movements in this century, see Kosiński's own "Yugoslavia and International Migration," Canadian Slavonic

Papers, vol. 20 (September, 1978), no. 3, pp. 314-38.

Chapter 12

1. "Koliko će nas biti," NIN, November 25, 1973, p. 24.

2. M. Macura, "Komponente populacione politike saobrazne sadašnjim i budućim potrebama Jugoslavije," Naše teme 1974, no. 4, p. 555.

3. For comprehensive critiques of the 1965 economic reforms from the viewpoint of manpower problems, see, e.g., T. Mulina, "Nezaposlenost, uzroci i karakteristike u sadašnjoj fazi razvoja privrede," Ekonomski Institut, Belgrade, Studia i saopštenja, Belgrade, n.d., and M. Knežević, "Neki socijalno-politički i ekonomski problemi zapošljavanja naših radnika u inostranstvu," Ekonomska misao, 1968, no. 2, p. 331.

4. See Ivo Vinski, "Privredna reforma i zaposlenost," Pregled, June 6, 1969, translated in Osteuropa, vol. 19 (1969), p. A347.

5. See Note 19 to Chapter 11.

6. D. Breznik, "Demografska komponenta razvojne politike," Ekonomist, vol. 23 (1970), no. 2-3, pp. 417-18.

7. See, e.g., D. Breznik and M. Sentić, "Radni kontingent stanovnistva i formiranje radne snage u Jugoslaviji do 1970 godine," Ekonomska misao, 1968, no. 1, p. 161; V. Simeunović, "Population of Working Age," Yugoslav Survey, 1966, p. 3717, fn. 1. See also Note 11.

8. See A. Wertheimer-Baletić, "Regionalne demografske implikacije zapošljavanja u inozemstvu," Ekonomski pregled, 1969, no. 7-8, p. 703.

9. I. Vinski, op. cit., p. A349.

10. For an analysis of the role of students in the events of 1968, see Ralph Pervan, Tito and the Students, Perth, 1978.

11. "The economic reform, rationalization, and the shift to a more intensive system of production have lessened the need for new labor, and that at precisely the moment when the sources of labor supply had grown quite exceptionally." D. Vogelnik, "Demografski procesi i stabilizacija," Ekonomist, vol. 19 (1966), no. 1-4, p. 385. In March 1968 the Serbian Economic Association (Savez ekonomista Srbije) organized a conference on employment problems at which the causes and consequences of the employment crisis were forthrightly analyzed. See "Savetovanje o problemima zaposlenosti," Stanovništvo, vol. 6 (1968), no. 1-2, p. 90, and Ekonomska misao, 1968, nos. 1 and 2.

12. For a discussion of some of these aspects of the reforms, see P. Shoup, Communism and the National Question, New York, 1968, chap. 6.

13. "Though the number of unemployed is up by 11% over December 1964, a comparison will show that nothing exceptional is taking place in this field." "Leto 1965 v luči statistike," Delo, January 5, 1966. The above excerpt from the Slovenian party daily is a good example of the insouciant style of postreform official thinking on employment problems.

14. See Appendix Table 30, p. 299.

15. For a general survey of trends in industrial productivity, see Miodrag Nikolić, "Labour Productivity in Industry, 1952-1973," Yugoslav Survey, 1975, no. 1, p. 119. Between 1965 and 1971 productivity increase was greater than that of employment. Since then the trends have been reversed (see Nikolić, op. cit., table 1, p. 120). According to Politika of February 20, 1976, p. 7, the increase in real wages during 1971-75 was the lowest for twenty years. On employment levels, see Appendix Table 29, p. 298.

16. Labels like "Westernizers," "technocrats," or "Partisans" obviously cannot totally encapsulate the truth, although they contain an important element of it. Their use does not imply a belief that they explain everything.

17. The martial terminology of the postwar years has been greatly revived since 1972. See, e.g, "Bitka za zapošljavanje mladih" [Battle for the Employment of the Young], Borba, September 20, 1974. On the growing prominence of former Partisans within the LCY leadership since 1971, see Robert F. Miller and E. Vance Merrill, "Yugoslav Central Committee Memberships: What the Figures Show," Politics, vol. 14 (1979), no. 1, pp. 75-76.

18. One example among many speaks of Yugoslavia's deep-seated and secularly worsening unemployment as "temporary" unemployment. "Employment and Temporary Unemployment," Yugoslav Survey, 1974, no. 2, p. 1.

19. See, e.g., Politika, February 20, 1976, p. 7; "Prividi i stvarnost nezaposlenosti," Kommunist, December 8, 1978, p. 7 (where a case is cited of a factory forced to take on the local unemployed and deteriorating sharply as a result).

20. Politika, May 21, 1976, p. 12.

21. See the speech by the president of the Federal Executive Council, Veselin Djuranović, to the Federal Assembly on December 26, 1978, reprinted as a supplement to Kommunist, January 19, 1979 (supplement), pp. 2-3.

22. See Appendix Table 30, p. 299.

23. For examples of apparently quite unrealistic optimism, see "Značajni izgledi za zapošljavanje povratnika," Politika, August 7, 1976; "Employment and Temporary Unemployment," Yugoslav Survey, 1974, no. 2, p. 21. The Politika article claims to foresee jobs being available for 400,000 returnees by 1980. Among other confusions, it appears to assume that natural wastage creates a store of new jobs (rather than being outweighed by a greater influx of school-leavers).

24. Politika, May 16, 1976, p. 7, reported on a Dimitrovgrad survey which found that of 1,189 registered unemployed in that area, only 160 were "really" out of work. Recent press articles suggest there is a growing feeling in the leadership that the present rate of increase in employment is too high and a (no doubt related) feeling that unemployment statistics are inflated. A social compact (društveni dogovor) is being planned, the effect of which will be to redefine some of the unemployed out of the statistics. See "Diploma ne garantuje posao," Politika, April 3, 1979, p. 7.

25. NIN, December 28, 1975, p. 8, reported an estimate that two thirds of the returnees are not seeking work in the socialized sector of the economy.

26. Given the difficulties on the labor market, it would be understandable if unemployed resident Yugoslavs were to resent the returnees, and harassed firms were to resist pressures on them to take on returnees on any kind of quota basis. Such resentments sometimes find reflection in Federal Assembly debates and seem very likely to affect grass-roots decision-making. See Politika, October 10, 1975, p. 7, and April 22, 1976, p. 8.

27. The draft long-term plan (dugoročni plan) for the ten-year period to 1985 speaks of a growth in the work-age population of 0.9% per annum and in the economically active population of 0.6% per annum, or a total in absolute terms of 660,000 (Borba, October 26, 1974, supplement, p. XIV). An analysis published in 1969 (when most of the relevant demographic magnitudes were already definitely known) suggested an increase in the economically active population over the same period of 865,000 (even assuming a decline in the work-force participation rate). D. Breznik, "Demografski i drugi aspekti formiranja radne snage

u Jugoslaviji za narednih 20 godina," Ekonomist, 1969, no. 1, pp. 139-40.

28. In 1961 women comprised 26.4% of all (nonrural) employees; in 1971 they made up 31.7%. Currently the figure is 34%. "Mladi dugo čekaju posao," Politika, April 13, 1979, p. 11.

29. Discrimination on the basis of sex is evidently not uncommon, but official publications always deplore the practice. See "Posao za žene," Borba, January 18, 1975.

30. B. Jovetić, "Šta s mladima na selu," Kommunist, December 25, 1969, translated in Osteuropa, 1970, no. 11, p. A817. Jovetić's estimate was made "from the point of view of modern agriculture." Western sources have estimated that up to one million rural workers could be shifted out immediately without appreciable loss. See L. Tyson, "The Yugoslav Economy in the 1970's," in U.S. Congress Joint Economic Committee, East European Economies Post-Helsinki, Washington, 1977, p. 964.

31. V. Puljiz, "O socijalnom i još nekim srodnim problemima poljoprivre-dnog i seoskog stanovništva," Naše teme, 1973, no. 10, p. 1672.

32. Politika, February 20, 1976, p. 7, reported a statement by a delegate to the Federal Assembly to the effect that "there are not a few enterprises where there are up to 20% more workers than is necessary."

33. The burden of maintaining unemployment benefits is naturally felt to be greater in the less-developed republics. Kosovo appears to solve its problem by simply not providing the benefits. Of the 32,879 registered unemployed in Kosovo in 1970, only 6% were receiving cash unemployment benefits, and only 20.5% were covered by health insurance. M. Karan, op. cit., p. 13. In Macedonia it was proposed to remove certain categories of unemployed from the registers, as not all qualify as "really unemployed," and some have other sources of income or support (Politika, March 9, 1976, p. 9). Slovenia and Croatia can better afford a liberal approach to these problems. See Note 24.

34. During the period of Soviet-Yugoslav rapprochement in 1972, the USSR undertook to supply nearly one billion dollars in credits. Difficulties arose subsequently over the implementation of this agreement, however. See S. Stanković, "Yugoslav Foreign Minister Visiting Moscow," RFE Research, RAD Background Report 1171 (Yugoslavia), December 8, 1975.

35. See "Migracije u Istočnoj Evropi," VUS za naše gradjane u svijetu, March 5 and 12, 1975.

36. Slovenia is the only republic that has been experiencing an overall labor shortage. See "Pomanjkanje radne snage," VUS za naše gradjane u svijetu, April 3, 1974. See Note 47.

37. A. Milojević and V. Sultanović in "Zapošljavanje u inostranstvu," Pregled, 1972, no. 1, p. 33, for example, refer to the "inherent political and economic weaknesses" of state-socialism and suggest that if there were to be a liberalization of its economic system, "very powerful migratory movements" might be unleashed, which would bring with them "very deep political and economic implications" (p. 35).

38. There seems to have been over the years a long-term trend toward greater uravnilovka in wages. In 1955 unskilled and semiskilled workers received 50% of the average wage, whereas by 1974 they received 75% (Politika, October 11, 1975, p. 9). During the reform period 1965-71, some attempt was made to counteract leveling tendencies. It was not evidently very successful. Although the post-1971 official mood has been again more egalitarian, articles deploring uravnilovka are still appearing regularly in the press. See, e.g.,

"Jednakost sa više lica," NIN, March 7, 1976, p. 14; "Zamršena mreža uravni-lovke," VUS, December 25, 1976, p. 12.

39. "Nerad na udaru," NIN, October 26, 1975, p. 7.

40. D. Breznik "Demografska komponenta razvojne politike," Ekonomist, vol. 23 (1970), no. 2-3, p. 413.

41. M. Milenović "Neke karakteristike zaposlenosti i zapošljavanje u 1972 godini," Socijalna politika, 1973, no. 4, p. 17.

42. See Appendix Tables 29 and 30, pp. 298-99.

43. A Croatian estimate made in 1968 put the joint Croatian and Slovenian contribution to the emigration at 69% (compare 30.3% of the total population as of 1971) and the combined Moslem-"Yugoslav"-Albanian contribution at 4.1% (compare the 14.8% of the population constituted by Albanians and Moslems in 1971). See Z. Komarica, Jugoslavija u suvremenim evropskim migracijama, Zagreb, 1970, p. 20.

44. The 1971 Census data on Yugoslav workers abroad (see Table 24, p. 292) suggest a marked rectification of the ethnic distribution of emigrants had oc-curred by that time. However, the census figures almost certainly understate the older emigration (which was heavily Croatian).

45. Ustav Socijalističke Federativne Republike Jugoslavije, Belgrade, 1974.

46. This is likely to be a controversial issue. Should migration from less-developed to more-developed regions be encouraged, or would it be better to increase the flow of capital to the less-developed regions? What should be the relationship between migration policy and other population policies? By what means can migratory flows be legitimately and efficaciously controlled and directed? Whatever federal policies are adopted, republic resistance or the pressure of events may in any case subvert them. Unfortunately, considerations of space preclude further discussion of this interesting theme. For what is prob-ably a fairly official, federal, view, see M. Jeličić, "Neki aktuelni problemi unutrašnje migracije radnika," Socijalna politika, 1973, no. 1, p. 18; Migracije stanovništva Jugoslavije, chap. 8. For clear signs that the controversy is in-deed raging, see "Kuda smo se selili," NIN, January 21, 1979, p. 13.

47. See, e.g., A. Wertheimer-Baletić, "Populaciona politika i politika radne snage," Naše teme, 1974, no. 4, p. 578. See also J. Lojk, "Postojeća struktura rada u SR Sloveniji ograničavajuće deluje na medjurepubličko zapošljavanje," Socijalna politika, 1973, no. 1, p. 21.

48. See, e.g., the account in Komunist, July 7, 1975, p. 11, of a meeting of the Kosovo Presidium of the Socialist Alliance, which says that "it is thought that more could be done in this country to provide work for people from Kosovo in other republics."

49. According to a reliable source, would-be immigrants from less-developed regions arriving in Slovenia without guarantees of employment are given a meal and a bed for the night and are then sent home again. Slovenia does, however, accept an agreed number of Gastarbeiter from the other republics, including, according to a recent report, 10,000 workers a year from Kosovo (this presum-ably is not fully cumulative). Politika, January 6, 1979, p. 5.

50. "Regionalni razvoj i diferencijacije," Borba, September 29, 1974. Kosovo, at least, is continuing to fall further behind. See, e.g., Politika, January 4, 1979, p. 5; NIN, March 4, 1979, p. 11.

51. See Note 3, Chapter 14, and Note 33, Chapter 15. While spokesmen from the wealthier and poorer regions ostensibly agree that the development gap is regret-table and ought to be struggled with, their diagnoses and recommended therapies

differ. Ethnoregional disputes over such issues have survived the crackdown on nationalist extremisms of 1971-72. Both the 1976 plan and the 1976-80 plan ran into major difficulties because of differences between the republics and provinces. See, e.g., Politika, December 26, 1975, p. 1, and March 11, 12, 16, and 18, 1976.

Chapter 13

1. Demografska statistika 1972, p. 29.
2. Migracije stanovništva Jugoslavije, p. 86, fn. 19.
3. M. Begtić, "Yugoslav Nationals Temporarily Working Abroad," Yugoslav Survey, 1972, no. 1, p. 17, fn. 1.
4. Politika, December 19, 1975, p. 9.
5. F. Stare, "Nekateri pogledi na problematiko zaposlovanja naših delavcev v tujini," Ekonomska revija, 1969, no. 1, p. 94.
6. See, e.g., Z. Komarica, Jugoslavija u suvremenim evropskim migracijama, pp. 103-4.
7. Komarica, writing in 1970, drew attention to the enormous disparity between the tiny number of official Yugoslav social centers for migrants and those provided by international religious agencies for the (Catholic) Croats alone. Komarica, op. cit., p. 111.
8. See Franci Stare, op. cit., p. 83; F. Kožul, "Po kateri poti," Naši razgledi, 1970 (September 11), no. 17, p. 499.
9. Nearly all the serious work on economic emigration being done in the late 1960s and early 1970s was Croatian. See, e.g., V. Komarica, op. cit.; V. Holjevac, Hrvati izvan domovine, Zagreb, 1968; I. Baučić and Z. Maravić, Vraćanje i zapošljavanje vanjskih migranata iz SR Hrvatske, Zagreb, 1971; and Stanovništvo: emigracija i zaposlenost u Hrvatskoj, Zagreb, 1971. By 1970-71 the popular Croatian press was spelling out the message in clear and forceful terms. See, e.g., "Biološkom osiromašivanju pridonijela je i ekonomska emigracija," VUS, February 18, 1970, and "Sve o popisu," Vjesnik, March 27, 1971.
10. Komarica cites one study done in 1966 which suggested that 63% of the migrants might be ethnic Croats (while himself placing the figure at 54%). Komarica, op. cit., pp. 19 and 20. See also Notes 42 and 43 to Chap. 12.
11. Ninety-two percent, insofar as the Census results can be taken as a guide. M. Begtić, op. cit., table 3, p. 20.
12. A. Wertheimer-Baletić, "Demografske implikacije zapošljavanja u inozemstvu," in Stanovništvo SR Hrvatske, pp. 79-80.
13. See Appendix Table 21, p. 290.
14. Miloje Nikolić, "Some Basic Features of Yugoslav External Migration," Yugoslav Survey, 1972, no. 1, p. 1.
15. M. Nikolić, op. cit., p. 8.
16. Politika, December 19, 1976, p. 9.
17. Politika, June 27, 1973.
18. Few emigrants appear to have gone abroad with the intention of acquiring new qualifications. M. Nikolić, op. cit., p. 9.
19. As of 1966 Yugoslav hard-currency remissions averaged $200-250 per worker (Franci Stare, op. cit., p. 95). By 1975 the average Yugoslav worker was remitting $1,900 a year. The annual total increased from $35 million in 1964 to $1.6 billion in 1975 (S. Letica, "Mit ili realnost," VUS, October 1, 1975). In 1977, despite the decline in numbers (though boosted no doubt by inflation), the figure reached $1.9 billion (Vjesnik January 22, 1978).

20. See, e.g., VUS za naše gradjane u svijetu, October 17, 1973, p. 62; Politika, April 12, 1976, p. 9.

21. See, for example, the articles by M. Mišović, "Ko se brine o njima," NIN, January 11, 1976, and "Sedma republika," NIN, October 19, 1975, p. 10. See also "Učinjeno dosta ali se mora još više," Komunist, January 12, 1979, p. 10.

22. Speech at Gnjilano, April 13, 1971, cited in Socijalna politika, 1971, no. 3-4, p. 5.

23. Croatia at least had already formulated a program for accelerating the return of economic emigrants in 1972. "Programi i ulaganja — više radnih mjesta," VUS za naše gradjane u svijetu, February 14, 1976.

24. Borba, December 9, 1972.

25. See S. Stanković, "Impact of Yugoslavs Working Abroad on National Defense and the Economy," and "Yugoslavia's Manpower Export: An Analysis," RFE Research, Yugoslavia, July 9, 1973, and February 4, 1974.

26. A reproach evidently made in or near official circles. See M. Begtić, "Vraćanje Jugoslovenskih gradjana s rada u inostranstvu kao element politike zapošljavanja u inostranstvu," Socijalna politika, 1973, no. 4, p. 10.

27. The West Germans (where more than half of all the Yugoslav emigrants were employed) were the first to ban further intakes, on November 23, 1973. Most other European countries had adopted similar restrictions by the end of 1974. S. Letica, loc. cit., VUS za naše gradjane u svijetu, November 27, 1974, p. 25.

28. See, for example, the article "Masovnog otpuštanja neće biti," VUS, December 26, 1973.

29. Komunist, September 15, 1975, p. 14.

30. See Notes 33 and 34 to Chapter 11 from which this rough estimate is derived. Compare Kosińksi, "Yugoslavia and International Migration," p. 335, who quotes an estimate from the Zagreb Centar za istraživanje migracije of a net return of 145,000 in 1974-76, evidently from Western Europe only.

31. See M. Begtić, op. cit.

32. Mišović, "Sedma republika," NIN, October 19, 1975, p. 11.

33. Ustav Socijalističke Federativne Republike Jugoslavije, Član 159, p. 93.

34. See VUS, October 21, 1970, p. 6.

35. S. Letica, "Mit ili realnost," VUS, October 1, 1975.

36. Politika, August 25, 1976, p. 7.

37. Politika, April 19, 1976, p. 5.

38. See, among many examples, "Cena povratka," Politika May 6, 1979, p. 10.

39. "Predlog zakona o zaštiti gradjana SFRJ na privremenom radu u inostranstvu," Politika, May 19, 1979, p. 5.

40. One of the most widely publicized instances of this occurred in the Dalmatian commune of Imotski, which had the highest emigration rate in the country. See Komunist, January 13, 1975, p. 10. There evidently remains a good deal of opposition to this ideologically risqué approach.

41. Thus, for example, a Croatian official emphasized that investment credits and the introduction of a system of social security for private farmers in that republic in 1976 were meant to encourage employment there and thus reduce the pressure of returnees on the urban labor market. VUS za naše gradjane u svijetu, February 14, 1976.

42. One observer claimed to see the possibility of creating 150,000 new jobs by increasing second and third shifts by only 10%. Komunist, February 4, 1974, p. 4.

43. See Note 35 to Chapter 12. Labor exports to the Third World are associated with capital construction projects there.

44. "Mesto u domovini," Politika, December 19, 1975.

45. "Skraćenje staža i zapošljavanje," Politika, May 18, 1976.

46. See, for example, "Program povratka," Politika, May 21, 1976.

47. NIN, September 21, 1975, p. 11.

48. The situation varies between republics, but in most parts of the country it is bad. Thus in Serbia, the largest republic, by the end of the first three years of the 1976-80 medium-term plan, only 34% of the planned number of dwellings had been built. NIN, January 28, 1979, p. 17. See also "Sporo i nee- konomično," Komunist, February 23, 1979, p. 9.

49. Politika, April 22, 1976, p. 8.

50. Politika, October 10, 1975, p. 7.

51. See Note 40.

52. Despite innumerable proposals (for special concessions for returnees) the old Customs Law, which dated from 1965, the year when the main flow of emigration began, had been altered little before it was finally superseded in 1976. Politika, March 2, 1976, p. 5. See also VUS za naše gradjane u svijetu, February 14, 1976, p. 67.

53. See S. Stanković, "Slovenia Passes New Law on Private Enterprise," RFE Background Report/272 (Yugoslavia), December 4, 1978.

54. An article in Politika (June 15, 1976, p. 5) describes some of the dis- criminatory measures that have been taken against tradesmen in recent years. VUS for February 21, 1976, p. 15, declares that "small-scale production (mala privreda), despite declaratory support, is not given a chance in this country." See also "Daleko od pameti," Politika, March 19, 1979, p. 5 and the aptly titled " 'Neprirodna pojava' u socializmu" [" 'An Unnatural Phenomenon' under So- cialism"], NIN, May 21, 1978. Again Slovenia is probably the sole exception.

55. Statistički godišnjak Jugoslavije 1975, p. 110.

56. Statistički godišnjak Jugoslavije 1978, p. 80.

57. See, e.g., "Zanatstvo u zapećku" and "Talas dopunskih zarada," in Poli- tika, January 9 and 10, 1976, and "Zanatlije ostavljaju radnje," Politika, Jan- uary 7, 1978.

58. As of early 1972, Yugoslav workers were estimated by West German sources to be holding some 4 billion DM in West German banks alone. VUS, January 26, 1972, cited in Z. Antić, "Yugoslavia Curbs Labour Exports to West- ern Countries," RFE Research, Yugoslavia, February 7, 1973, p. 3.

59. This appears to be the Federal line on internal migration generally, and it is often urged in the specific context of the returnee problem. See, for ex- ample, the statements by the Croatian undersecretary for labor in VUS, August 20, 1975, p. 3.

60. Hitherto, very little of West German investment has gone to the countries from where its Gastarbeiter stem. Greece, Turkey, and Yugoslavia provide two thirds of all the migrants but received only 1% of all West German foreign investments in the decade before 1974. "Pouke jedne recesije," NIN, February 2, 1975, p. 36.

61. See Notes 47 and 48 to Chap. 12 (and corresponding text), and also the discussion in Chap. 14 below.

62. "Ne kao stari pečalbar," Politika, January 18, 1976. There is a likeli- hood that if credits are forthcoming, they will be made conditional on the accel- erated return of Yugoslav Gastarbeiter to their own country. See "Strana sre- dstva za povratnike," Politika, March 22, 1978, p. 7.

63. After 1972 Kosovo was given formal priority in emigration opportunities

as a matter of policy (Miloje Nikolić, op. cit., p. 12). It has also sought special treatment in <u>internal</u> migration policy (see the remarks by a Kosovo delegate in a Federal Assembly debate on returnee policy, <u>Politika</u>, April 1, 1976, p. 6). Here, too, there is some disposition at the Federal level to meet their demands. But, again, compare Notes 47-49 to Chapter 12.

64. <u>VUS</u>, May 28, 1975, p. 8. Direct investment in Kosovo by enterprises from other republics is still very modest, however.

65. According to one Yugoslav analysis, this will result in a further net return of 150,000 workers by 1985. <u>Politika</u>, March 25, 1979, p. 10.

66. See Appendix Table 24, p. 289.

67. The overworked Yugoslav consular network would find gathering the emigration's vital statistics a difficult task, but until recently in fact it was not required to do so at all. Nor, apparently, did the Federal Institute for Statistics do anything to fill the gap. Mišović, "Ko se brine o njima," <u>NIN</u>, January 11, 1976, p. 17.

68. See Begtić, "Yugoslav Nationals Working Abroad," p. 22.

69. Compare the tables in Statistisches Bundesamt, <u>Statistisches Jahrbuch</u>, Wiesbaden, for 1975 and 1978, pp. 65 and 66 respectively.

70. See, e.g., <u>VUS za naše gradjane u svijetu</u>, January 30, 1974, p. 34, and May 29, 1974, p. 30; "Kuda druga generacija," <u>Politika</u>, June 13, 1976; <u>NIN</u>, September 4, 1977, p. 26, December 10, 1978, p. 10, and March 18, 1979, p. 18.

71. <u>NIN</u>, December 10, 1978, p. 11.

72. Ibid. There is an ambivalent impulse to partially accept the Church's assistance, though with misgivings ("Crkva može da pomogne," <u>NIN</u>, January 14, 1979, p. 15); but only in the case of Macedonia does there seem to be a real identity of interest (<u>NIN</u>, November 18, 1978, p. 16).

73. Between late 1973 and late 1977, for example, despite the restrictions that had been placed on foreign workers in the meantime, the registered number of Yugoslavs in West Germany fell only from 673,000 to 630,000. (See <u>Statisches Jahrbuch 1975</u> and <u>1978</u>, pp. 65 and 66 respectively.) It has often been suggested in the Yugoslav press that there may be significant numbers of Yugoslavs staying on illegally in West Germany.

74. According to one estimate the number of Yugoslav dependents abroad increased by 115,000, or almost one third, between 1973 and 1976, thereby all but nullifying the effect of the return of 135,000 workers in the same period. <u>Vjesnik</u>, January 22, 1978.

75. Between late 1973 and late 1977 the number of Yugoslav citizens under the age of six in West Germany increased from 37,800 to 63,000. Compare <u>Statistisches Jahrbuch 1975</u>, p. 65, and the corresponding table in the 1978 volume.

76. "Izgubljene duše," <u>Delo</u>, July 13, 1971. This article in the Slovenian party daily declared that the census had missed "half" of the Croats abroad. See Note 44 to Chapter 12.

77. <u>Komunist</u>, September 15, 1975, p. 14.

78. Judging on the basis of the 1971 Census results, only 4% of the emigrant workers from Kosovo were women (compare 18% from Macedonia, 37% from Croatia, and 40% from Slovenia). Begtić, "Yugoslav Nationals Temporarily Working Abroad," p. 20.

Chapter 14

1. The Yugoslavs have, of course, rejected Stalin, but not Lenin.

2. Both historically, and in recent years, Soviet nationalities policy has equivocated between Great Russian chauvinism thinly disguised and greater or lesser measures of ethnic pluralism. But Bulgaria and Romania have been perhaps even more given to unitaristic assimilationism at times than their Soviet mentors. On Romania's assimilationist phase (and the strategic reasons for their partial retreat from it), see R. King, Minorities under Communism, chap. 7; see also "Ceausescus Nationalitätenpolitik," Osteuropa, 1975, no. 5, p. A282. By contrast, Bulgaria's Staatsvolk nationalism seems to be growing unchecked at present. Presumably this is a sign of Moscow's special favor. See the discussion of the Macedonian question in this chapter and RFE Research, Bulgarian Situation Report/13, April 28, 1976, p. 5, and no. 31, December 8, 1977, p. 1. On the other hand, Hungary, Yugoslavia, and Czechoslovakia have all treated their national minorities remarkably well in at least some respects. Even an ethnically almost homogeneous state like East Germany observes certain decencies in relation to its tiny Lusatian Sorb minority. (See K. J. Dippman, "The Legal Position of the Lusatian Sorbs since the Second World War," Slavonic and East European Review, vol. 53 [January 1975], no. 130, p. 62.) On the situation in Poland, compare the section in Chapter 10 on ethnic relations.

3. "Calculations show that Kosmet's falling behind Slovenia in economic growth is two thirds due to its faster population growth and only one third due to its slower economic growth." Janez Škerjanec, "Mednacionalni ekonomski odnosi v Jugoslaviji," Teorija in praksa, 1969, no. 1, p. 31.

4. On the theory, see "Deveto rešenje," "Formule odgovornosti," and "Život ispravlja greške," in NIN, March 23, 1975, May 18, 1975, and May 2, 1976, respectively. On the practice, compare Note 51 to Chapter 12 and Note 71 to Chapter 13.

5. Including employment and unemployment. See the article on Kosovo employment policy, "Medjunacionalni odnosi, zapošljavanje i razvoj," Politika, March 12, 1979, p. 6. For further details, see J. F. Besemeres, "The Demographic Factor in Inter-Ethnic Relations in Yugoslavia," Southeastern Europe, vol. 4 (1977), no. 1, p. 3, fn. 6.

6. R. Petrović, "Ethnically Mixed Marriages in Yugoslavia," Sociologija: Selected Articles 1959-1969, Belgrade, 1970, p. 185, especially p. 198, note 14. As in the Soviet Union, people of Moslem faith are much less likely to contract ethnically mixed marriages, especially the women. And when they do, it is usually with other Moslems, if the latter are, territorially speaking, "available." For further details, see Besemeres, op. cit., pp. 4-5, fn. 7.

7. On this point, compare Note 77 to Chapter 6.

8. For a rough guide, see Appendix Tables 20 and 21, pp. 289-90. See also Notes 7, 8, 12, and 14 to Chapter 11 (and the corresponding text).

9. For some examples of this kind of writing, see Besemeres, op. cit., fns. 11 and 12.

10. See Notes 9 and 10 to Chapter 13, and Appendix Table 24, p. 292.

11. For details, see Besemeres, op. cit., p. 6, fn. 13.

12. See Appendix Table 29, p. 298.

13. See, e.g., "Izmedju umiranja i 'eksplozije,' " VUS, March 12, 1969. In those heady times it was normal to speak of Croatia as if it were the same kind of entity as Greece or Portugal.

14. Komarica, op. cit., p. 25, estimated that (as of 1968) only 0.42% of the population of Serbia was abroad, compared with 3.30% from Slovenia and 4.21% from Croatia.

15. See Esad Čimić, "Mednacionalni odnosi na razpotju," Teorija in praksa, 1969, no. 10, p. 1479, especially pp. 1484-85. Pressures against the Moslems seem to still come more from the side of the Serbs. (See "Streit um die Anerkennung der bosnisch-herzegowinischen Mohammedaner als Nation," Osteuropa, 1975, no. 4, p. A236.)

16. See Note 47 to Chapter 12. Compare, too, the following comments by Šuvar: "As we know, there is among the Serbian, Croatian, and Slovenian communities a certain distaste for the 'rapid multiplication of the Shiptars'"; and, "I know that Djodan and people who think like him secretly do not wish that, let's say, half a million Albanians should settle in Croatia." S. Šuvar, "Da li je Hrvatska eksploatirana," Naše teme, 1969, no. 12, pp. 2055 and 2062.

17. See Appendix Table 21, p. 290, and Notes 7 and 8 (and the corresponding discussion) in Chapter 11.

18. See, e.g., "Ali Slovenci izumiramo?" Delo, February 5, 1972; "Bomo Slovenci res izumrli?" Delo, October 27, 1973.

19. During the period of acute interrepublic tension before 1972, these sentiments found considerable overt expression. See, e.g., "Hoće li slovenci u vojsku?" NIN, October 31, 1971 (for a Slovenian initiative to create separate republic armies).

20. See Note 8 to Chapter 13.

21. VUS za naše gradjane u svijetu, April 3, 1974; Politika, July 26, 1976.

22. If only because of Slovenia's reported acceptance of 10,000 workers from Kosovo annually (see Note 49 to Chapter 12).

23. As was noted earlier, census statistics locate people at their "permanent" residence, not their work residence. In 1972, 26,600 of the 28,700 babies born in Slovenia were reported as being born to Slovenian mothers (Demografska statistika 1972, p. 148).

24. "It is not known precisely how many workers from other republics there are in Slovenia at present: from political sources we were informed that there are about 100,000 but the Institute for Sociology put forward an estimate of 120,000 to 140,000." P. Stojanović, "Senke visokog standarda," NIN, August 4, 1974, pp. 12-13.

25. One in four employed workers in Slovenia is not Slovenian ("Štorkljo v slovenski grb!" I.T.D., January 15, 1974). If one were to regard Slovenia as an independent country, this proportion of Gastarbeiter would place it in the Liechtenstein class.

26. "Pečalbari bez pasoša," VUS, May 1, 1976, p. 18.

27. See the earlier discussion of the same dilemma in the Croatian case. Once granted minority rights, the immigrants could form permanent and unassimilable communities. One reason why official statistics are not reorganized to give a realistic picture of the residential ethnic structure of Slovenia may be that if this were done, it could become difficult to resist demands for the rigorous application of the nacionalni ključ in the republic.

28. The prominent Slovenian sociologist Stane Saksida is quoted in P. Stojanović, op. cit., as comparing the Slovenian immigrants with European Gastarbeiter and saying that "the work force from the south of our country is not offered adequate living conditions in Slovenia."

29. "It is clear that she is nationally oriented toward Slovenia, but without any special sharpness toward the 'south'; but the thought of danger from workers from the south is more compelling. That's why she mostly stays home in the evening.... She is much more interested in locking the doors than in changes in

the federation, so she does not know who the commune president is, but she is greatly disturbed about the question of construction near her home." The above is extracted from a Yugoslav sociologist's composite portrait (based on survey results) of a type of person who has withdrawn from active political life. It is quoted by Sharon Zukin in her Beyond Marx and Tito, London, 1975, p. 121. Perhaps the only comment that needs to be added to this evocative pen sketch is that in Slovenia, migrant workers from other republics form 42.4% of all employed in the construction industry (VUS, May 1, 1976, p. 19).

30. See Note 47 to Chapter 12.

31. According to Politika, December 5, 1975, p. 14, Slovenia has a labor deficit of 80,000 and is prepared to accept 10,000 workers a year from other republics. See Note 49 to Chapter 12.

32. See Popis stanovništva i stanova 1971, vol. 1, pp. XIV-XVI; Besemeres, op. cit., p. 12, fn. 32.

33. It was repeatedly emphasized by the highest political authorities in Bosnia and Hercegovina that Moslems were to feel absolutely free to so identify themselves. See, e.g., the article by the Bosnian party secretary Hamdija Pozderac in Komunist, March 4, 1971.

34. See Appendix Table 28, pp. 296-97.

35. In the 1948 Census 37,000 Slavonic Macedonians identified their religion as Islam. For an account of their ethnic makeup and some of the pressures to which they have been subjected, see Mustafa Imamović "Nesporazumi oko Muslimana," Gledišta, 1971, no. 2, p. 247. For the Macedonian view, see Nova Makedonija, January 21 and February 14, 1971.

36. See Note 12 to Chapter 11. In 1975 the NRR for Bosnia and Hercegovina was 1.06, compared with 0.89 and 0.87 for Croatia and Serbia proper. Demografska statistika 1975, Belgrade, 1977, p. 56. In the same year in Bosnia and Hercegovina there were 36,822 Moslem births but only 23,919 children born to Serbian mothers (Demografska statistika 1975, p. 145). In 1971 Moslems formed 39.6% and Serbs 37.2% of the republic's total population.

37. See Notes 31 to 33.

38. It is possible that their numbers are now growing and are simply not adequately registered owing to the "permanent residence" criterion. One estimate in 1970 put the total number of Moslems living in Slovenia and Croatia at 100,000 (VUS, July 22, 1970, p. 22). A letter writer to Vjesnik (May 7, 1971) claimed there were over 100,000 Moslems in Croatia alone. According to the census results, there were only 18,457 in Croatia and 3,231 in Slovenia (Popis stanovništva i stanova 1971, vol. 1, pp. 24 and 32).

39. With 120,000 members, as compared with the Moslems 87,000. The preponderance of Serbs in key republic bodies is less marked. Večernje novosti, May 9, 1978. For further and earlier details, see Besemeres, op. cit., p. 14, fns. 39 and 40.

40. See Slobodan Stanković, "A Moslem Finally to Become Member of the Yugoslav Party Presidium," RFE, RAD Background Report/49 (Yugoslavia), March 6, 1979.

41. The Australian, April 21, 1979.

42. On Mihajlović's plans, see M. Hadžijahić, "Krivo svedočanstvo," VUS, August 26, 1970. During World War II the Sandžak area was the center of particularly confused and violent exchanges between various armies and local bands of ethnic militants. Četnik and Moslem detachments were heavily involved in communal reprisals in the area. See S. Pavlo-

witch, Yugoslavia, London, 1971, Chap. 3.

43. They were 383,988 (81.4% of the total) in 1961 and only 355,608 (67.1%) in 1971. "Nacionalni sastav stanovništva po opštinama," Statistički bilten, 727, April 1972, p. 8.

44. See Appendix Table 21, p. 290, and Notes 7, 8, 9, and 10 to Chapter 11.

45. G. Žarković, N. Stojkov, G. Todorović and M.(irjana) Džumhur, Projekcije stanovništva SFR Jugoslavije po republikama i narodnostima do 2030 godine, Sarajevo, 1971. The book was given prominence in at least the Slovenian and Croatian press. See Vjesnik, August 14, 1971, and Tovariš, August 30, 1971.

46. Žarković et al., op. cit., p. 83.

47. They derived their figure for the Moslems from the 1961 Census results which, as later became apparent, greatly underestimated their real numbers. But they continued extrapolating very rapid (and almost certainly unrealistic) increase rates for them to 2030. Ibid., p. 81.

48. For some critical comments, see Besemeres, op. cit., p. 16, fn. 47.

49. The complete stagnation of the Serbian population in Kosovo (227,000 in 1961, 228,000 in 1971), in combination with the relatively higher fertility of the Serbs in the area (GFR 130 in 1961, compared to 75 for Yugoslavia as a whole in the same year; Fertilitet ženskog stanovništva 1950-1967, p. 22), suggests either high emigration, or changes in ethnic self-identification, or both. The 1971 Census recorded a net migratory balance of 49,000 Serbs from Kosovo (plus 6,000 Montenegrins from Kosovo). See Note 28 to Chapter 11. See also "Uzroci migracije stanovništva," Politika, June 22, 1971, tr. in Osteuropa, vol. 22 (1972), no. 3, pp. A196-97.

50. Borba, May 30, 1968.

51. Ćosić is continuing his recidivist career. In late 1977 he was twice severely criticized in the party weekly Komunist for a speech he had made while accepting membership in the Serbian Academy of Sciences, in which he said, inter alia, that various disasters had brought the Serbs to "the verge of biological extinction." Komunist, October 3 and December 5, 1977. But the criticism was very slow in coming. And Ćosić is still apparently a member of the Academy.

52. Politika, May 11, 1978. For further details, see Besemeres, op. cit., fn. 50.

53. On the development of republic and autonomist aspirations, see R. King, Minorities under Communism, Cambridge, Mass., 1973, especially pp. 137 ff., and L. Zanga, "Jugoslawische Nationalitätenpolitik im Fall Kosovo," Osteuropa, vol. 25 (1975), p. 503. The 1974 Constitution goes some of the way toward granting Kosovo republic status. Meanwhile autonomist pressures continue, e.g., for further increasing the status of the Albanian language within the province and for preventing any discrimination against people who do not know Serbo-Croatian. See Politika, March 6, 1976, p. 6.

54. These aspects of the problem will be further discussed in Chapter 16.

55. See Appendix Table 28, pp. 296-97.

56. See Demografska statistika 1972, p. 147; Popis stanovništva i stanova 1971, vol. 1, p. 28. See also Note 10 to Chapter 11.

57. See RFE, Bulgaria/28, October 16, 1969, Bulgarian Situation Report/13, April 28, 1976, and Bulgarian Situation Report/31, December 8, 1977. For the emigration data, see Migracije stanovništva Jugoslavije, p. 89.

58. See Note 6.

59. There may also be a large (and rapidly growing) number of Gypsies in Macedonia who would welcome recognition as a distinct ethnic group. See Note 74 to Chapter 17.

60. See Note 37 to Chapter 15.

61. Since 1950 some 39,000 Macedonians have been repatriated from the Soviet bloc. Bulgaria has been, but is not apparently at present, one of the source countries. NIN, October 15, 1978, p. 8. Most of these returnees are being settled in the Western communes of the republic whence the Turks have emigrated and where the Albanians are concentrated. Special successes are also claimed with economic emigrants of more recent date (the Eastern bloc repatriates are presumably in many cases fugitives from the Greek civil war of the late 1940s). In this endeavor the full cooperation of the Macedonian Orthodox Church is actively solicited. NIN, November 19, 1978, p. 16.

62. These problems are discussed further in Chapter 16.

63. See Borba, September 12, 1970; Nova Makedonia, December 24, 1970; and "Muslimani: nacija ili vera?" NIN, February 7, 1971.

64. For a brief discussion of this question, see Besemeres, op. cit., p. 20, fn. 60.

65. It is also possible that the Macedonians are eager to forestall any claim to ethnic separateness by the 10% or so of Macedonians in Bulgaria who may be Moslems. See Besemeres, op. cit., p. 21, fn. 59.

66. See the discussion in Chapter 16.

Chapter 15

1. "Živimo šest godina duže," Vjesnik, June 3, 1957.

2. "Zemlja mladih ljudi," Vjesnik, August 18, 1957.

3. "Dinamizam savremenog Jugoslovena: sve jače kretanje našeg stanovništva," Oslobodjenje, July 12, 1959.

4. Vjesnik, August 18, 1957.

5. Savezni zavod za statistiku, Fertilitet ženskog stanovništva 1950-1967, Belgrade, 1971, p. 18.

6. Oslobodjenje, July 12, 1959.

7. From an editorial note appended to the first issue of Stanovništvo, in which the reasons for its formation were outlined.

8. T. Mulina, "Tretman stanovništva i radne snage u kontekstu privrednog razvoja Jugoslavije," Belgrade Population Policy Conference (Savetovanje o izgradnji društvenih stavova o populacionoj politici), 1973, mimeographed paper, p. 2.

9. In 1964 the party daily Borba devoted a lengthy round-table discussion to the declining birthrate. See "Zašto opada natalitet," Borba, February 2 and 3, 1964.

10. See, e.g., J. Klauzer, "Jedan aspekt ocenjivanja potrebe za populacionom politikom u Jugoslaviji," Stanovništvo, vol. 6 (1968), nos. 1-2, pp. 7-8.

11. See, e.g., the draft Long-Term Development Plan of Yugoslavia to 1985 (published as a supplement to Borba, October 26, 1974).

12. This same conclusion is also supported by a consideration of trends in domestic population policies at the federal and republic levels. See Chapter 17.

13. For a Yugoslav perspective on international population politics, see Hristina Pop-Antoska, "Razvoj pogleda na populacionu politiku sa osvrtom na planiranje porodice u Ujedinjenim Nacijama" (sic), Naše teme, 1974, no. 4, p. 603.

14. For a complete text of the statement, see Studies in Family Planning, no. 16 (January 1967).

15. See, for example, President Tito's message to the Bucharest Conference (UN World Population Conference Press Release, POP/CONF/10, August 19, 1974); the report on the head of the Yugoslav delegation, Deputy Premier Anton Vratuša's address to the Conference in Borba, August 22, 1974; and the inter-

view with Vratuša, "Sve nas je više, ali izlaz postoji," VUS, September 11, 1974.

16. Anton Vratuša, in VUS, September 11, 1974.

17. For an account of these developments, see Richard Symonds and Michael Carder, The United Nations and the Population Question, London, 1973, chaps. 12-14.

18. See J. Finkle and B. Crane, "The Politics of Bucharest," Population and Development Review, 1975, no. 1.

19. Pop Antoska, op. cit., p. 617.

20. Symonds and Carder, op. cit., pp. 181-83.

21. Though the proportion of all aid going to population programs worldwide increased rapidly during the late 1960s and early 1970s, it had not reached much more than 2.5% of the whole at the time of the Bucharest Conference. See United Nations World Population Conference 1974 E/CONF. 60/CBP/24, The Role of International Assistance in the Population Fields, annex table 1. It has been estimated that in 1971, the major international donors contributed no more than one tenth of the cost of the fertility-control programs then in operation in developing countries (and these are widely held to be modest enough in scope). See International Bank for Reconstruction and Development, Population Policies and Economic Development, Baltimore, 1974, pp. 80-81.

22. India, Yugoslavia's voting partner at Bucharest, to cite one glaring example. See Mauldin et al., "Report on Bucharest," Studies in Family Planning, 1974, no. 12, especially pp. 371-72.

23. "With such prestige all doors were open to us; all delegations were ready to cooperate with us and sought our cooperation. We took, if I may say so, full advantage of this." VUS, September 11, 1974.

24. "At this conference we witnessed the transition of militant opposition into an active posture, and I think that this is an important result of the Bucharest Conference. The developing countries succeeded in imposing their view because they were organized and united in their activities and submissions." Ibid. It should be noted that the word "impose" (nametnuti) used by Vratuša on this occasion is a very negative one in Yugoslav political vocabulary, usually being used to describe the hegemonist activities of East or West. World population problems are evidently now seen essentially in terms of Lenin's kto kogo.

25. "Priraštaj — briga sveta," Borba, August 2, 1974. Compare also "Eksplozija stanovništva," Borba Reflektor, September 17, 1969.

26. "Bitka bogatih i siromašnih, Borba, August 22, 1974.

27. For an example of anti-Malthusianism worthy of the best the Soviet Union could offer, see Željka Zalar, "Maltuzianizam i ekologija," Naše teme, 1973, no. 4, p. 886.

28. Yugoslavia has also maintained a distinct stance politically, caucusing and voting with its nonaligned allies and not with the Soviet bloc. See Mauldin et al., op. cit., pp. 363 and 372.

29. Note the following phrase from a Yugoslav commentary on world population problems: "to diminish the 'explosion' of which, it seems, it is only the developed nations who are afraid" (NIN, August 18, 1974, p. 34).

30. See, e.g., D. Breznik, "Neki problemi porasta svetskog stanovništva," Medjunarodni problemi, vol. 20, no. 2, p. 45; M. Rašević, "The Development of World Population with Special Reference to the Modern Period," a paper (in Serbian) presented to the Belgrade Population Policy Conference, 1973.

31. See, e.g., S. Krašovec, "Razvitak marksističkog pristupa teorii i politici populacije," Naše teme, 1974, no. 4, especially p. 551, and the same author's

Človeštvo kruh in lakota, Ljubljana, 1970; R. Njegić and L. Radović, "Novi pogledi sovjetskih autora na zakon razvitka stanovništva u socializmu," Ekonomski Analiz, no. 35 (June 1972), p. 44; R. Supek, Ova jedina zemlja, Zagreb, 1973.

32. See the instances cited by Macura (of such inadequacies and of such criticism) in "Komponente populacione politike," Naše teme, 1974, no. 4, especially pp. 554-58.

33. K. Miljovski, "Kretanje stanovništva, ekonomski razvoj i nedovoljno razvijena područja," paper presented to the Belgrade Conference on Population Policy, 1973.

34. G. Žarković, "Smanjivanje prirodnog priraštaja stanovništva i ekonomski i socijalni razvoj," paper presented to the Belgrade Conference on Population Policy, 1973.

35. I. Popit, "Povprečje zdaj: dva otroka," Delo, September 9, 1972. Since that time Delo articles on demographic themes have become much more tactful.

36. For an instance of fully "official" Malthusian thinking by a Macedonian, see the Macedonian Central Committee member Aleksandar Donev's article, "Kako da presahnu izvori nezaposlenosti," Komunist, January 7, 1974, p. 11.

37. N. Stojkov, "Determinante visokog i niskog nataliteta u Jugoslaviji." See also V. Starova, "Vlijanieto na zdravstvenata zaštita na demografskite dviženja," and K. Miljovski, op. cit.

Chapter 16

1. A Komunist article (August 26, 1974, p. 17) on the "education" of workers abroad remarks that adoption by workers of foreign ways draws them away from their homeland and threatens them "either with assimilation or other negative influences." The article goes on to say that studies of "temporary" emigrants point "more than clearly" to widespread "temporary" assimilation. See Notes 21, 70, and 72 (and corresponding text) to Chapter 13.

2. S. Vidaković, "Popis stanovništva i mogućnost korišćenja rezultata za potrebe narodne odbrane," Vojno-ekonomski pregled, vol. 17 (1971), no. 4, p. 484.

3. See Notes 24 and 25 (and corresponding text) in Chapter 13.

4. Press expositions of the doctrine by senior officers are quite common. See, for example, the interview with General Pejnović (head of the Center for Strategic Research of the General Staff) in VUS, December 24, 1975. For a very good short account by a Western observer, see A. Ross Johnson, "Yugoslav Total National Defence," Survival, vol. 15 (1973), no. 1, p. 54.

5. The above calculations are based on the figures supplied by Begtić, "Yugoslav Nationals Temporarily Working Abroad," p. 20, and Popis stanovništva i stanova 1971, vol. 1, p. 2.

6. This is samozaštita (literally "self-defence"), the self-managing dialectal form of the Soviet bditel'nost'. Calls for intensified samozaštita multiplied after 1975, when the renewed wave of "cominformist" activities was publicly acknowledged. See "Samozaštita, šta je to?" Politika, January 11, 1976, p. 7.

7. A. Ross Johnson, op. cit., p. 58.

8. See VUS, November 19, 1975, and Komunist, September 22, 1978, p. 22.

9. For a Slovenian study giving data on the declining numbers identifying as Slovenians in Italy (and apparently accepting this trend as inevitable), see J. Jeri, "Etnična, gospodarsko-socialna in kulturno-prosvetna struktura slovenske narodnostne skupnosti v Italiji," mimeographed paper presented to the 1974 Slovenian Demographic Symposium (Raziskovalni Center Ekonomske Fakultete

Univerze v Ljubljani, Slovenski demografski simpozij, Ljubljana, 1974).

10. See Zdenko Antić, "Karamanlis to Visit Belgrade," RFE, RAD Background Report/62 (Yugoslavia), March 15, 1979.

11. Politika, May 25, 1976.

12. See, e.g., "Manevri znani kao 'poseban popis,'" Borba, February 26, 1975; "Meta napada antislovenačkih snaga," Komunist, February 27, 1978, p. 14.

13. See, e.g., Politika, August 12, 1976, p. 4.

14. For the official Yugoslav view of the treaty, see "Nezadovoljena prava nacionalnih manjina," Komunist, January 27, 1975.

15. Politika, August 5, 1976.

16. Clissold, op. cit., p. 122. The Vojvodina referred to there does not correspond precisely to the present province of that name.

17. Hungarians formed 25.8% of the population of Vojvodina in 1948, but only 21.7% in 1971 ("Nacionalni sastav stanovništva po opštinama," p. 11). They were 10% of the Romanian population according to the 1930 Census, but only 8.5% by 1966 (the percentage of Romanians having increased in that time from 77.9% to 87.7%): Anarul demografic al Republicii Socialiste Romania 1974, pp. 106-7. There were 658,000 Hungarians recorded by the 1921 Czechoslovak Census, 597,000 in 1930, and 578,000 in 1971. As a percentage they had fallen from 5.1% in 1921 to 4% in 1971, while the Czechs and Slovaks combined had increased from 67.6% in 1921 to 94.3% in 1971 (Demografie, vol. 10 [1968], no. 4, p. 302, and vol. 14 [1972], p. 183). The data are not strictly comparable and not, perhaps, wholly reliable either. Moreover, in recent years the Hungarian population has been increasing modestly. But the long-term trend has been clearly toward relative decline.

18. King, op. cit., pp. 163 ff.

19. Reuter and dpa, January 8, 1976, cited in Z. Antić, "Yugoslav Leader Accuses Cominformists of Having Foreign Ties," RFE Research, RAD Background Report/1 (Yugoslavia), January 9, 1976.

20. In 1976 Hungarian news media were given a curiously monopolistic role in reporting certain recent perturbations in Sino-Albanian relations. See L. Zanga, "Whither Albania," RFE Research, RAD Background Report/112 (Albania), May 18, 1976, especially pp. 3 and 9.

21. "Privatni kanali," NIN, July 7, 1974, p. 20.

22. The Macedonians made their last significant census appearance in Bulgaria in 1956, when 178,000 of them were registered. According to Komunist, December 8, 1975, p. 7, the Sofia party daily Rabotničesko Delo once estimated that there were 500,000 Macedonians in Bulgaria.

23. The Macedonian dispute has been long and acrimonious and has passed through numerous phases. A considerable literature has developed on the subject. See, e.g., P. Shoup, op. cit., chap. 4; R. King, Minorities under Communism, chap. 10; Stephen E. Palmer, Jr., and Robert R. King, Yugoslav Communism and the Macedonian Question, Hamden, Conn., 1971; RFE Research RAD Background Report/99 (Yugoslavia), June 6, 1975; RAD Background Report/98 (Bulgaria), June 6, 1975; RAD Background Reports 148 and 155 (Yugoslavia), July 3 and 10, 1978; and Bulgarian Situation Report/14 (Bulgaria), July 27, 1978.

24. See RFE Research, Bulgarian Situation Report/13, April 28, 1976, p. 5.

25. "The favorite theme of the present-day agitpropites is the 'falling apart' of Yugoslavia! There is never a political meeting in Pirin Macedonia, it seems, where there isn't some well-paid agitator to devote a good deal of attention to that theme." "Šta se krije iza popisa u Bugarskoj," VUS, November 26, 1975,

p. 6 (translated from an article in Nova Makedonia).

26. In 1973 the Belgrade children's magazine Kekec published a linguistic map which depicted a large part of Macedonia (including Skopje and also some regions of strongly Albanian settlement) as falling within the area in which the Ekavian dialect of Serbo-Croatian is spoken. See Borba, November 23, 1973, where the episode was described as a "political maneuver" (but only after the Macedonian Public Prosecutor had demanded that a ban be placed on that issue of the publication). Kekec and Borba are published by the same enterprise.

27. See, e.g., "Šta hoće," NIN, November 9, 1975.

28. According to one Yugoslav source, a wave of arrests began in late 1973, suggesting that it was part of a systematic buildup toward attaining a "good" result in the 1975 Census. "Zvanično nestali," NIN, January 5, 1975, p. 47.

29. See Note 53 to Chapter 14.

30. Though Albanians and Turks formed some 24% of the Macedonian population in 1971, only three of the twenty-one members of the republic party presidium were, apparently, Moslems. In the Central Committee the relationship was even more unfavorable for the Moslem ethnic groups — only nine of a total membership of eighty-four. Albanians and Turks combined form less than 10% of the total Macedonian party membership. These disparities should be contrasted with the rapidly changing situation in Kosovo (see Note 52 to Chapter 14).

31. In early May 1976 Enver Hoxha announced that a clique of pro-Soviet elements had been uncovered. Among their other crimes, this clique was said to have been plotting to undermine the alliance with China ("Smenjivanja u vrhu," NIN, May 9, 1976). Since that time, of course, the alliance with China has collapsed. While Hoxha remains, reconciliation with Moscow will be difficult. But given the withdrawal of China's support and the continuing reserve toward the Yugoslav Federal government (as opposed to local accommodation with republic and provincial authorities, especially in Kosovo), Albania seems to have only one move open to it. It tends to be forgotten that Albania was once a loyal member of the Soviet bloc. In 1958, for example, Albanian papers were writing of "joint wars of liberation" with their Bulgarian allies (Carl Ströhm, "Der Ostblock und das Jugoslawische Nationalitätenproblem," Osteuropa, 1958, p. 719). Though the ageing and ailing Hoxha-Shehu leadership may be irrevocably set against it, Soviet-Albanian rapprochement seems quite likely to be ultimately seen as of advantage to both parties. Any such development would be a dark omen for Yugoslavia.

32. Rilindja (the Priština Albanian-language party daily), February 24, 1976, abstracted in ABSEES, vol. 7 (July 1976), no. 3, p. 245. See also "Sprache und Politik in Albanien," Osteuropa, vol. 23 (1973), no. 8, p. A582.

33. Louis Zanga, "Sharp Upswing in Yugoslav-Albanian Economic Cooperation," RFE, RAD Background Report/56 (Albania), March 9, 1979.

34. In 1975-76 there were repeated references in the Yugoslav press to the activities of Albanian "irredentists." Politika, December 5, 1975, p. 7, reports the Federal Public Prosecutor as saying that thirty-three irredentists had been proceeded against in Kosovo during that year. See also Politika, January 16, 1976, p. 8, and April 24, 1976, p. 8. For an account of a trial of eighteen Albanian "irredentists" (all of them apparently with some higher education), see Politika, February 8, 1976, p. 9.

35. Four-pronged in the event that a (post-Ceausescu?) Romanian leadership were induced to participate in the adventure. Romania, like Albania, though to a lesser extent, has been betraying signs of internal dissension in recent years.

36. "There does not seem to be much doubt that the Soviets will not send troops into Yugoslavia while Tito is alive; there is serious doubt that they will do so even after his passing, unless internal disorders should break out." J. Walkin, "Yugoslavia after the Tenth Party Congress," Survey, vol. 22 (1976), no. 1, p. 69. Walkin spent some time as a U.S. diplomat in Belgrade.

37. The Yugoslavs interpreted the Sonnenfeldt affair as a deliberate signal from the USA to the USSR that any settlement they wish to make of the Yugoslav problem will be satisfactory provided that the American sphere of interest is not threatened. See, e.g., "Prazan rulet," NIN, April 18, 1976, p. 423. It seems fairly clear that if the Soviet Union attempts overt aggression against Yugoslavia at some appropriate moment, the American response will be restrained (see Note 36).

38. This passage has been retained as it was first formulated in 1976. The partial aberration of Carter's stress on human rights seems unlikely to prevail for long. In any case, judging by his lamentable performance on his official visit to Poland, he does not appear to have ever intended the doctrine to be taken too seriously in the East.

Chapter 17

1. For a comprehensive discussion of many aspects of Yugoslav population policy, see (if possible) the mimeographed proceedings of the 1973 Belgrade Conference on Population Policy, Savetovanje o izgradnji društvenih stavova o populacionoj politici u Jugoslaviji. Several key contributions to this conference were published in Naše teme, 1974, no. 4, including the admirable summary by Miloš Macura, "Komponente populacione politike saobrazne sadašnjim i budućim potrebama Jugoslavije." Important republic conferences have been held in Croatia and Slovenia: see Stanovništvo, emigracija i zaposlenost u Hrvatskoj, Zagreb, 1971, and Raziskovalni Center Ekonomske Fakultete Univerze v Ljubljani, Slovenski demografski simpozij, Ljubljana, 1974, mimeograph. There is a good short account in D. Breznik and M. Rašević, "Razmatranja o populacionoj politici u Jugoslaviji," Stanovništvo, vol. 10 (1972), no. 1-2, p. 5, and a useful one in English by Stanka Krajnc-Simoneti et al. in M. Kirk, M. Livi Bacci, and E. Szabady, eds., Law and Fertility in Europe, Dolhain, 1975, vol. 2, p. 665.

2. See Notes 1 and 2 to Chapter 12.

3. Compare the discussion in Chapter 15.

4. Family allowances seem to have had a significant pronatalist impact in the postwar years, when they were quite large in relation to the incomes of the time. See D. Breznik and M. Rašević, op. cit., p. 6.

5. See J. Klauzer, "Jedan aspekt ocenjivanja potrebe za populacionom politikom u Jugoslaviji," Stanovništvo, VI (1968), no. 1-2, p. 5, at p. 8.

6. See M. Bešter, "Nekateri vidiki politike reprodukcije prebivalstva," Ekonomska revija, vol. 16 (1965), no. 2, p. 127.

7. For English texts of the 1952 and 1960 decrees, see H. P. David, Abortion and Family Planning in Socialist Countries of Eastern Europe, pp. 216 and 219. For accounts of the reform movement that made them possible, see A. Milojković et al., "Historijat liberalizacije pobačaja u Jugoslaviji," and F. Novak et al., "Prikaz razvoja odnosa do celokupne problematike planiranja porodice u medicinskim krugovima," papers presented to the 1973 Belgrade Conference on Population Policy (mimeograph). See also Note 11.

8. See, e.g., S. Krašovec, "Stihijnost ili kontrola kretanja stanovništva,"

p. 36; Breznik and Rašević, op. cit., pp. 6-7; Klauzer, op. cit., p. 8.

9. See M. Macura, "Demografska analiza u pripremama za Sedmogodišnji plan," Stanovništvo, vol. 1 (1963), no. 2, p. 179; M. Sentić and D. Breznik, "Demografska kretanja i projekcije u Jugoslaviji," Stanovništvo, vol. 2 (1964), no. 2, p. 101.

10. See Note 9. See also Macura's contribution to the round-table discussion, "Zašto opada natalitet?" Borba, February 2 and 3, 1964, and M. Bešter, op. cit.

11. The group I have chosen to identify as "family planners" was of course made up of disparate elements, including party feminists, the reforming minority of the medical profession, and a variety of other social policy liberals. For an account of their successful campaign, see N. Petrić, "Društveno-politički aspekt razvoja planiranja porodice u Jugoslaviji," paper presented to the 1973 Belgrade Conference on Population Policy (mimeograph).

12. See Note 14 to Chapter 15.

13. See F. Novak et al., op. cit.

14. Službeni list SFRJ, 1969, no. 20.

15. The resolution and the new Abortion Law were obviously regarded by the regime as a parcel of measures. For an English text of the resolution, see Yugoslav Survey, 1969, no. 3, pp. 103-6. The resolution was evidently passed in the teeth of stiff opposition. See S. Stanič, "'Pobuna' ginekologa," NIN, December 8, 1974.

16. "Federal Assembly Resolution on Family Planning," Yugoslav Survey, 1969, no. 3, p. 103.

17. Stane Krašovec, "Hrvatski posvet o prebivalstvu, emigraciji in zaposlitvi," Ekonomska revija, vol. 22 (1971), no. 2, p. 241.

18. For citations for all three conferences, see Note 1.

19. See Note 11 to Chapter 15. The 1974 Long-Term Development Plan of Yugoslavia to 1985 was apparently the first planning document to contain a rubric specifically devoted to population policy. See "Bolj človeško, bolj razumno," Delo, June 22, 1974.

20. For an account of the preparations for and course of these Assembly proceedings (an account which demonstrates very clearly the influence of the Federal Council for Family Planning on policy formation), see B. Vesić, "Ostvarivanje načela i ciljeva Rezolucije Savezne Skupštine o planiranju porodice," Socijalna politika, 1974, no. 4, p. 17.

21. Ustav Socijalističke Federativne Republike Jugoslavije, p. 99, article 191. Identical formulations were entered in all the republic and provincial constitutions as well. The Slovenian Constitution also contains an additional guarantee of the right to information and appropriate social security in family planning. "'Pobuna' ginekologa," NIN, December 8, 1974.

22. See "Jednaka prava za bračnu i vanbračnu decu," Borba, September 27, 1973.

23. See the instances cited by Macura in "Komponente populacione politike," pp. 554-55.

24. Vida Tomšič, "Planiranje porodice i populaciona politika," paper presented to the 1974 Slovenian Demographic Symposium (mimeograph), especially p. 16. Tomšič is president of the Federal Council for Family Planning, a member of the LCY Central Committee, and a frequent spokeswoman for Yugoslavia at international conferences on demographically relevant topics. Given her high political standing and the Federal Council's overwhelming influence on policy-making in this area, her views on this as on other issues can be safely regarded as at least semiofficial.

25. See Tito's support for child-care services in an interview published in Komunist, February 2, 1976. The emphasis is always on solving social problems not demographic ones. See, e.g., "Socijalna karta za celu porodicu," Borba, February 23, 1975.

26. See "Kako se snaći," NIN, November 30, 1975; "Razvod sa starim brakom," NIN, March 26, 1978; Politika, May 9, 1979, p. 7.

27. The draft Long-Term Plan speaks only of a "gradual overcoming of regional demographic differences," Osnova zajedničke politike dugoročnog razvoja SFR Jugoslavije do 1985 godine: Predlog za javnu diskusiju, published as a supplement to Borba, October 26, 1974, p. XIV.

28. For the constitutional position of the new "interest communities," see Ustav Socijalističke Federativne Jugoslavije, articles 51-59 and 110-13. For an interesting general discussion, see S. Nikšić, "Kraj znači početak," NIN, December 22, 1974.

29. See, e.g., "Muke zrelog doba," NIN, December 11, 1978; "Ko troši tudje? Otvoreno pismo vladi," NIN, October 15, 1978. NIN was subjected to official censure for articles like these. See Politika, January 30, 1979, p. 6.

30. See, e.g., G. Žarković et al., "Znanje, stavovi i praksa planiranja porodice kod ženskog stanovništva u fertilnoj dobi," and D. Štampar, "Planiranje porodice u Jugoslaviji — razvoj i problemi," papers presented to the Belgrade Population Policy Conference; Krajnc-Simoneti et al., "Law and Fertility in Yugoslavia," in Kirk et al., op. cit., vol. 2, especially pp. 674-75.

31. Of 8,000 women in a 1970 survey, 70% relied basically on coitus interruptus. Žarković et al., "Znanje, stavovi i praksa," pp. 13-14.

32. Data concerning abortions in Yugoslavia are not published regularly. One estimate put the annual total of registered abortions in the country at about 300,000, of which 120,000 occurred in Serbia proper and 45,000 (compare 19,000 live births in 1973) in Belgrade ("Pismo nerodjenom detetu," NIN, February 8, 1976). The total figure (including illegal abortions) may be higher by 100,000 (B. Vesić, op. cit., p. 19). In Serbia, at least, the situation may be worsening. See Politika, May 2, 1979, p. 7.

33. There were 146 deaths consequent on abortion in 1966, for example (Fertilitet stanovništva u Jugoslaviji, p. 329). Reportedly, all cases of death from abortion since 1963 have resulted from illegal abortions. Krajnc-Simoneti et al., op. cit., p. 677.

34. Žarković et al., "Djelatnost zdravstvenih ustanova na planiranju porodice u Jugoslaviji," paper presented at the Belgrade Population Policy Conference.

35. Žarković et al. found that social insurance funds in fact covered less than half the total sum required for actual current expenditure on contraception and less than 1% of what might be regarded as a satisfactory program. Ibid, pp. 2-3.

36. See, e.g., F. Novak et al., op. cit.; "Pismo nerodjenom detetu," NIN, February 8, 1976.

37. See, e.g., "Zašto kasne stanovi," NIN, April 14, 1974, and "Korakom puža," Komunist, September 22, 1975, p. 15. Yugoslav construction rates are among the very slowest in Europe.

38. "Generacija podstanara," NIN, May 23, 1976.

39. See, e.g., "Kome stanarina s popustom?" VUS, November 19, 1975; "Prava cena stanovanja" and "Stan iz svog džepa," NIN, October 15, 1978, and January 28, 1979.

40. See, e.g., "Ko je privilegovan," NIN, November 16, 1975; "Ukleto vlasništvo," VUS, February 7, 1976.

41. A good deal of the inflation appears to have been due to the monopolistic position held by construction enterprises which, particularly since the 1965 reforms, have apparently often taken advantage of the housing shortage and market conditions to raise their charges inordinately. See Borba, November 20, 1971, pp. 1 and 4.

42. Politika, March 26, 1976, p. 7, reported that as of 1975, housing cost 3,182 dinars per sq. m. in Bor, but 7,202 dinars per sq. m. in Sarajevo.

43. See, e.g., "Spriječiti, legalizirati ili rušiti," VUS, September 17, 1975.

44. Komunist, February 2, 1976, p. 8.

45. See, e.g., "Kad se zakida na deci," Politika, April 20, 1976; "Dok vi radite, vrtići spavaju," VUS, February 19, 1977; "Dotacije imućnima," NIN, May 15, 1978.

46. In this as in many related fields, Serbia lags far behind Croatia, Slovenia, and Vojvodina. See NIN, February 15, 1976, p. 27.

47. Compare the discussion in Chapter 9, pp. 104-115.

48. Osnova zajedničke politike dugoročnog razvoja, p. XIV.

49. Macura, "Komponente populacione politike," p. 558.

50. Perović participated in the 1964 Borba round-table debate on population policy, taking a strongly feminist and "anti-pro-natalist" line (Borba, February 2 and 3, 1964). The case of Vida Tomšič of Slovenia is also significant (see Note 24).

51. M. Macura, "Komponente populacione politike," pp. 573-74.

52. According to a major fertility survey conducted in 1970, the ideal number of children varied by republic and province between 2.3 in Serbia proper and 3.8 in Kosovo; the number actually desired varied between 2.0 in Serbia proper and 3.6 in Kosovo. G. Todorović, "Idealni i željeni broj dece," Stanovništvo, vol. 9 (1971), no. 304, pp. 301 and 305.

53. V. Tomšič, "Planiranje porodice i populaciona politika," (mimeograph), especially pp. 15-18.

54. Perhaps it should be emphasized once more that Yugoslavs are intensely conscious of (though not necessarily well-informed about) ethnodemographic trends. For a sense of the keen expectancy with which the census results by nationality were awaited in 1971-72, see the two articles entitled "Nacije u popisu," in NIN, July 4, 1971, and May 28, 1972.

55. For an instance of Serbian opposition, see B. Stambolović, "Planiranje porodice i demografska situacija u opštinama Srbije," Srpski arhiv za celokupno lekarstvo, 1971, no. 7-8, p. 475. Stambolović, a doctor, speaks with the greatest anxiety about the threat posed by abortion to the biological future of the nation (by which he means the Serbs) and repeatedly compares a woman's moral and civic obligation to bear children with a man's duty to serve in the army. The article is also enlivened by some comical demographic logic. For an instance of Macedonian opposition, see A. Kjurčijev, "Niektóre aspekty polityki ludnościowej w Jugosławii," paper presented to the 1972 Warsaw Conference on Population Policy (mimeograph), pp. 12-14. Kjurčijev believes abortion laws should be made an instrument of differentiated population policy. Even more orthodox discussions of abortion policy betray at times more than a trace of ambivalence about the current legislation. See "Planiranje porodice kao čovekovo pravo," Politika, May 12, 1979, p. 7.

56. A problem previously discussed in the Polish context (see pp. 121-24). See, e.g., D. Štampar, "Planiranje porodice u Jugoslaviji — razvoj i problemi," especially pp. 12-17.

57. Compare earlier discussion in Chapters 12 and 15. This debate has been going on in that form for some time. See Migracije stanovništva Jugoslavije, p. 339.

58. See Politika, November 20, 1975, p. 10 (Macedonia); Politika, December 12, 1975, p. 9, and June 10, 1976, p. 8 (Montenegro); NIN, February 9 and 16, 1975, and March 18, 1979, p. 10 (Serbia proper); and Politika, April 2, 1979, p. 6.

59. See Note 39 to Chapter 14. Serbia proper feels aggrieved that it receives no support from the Federal Fund for the Development of Underdeveloped regions. See "Može li brže," NIN, March 18, 1979, pp. 10-14.

60. Recently there has been a tendency for some commentators to argue for transference of family allowance funds to the construction of child-care institutions. See NIN, May 15, 1977, p. 21; Žena (Zagreb), 1978, no. 6, p. 11.

61. M. Mladenović, Društvena zaštita porodice i dece, Belgrade, 1973, pp. 178-79.

62. See Appendix Table 33, p. 302.

63. See, e.g., Komunist, August 12, 1974, pp. 1-2.

64. See, e.g., Borba, July 26, 1974 (Montenegro); VUS za naše gradjane u svijetu, January 8, 1975, p. 32, and Politika, April 16, 1976 (Croatia); and Politika, August 2, 1974, p. 7, and February 1, 1979, p. 8 (Serbia proper). On Slovenia, see A. Radovan, "Zakonodaja o varstvu zena s področja dela in socijalne varnosti ter o otroškem varstvu," paper presented to the 1974 Slovenian Demographic Symposium (mimeograph), pp. 20-21, and Politika, April 11, 1979, p. 9.

65. It was reported in 1977 that two adjoining communes in the Croatian littoral had set tax concessions for unemployed spouses that differed by a factor of five. "Siječanjska halabuka," VUS, January 22, 1977, p. 16.

66. See "Čije su makaze oštrije," NIN, December 1, 1974, and "Različiti aršini," Politika, December 5, 1975. Slovenia seems a little more inclined to treat income tax as a natalist device. See also "Bodo davčne olajšave privabile štorklje?" Tedenska tribuna (Ljubljana), February 21, 1973.

67. See also "Koliko nam je socijalna politika socijalistička," VUS, February 21, 1976.

68. VUS, June 4, 1975. One can well imagine the ribald jocosities that must have been exchanged as these rules were being framed. Family allowances may also vary from enterprise to enterprise. See, e.g., "Pomoć radnicima s više dece," Borba, October 7, 1974.

69. In abortion legislation, as in the case of family allowances, there seems to be a tendency for new measures to be taken up by one republic after another, starting usually from Slovenia. See "'Pobuna' ginekologa," NIN, December 8, 1974, and "Strah od pobačaja," NIN, June 8, 1975. See also VUS, June 11, 1977, p. 39, and NIN, May 22, 1977, p. 15.

70. See Note 31.

71. K. Miljovski, "Kretanje stanovništva, ekonomski razvoj i nerazvijena područja," paper presented to the 1973 Belgrade Population Policy Conference. Another Macedonian contribution to the same conference argued for a differential population policy on the quite explicit grounds that such a policy was necessary to preserve ethnic harmony between Macedonians and Albanians. I. Josifovski, "Problemi populacione politike sa stanovišta razvoja etničkih grupa i njihovih medjuetničkih odnosa na jednom užem području u SR Makedoniji," Naše teme, 1974, no. 4, p. 590. Similar demands were voiced at the same conference in respect of Bosnia and Hercegovina, Montenegro, and Kosovo.

72. See Social Welfare Aspects of Family Planning in Yugoslavia (mimeograph), Belgrade, 1973, p. 27.

73. Montenegro and Macedonia, for example. Miljovski (op. cit.) calls for a "subtly differentiated policy," and Kjurčijev (op. cit.) for a policy differentiated by region (not just by republic or province). A Montenegrin contributor to the 1973 Belgrade Conference, having deplored the lack of any official support for family planning in his republic, went on to speak of the need for determining a population policy in Montenegro, "especially in the less-developed regions." These, of course, are the strongly Moslem communes of the Sandžak (see Note 59). M. Djurić, "Problemi planiranja porodice u SR Crnoj Gori" (mimeograph), pp. 1 and 2.

74. Der Spiegel, April 16, 1973, p. 153, reported that Yugoslav officials had been attempting to get rid of Gypsies as Gastarbeiter to Western Europe, especially to Austria. In the Bosnian commune of Kakanj, according to this report, some 30 Gypsy families had been given financial inducements by the authorities to go abroad. It is characteristic that the 1971 Yugoslav Census reported a total of twelve Gypsies in the whole of Kakanj ("Nacionalni sastav stanovništva po opštinama," p. 14). The Gypsy population in Yugoslavia may in actual fact be very large. One (Gypsy) estimate gives their numbers at 650,000, 200,000 of them allegedly in Macedonia (Gratton Puxon, Rom: Europe's Gipsies, Minority Rights Group Report No. 14, London, 1973). The 1961 Yugoslav census found 150,000 Romany speakers. A more recent Yugoslav source puts the figure at "over 300,000" (Politika, September 11, 1977). Most Yugoslav Gypsies are evidently identifying as Serbs or Macedonians. Should the Gypsies emerge as an independent ethnic group in Yugoslavia, the demopolitical consequences might be quite significant, especially in Macedonia.

75. Krajnc-Simoneti et al., op. cit., p. 693.

76. For some Slovenian talk, see, e.g., "Vzroki premajhnega števila rojstev v Sloveniji," Komunist (Ljubljana edition), November 24, 1972; "Kakšno populacijsko politiko potrebujemo?" Tovariš, October 8, 1973. The Croats talk rather less about population policy since 1971; but see, for example, "Korak ka društvu razvijenih," Politika, March 30, 1975, and "Skupi stanovi — mali natalitet," Borba, August 17, 1974.

77. Evidently for pronatalist reasons, among others. See Krajnc-Simoneti et al., op. cit., p. 680. For a review of the diverse republic provisions in this area, see "Zaštita materinstva u zakonu i praksi," Žena, 1978, no. 6, pp. 7-9.

78. The only pronatalist cris de coeur I have seen in the Belgrade press in recent years have not referred to Serbia. See, e.g., the article on French fertility in Politika, April 4, 1976. Articles like this may be Aesopian illusions to the Serbian situation, but if so they are well camouflaged.

79. Ankucić, op. cit., prilog 1.

80. Politika, October 7 and 21, 1975, p. 9 in each case.

81. Borba, October 27, 1973, p. 6.

82. Politika, July 31, 1976, p. 11.

83. On the lag, see Politika, May 27, 1976, p. 5, and NIN, May 15, 1977, p. 20. The Slovenian varuške are women who are licensed to run child-care institutions in their own homes. The Croatian authorities have adopted the scheme (Politika, March 3, 1979, p. 7), but the Serbs are still presumably more occupied by its ideological "dangers" than its social or demographic advantages. See Politika, March 22, 1979, p. 8.

84. See "Prazne zibelke," Delo, February 15, 1974 (a Slovenian translation of an article that had appeared in the Novi Sad paper Dnevnik), and "Kritična tačka za bebe," NIN, June 23, 1974.

85. "Nacionalistički pucnji u prazno," VUS, October 8, 1975.

86. Thus in 1976, for example, the increase in Kosovo was 30%, while the increase in Bosnia and Hercegovina was only 16.8% (Politika, February 24, 1976, p. 7).

87. Compare the report of a Swedish demographer after a visit to Albania: "In addition, one often encounters the nationalistic argument in favour of a population larger than it is at present. The Albanians feel that they are surrounded by enemies and that if their population was larger it would be easier for them to resist possible attacks." E. Hofsten, "Demographic Transition and Economic Development in Albania," European Demographic Information Bulletin, vol. 6 (1975), no. 5, p. 156.

88. See Note 73.

89. Borba, July 26, 1974.

Chapter 18

1. Here some of the less-developed countries with relatively recent histories of demographic transition and therefore relatively plentiful natural manpower reserves are well to the forefront, suggesting that an important element involved is the strength of liberal political culture in the country concerned. For some Bulgarian and Romanian essays into "administrative measures" in the field of labor policy, see RFE Research, Bulgarian Situation Report, April 23, 1970, October 22, 1971, and May 9, 1975, and Rumanian Situation Report, March 14, 1975.

2. 15.1% in 1921 (Srb, op. cit., p. 302) and 29.2% in 1970 (Statistická ročenka ČSSR 1972, p. 103).

3. For general discussions of the Slovak-Czech relationship in the Socialist period, see, e.g., H. Klocke, "Das slowakische Problem — gestern, heute, morgen," Osteuropa, 1971, no. 10, p. 10, p. 773; M. Zaninovich and D. Brown "Political Integration in Czechoslovakia: The Implications of the Prague Spring and Soviet Intervention," Journal of International Affairs, 1973, no. 1, p. 66; Robert R. King, Minorities under Communism, chap. 6. For some data on Slovakia's relative progress vis-à-vis the Czech lands, see RFE Research, Czechoslovakian Situation Report, September 4, 1974, and December 10, 1975.

4. See "The Gipsies," East Europe, vol. 14 (1965), no. 10, p. 20; RFE Research, Czechoslovakian Situation Report, September 23, 1971, March 8, 1972, October 17, 1973, July 31, 1974, and February 25, 1976; O. Ulč, "Communist National Minority Policy: The Case of the Gipsies in Czechoslovakia," Soviet Studies, vol. 20 (1969), p. 421; V. Pekelský, "Die Zigeunerfrage in den ost- und südosteuropäischen Staaten," Osteuropa, 1970, no. 9, p. 616.

5. See Note 2 to Chapter 14. In addition to the literature cited there, see W. Reiter "Die Nationalitätenpolitik der rumänischen Volksrepublic im Spiegel ihrer Statistik," Osteuropa, vol. 11 (1961), p. 189; "Zur Frage der Gleichberechtigung der Minderheiten im heutigen Rumänien," Osteuropa, vol. 25 (1975), p. 40; Robert R. King "Die Nationalitätenfrage in der Rumänischen Politik," Osteuropäische Rundschau, 1971, no. 10, p. 15, and no. 11, p. 10; RFE Research, RAD Background Report (Romania), February 12, 1976; RFE Research, Rumania, September 27, 1972; and Situation Report Rumania, March 1, 1971, March 17, May 11, and June 30, 1978; RAD Background Report (Romania), no. 75, April 19, 1978, and no. 224, October 11, 1978.

6. See RFE Research, Romanian Situation Report/12, April 16, 1977, and

RAD Background Report/94, May 9, 1977.

7. On the Hungarian Gypsies, see the two Hungarian articles translated in "Zigeuner in Osteuropa," Osteuropa, vol. 21 (1971), no. 2, p. A115. Like other East European states, the Hungarians do not accord recognition to the Gypsies as a national group, and official statistics are not available. Puxon, Rom: Europe's Gipsies, Minority Rights Group Report no. 14, London, 1973, has estimated the Hungarian Gypsy population at 480,000. Whatever their present numbers, as the articles referred to above make clear, they are growing very rapidly. On Hungary's very liberal policy toward its other minority groups (recently estimated to total 450,000, i.e., less than Puxon's estimate for the Gypsies), see the Hungarian articles translated in RFE Research, Hungarian Press Survey, January 7, June 2, and July 16, 1970, June 15, September 12, and September 26, 1973. See also Robert R. King, Minorities under Communism, chaps. 4 and 9; "Mehr Bewegungsraum für nationale Minderheiten in Ungarn," Osteuropa, vol. 22 (1972), no. 4, p. A262; and RFE Research, Hungarian Situation Report, December 11, 1973, March 11, 1976, March 8 and April 19, 1978.

8. Precise figures are not available. At their most recent census, in accordance with their new hard-line nationalities policy, the Bulgarians statistically abolished their ethnic minorities (RFE Research, Bulgarian Situation Report, January 28, 1976). See the discussions in Chapters 14 and 16 and Note 2 to Chapter 14. See also M. Costello, "Emigration of Bulgarian Turks: Foreign and Domestic Considerations," RFE Research, Bulgaria, October 16, 1969, and Bulgarian Situation Report, August 27, 1970, February 21, 1974, November 11, 1975, March 17, May 14, and June 24, 1976, December 8, 1977, and August 24, 1979.

9. See Note 2 to Chapter 14.

10. Compare the discussion in Chapter 10 on Polish ethnic relations.

11. Compare the discussion in Chapter 6, "Some Historical and Theoretical Considerations."

12. Consider, for example, the enormous divergence between European and Central Asian birthrates in the USSR and between "Christian Slav" and Shiptar and Magyar and Gypsy natality in Yugoslavia and Hungary respectively. Outside Socialist Europe (e.g., in Southern Africa) the same proposition usually holds also.

13. In addition to the chapters on Hungary in David, op. cit., Kirk et al., op. cit., and Berelson, op. cit., see E. Szabady, "Hungary," in The Population Council, Country Profiles, July 1974; "Ungarn propagiert die Drei-Kinder-Familie," Osteuropa, 1974, no. 5, p. A290; "Verbesserte soziale Massnahmen der ungarischen Regierung," Osteuropa, 1975 no. 10, p. A505. Among the reports on topics related to population policy that have been published by Radio Free Europe, see especially "Hungarian Demographic Policy at Turning Point" and "New Rules on Induced Abortion," in RFE Research, Hungary, October 18, 1973, and January 23, 1974; see also Hungarian Situation Reports, August 11, 1977, and August 8, 1978.

14. For Czechoslovakia, see David op. cit.; Kirk, et al., op. cit.; Berelson, op. cit.; Vladní populacní komise, Děti naše budoucnost, Prague, 1972; Population Policy in Czechoslovakia, Prague, 1974; V. Srb, "Population Development and Population Policy in Czechoslovakia," Population Studies, vol. 16 (1962-63), p. 147; A. Heitlinger, "Pro-natalist Population Policies in Czechoslovakia," Population Studies, vol. 30 (1976), no. 1, p. 123; K. Grzybowski, "Czechoslovakia," in Luke T. Lee and Arthur Larson, eds., Population and Law, Leiden, 1971, p. 235; "Sozial- und Bevölkerungspolitik in der Tschechoslowakei," Osteuropa, 1975, no. 2, p. A100; J. Adamiček, "Bevölkerungspolitik in der Tschechoslowakei," Osteuropa Wirtschaft, vol. 23 (1978), no. 3, p. 173.

15. According to Kirk et al., vol. 1, p. 157, contraceptives are still not advertised in Bulgaria and are available in pharmacies only on prescription. On Bulgarian policies, see in addition Berelson op. cit.; David, op. cit.; I. Stefanow, "Problemy polityki demograficznej w Bulgarii," in Polityka ludnościowa: współczesne problemy, p. 430; Bulgarian Ministry of Information and Communications, Naselenie i demograficheskaia politika Narodnoi Respubliki Bolgarii, Sofia, 1974; V. Kassabov, "La natalité en Bulgarie: résultats, perspectives, politique," Population, vol. 29 (1974), no. 2, p. 275. See also RFE, Bulgarian Situation Report, July 10 and 12, 1978.

16. On the 1966 legislation and its demographic impact, see H. David and N. Wright, "Abortion Legislation: the Romanian Experience," Studies in Family Planning, vol. 2 (1971), no. 10, p. 205, and M. Teitelbaum, "Fertility Effects of the Abolition of Legal Abortion in Romania," Population Studies, November 1972, p. 405. More generally on Romanian population policy, see H. P. David, op. cit.; Kirk et al., op. cit.; Berelson, op. cit.; I. Ceterchi et al., Le droit et la croissance de la population en Roumanie, Romanian National Demographic Commission, Bucharest, 1974; I. Marinescu et al., "Niektóre aspekty polityki ludnościowej w Rumunii," Polityka ludnościowa: współczesne problemy, p. 495; RFE Research, Rumanian Situation Reports, December 17, 1976, and May 5, 1978.

17. On East German population policy, see Henry P. David, op. cit.; Kirk et al., op. cit.; K. H. Mehlan, "Reducing Abortion Rate and Increasing Fertility by Social Policy in the German Democratic Republic," UN World Population Conference 1965, vol. 2, p. 223; G. Schulz, "German Democratic Republic," in L. Lee and A. Larson, op. cit.; H. Harmsen, "Abortion Laws: Stringency in Rumania and Relaxation in East Germany," Review of Soviet Medical Sciences, vol. 6 (1969), no. 2, p. 19; "Report of the Government of the German Democratic Republic on population policy and population development in connection with economic and social development," mimeograph, prepared by the GDR for the UN World Population Conference in Bucharest, 1974; P. Khalatbari et al., "Problemy polityki ludnościowej w NRD," Polityka ludnościowa: współczesne problemy, p. 480.

18. The new measures have achieved some success. See The Economist, May 13, 1978, p. 59.

19. See E. Hofsten, "Demographic Transition and Economic Development in Albania," European Demographic Information Bulletin, vol. 6 (1975), no. 3.

20. Yugoslavia is in fact one of only three countries in the world that have written the right to family planning into their constitutions. Population Reference Bureau, Intercom, December 1978, p. 4.

INDEX

Index

Index

Montenegro, 157, 162, 171, 173, 195,
    197-98, 204, 222-25, 240, 245-46
Morozovism, 27, 28
Mortality, 26, 30-31, 35-36, 119, 206
    infant, 31, 35-36
    in Poland, 119-21
    in USSR, 30, 31, 35, 36
    in Yugoslavia, 157-63
Moslems, xi, 33-34, 55-56, 65-72,
    77-78, 85, 89, 94, 157-60, 171,
    190, 192, 195-204, 240, 245, 256
    in Bulgaria (Pomaks), 201, 222,
    253-54
    in Romania, 197
    in USSR, 56, 197
    in Yugoslavia, 195-204, 240, 256
Multiracialism, 49, 53

Natality. See birthrate
Nationality. See ethnic relations
Nazism, 29, 261
Northern Ireland, 53
Nuptiality. See marriage

Optimum population, 138
Orphans, 27
Orthodox church, 80, 191, 197
Overemployment. See manpower
Overpopulation, 10, 11, 45, 95, 96,
    100, 162, 170

Pan-Iranianism, 89
Pan-Islamism, 56, 64
Pan-Moslemism. See Pan-Islamism
Pan-Turanianism, 64-65, 89
Pan-Turkism, 56
Pensioners, 45
Perevedentsev, V. I., 93, 115
Plural societies. See multi-
    racialism
Poland (Poles), xii-xiv, 5, 31-33,
    36-37, 43, 44, 80, 88, 110, 119-54,
    173, 234-35, 250, 252, 254,
    257-60, 262, 264-66
    in USSR, 132
Political science, 3-39
Pomaks. See Moslems and Bulgaria
Population doctrines, 95-103, 104, 123,
    134-54, 208, 257-58
    in Poland, 134-54
    in USSR, 95-103, 104

in Yugoslavia 205-15
Population policies, xii-xiii, 21-29,
    60, 71, 72, 104-16, 121-25,
    137-54, 227-46, 260-68
    in Poland, 121-25, 137-54
    in USSR, 104-16
    in Yugoslavia, 227-246
Productivity, 47, 48, 126, 164, 167,
    170, 173
Pronatalism, xii-xiv, 7, 34, 43, 58,
    91, 105-7, 113, 115, 144, 146,
    149-54, 173, 228, 232, 235-36,
    241-42, 245-46, 251, 260-67
Purges, 31, 56

Racial relations, 49, 75, 81, 254-56
    and ethnic relations, 49, 254-56
Repatriation, 132, 167, 178-79, 182,
    184, 186
Romania (Romanians), 31, 33-34,
    37-38, 88, 109-11, 145, 177,
    197, 216, 220, 232, 235, 245-46,
    250, 253-54, 257-58, 260,
    262-63, 266
Russians, xi, 31-35, 46, 52, 55-56,
    58, 60, 63-64, 66-67, 69-71,
    78-79, 81-83, 91, 133, 190, 196,
    254, 264
Russification, 58, 61-62, 76, 82
RSFSR, 46
Ruthenia, 252

Sandžak area, 240
Self-management, 231, 233-35,
    238-42
Serbia (Serbs), 34-35, 55, 70, 74,
    157, 159-62, 190-93, 196-98,
    200-4, 205, 213, 221-25, 234-36,
    240-41, 244, 246, 256
Sex education, 207, 230, 233, 235, 265
Shiptars. See Albania
Siberia, 44, 58, 72, 88-89, 91
Slavs, 59, 254, 256
Slovaks, 55, 252, 254, 256
Slovenia (Slovenes), 157, 159, 162-63,
    170, 172, 174, 175, 182, 184,
    192-93, 196-97, 200-4, 213,
    218-19, 230, 234, 239, 241, 244,
    246
Sorbs, Lusatian, 254
Soviet Union. See USSR

ABOUT THE AUTHOR

John Besemeres was trained in Russian studies and political science at Melbourne and Oxford Universities and the Australian National University, from which he received his doctorate in 1976.

He has taught Soviet politics at Monash University and spent five years in Eastern Europe, where he worked as a translator from Polish and Serbo-Croatian. His articles on the Socialist world have been published in academic journals in the United States as well as in the <u>Australian National Times</u> and <u>The New Statesman</u>. Currently he works in the Department of Prime Minister and Cabinet in Canberra.